War in the Desert

WAR
IN THE DESERT

AN R.A.F. FRONTIER CAMPAIGN

Lieutenant-General
Sir John Bagot Glubb,
K.C.B., C.M.G., D.S.O., O.B.E., M.C.

Bear with my foolishness for a little, for I want to tell you
how these things took place in me. This is indeed of no
importance; I put myself forward only in order to be useful
to you, and if you are helped I am consoled for my egoism;
if not, I shall have exhibited my folly.

SAINT BERNARD OF CLAIRVAUX

W · W · NORTON & COMPANY · INC ·
NEW YORK

*To my comrades of the Royal Air Force
who served in Iraq from 1921 to 1930:
and to the tribes, with whom I lived,
and whose anxieties I shared.*

PREFACE

TO many people, the study of minor frontier hostilities against wild tribes, thirty or forty years ago, may seem today a profitless occupation. Those interested in the military aspect of the narrative may consider that, with the modern revolutionary developments in weapons, such campaigns are too primitive to contain any lessons. Others may deny any interest in events which took place in what they consider to have been the bad old days of "imperialism". Those more familiar with the Arabic-speaking countries today may point out that bedouins no longer play an important part in the Middle East political scene.

In spite, however, of these possible objections, I have thought it worth while to tell this story. It provides a narrative of service rendered by British forces, principally the R.A.F., to which scant justice has been done. While everybody knows what we owed to the Royal Air Force in the Battle of Britain, its services in frontier wars in remote countries have not received adequate recognition.

To those who still feel a guilty suspicion that British action in Asia was, in former times, oppressive or unscrupulous, this account may give a different viewpoint. For here, it seems to me, British intervention was purely beneficial. It saved a poor, simple and hardy community from the terror of constant massacre, and established a peace which has never since been broken. This result could only have been achieved by the defeat of the militant Ikhwan, and such a defeat could not have been achieved without British help.

Yet these operations were scarcely heard of in Britain. The desert in those days was remote and uncomfortable and no press correspondent ever visited the scene of our struggles. Perhaps the British Government itself avoided publicity, for "colonial wars" were a delicate subject, liable to call forth the indignation of sentimental but ill-informed philanthropists and providing useful propaganda material to our enemies. Even among those better informed, these troubles were too often interpreted as a dynastic conflict between the Saudi and sherifian dynasties. In reality, the successful outcome of the operations saved Nejed and Iraq alike from chaos. Far from attacking Ibn Saud, British forces were largely instrumental in saving him.

I cannot help feeling, therefore, that these events, far from being hushed up, deserve wider publicity, for they provide an example of an intervention by British forces, which rendered signal service to both Nejed and Iraq.

If these reasons be insufficient to justify this story, then I must add that I wrote it because to do so, and to renew the memory of old friends, has caused me pleasure. If it can likewise give enjoyment to the reader, I shall be perfectly satisfied.

J. B. G.

West Wood St. Dunstan,
  Mayfield,
    Sussex.

Author's Note

In transliterating Arabic words and names, I
have endeavoured as far as possible to help
the English reader to pronounce the word
correctly. As a result, I have not followed
any regular system. In cases where there
is already a well-known anglicized form,
however, I have preferred to adhere to that.

ACKNOWLEDGMENTS

I am grateful to the historical section of the Royal Air Force for much assistance and also for permission to publish a number of R.A.F. official photographs. Some of these pictures were obtained from the late Lady Trenchard and I would like to record my debt to her. Some of the earlier photographs were taken by myself, but a few of those included were found by me among some old papers. I have no trace of the origin of these pictures. If I have used any of them without the authority of the owners of the copyright, I beg herewith to tender my apologies.

CONTENTS

LIST OF MAPS

I

Dramatis Personae

No arts, no letters, no society: and which is worst of all, continued fear and danger of violent death; and the life of man is poor, nasty and short.　　　　　　　　　　　　THOMAS HOBBES, *Leviathan*

The Arabs before the time of Muhammad had been a collection of rival tribes or clans, excelling in the savage virtues of bravery, hospitality and even chivalry, and devoted to the pursuit of booty.
　　　　　　　　　　　　　　　　STANLEY LANE-POOLE

Thou shalt call his name Ishmael; . . . He will be a wild man; his hand will be against every man, and every man's hand against him.
　　　　　　　　　　　　　　　　　　Genesis xvi. 11

The wonders of earth, and air, . . . and sky, were a real intelligible language in which they heard Almighty God speaking to them.
　　　　　　　　　　FROUDE, *England's Forgotten Worthies*

Contentment consists not in great wealth, but in few wants.
　　　　　　　　　　　　　　　　　　EPICURUS

I

DRAMATIS PERSONAE

IT was a cold blustery morning in March 1924, as we rode our camels across the endless rolling grey wastes of the Syrian desert. A raging north-westerly gale howled around us, as it can across those exposed and treeless plains. I wrapped my sheepskin cloak tighter round my legs, bending my head to avoid the storm. On my right, Burjas al Dhafeeri, our guide, crouched low on the back of his camel, as though huddling up his body to keep warm. My servant, Ali, rode on my other side. Suddenly I saw moving figures coming over a low ridge on our right. Burjas, though he knew all the desert by heart, was losing his eyesight and could no longer see distant objects. I kicked my camel to a trot and rode over beside him, tapping the camel's neck with my cane to steer her alongside of his.

"I see figures on our right," I shouted.

"How many and what are they?" asked Burjas.

"*Ahel thentain*," I answered, "people of two"—a bedouin idiom for two camel-riders.

He struck his camel sharply on the neck with his cane, and turned down a narrow depression, calling quickly, "Come on, this way."

We dropped into a dry water course strewn with boulders, couched our camels and slipping from their backs, scrambled up the rocky bank and threw ourselves down on our faces, peering over the top. The camel-riders were crossing our front from right to left, but had apparently not seen us. Two more figures appeared, a third camel-rider and a horseman. They were riding quietly and steadily at a walk, and were perhaps six hundred yards away. I slipped a round into the chamber of my rifle and pulled the safety catch back.

"Look to the right," said Ali, who was now lying beside me.

He had been sharper than I was. A fresh group of figures had appeared in view. Obviously the four leading riders were the advanced guard of a larger party. But as the new group drew closer, we relaxed our tense muscles, for we could see on the camels the swaying litters in which women travelled—it was a nomadic tribe on the move, not a raiding party.

We walked back to our camels and remounted. Burjas seemed to grow thoughtful over the constant alarms and vicissitudes of desert life.

"Are there many raiders in your country?" he suddenly asked me.

"There are none," I answered. "Firstly because there is a government and secondly because there are no camels to raid."

"As God pleases! *Ma sha Allah!*" he exclaimed in astonishment. "A country where there are no camels?"

"What is more," I added, piling Pelion upon Ossa, "there are no deserts and it rains all the year round."

"Rain in the summer!" cried Burjas, half incredulous. "That indeed is a land blessed by God"—an expression of admiration to which the English climate must be unaccustomed.

He rode for a few minutes in silence, considering these extraordinary statements. "*Subhan Allah,*" he said philosophically. "Glory be to God, Who has created so many different kinds."

Again he rode for some minutes without speaking until a new idea occurred to him. "And what do they say of us bedouins in your country?" he asked.

"I don't think they say anything particular," I answered. "Most of the people do not know much about bedouins."

"But you know them," he said. "It is for you to tell your people about the bedouins, their wars, their raids, their tents and their flocks. I conjure you by Allah to tell them."

"Some day, if God wills, if I go back to my country, I will tell them," I promised.

Thirty-six years have elapsed since that promise was given. Now I have returned to my native country and the time has come to fulfil it.

*   *   *   *   *

Forty years ago, the economy of northern Arabia was comparatively simple. Oil had not, as yet, been discovered and there was no industrialism.

Round the outer rim of Arabia lay a narrow belt of cultivated and settled country. In general, the agricultural area of Palestine, Jordan, Lebanon and Syria was some one hundred miles wide from east to west, and was dotted with towns and villages. It was watered in winter by rain, which came with a west wind from the Mediterranean, and which fell, generally speaking, from November to March. No rain fell in summer. At a distance of a hundred to a hundred and twenty miles from the Mediterranean coast, the rainfall so far decreased that agriculture became impossible. Thereafter the desert extended for five hundred miles to the banks of the Euphrates.

In Iraq, the rainfall was insufficient for agriculture except in the extreme north. Elsewhere it depended solely on irrigation, particularly from the great rivers, the Tigris and Euphrates, the valleys of which were closely cultivated. On the Arabian shores of the Red Sea and the Persian Gulf, the desert ran down to the sea, except for a few oases, consisting of clusters of mud-brick houses and plantations of date palms. On the south coast, however, the Yemen,

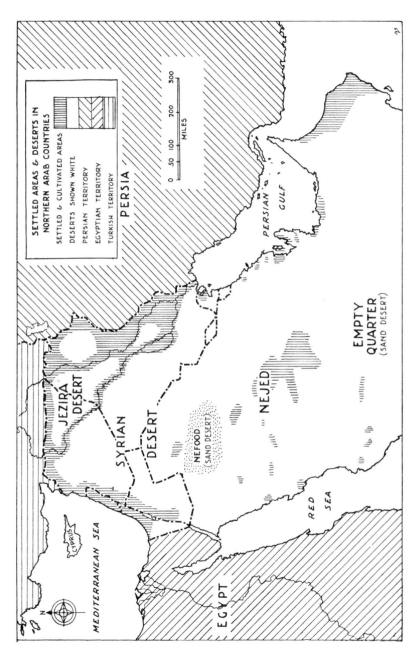

SETTLED AREAS & DESERTS IN
NORTHERN ARAB COUNTRIES

SETTLED & CULTIVATED AREAS
DESERTS SHOWN WHITE
PERSIAN TERRITORY
EGYPTIAN TERRITORY
TURKISH TERRITORY

0   50 100   200   300
MILES

PERSIA

MEDITERRANEAN SEA

CYPRUS

JEZIRA DESERT

SYRIAN DESERT

NEFOOD
(SAND DESERT)

NEJED

EGYPT

RED SEA

PERSIAN GULF

EMPTY
QUARTER
(SAND DESERT)

N

Hadhramaut and Oman enjoyed the rains from the Indian mon-
soons and they also were thereby enabled to practise agriculture and
build towns.

Thus, with the exception of Nejed, all the settled, populated and
cultivated areas were arranged in narrow strips round the circum-
ference of the Arab countries. Nejed, however, was in the middle of
the Arabian sub-continent. Here springs of water or shallow wells
produced groups of oases, towns and gardens. The settled area of
Nejed differed from, for example, that of Palestine or Syria. In the
latter, the fields of cultivation, the orchards, the villages and the
towns were contiguous to one another, as they are in Europe. The
oases of Nejed, however, resembled rather an archipelago in the
desert sea, with long bays and creeks of wasteland running in between one settlement and the next.

Briefly, therefore, we may remember that the settled areas of the
Arabian sub-continent were divided into four groups:

The Mediterranean group, including Syria, Palestine, Jordan
and Lebanon
Iraq
The south coast group, consisting of the Yemen, Hadhramaut
and Oman
The central group, called Nejed, consisting of oases, towns and
cultivation, but entirely encircled by desert, cutting it off from
the rest of the world.

Apart from these four areas, the rest of the Arabian sub-continent
was desert. In so far as the northern area was concerned, namely
the triangle of desert enclosed between Syria, Iraq and Nejed, there
was little sand except in the Nefood, in the extreme south and south-
west of the triangle. The greater part of the area consisted of vast
undulating plains, with ranges of hills almost, in one or two places,
achieving the status of mountains. The sub-soil in the greater part
of this northern desert was limestone.

The definition of desert in the Arab countries was that it consisted of land the rainfall of which was inadequate for agriculture.
Part of the desert country was indeed cultivable in years of good
rains, and most of it received sufficient rainfall to support shrubs
and, in the winter and spring, a cloak of grass and flowers.

*   *   *   *   *

These contrasting areas of cultivation and desert had divided the
Arabs from time immemorial into two communities, the settled and
the nomadic. Now, in 1960, industrialism, oil fields and city life are
on the increase, but forty years ago, the great majority of Arabs were
either cultivators or nomadic bedouin. Each community was essen-

tial to the well-being of the other. The land capable of cultivation was rarely if ever sufficient for the needs of the population, and thus no part of it could be made available for grazing. Grass fields, such as are to be seen on farms in England, were unknown in the Arab countries. Any field capable of growing such grass would have been ploughed up and sown with grain crops.

In spite of this, however, the cultivators and the city dwellers needed meat, milk, cooking oil and wool. The nomadic tribes employed themselves in the breeding of livestock to satisfy these needs. The farmers ploughed and sowed in the autumn, and thereafter would not allow flocks of animals to graze on their land. At the same season, however, the winter rains began to fall in the desert, and the nomads moved out from the cultivated area with their flocks. The harvest was over by July and thereafter some of the nomads could infiltrate once more into the farming area, grazing their animals in the stubble fields until October or November, when they would vanish once again over the blue desert horizon. Others remained all the year round in the desert.

The bedouin took advantage of his autumn contact with the settled population to sell as many of his animals as he found necessary in order to support his family and to purchase as much food and clothing as would suffice his simple needs for six months or more. In 1920, the average bedouin family, which might have owned a dozen camels as its stock in trade, would probably only sell one each year, but possibly two. The price of each camel might have been fifteen to twenty pounds, and the annual income of the family might thus vary from fifteen to thirty or forty pounds sterling.

Should the family have no camel to sell, one or other of its male members would attempt to secure one by theft from a hostile tribe or by joining in a raiding party and receiving a share of the loot. The bedouins obviously could not live by raiding one another, any more than by taking in each other's washing. Raiding, however, did on the whole tend to equalize wealth among them, for the poor would obviously tend to raid more actively than the rich. In the days of uncontrolled tribal wars, no man need despair of a livelihood, no matter what material disasters might overtake him. He could always recoup his fortunes at the expense of another tribe. Only with the prohibition of raiding, thirty years ago, were poor bedouins for the first time reduced to hunger and despair.

In many different spheres of life, primitive conditions seem to lead to a natural and self-adjusting balance, tending to produce a rough and ready form of social justice. Amongst the nomadic Arab tribes, the impossibility of transporting furniture across the desert on camels obliged all to sit on the ground, a custom producing a democratic levelling of social distinctions. The size of the tent was limited by its portability, preventing one family from living in a mansion and another in a slum. The prevention of raiding, to a description of which the greater part of this book is dedicated, heralded the destruction of this virile, democratic equalitarian society. Since the 1930's, the more prosperous tribesmen have tended to abandon the nomadic life, the poorer bedouins to sink below the starvation level. Yet, in the 1920's, when we set ourselves enthusiastically to the task of reducing chaos to order, we had no forebodings. We embarked with enthusiasm upon a programme which appeared to us entirely benevolent and humanitarian, the substitution of peace and security for endless bloodshed and violence.

As I have already explained, the cultivable areas of the Arabian sub-continent were so restricted that no land was available for grazing purposes. In the desert, the grass was so thin and scanty throughout most of the year that the camels or sheep would eat down any given area in a few days, rendering a move to fresh grazing essential. The desert, however, was immense, and virgin soil could usually be found a few miles farther on. Thus the herds of camels and the flocks of sheep inevitably spent the winter and spring in constant movement, and their owners had no alternative but to live in tents. However much the Arab countries become modernized or industrialized, the need for meat to feed the cities will probably continue to render the nomadic life necessary for the breeding of sheep, unless indeed some cheap artificial means of feeding can be devised. The end of tribal wars and raiding, and the general progress of modernization, have already stripped the nomads both of their romantic glamour and of their armed power, but nomadism as a means of livelihood has not disappeared.

In the West, it was once a common illusion that all Arabs rode camels and lived in tents. In the sense in which the word Arab is now used, to signify the whole populations of Iraq, Syria, Lebanon, Jordan and even Egypt (let alone North Africa), this idea would be as ridiculous as the belief that the people of the United States are all cowboys. In reality, nomadic tribes have never constituted more than a fraction of the population of the Arabian sub-continent and their numbers are decreasing in relation to the settled inhabitants.

*　　*　　*　　*　　*

The Mediterranean Arab countries have always been exposed to invasion from Asia Minor, from Egypt and across the sea from Europe. Indeed Palestine, Lebanon and Syria have been a highway for invading armies. The peoples of these countries, therefore, are of mixed origin and have borrowed from many different cultures.

The vast expanses of the desert, however, have never proved tempting to invaders, with the result that Nejed is one of the few countries known to us which have seldom been invaded, and the population of which has never been mingled with another race. Every European nation has undergone extensive admixture during the last two thousand years, much more in the last four thousand, and a race almost unmixed for several millennia must indeed be a rare phenomenon. This book is almost solely concerned with this isolated and inbred race of Central Arabia.

The characteristics of the bedouins forty years ago were strongly marked. We have descriptions of their customs and mentality fourteen hundred years ago, before the appearance of Islam. The striking resemblance between the Arab nomads of the sixth century A.D. and those described in my story, emphasizes the remarkable isolation in which the latter had lived, at least for a millennium and a half.

The first and most striking characteristic of desert life was its hardship, its poverty and the desperate struggle needed to keep alive —particularly the battle with hunger, thirst and vast distances. The intense poverty of Central Arabia resulted in the virtual impossibility of forming a stable government, the machinery of which— officials, soldiers, buildings, communications—inevitably presupposed a regular revenue. But individual men are afraid to live in isolation, and invariably seek security by joining some organization which will afford them support and protection. The Arab nomads consequently banded themselves into tribes. In theory the tribe consisted of one family, all descended from a single ancestor. In practice, as tribes grew larger, a certain adulteration took place. For example, fugitives from other tribes were given protection and eventually married into the tribe. In general, however, all the members were related to one another and inter-married within the tribe. As a result, the tribe enjoyed the great advantage over a political state that, being a single family, it could command the services and the allegiance of its members without paying them. Thus among so poor a people, the tribe was the only workable unit and did actually play the part of a miniature state.

Even the tribe, however, suffered in its efficiency from lack of money. The tribal shaikh was unable to exercise strict authority, for all his fellow-tribesmen were socially his equals and he had no funds with which to support armed retainers to enforce his commands. In the absence of force to ensure the execution of his orders, the tribal chief was fain to base his authority on the obligation of family relationship between himself and his tribesmen. The impotence of the tribal shaikh gave rise to the principal characteristic of tribal life—the absence of enforceable discipline. The tribal chief, for example, was normally the judge of tribal "law". In the absence of any legislative body authorized to enact legal measures, tribal law was simply recognized custom. As such, it was built on precedent and the bedouin judge would support his decisions by quoting similar cases from the past. But the problem confronting the tribal judge was always one of enforcement. All that he could do was to inform the parties to the case and their fellow-tribesmen (for all cases were heard in public) what custom prescribed in such circumstances.

The absence of any force to implement the decision meant that there could be no question of punishment. Law was concerned solely with redress for the injured party. Perhaps the pressure of public opinion might be sufficient to cause the offenders to make the necessary amends, but frequently it was not. Where the defendant proved recalcitrant, the injured party could call on his relatives to assist him in enforcing the judge's ruling, or could himself endeavour to secure payment by forcibly seizing his rival's possessions. A system under which the aggrieved party was authorized to recover his property by force, obviously set a premium upon violence. In any case, the constant uncertainties and dangers of desert life tended to produce an extremely self-reliant type of man, full of initiative and long inured to violence. Thus boldness, turbulence, independence and obstinacy were often typical characteristics.

The tendency to violent and arrogant self-assertion was, however, constantly checked by the dependence of the individual upon the tribe. Where no state existed to protect him, the man driven out of his tribe was defenceless. Anyone could plunder or kill him without fear. His tribe, on the other hand, was to the tribesman not only his "country", but his trade union, his club, his insurance policy and his old age pension. If he were killed by an outsider, the tribe would avenge him, and feed and care for his wife and children. No tribesman or woman could starve—the tribe would care for them.

Crimes of violence were restrained by the laws of revenge. Any man who killed another could himself be legitimately murdered by the relatives of his victim. To kill a man of his own tribe was the action which entailed the direst penalties, for the murderer would be obliged to flee to another tribe for refuge. The tragic plight of such people gave rise to the custom of sanctuary. The man driven from his tribe would seek out a leading personality of another tribe and appeal to him for asylum. But if circumstances did not allow him to reach a leader, any tent, no matter how humble, would give him sanctuary. An Arab tribal family, to which even a complete stranger appealed for protection, was bound to defend him. The tent owner, or any of those living in the tent, would leap to his support, and would defend the guest, even with his own life.

*   *   *   *   *

The life of a herdsman involved little hard intellectual work and allowed much time for contemplation. Long periods of leisure, the immensity and simplicity of the desert and the constant proximity of death caused the Arab to speculate on the existence of God and the meaning of life. In the God of his meditations, he tended to emphasize vastness, power and simplicity, rather than tenderness. The thought processes of the tribesman were simple and direct. He was devoted to his relatives and friends, but made no bones about hating his blood enemy and pursuing him with a ferocious thirst for vengeance, in which he actually took pride, and which he nursed within himself with relish. His simple outlook made him indifferent to the metaphysical hair-splitting which has divided Christian against Christian and Muslim against Muslim. He was apt to conclude that those who differed from him were the enemies of God, whom he proposed to treat as he would like to treat his own blood enemies, that is to kneel on their chests and cut their throats.

But however sublime might be the speculations of the Central Arabian about God and death, as he sat gazing over the vast blue distances of the desert, the pressing pangs of hunger soon re-asserted themselves, and his most noble religious movements usually ended in a quest for plunder.

If these qualities appear hard, ruthless and savage, there were compensating virtues. In a country where a man lived in such constant insecurity, a true and loyal friend was indeed a pearl of great price. If the Arabs were merciless to their enemies, they were capable of extraordinary loyalty to their friends. The immense empty spaces of the desert and the toils and dangers to which travellers were exposed, made hospitality to the stranger and the wayfarer a sacred duty. Probably in the history of the world, no race has equalled the Arabs in hospitality—it is the Arab virtue par excellence.

There was much that was savage, arrogant, greedy and violent in the bedouin of fifty or more years ago. Particularly was he liable to behave with an insufferable arrogance towards those—in his view—lesser breeds, who were not nomads. To be a farmer or a city dweller and to fall into the hands of bedouins was to meet with hard-hearted and haughty masters. But to obtain a balanced picture, it is well for us also to remember the gentle, the hospitable and the romantic sides of their nature. Charles Doughty, the greatest of all Arabian travellers, wandered for two years penniless among the bedouin tribes.

"In the adventure thus begun," he writes, "there passed over me, amongst the thinly scattered, generally hostile and suspicious inhabitants of that land of wilderness, nearly two long and partly weary years; but not without happy turns, in the not seldom finding, as I went forth, of human fellowship amongst Arabians and even of some very true and helpful friendships.''

* * * * *

The frequent absence of any central authority was the cause of the principal peculiarities of bedouin society, especially that of perpetual war. As the following chapters will show, Central Arabia was, from time to time, brought under a single ruler, but the establishment of this central authority was invariably due to the personality of one outstanding man. With his death, the edifice usually collapsed, because it was unsupported by a regular organization and paid officers. In the absence of a government, the bedouin tribes were like the nations of the world today, often anxious to avoid war yet unable to do so, owing to the lack of any overruling power capable of doing justice between them. But unending war, if conducted with the ruthless savagery of modern warfare between "civilized" countries, would end in the extermination of the race. Nowadays a world war must inevitably be succeeded by an interval of peace and recovery.

Bedouin tribal wars, on the other hand, involved comparatively few casualties in any one encounter, but their endless hostilities were rarely, if ever, interrupted by periods of peace. In the long run, the percentage of their men killed in battle was perhaps not very different from the proportion of Europe's manhood which has fallen in the wars of the last fifty years.

The limited number of casualties suffered in bedouin tribal battles was not due to a deliberate policy designed to avoid losses, but to the fact that these encounters were governed by strict rules. A clear distinction must here be drawn between nomads on the one hand and the oasis dwellers of Central Arabia or the cultivators along the fringes of the settled areas in Iraq, Syria or Trans-Jordan on the other. The worldly wealth of the nomads consisted of mobile flocks of animals, that of the cultivators of lands, houses and gardens. A nomad, if threatened by a superior enemy, could elude attack by moving hastily away, driving his flocks with him. Indeed, as long as there was still open desert in front of him, he could escape from his persecutors by seeking entirely new pastures, beyond the reach of his adversaries. The cultivator, however, must needs stand his ground and fight it out. If he fled, he became a penniless refugee, abandoning his land and his buildings to the conqueror. War, therefore, to the nomad was never the same grim struggle for survival which it represented to the farmer. Indeed to the bedouin, war sometimes seemed little more than a sport, which provided the colour and excitement needed to counteract the monotony of the pastoral life.

The ostensible object of tribal warfare was loot, usually in the form of the enemy's herds of camels or flocks of sheep. But in reality loot was sometimes merely the symbol of victory, as a silver cup is to a football team. The most successful fighters were often among the poorest men in a tribe. The reckless character of the famous raider often went with equally heedless generosity and hospitality. In both cases, the principal object was not to acquire or to accumulate wealth, but to achieve personal glory. The bedouin was not a materialist but he was a complete egoist. He was avid of praise and his passion was self-glorification. His only allegiance was to his tribe, for he had no country or government. But even his loyalty to his tribe occupied less of his thoughts than did his own fame and dignity. Fighting thus largely for self-glorification, the most important object of his warlike actions was to draw attention to himself by performing startling exploits. He would therefore challenge the enemy to single combat or warn him of his intention to attack. If his enemy fell into his hands, if no blood feud divided them, he would often treat him with generous chivalry, prepare a feast in his honour, allow him to rest as a guest in his tent and send him away to his tribe with provisions for the road.

We must not, however, idealize Arab chivalry. The artificial glamour and romance which attaches to the word chivalry in Western Europe today is a later refinement. The bedouin would have thought little of Chaucer's gentle perfect knight, whose port was meek as is a maid. The nomad warrior was anything but modest, indeed he would have struck any Englishman as unpleasantly arrogant and boastful.

If, however, war for glory was peculiar to the nomadic tribes, the oasis dwellers of Nejed, who owned immovable property, took a more sober view. Life in urban communities naturally imposed a measure of discipline which would have been felt as irksome by the wild nomad of the great desert spaces. Yet the vast majority of the oasis dwellers were descended from the tribes, though the more regular and static nature of their occupations had rendered them more stable in character. The nomadic life, moreover, set a limit to culture and education, for books, papers and writing materials were preserved with difficulty in constantly moving tents. In the towns and villages of Central Arabia the opportunities of learning were greater, though the surrounding deserts formed a barrier to the introduction of foreign culture.

Nejed, however, was never self-supporting. It exported camels and, to a lesser extent, sheep, but it was obliged to import rice, flour, tea, coffee, sugar and clothing. This trade was in the hands of the oasis dwellers of Central Arabia, who were obliged, in order to conduct this commerce, to visit Egypt, Syria, Iraq and the Persian Gulf. Thus the towns of Central Arabia produced a culture distinctively their own, on the one hand deeply imbued with the warlike traditions of the tribes, on the other in just sufficient contact with the outside world to prevent it from relapsing into savagery.

The settled lives of the merchants and the oasis dwellers rendered them less fickle and unreliable than the bedouins, while it also made them more sober and more determined in war. They entered unwillingly on war, but if they fought they did so with greater obstinacy than did the nomads.

Although the bedouins were so magnanimous and so chivalrous in war, the intensity of their personal jealousies and ambitions often led them to commit murder. Many an Arabian prince or tribal chief had seized power by assassinating his rivals or even his own brothers. Indeed the tribesmen often appeared to be like children—for a long time they would play at war together with perfect good humour and enjoyment. Then something would suddenly go wrong. One would accuse the other of cheating, some flash of jealousy would incense them, and a furious struggle would follow. Especially in the pursuit of their blood feuds did they show an unrelenting vindictiveness.

*   *   *   *   *

Such were the bedouins who formed the bulk of the inhabitants of Central Arabia and whose territory extended northwards almost to Aleppo, in the triangle between the Euphrates and the settled areas of Syria and Trans-Jordan.

But Arabia had always been one of those hard and arid lands which gave birth to more people than they could support. The surplus population was tempted to seek easier conditions of life in the neighbouring richer lands to the north. Sometimes individuals or families migrated to Syria or Iraq, sometimes whole tribes emerged from the desert and fought their way into the surrounding settled countries. Probably more often than not, these irruptions of desert tribes into the fertile northern areas were the result of some internal war in Arabia. A year of drought, or overcrowding of the scant pasture or at the desert wells, would cause some weaker tribe to be driven northwards. It in turn attacked the tribes barring its way and so the pressure was passed on from tribe to tribe.

These age-old movements towards the fertile countries had produced, in the Syrian and Iraqi deserts, a secondary group of nomadic tribes, known as sheepmen or shepherds, probably themselves originally bedouins, but changed in their manners and outlook by several centuries of contact with the settled and agricultural communities. The towns and villages of Syria and Iraq had always been influenced by foreign civilizations, Roman, Persian, European or Turkish. When a bedouin tribe, driven from Central Arabia, came into contact with these influences, subtle changes began to take place in the outlook of the tribesmen. They became less willing to endure the constant hardships and privations of the desert life. They began to enjoy the greater comfort of a permanent water supply during the summer heats, on the banks of the mighty Euphrates or by the springs of Syria. They discovered that sheep provided a more comfortable livelihood than did camels. The bedouin sold one or two camels a year and with the proceeds purchased a year's supply of flour, rice or dates, on which he and his family were obliged to live, for there were no shops in the great desert. In the whole of his life, he hardly ever tasted fresh fruit or vegetables. Sheep, however, at all times found a ready market in towns and villages in the cultivated area, and the shepherd could sell one as often as he wished, to add to his supplies or to purchase small luxuries. Sheep, moreover, kept their owner constantly supplied with milk, butter and cooking oil, and in the spring, their wool was a valuable source of additional income.

Camels and sheep, however, did not do well together. The camel migrated far and fast, crossing long stretches of waterless deserts which would have proved fatal to flocks of sheep. Camels, throughout most of the year, grazed on the desert shrubs, but sheep preferred grass. As a result, the tribe which made sheep its chief source of income gradually abandoned its camels and took to donkeys as its beasts of burden. It thereby ceased to be bedouin, for the latter are by definition camel people. Nevertheless the shepherds still remained largely nomadic, using donkeys to carry their tents, supplies, cooking pots, water and other impedimenta. The men and women went on foot, only a few of the more prosperous tribesmen riding horses.

The background and culture of the shepherds were founded on those of the camel bedouins, though modified by their greater contact with the towns and villages which had been affected by foreign civilizations. The shepherds normally spent some seven months of the year in, or on the verge of, the cultivated area, and only some five months in the desert.

While in the desert, the shepherds were almost entirely dominated by the bedouins, for the camel was the only means of transport which could be used for raiding. It is true that bedouins also used horses in war, for the horse was the only animal from the back of which the rider could fight. Camels were too cumbrous for fighting at close quarters except in a single wild charge. In a serious battle, the camelmen dismounted and fought on foot. The bedouin who took his mare with him on a raid rode a camel and led the mare when on the march. Moreover the camel carried water and possibly also forage for the mare. Thus horses could only be used on raids by tribes which also owned camels.

Shepherd tribes were therefore unable to raid. In theory, if they could concentrate, they should have been able to defend themselves against bedouin attack, but the fact that they possessed no camels made it difficult for them to obtain prior information of the approach of an enemy. The sheep tribes, therefore, while in the desert, were inevitably at the mercy of the bedouins, becoming as it were their clients and paying tribute to them for protection.

*   *   *   *   *

One of the most striking qualities of the old-time bedouin was his devotion to poetry. Many nations doubtless have produced poets, who have usually been men of culture and letters. But among the bedouins, poor and illiterate as they were, poets were innumerable. Yet their compositions were not the uncouth rhymes of peasants, but were governed by ancient artistic conventions, employed an extensive and varied vocabulary, and were both stirring and musical in their rhythm and diction. One of the characteristics of the old-fashioned bedouin was his outspoken frankness and absence of subtlety. The same characteristics were observable in his poetry, which consisted mostly of heroic ballads. It contained many descriptions of nature, the sky, the clouds, a passing shower falling on the parched earth, and of course an intimate knowledge of animals. There was little, perhaps, of what we should call the really spiritual, nor was the tribesman a subtle psychologist. The bedouins accepted men as they found them, without analysing their mental processes. Their poems dealt in a heroic vein with their principal interests, war, generosity, hospitality and love. Couched in a magnificently sonorous language and rendered with spirit and feeling by the bedouin poet, they were intended essentially for vocal recitation and look cold and dull in print, especially in translation.

Here is a quotation from a bedouin poem of twelve hundred years ago:

UMAYMA

> She charmed me, veiling bashfully her face,
> Keeping with quiet looks an even pace;
> Some lost thing seemed to seek her downcast eyes:
> Aside she bends not—softly she replies.
> Ere dawn she carries forth her meal—a gift
> To hungry wives in days of dearth and thrift.
> No breath of blame up to her tent is borne,
> While many a neighbour's is the house of scorn.
> Her husband fears no gossip fraught with shame,
> For pure and holy is Umayma's name.
> Joy of his heart, to her he need not say
> When evening brings him home, "Where passed the day?"

Slender and full in turn, of perfect height,
A very fay were she, if beauty might
Transform a child of earth into a fairy sprite.[1]

As complement to this little portrait of a bedouin wife of one thousand two hundred years ago, here is a poem by Dughaiyim al Dhalmawi, a man of the tribe of Shammar, composed about the end of the nineteenth century. Dughaiyim had grown poor and lost his camels and as a result had abandoned the nomadic life and had built himself a little mud-brick house in one of the oases of Nejed; but in spite of his poverty, his hospitality to passers-by became famous. The poem records an incident in which a party of travellers arrived as guests after midnight. Some of the wayfarers, however, seem to have rejected the poet's hospitality or to have made disparaging remarks about his mud dwelling. Dughaiyim apostrophizes his henchman, Klaib.

Light the fire O Klaib! light it well, my son,
If you light it more wood will be brought.
I will fetch coffee and cardamon,
You the coffee pots, always eagerly sought.[2]

The beans on a bright wood fire roast,
While the eyes of the fair sleep light,
Then pound the brass mortar, good host,
Like a wolf's howl, ringing out in the night.[3]

When the fire flames up, well-lighted,
(While weaklings nestle with their wives in bed)[4]
May it bring us weary travellers benighted,
How sweet the tap of cane on camel's head.[5]

Make haste, O Klaib, the ready brew to poor,[6]
(Life comes from Him who drives the clouds above)[7]
Though some may scorn our humble cottage door,
Speak to them Klaib in kindly words of love.

[1] *A Literary History of the Arabs.* R. A. Nicholson.
[2] Coffee was the first thing immediately served to guests on arrival — as in Europe they would first be invited to a drink.
[3] The Arabs always used coffee beans which they roasted themselves and then pounded with a pestle and mortar.
[4] Bedouins professed to despise sleep at night, which was more suitable for women (see four lines above). Their warriors compared themselves rather to wolves, who prowled at night and slept by day.
[5] The ringing sound of the pestle and mortar and the flickering flame of the fire were an announcement that their owner was making coffee and thus an invitation to passers-by to call in. The rider tapped his camel on the head to make it kneel and thus the sound of tapping canes meant that guests were dismounting at the door.
[6] Pour out to the guests what is ready in the pot and then make a fresh brew.
[7] This is an exhortation to generosity—God will make good whatever we lavish on the guests.

A language than fresh Jubba dates more sweet,[1]
Than melted Arab butter far more clear,
For in the way of love both shaikh and herdsman meet.
All creatures stand 'fore God in equal fear.
For guests are sent by God for us to serve
So from the path of love we must not swerve.

This little poem, advocating love in return for the rudeness of an arrogant guest, illustrates another side of the often hasty and vindictive bedouin character.

For the composition of the ballad, there were certain recognized forms, some of them undoubtedly thousands of years old. One such form which constantly recurred in bedouin poetry was that of the messenger. The poet began by addressing himself to a camel-rider who had just arrived with news, or to one who was about to leave and could be entrusted with a message. The first four or six lines of the poem were occupied with a description of the rider's swift camel, its broad chest, deep girth, strong ribs, light stride and fine well-bred head. The camel was the bedouin's passion and no non-bedouin could ever challenge his technique in describing it. These preliminaries over, the poet then begged the rider to deliver a message, perhaps to his sweetheart, perhaps to some great shaikh, whose noble deeds and princely generosity could then be suitably retailed.

The following poem, also probably some fifty or sixty years old, was composed by an old Shammar bedouin in Nejed, whose two sons had gone to Syria to work and make money. It begins with a variation of the messenger form of introduction.

O ye riders on ten camels all of one hue,
Tawny sisters who shy at every shade,
Ten riders on ten mounts, side by side they flew,
Their long necks straight as palm fronds displayed.

Their nostrils wide stretched, all of equal height,
Their ribs like barrels, their great shoulders strong;
O lads! if you are leaving for Hauran tonight,
May you meet good luck! bear the burden of my song.

Bear my words in your minds as in caskets safe,
Words sweeter than the milk of young girls,
Delay, by Allah, while you smoke one more pipe,
And I'll put pen to paper—though my mind swirls.

Then saddle your mounts when you're prepared to start,
Put your desert gear ready for time of need,
Keep the north star on your right, do not far from it part,
To the seven stars of the bear give good heed.

[1] Jubba is an oasis west of Hail, famous for its dates.

Give my love to those who set out and left me alone,
Saif and Shwardi, light of my eyes, my heart's joys,
Tell them their old father has sworn they must come home,
If they return not, he will ride to seek his boys.

If they complain of lack of money or wealth,
Tell them riches cannot prolong a short life,
Riches did not keep the Aida or Sadoon in health,[1]
So spit upon this world—death soon will end our strife.

The majority of bedouin poems, however, treated of war rather than of love. Here in conclusion is a short fragment on the subject of a bedouin raid. The poet, like the fighters of all nations, however unscrupulous their wars, begins by asking God to give him success in his search for plunder, which will suffice to provide him with a livelihood.

O God! I beg Thee (Thou dost swiftly hear us)
Open the gate of fortune with thy keys;
Prayer of His slave to God who still will bear us,
The life of Arabs[2] and of the towns he sees.

Sleep is disgrace, mark of the coward's shame,
The eyes which seek great deeds must sleep in snatches,
He tires his mount who rides in quest of fame,
Who journeys far the fairest plunder catches.

They raced for the hilltop like a ravening wolf pack,
They strove like free men bearing noble names:
The camel escorts drew their swords for attack,
Men said they fought for love of black-eyed dames.
How many pressed their wounds to keep the blood back,
Wounds given by hands which never missed their aims.

The actual existence of an idyllic pastoral state of innocence, so frequently extolled in antiquity, seemed to me to be partly realized in the bedouins. Not indeed that the bedouins were innocent, in the sense of being harmless or gentle, for, according to our standards, most of them were robbers and many were murderers. Their innocence was rather a lack of sophistication, like the innocence of animals who prey upon one another, like the innocence of man before he ate of the fruit of the tree of knowledge. There was about them an indifference to material considerations, a lack of self-consciousness, an acceptance of the world as it is, a childlike cheer-

---

[1] Al Aida was shaikh of the tribe of Aneza in the Hejaz. Sadoon will be frequently referred to in this narrative.
[2] Note the use of the word Arabs to mean tribesmen as contrasted to townsmen. This was before the renaissance of Arab nationalism.

fulness in surroundings full of bloodshed and violence, a truthfulness and a directness of speech and a certain simplicity which made them all poets. Moreover as soon as they abandoned the primitive life of complete nomadism for the status of shepherds, the tribes lost this freshness of outlook. Thereafter they ceased to produce spontaneous poetry.

The bedouin was hardy and warlike, but too fickle or easy-going to desire to annihilate his enemies or even to extend his territory. His desultory and plundering wars were half sport. One thing alone could make the bedouins ruthless and compel them to combine to serve a single cause—and that thing was religion. Now and again a fire of religious enthusiasm would sweep across the arid peninsula, as it had done at the first rise of Islam in the seventh century of our era. On such occasions, the bedouin would for a while be carried out of himself, would forget his glory or his greed, and would fight with fanaticism for a cause which he believed to be divine. But at last the enthusiasm would evaporate and twenty, thirty or fifty years later, the tribes would have reverted to their immemorial way of life.

This book deals with one such outbreak, in the form of the revival of Wahhabi-ism early in the present century. Before, however, relating my own story of this convulsion and its consequences, I must first give some slight account of the history of the sect of the Wahhabis.

II

The Rise, Decline and Revival of the Wahhabis

The Semitic religions would have none draw breath of life in the earth beside themselves.　　DOUGHTY, *Travels in Arabia Deserta*

In delivering his new doctrines to the Arabs, it cannot be denied that Abdul Wahhab conferred on them a great blessing . . . for although the bedouins at all times devoutly worshipped the Divinity, yet the deistical principle alone could not be deemed sufficient to instruct a nation so wild and ungovernable in the practice of morality and justice.　　BURCKHARDT, *History of the Wahabys*

We may as well tolerate all religions since God himself tolerates them.
　　FÉNELON

> With devotion's visage and pious action,
> We do sugar o'er the devil himself.
> 　　SHAKESPEARE

The perpetual independence of the Arabs has been the theme of praise among strangers and natives . . . The obvious causes of their freedom are inscribed on the character and country of the Arabs. Many ages before Mahomet, their intrepid valour had been severely felt by their neighbours . . . The long memory of their independence is the firmest pledge of its perpetuity, and succeeding generations are animated to prove their descent and to maintain their inheritance.
　　GIBBON, *Decline and Fall of the Roman Empire*

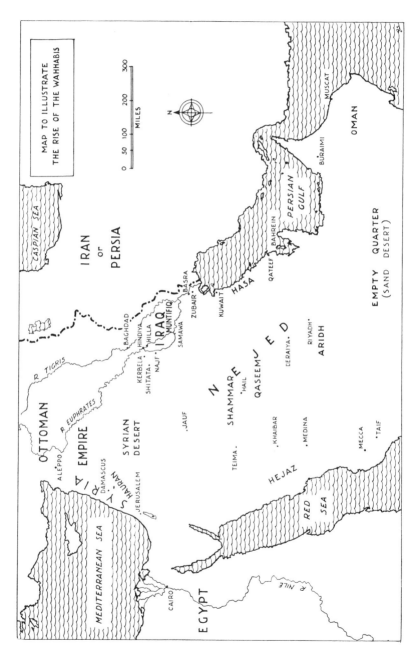

MAP TO ILLUSTRATE
THE RISE OF THE WAHHABIS

N

0 50 100 200 300
MILES

CASPIAN SEA

IRAN or PERSIA

OTTOMAN EMPIRE

ALEPPO

R. EUPHRATES

R. TIGRIS

SYRIA

DAMASCUS

HAURAN

JERUSALEM

SYRIAN DESERT

BAGHDAD

KERBELA

SHITATA

HINDIYA

HILLA

NAJF

IRAQ

MUNTIFIQ

SAMAWA

ZUBAIR

BASRA

KUWAIT

HASA

QATEEF

BAHREIN

PERSIAN GULF

BURAIMI

MUSCAT

OMAN

TEIMA

JAUF

SHAMMAR

HAIL

QASEEM

KHAIBAR

NEJED

DERAIYA

RIYADH

ARIDH

EMPTY QUARTER (SAND DESERT)

MEDINA

HEJAZ

MECCA

TAIF

RED SEA

CAIRO

EGYPT

R. NILE

MEDITERRANEAN SEA

II

THE RISE, DECLINE AND REVIVAL
OF THE WAHHABIS

THE Semitic races have originated the three greatest religions of the modern world, Judaism, Islam and Christianity. Moreover all three found their source in a social structure of extreme simplicity. Amongst the bedouins the daily struggle for existence under the hard conditions of life in a vast land almost without water, compelled them to be strictly realistic. The simplicity of their existence preserved them from developing their religious ideas into ritual, ceremony or architecture. This combination of realism with speculation caused the first Muslims to emphasize one of the grandest and yet simplest aspects of religion—the Unity of God.

In the seventh century of our era, the preaching of the Prophet Muhammad stirred the latent emotion of the bedouins. Carried away by an enthusiasm which made them forget their tribal feuds and their greed for loot, they burst out of their deserts, bearing before them like a banner the phrase, "There is no god but God." With this sign they conquered an empire extending from southern France to northern India. The plain and simple creed of the desert was adopted by great empires and complicated civilizations, from the fountains and gardens of Andalusia to the palaces of Persia and the great Moghul. Meanwhile, however, the fiery passion and the warlike zeal of the primitive inhabitants of Central Arabia had spent their force. Some Arab tribesmen had been borne on the crest of the wave to Persia, North Africa or Spain, where they had become merged in the local populations. Those still remaining in Central Arabia returned to their time-honoured way of life, cut off from the world at large by their surrounding circle of desert. The glittering new Muslim empires and kingdoms had no interest in the barren steppes from which their faith had emerged. No non-Arab race desired to penetrate those inhospitable wastes. Central Arabia, which had originated this world-shaking movement, returned to its former isolation.

Ancient tribal customs, remnants of earlier ages, which had been scotched rather than destroyed by the first Muslim fervour, now regained their sway. The centre of the Muslim religion moved to Damascus, to Baghdad, to Granada and to Cairo, to Constantinople or to Delhi. The prevalent illiteracy of the Central Arabians prevented the study or elaboration of that religion which they themselves had originated and which they still nominally professed. The warring bedouin tribes gradually relapsed into that anarchic freedom and ignorant insularity which had characterized them before the rise of Islam. The religion which they had propagated united them only for a short time to the far-reaching Arab empire which they themselves had founded.

$$* \qquad * \qquad * \qquad * \qquad *$$

Many centuries later, in 1703, or, as some say, in 1691, there was born in Nejed a boy of the Beni Tameem tribe, whose name was Muhammad Ibn Abdul Wahhab. His father is believed to have been, at any rate by Central Arabian standards, a man of learning, who early instructed his son in the principles of the Muslim religion. The family were of settled stock, living in one of the oases of Nejed. Performing the pilgrimage to Mecca at an early age, the young Muhammad remained to devote himself to religion at Medina and subsequently at Basra and Damascus. By fervent study of the Qoran and of the traditions of the Prophet Muhammad, he became convinced of the abuses which had crept into Islam, as practised by the Turks and the Persians. In or about 1742, he came back to Nejed and began to preach a religious revival based on a return to the Qoran and the sayings of the Prophet and excluding, as man-made innovations, all practices for which authority could not be found in the orthodox writings. Meeting with little sympathy in his native village, he transferred his activities to the neighbouring small town of Deraiya.[1] The headman of this settlement was a certain Muhammad Ibn Saud, by birth of the Aneza tribe, who soon declared himself a convert to the preaching of the reformer. Nejed was at the time without a central government and its people were occupied in endless petty wars. The close alliance which was now cemented between the reformer Muhammad Ibn Abdul Wahhab and the shaikh of Deraiya, Muhammad Ibn Saud, led to the rapid growth of the latter's power.

Muhammad Ibn Saud died in 1765, and was succeeded by his son Abdul Aziz.[2] By 1770, the greater part of the inhabitants of Nejed, whether owing to the persuasiveness of the preacher or to coercion by the chieftain, had joined the new movement, the professors of which had become known as Wahhabis,[3] after the name of Muhammad Ibn Abdul Wahhab. A new wave of religious en-

[1] Pronounced Dera-eeya—the a and i being separate syllables.
[2] For chronological table of Saud and Rasheed dynasties see page 65.
[3] The accent is on the second syllable. For English people, who usually do not pronounce their r's, the phonetic spelling might be "Waharbies".

thusiasm swept through Nejed, consciously modelling itself on the original rise of Islam eleven hundred years earlier.

The neighbours of the newly formed Wahhabi confederation in Nejed were the shaikhs of the Beni Khalid tribe in the Hasa on the east and the sherifs[1] of Mecca on the west. In the holy city, the Turks claimed suzerainty in the name of the sultan of Turkey, but in practice the sherifian family, the lineal descendants of the Prophet Muhammad, the founder of Islam, ruled the Hejaz as secular Arab princes, in addition to enjoying the religious prestige which they derived from their genealogy.

In 1792, war broke out between the Wahhabis and the ruler of Mecca, Sherif Ghalib. Meanwhile the Wahhabi dominions were expanding in every direction. Between 1793 and 1795, several attacks were made on Kuwait, but all were repulsed. In 1795, the province of the Hasa was annexed after the defeat of Beni Khalid, and the Wahhabis proceeded to press on down the coast of the Persian Gulf towards Bahrein and Muscat. In the same manner, raids against the Euphrates area from Basra to Kerbela continued unabated from 1765 to 1803.

The Ottoman Empire during this period was in a condition of confusion and exhaustion. Successive wars with Russia, Napoleon's invasion of Egypt and the repeated mutinies of Turkey's regular troops, the Janissaries, almost destroyed the fabric of the state, and made it quite impossible for the Constantinople Government to send troops to Arabia. In Baghdad, a mameluke government, staffed by Circassian slaves, was virtually independent. The Sublime Porte, though itself helpless, ordered the Baghdad rulers to take action against the Wahhabis.

Accordingly, in February, 1797, the wali (or governor) of Baghdad nominated Thuwaini Ibn Sadoon, prince of the Muntifiq tribal confederation, to be governor of the province of Basra,[2] on condition that he raised a force to fight the Wahhabis. In the eighteenth century, so loose was the organization of the Ottoman Empire that the Wali of Baghdad was virtually independent of Constantinople, while his own authority extended only a few miles outside the city. The remainder of the country which now constitutes Iraq was ruled by semi-independent Arab princes, who paid little more than lip-service to either Constantinople or Baghdad. Of these princely Arab dynasties, that of the Sadoon family of the Muntifiq confederation was one of the most powerful. Thuwaini Ibn Abdulla Ibn Sadoon raised a large force and marched southwards to the

[1] Pronounced shereef.
[2] See map opposite first page of this chapter. Unless otherwise stated, the first map appearing in each chapter throughout this book shows all the places referred to in the chapter in question.

Hasa province. But on the evening of 1st July, 1797, he was assassinated in his tent by one of his own negro slaves, and his army disintegrated.

A year later, a fresh force was organized in Baghdad, consisting
of five thousand Turks, supported by tribal contingents from the
Dhafeer, Shammar and Muntifiq tribes, amounting to perhaps ten
thousand men. After occupying the Hasa province, the army withdrew again towards Basra, having accomplished nothing. Then
negotiations were opened, and a six-year truce was signed. The
truce, however, was soon broken by a renewal of raids by the Wahhabis, whose aggressiveness had been increased by the contempt
which they had conceived for the Turks, as a result of this abortive
campaign.

One morning in April, 1801, a Wahhabi force estimated at some
ten thousand men on six thousand camels, appeared in the date
palm gardens which surrounded the holy city of Kerbela, and
immediately carried the gateway of the town by assault. The inhabitants, utterly unprepared, fled here and there in panic, while
the Wahhabis seized and massacred all whom they met. They broke
into the great mosque which covers the tomb of the martyred
Husain, grandson of the Prophet himself, and where immense wealth
was reputed to have been accumulated from the centuries-old
offerings of the faithful. The iconoclastic bedouins did what they
could to wreck the splendid building, the glazed coloured tiles and
the golden dome.

The whole tragedy of the sack of Kerbela occupied only eight
hours. On the evening of the same day the raiders withdrew, vanishing once more into the desert, driving before them two hundred
camels laden with treasure. Five thousand persons were reported to
have been massacred in cold blood.

In 1802, the year after the sack of Kerbela, the Wahhabis invaded the Hejaz and captured Taif, massacring the inhabitants one
and all. In May, 1803, they occupied the city of Mecca itself.
Sherif Ghalib retired to Jidda, on the coast of the Red Sea. In July,
1803, when the Wahhabi forces had withdrawn to Nejed, he sallied
forth from Jidda and suddenly reappeared in the holy city. Negotiations ensued, as a result of which Sherif Ghalib was allowed to
remain as the ruler of Mecca, under the suzerainty of Ibn Saud, a
remarkable example of broadminded leniency on the part of the
latter.

On 4th November, 1803, the aged Abdul Aziz Ibn Saud was
leading the public prayers in the mosque of Deraiya, when he was
suddenly struck in the back with a dagger and died instantly. The
murderer was a Persian whose three sons had been massacred by
the Wahhabis in the sack of Kerbela two and a half years earlier.

Their father had somehow travelled to Deraiya and professed conversion to the Wahhabi sect. For more than a year he had worked in the Wahhabi capital, awaiting the opportunity to avenge the murder of his children. He was seized, burnt alive and then decapitated.[1] The Wahabbis might wreak their vengeance on the unfortunate Persian, but they could scarcely condemn the immorality of his action. Wholesale massacre had become the corner-stone of their policy. Indeed the reformer Muhammad Ibn Abdul Wahhab himself had not scrupled to arrange the assassination of his opponents in Nejed, in the early years of the movement.[2]

Saud Ibn Saud, who for many years had led the Wahhabi attacks on Iraq and the Hejaz, succeeded his father. He was handsome, a good speaker, and straightforward and frank in manner and speech, though of a quick temper. He was careful to be readily accessible to all, simple in dress, free from any desire for ceremonial, and famed for his lavish hospitality. These had been the typical and most attractive qualities of the bedouin prince in all ages. Under the title of Saud the Wahhabi, he appears to have been the first leader of the new movement to become known to the world at large outside Arabia.

In 1808, a Wahhabi force seized the oasis of Shitata, a few miles west of Kerbela, and thence raided the Euphrates bank near Hilla. A partial panic took place in Baghdad and the Wahhabis were momentarily expected in the capital. In 1810 again, a Wahhabi raid under Abdulla Ibn Saud, the eldest son of Saud the Wahhabi, almost reached Baghdad. In 1812, a Wahhabi tax-collector taxed the assembled Iraqi tribes at Hindiya on the Euphrates, only forty miles from the capital. The Wali of Baghdad, unable to face the Wahhabis in the field, was the helpless spectator of the devastation of his province.

Meanwhile in 1810, a raiding force six thousand strong broke into the Syrian province of Hauran, immediately south of Damascus. Although the raiders had taken thirty-five days to reach Hauran from Nejed, the governor of Damascus only heard of their approach forty-eight hours before their arrival. A panic ensued in Damascus and, if the Wahhabis had advanced boldly, they could probably have captured and looted that great and ancient city. As it was, they limited themselves to sacking thirty-five villages in the course of three days. They then vanished into the desert once more, without meeting with any opposition. The same year, they collected taxes from the Ijlas division of the Aneza tribe, only forty miles south of Aleppo.

The first Wahhabi dominion was at the height of its power from 1804 until 1812, coinciding with the zenith of Napoleon's domin-

[1] H. St. J. Philby. *Arabia*.   [2] H. St. J. Philby. *op. cit.*

ation of Europe. The two were doubtless not unconnected, for the pre-occupation of the Ottoman Empire and the European Powers with the struggle against France left Arabia to the mercy of the Wahhabis.

In the conduct of the affairs of the state, the ruling prince of the Saud dynasty exercised complete power, but it was the custom for the reformer, Muhammad Ibn Abdul Wahhab, as long as he lived, to be called into council with the prince for all major decisions. After his death, his descendants, known as the "sons of the shaikh", remained as a kind of unofficial council of state.

The Wahhabi dominion undoubtedly put an end to the tribal warfare and robbery which had previously been endemic in Arabia. The fact that the hands and feet of offenders were amputated with a hatchet may have constituted a deterrent, but the force of the religious revival also doubtless contributed. More serious offences were punished by death, those of less gravity by fines, the proceeds of which constituted a substantial part of th state revenues. Any man who failed to repeat his prayers five times a day was beaten with sticks.

The tradition of hospitality has always been deeply respected by the Arabs, who lead the world in this quality. Saud Ibn Saud, it was estimated, daily fed five hundred guests. In addition, many of them received sums of money or suits of clothing. The tradition of "visiting the prince" survives to this day in Arabia. Nearly every bedouin chief, great or small, paid a visit to the ruler to whom he owed allegiance once or twice a year, in the hope of receiving the traditional cash present and suit of clothing, or at least a new cloak. The Prophet Muhammad himself is alleged to have employed the same methods in dealing with bedouin chiefs. Often the "visitors" were accompanied by relatives or retainers, whose greed had likewise to be satisfied with gifts.[1]

Saud Ibn Saud was said to have a paid bodyguard of three hundred men, who in battle, according to their contemporary chronicler Burckhardt, were clad in complete armour. Apart from this *corps d'élite*, his only force was derived from the tribal levies. Every Wahhabi could be compulsorily called out for service. No military training whatever was considered possible or even desirable. Thus the revenue of the Wahhabi state, amounting perhaps to £100,000 a year, was principally expended on hospitality and on gifts or allowances to tribesmen and their chiefs. As the tribes constituted the sole army and police force of the state, to keep them contented and loyal was the prince's first preoccupation.

When the prince desired to set out on a campaign, orders were

---

[1] Compare the present given to Gehazi by Naaman the Syrian, "two talents of silver and two changes of garments." *II Kings* v. 23.

sent to the tribes to assemble. Each man brought his weapons and his own camel or horse or both; there could be no question of marching anywhere on foot across the deserts of Arabia. Every levy was required to bring his own food in his saddle-bags. His provisions normally consisted of flour, dates and oil, and a goatskin slung from the saddle to carry water. Little attempt was made to evolve a system of tactics, but each tribal contingent fought as a separate unit, under the war-banner of its chief, a system employed by the Prophet Muhammad in the seventh century. The contingents from the towns and oases of Nejed formed slightly less fickle elements than did the nomadic tribes. Neither the tribal nor the town contingents received pay for their services, but four-fifths of the loot taken were distributed amongst those serving on the campaign.

So primitive a military system was adequate enough for raiding purposes, but as each man was obliged to carry with him his rations for the whole expedition, no campaign could be prolonged. Moreover the Wahhabis were unable to provide garrisons for distant outposts or conquered provinces, because they employed no paid soldiers. Their policy of wholesale massacre, however, induced such terror that conquered populations hesitated to revolt, even if left without a garrison of Nejdis. The Wahhabis murdered in cold blood every male human being, even small children, but women were rarely, if ever, molested. Not only were they not assaulted but they were never taken prisoners.

From the point of view of the Muslim religion, the Wahhabi doctrines were strictly guided by the Qoran and traditions of the Prophet, and Muslim theologians could find little fault with them. But in the practical application of their principles, the savagery of their massacres of other Muslims, their greed for loot and their iconoclastic destruction of tombs and holy places, caused them to be regarded with hatred and repulsion by other professors of the Islamic faith. To the horror of the Muslim world, they even ventured, with sacrilegious hands, to desecrate in Medina the very tomb of the Prophet himself. Like Communism today, the Wahhabi movement sounded well enough when defended in argument, but the cruelty and the brutality of its practice obliterated the benefits which might have been anticipated from a study of its theories.

The unity of God had for centuries been an aspect of religion which had appealed to the Semites. It was the principle article of the Wahhabi revival. The members of the sect carried it to extremes and the most opprobrious term which they employed for their enemies was that of *mushrikeen* or "associaters" of other things with God.

* * * * *

The Sultan of Turkey had been deeply incensed at the capture of Mecca and Medina by the Wahhabis, and at their repeated outrages against the provinces of Iraq and Syria. Appeals to the Baghdad Government had been fruitless, and orders were sent to the Pasha of Egypt to restore the holy cities to their loyalty to the Khalif of Islam.

Napoleon had invaded Egypt in 1798 and had defeated the Mamelukes, the former slaves who had usurped the government of the country. The withdrawal of the French left Egypt in anarchy until, in 1805, an Albanian soldier of fortune, Muhammad Ali, secured his own elevation to power. Further internal conflicts ensued until, in 1811, he finally consolidated his power by a general massacre of the Mamelukes. It was to Muhammad Ali Pasha that the Sublime Porte turned for help against the Wahhabis. As soon as he had established his authority by eliminating the Mamelukes, he began serious preparations for a campaign in Arabia, by collecting a fleet of naval transports in Suez. Tusun Beg, his son, was appointed commander-in-chief, though he was only eighteen years old.

In October, 1811, a thousand Albanian infantry sailed from Egypt and landed at Yenbu. Fourteen days later, Tusun Beg reached the same town, having marched by land through Aqaba with eight hundred cavalry, the personnel of which were partly Turks and partly bedouin Arabs. In January, 1812, while Napoleon's army was struggling through the snows of a Russian winter, Tusun Beg led his little force up the Arabian mountain gorges to attack Medina. In the narrow pass of Judaida, he was ambushed by a large Wahhabi force, which, apparently unknown to Tusun, had just arrived from Nejed. The Wahhabis suddenly appeared on the mountains on both sides of the pass, and fired down upon the troops from every side. First the infantry and then the cavalry panicked and fled, while the nimble bedouins ran lightly along the mountain slopes, firing down continuously on the soldiers crowded into the gorge below.

Tusun Beg displayed considerable gallantry in this crisis, exposing himself in person to the fire of the Arabs until he succeeded in partially halting the flight of his troops. In this he was assisted by a certain Ibrahim Agha, whose original name had been Thomas Keith. He was a native of Edinburgh and had landed in Egypt in 1801 with General Abercrombie's army, in which he was an armourer in His Majesty's 72nd Highlanders. He was taken prisoner, became a Muslim and found his way into the service of Tusun Beg. His new master, however, in a fit of ill-temper one day, gave orders that the young Scot be put to death for some trifling neglect of duty. When Tusun's retainers arrived to execute the sentence, Thomas Keith defended the entrance to his room, sword in hand, against all comers,

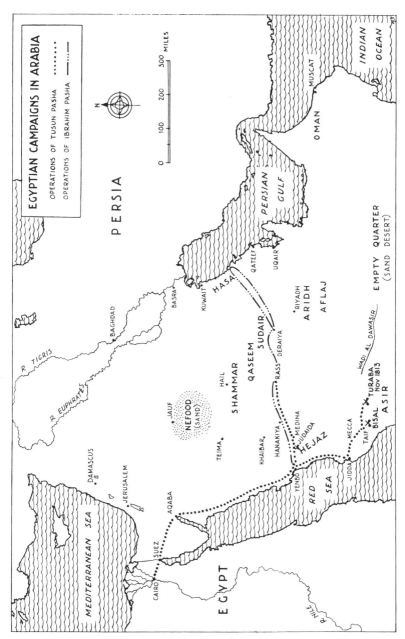

EGYPTIAN CAMPAIGNS IN ARABIA

OPERATIONS OF TUSUN PASHA ········
OPERATIONS OF IBRAHIM PASHA ─·─·─

500 MILES
0   100   200

N

PERSIA

INDIAN OCEAN

OMAN

MUSCAT

PERSIAN GULF

QATEEF

UGAIR

KUWAIT

BASRA

HASA

*RIYADH

ARIDH

AFLAJ

EMPTY QUARTER
(SAND DESERT)

BAGHDAD

R TIGRIS

R EUPHRATES

SUDAIR

RASS DERAIYA

QASEEM

HAIL

SHAMMAR

WADI AL DAWASIR

JAUF

NEFOOD
(SAND)

TEIMA

KHAIBAR

HANAKIYA

MEDINA

JUDAIDA

HEJAZ

MECCA

TAIF

BISAL

TURABA
NOV 1813

ASIR

DAMASCUS

JERUSALEM

AQABA

YENBO

RED SEA

JIDDA

SUEZ

CAIRO

EGYPT

R NILE

MEDITERRANEAN SEA

49

and eventually threw himself out of the window and took refuge with
the wife of Muhammad Ali Pasha, who caused him to be reconciled
with his young master. Eventually Tusun Beg himself came to appreciate the courage of his Scottish retainer, and appointed him to
be the chief agha of his mamelukes. After his heroism at the rout of
Judaida, Thomas Keith became virtually Tusun's second-in-
command.

The Egyptian army had suffered at Judaida a complete disaster,
losing one thousand two hundred men, two hundred horses, four
guns and all their baggage. If the Wahhabis had followed up their
victory, the expeditionary force could probably have been completely destroyed and the invasion of Arabia nipped in the bud.
But, bedouin-like, the victors were engrossed in the division of the
spoils and the opportunity was lost.

Nine months after his defeat at Judaida, Tusun Beg, now reinforced, again advanced on Medina, which he reached without en-
countering opposition. The walled town resisted for fourteen days.
A breach was then opened in the wall by a mine, and the irrepress-
ible Thomas Keith, sword in hand, led the assault, carrying the
town by storm and killing a thousand Wahhabis in the process. A
further one thousand five hundred of the enemy retired to the citadel.
but surrendered three weeks later.

In January, 1813, Mecca was occupied without opposition and
Taif a fortnight later. Sherif Ghalib joined the Egyptians, with whom
he had been in secret correspondence since the commencement of
the invasion. To celebrate these successes, Tusun Beg was raised to
the dignity of a pasha.

On 28th August, 1813, Muhammad Ali Pasha himself landed at
Jidda, bringing with him reinforcements of two thousand cavalry
and two thousand infantry. In November, 1813, he ordered his
son Tusun Pasha to advance from Taif to Turaba, but the column
was repulsed, beat a confused retreat and was once more only saved
by the personal bravery of Tusun and Thomas Keith.

But although the Egyptian army had retaken Mecca and Medina,
Muhammad Ali found himself faced with formidable difficulties.
The forces in the Hejaz amounted only to some five thousand men.
Burckhardt, the explorer, who saw them at this time, wrote that
"discontent and a kind of panic was universal among the soldiers".
In the autumn of 1814, another one thousand Turkish cavalry
arrived from Egypt. Meanwhile the Wahhabis had suffered a
grievous loss for on 17th April, 1814, Saud Ibn Saud died of a fever
in Deraiya, at the age of 68 years. His son Abdulla Ibn Saud succeeded him.

Meanwhile emissaries from the province of the Qaseem in Nejed
visited Tusun Pasha to ask him to advance into their country. The

tide of Wahhabi domination seemed to be on the ebb. Tusun left for the Qaseem at the end of March, 1815, with only six hundred cavalry and four hundred infantry, but this time he was supported by contingents of the Harab and Mutair tribes, hitherto themselves Wahhabis. He occupied the oasis town of Rass, but his communications with Medina were quickly cut behind him. The indomitable Thomas Keith, lately appointed governor of Medina, with two hundred and fifty cavalry reinforcements coming up from Medina, was surrounded by a large force of Wahhabis, and met his death after killing four of the enemy with his own hand. Tusun's position, cut off in the Qaseem from his base at Medina, was for a time precarious. But Abdulla Ibn Saud also faltered. He asked to negotiate and Tusun, perhaps with relief, consented. An agreement was concluded in June, 1815 (when the British army was driving Napoleon back from the blood-soaked ridge of Waterloo). The Wahhabis abandoned all claim to Mecca and Medina, and recognized the Sultan of Turkey as their overlord. Tusun Pasha, on his part, agreed to withdraw from the Qaseem to Medina. Muhammad Ali Pasha, who had meanwhile left for Egypt, refused to ratify the treaty. Tusun Pasha returned to Cairo under a cloud, and died of the plague a year later.

In September, 1816, Ibrahim Pasha, another son of Muhammad Ali, landed in the Hejaz and assumed command, bringing with him two thousand soldiers and one thousand five hundred Libyan bedouin horsemen. In December, 1817, he advanced to Hanakiya, east of Medina, where he was joined by the greater part of Ataiba, Harab and Mutair, and portions of the Shammar tribe. In June, 1817, he advanced into the province of the Qaseem, which had been reached by his brother Tusun, two years earlier.

On 22nd March, 1818, Ibrahim Pasha led his army from the Qaseem over the pass into the Wadi Haneefa, in which lay the Wahhabi capital. It was estimated that Ibrahim's army consisted by this time of one thousand nine hundred and fifty cavalry and five thousand six hundred infantry, with twelve guns. On 6th April, 1818, the Egyptian army stood beneath the walls of Deraiya, the Wahhabi capital, which, however, it failed to seize by a *coup de main*. The struggle for the town lasted for five months. On 9th September, Abdulla Ibn Saud asked for an interview and the two commanders met. Ibrahim presented him with an ultimatum demanding that he give himself up within twenty-four hours, to be sent into exile in Egypt. He complied. In Egypt he was well received by Muhammad Ali, but being sent on to Constantinople, he was ultimately beheaded in public in the square of Santa Sophia. His capital of Deraiya was razed to the ground and has never since been rebuilt. Ibrahim went on down to the Hasa and the Persian Gulf.

Within less than a year of the fall of Deraiya, Ibrahim Pasha had decided that direct rule of Central Arabia was not worth while. In June, 1819, the Egyptians evacuated the Hasa, which was given back to the Beni Khalid chiefs who had ruled it until the Wahhabi conquest in 1795. On 13th August, 1819, the Egyptians evacuated the Aridh province, retaining a garrison only in the Qaseem.

We are fortunate in the fact that Captain Sadleir of His Majesty's 47th Regiment accompanied the Egyptian withdrawal. The appearance of Ibrahim on the shores of the Persian Gulf had aroused the interest of the Government of India, which had sent Captain Sadleir on a mission to ascertain the intentions of the Egyptian commander. Sadleir arrived in the Hasa as the Egyptians were leaving it, and accompanied their retreat across the whole width of Arabia to the Red Sea. He has left a description of this mercenary army, clad in its ragged and worn-out uniforms and living in considerable squalor. The force which invaded Nejed consisted principally of Albanians, Turks and Libyans, assisted, when the tide began to turn against the Wahhabis, by an increasing number of Nejdi bedouins. Muhammad Ali kept his own recruiting organization, which hired mercenaries in the Balkans.

Ibrahim Pasha sailed from the Hejaz for Egypt on 17th November, 1819.

*   *   *   *   *

After the exile of Abdulla Ibn Saud in 1818, Nejed remained for twenty-four years in confusion. In 1834, a certain Feisal Ibn Saud seized power, and the people of Nejed rallied quickly to his leadership. In 1838, however, a fresh Egyptian expedition defeated Feisal and drove him into exile, but he reappeared once more in March, 1843, and reassumed control. Thereupon, after twenty-four years of instability, Egyptian intervention in Central Arabia came to an end.

During his early struggles, the new ruler, Feisal Ibn Saud, had been faithfully served by one of his retainers, a certain Abdulla Ibn Rasheed of the Shammar tribe. These services were rewarded by the appointment of Abdulla to be the governor of the northernmost province of Nejed, that of Jebel Shammar, of which the capital was Hail. Abdulla Ibn Rasheed remained, until his death, outwardly loyal to his patron Feisal Ibn Saud, although he was in reality independent in all but name. He died in 1847 and was succeeded as ruler of Hail by his eldest son Telal.[1]

The new Rasheed prince was a man of peace and inaugurated his reign of twenty-one years by openly acknowledging the suzerainty of the Wahhabi ruler of Riyadh, where Feisal had established his capital. Verbal acknowledgement, however, was the extent of his

---

[1] For table of Sauds and Rasheeds see end of this chapter.

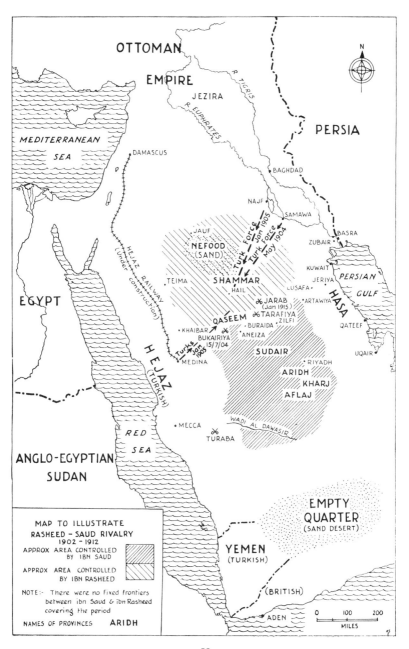

MAP TO ILLUSTRATE
RASHEED – SAUD RIVALRY
1902 – 1912

APPROX AREA CONTROLLED
BY IBN SAUD

APPROX AREA CONTROLLED
BY IBN RASHEED

NOTE:- There were no fixed frontiers
between ibn Saud & ibn Rasheed
covering the period

NAMES OF PROVINCES   **ARIDH**

53

submission and in all else he was an independent ruler. During his reign, which ended in 1868, the Shammar state extended its dominions, but, in order to avoid a clash with Ibn Saud, it did so towards the north and west by annexing the oases of Jauf, Khaibar, and Teima. Nejed became thereby divided into two states, ruled by two separate dynasties.

The venerable Feisal Ibn Saud was succeeded by his eldest son Abdulla, who had already been acting for his father, and who appeared to be a reasonably capable ruler, though apparently possessing an unattractive manner. Feisal's second son, Saud, was of different metal. Gifted with a magnetic personality, ambitious, generous and popular, he had acted as governor of the southern provinces during the reign of his father, and was already on bad terms with his elder brother Abdulla.

The year after the succession of Abdulla Ibn Saud in 1867, considerable friction arose with the Wali of Baghdad, as the result of Wahhabi raids on the Dhafeer and Muntifiq tribes—a situation which was to recur in the nineteen-twenties, as this narrative will show. In 1869, however, as a result of the weakening of Saudi policy under Abdulla Ibn Saud, the Wahhabis evacuated the Buraimi oasis on the borders of Oman.[1] Ever since the first great period of their expansion in 1800, they had periodically laid claim to Buraimi and at times had occupied or taxed it. After 1869, they were not to renew their claims until 1953, eighty-four years later.

Telal Ibn Rasheed had died in 1868, his brother Muhammad seizing power after a bitter family conflict, in which the new ruler caused every rival claimant to be butchered. Three years later, Saud Ibn Saud, the second son of Feisal, rebelled against his elder brother Abdulla, who appealed for support to the Ottoman Government in Constantinople.

On 26th May, 1871 (while Germany celebrated her triumph over France and the rising of the Commune was being suppressed in Paris), a Turkish army landed on the shores of the Hasa. Qateef surrendered on 3rd June. By July, the whole province of the Hasa was under effective Turkish control. The Ottoman Government, however, soon tired of its occupation of so remote a province and, in 1874, withdrew its troops, leaving the two Arabian dynasties to their own devices.

Thus between 1867 and 1887, Sauds and Rasheeds alike were torn by palace revolutions and fratricidal strife. Muhammad Ibn Rasheed, by the ruthless massacre of his relatives, was the first to restore order, and soon became the most powerful figure in Arabia. In 1887, a fresh schism broke out in the Saud family. The opportunity was too good to be missed by Ibn Rasheed, who marched on Riyadh and seized the town. The Sauds were carried prisoner to

---

[1] See map, page 40.

Hail or escaped abroad, and Muhammad Ibn Rasheed became the undisputed ruler of all Nejed.

The reign of Muhammad Ibn Rasheed was one of those periods of prosperity and contentment which came to Nejed whenever a great ruler arose, but which, in the past, so often alternated with periods of war and confusion after his death, until another outstanding man appeared, equal to the task of government.

The great Muhammad Ibn Rasheed died childless in 1897, and was succeeded by his nephew, Abdul Aziz Ibn Mitab Ibn Rasheed, a figure of romance, the embodiment of Arab chivalry, a Nejed Richard Cœur-de-Lion. His sole pleasure was raiding. Year after year he lived in the desert, raiding and hunting, but neglecting the duties of government. In spite of his gallantry, Abdul Aziz Ibn Rasheed lacked the political skill of which all the great rulers of Nejed have been masters. The people of Nejed are too virile to be ruled by force alone.

Towards the close of 1901, a certain Abdul Aziz Ibn Saud left Kuwait, where he had been in exile, with a party of forty camelmen, ostensibly for a raid. He wandered for some time in the Hasa and towards southern Nejed, without accomplishing anything notable. Early in January, he suddenly set out for Nejed with sixty men. On January 15th, 1902, he left thirty of his men in the desert not far from Riyadh, with orders to return to Kuwait if they received no news of him in twenty-four hours. When he reached the palm gardens immediately outside the city walls, he posted another twenty men. Then, with his remaining ten followers, he entered the city, apparently through a ruined and uninhabited quarter. Under cover of darkness, the little party occupied a house on the main square of Riyadh, on the other side of which lay the castle. The governor of the town, a certain Ajlan, who represented the authority of Ibn Rasheed, slept each night in the castle, but every morning held a levée in a house on the other side of the square. Abdul Aziz Ibn Saud and his ten followers lay all night in the house which they had occupied, observing the gate of the castle.

Soon after dawn, the gate was thrown open according to the daily routine, of which the raiders were of course fully aware. No sooner did the governor and his retainers emerge from the gateway to walk across the square to the hall where he held his morning court, than Abdul Aziz Ibn Saud and his ten men ran out upon them suddenly from their hiding place. The surprise was complete. Ibn Saud's little party fell upon the governor's escort, attacking them desperately with sword and dagger. Ajlan and several of his retainers were killed before they could prepare to defend themselves. Meanwhile, Abdulla Ibn Jiluwi, a cousin of Ibn Saud and one of his most devoted followers, accompanied by a few others, rushed the gate of the castle before the astonished garrison could close it.

The townspeople were, of course, favourable to the Sauds, the native dynasty under whom their town, not Hail, had previously been the capital of Arabia. The desperate fight in the square had occupied only a few minutes. In a short time order was restored in the town, and the Sauds were again in control after eleven years of exile. This enterprise, carried out with such courage, initiative and careful planning, revealed that a new personality had arisen in Nejed. Soon Abdul Aziz Ibn Saud was to prove that his wisdom and statecraft exceeded even his courage. Abdul Aziz Ibn Rasheed was no match for him as a statesman.

On 7th January, 1904, Ibn Rasheed telegraphed the Ottoman Prime Minister in Constantinople, claiming that the British were supporting Ibn Saud and asking for Turkish help. Meanwhile in March, 1904, Ibn Saud occupied the Qaseem.

Early in 1904, Turkey, having secured the support and friendship of Imperial Germany, was bent on the modernization and expansion of her empire, and had just embarked on the construction of a railway from Damascus to Medina, under the supervision of German engineers. A hostile Nejed could easily render the construction of the railway impossible. The Turks decided to act forthwith. In May, 1904, a Turkish force about two thousand strong, with six guns slung in litters between mules, set out for Hail from Samawa on the Euphrates.

On 15th July, 1904, a pitched battle took place at Bukairiya between Ibn Saud and the people of the Qaseem on the one hand and Ibn Rasheed and the Turks on the other. The result was indecisive. The fighting was extremely heavy by Arabian standards, each side suffering about a thousand killed.[1] As a result, the morale of both sides seems to have fallen low after the battle. The Turks had suffered heavy casualties, from sickness, desertion and battle, their numbers having fallen in a few weeks from two thousand to seven hundred. But Ibn Saud seems also to have lost his nerve, and sent his submission to the Turks. For the moment the Turks, though their expeditionary force was almost destroyed, were receiving protestations of loyalty from Ibn Saud and Ibn Rasheed simultaneously.

In January, 1905, a further Turkish force of three thousand men with six guns left Nejef in Iraq for Central Arabia. Simultaneously another column of seven hundred and fifty and one battery of artillery set out from Medina for the Qaseem. On 15th April, the Turks occupied Buraida in that province. A senior Turkish officer, who had negotiated with both the rivals, described Abdul Aziz Ibn Rasheed as the desert warrior, but Abdul Aziz Ibn Saud as the desert

[1] H. St. J. Philby. *Arabia*.

diplomatist. Ibn Rasheed was reported on more than one occasion to have challenged Ibn Saud, with old-fashioned chivalry, to decide the issue by personal combat, but his patient and cautious rival was not attracted by hare-brained romantic schemes.

On 11th April, 1906, a Saudi force surprised Ibn Rasheed in his camp, under cover of a dust storm. The Amir could have saved himself by flight but refused. He chose to die, calling out his war-cry and surrounded by enemies. His son Mitab, aged eighteen, succeeded his father. The Turks at this time, it appears, were paying a subsidy of £200 a month to Mitab Ibn Rasheed and £90 a month to Ibn Saud.

Meanwhile the Turkish troops, like the Egyptians before them in the time of Muhammad Ali Pasha, were reduced to the rags of their uniforms and were even in need of food. Many, it was reported, sold their arms to supplement their rations. (The majority of the soldiers in the Turkish forces in Nejed were actually Arabs of Iraq or Syria.) In November, 1906, the Turks decided to make the best of a bad job, and to evacuate Nejed altogether, as the Egyptians had been compelled to do sixty-six years earlier.

The great Muhammad Ibn Rasheed had raised his family to the highest pinnacle of greatness, but he had seized power by murdering nearly all his male relatives. It was a precedent which was to prove fatal to the dynasty. Mitab Ibn Rasheed had scarcely ruled for a year when he was assassinated by his cousin Sultan, who himself was murdered by his brother Saud Ibn Hamood. Nine months later, he also was assassinated, and a child, Saud Ibn Abdul Aziz, was proclaimed. Under the nominal rule of the infant Saud, and the regency of Zamil Ibn Subhan, the Shammar state enjoyed a few much needed years of peace, a St. Martin's Summer during which, for a brief period, something of the old spirit seemed to revive.

From 1902 to 1912, Abdul Aziz Ibn Saud had fought against the Rasheed family, more or less as the wars of Nejed had always been fought. Abdul Aziz Ibn Rasheed was actuated by something of the old spirit of fighting for fighting's sake, as a means of performing heroic deeds, to be celebrated in verse and song. Abdul Aziz Ibn Saud, in this direction, was more realist—more modern perhaps. He fought to win. In spite of this, however, he had carried on the war on a personal or a dynastic, not on a religious, basis. Perhaps the fact that, when a youth and a young man, he had lived with the Turks in the Hasa, and with Ibn Sobah in Kuwait,[1] had made him more tolerant than the old Wahhabis had been. Having lived and ruled thus for ten years, in 1912 he suddenly inaugurated a revival of Wahhabi extremism. His introduction of fanaticism at this stage and his abandonment of it twenty years later, when it proved

[1] The Sobah were and are the hereditary rulers of Kuwait.

inconvenient, seemed to prove indisputably that he employed it for purposes of policy.

Whatever may have been the motives of Abdul Aziz Ibn Saud, the fact remains that in 1912 he appears to have definitely, and even enthusiastically, sponsored a revival of Wahhabi fanaticism, based on the precedent of the first sectaries, in the latter years of the eighteenth century. But if the religious revival of 1912 was something of an imitation, another of Ibn Saud's plans was original. Doubtless he had been impressed by the greater steadiness in battle of the people of the Nejed oases, as opposed to the nomadic bedouins. "Unstable as water thou shalt not excel"[1] had always epitomized the character of the tribes. Why not then transform the tribes into oasis dwellers?

It was perhaps a somewhat superficial solution to the problem, for nobody knew if sufficient water were available to make new oases possible. The order to the bedouins to settle, to build huts and engage in agriculture was given religious sanction by the new Wahhabi revival. The true believers were told that to sell their camels and to live in mud huts in place of tents was a religious duty. The new settlements were definitely religious communities, bound together in a religious brotherhood, in proof of which they assumed the title of the brethren—Al Ikhwan. They foreswore tobacco, music, silk, gold thread on their cloaks and the vanities of the world in general. The Mutair tribe had been one of the first to adopt, at least outwardly, the new Wahhabi fanaticism, and the first Ikhwan bedouin colony was founded at their wells of Artawiya, by their tribal chief Feisal al Duweesh.

During the winter of 1913–14, Captain W. H. I. Shakespear, then British Political Agent at Kuwait, visited Ibn Saud in Riyadh, and discussed with him a treaty of alliance with Great Britain. When the First World War commenced, and Turkey joined Germany, Ibn Rasheed immediately declared his devotion to the Ottoman Empire. Captain Shakespear was sent back to Nejed, this time as permanent British representative to the court of Riyadh, with the task of securing Ibn Saud's adherence to the Allied cause. He was so far successful that, in January, 1915, Ibn Saud led out his forces against Ibn Rasheed. Thus the dynastic rivalry in Arabia fell into line with the two sides in the First World War.

An indecisive battle was fought at Jarab. The Wahhabi horsemen drove the Shammar mounted men from the field, but a dismounted force, possibly the townsmen of Hail or the villagers of Jebel Shammar, defeated Ibn Saud's foot soldiers. Shakespear, wearing a British army uniform, was assisting to fire Ibn Saud's solitary mountain gun when Ibn Rasheed's army drove the Wahhabis from their

[1] *Genesis* xlix. 4.

positions. He refused to take to flight, and selling his life alone as dearly as he could, he was overwhelmed and killed.

Few people in England have ever heard of William Henry Irvine Shakespear, yet it may scarcely be an exaggeration to say that his death changed history. He possessed remarkable influence over Abdul Aziz Ibn Saud. Fourteen years later, I myself was to hear the latter exclaim that Shakespear was one of the greatest men he had ever known. If the battle of Jarab had ended differently, Ibn Saud and Shakespear might have played a part in the First World War no less distinguished than that of the Amir Feisal and T. E. Lawrence.

After Shakespear's death, however, Ibn Saud withdrew to Riyadh, and played no further part in the First World War. In December, 1915, the British Government concluded an agreement with Sherif Husain of Mecca for an Arab rising against the Turks. Unfortunately relations were already strained between Ibn Saud and the sherifs, with the result that the latter tended to favour Ibn Rasheed. The local power politics of Arabia, thereafter, conflicted with the alignment of these princes in reference to the Allies on the one hand, and Germany and Turkey on the other. The sherif, now Britain's first champion, was a friend of Ibn Rasheed, the ally of Turkey, but hostile to Ibn Saud, Britain's other friend. Indeed Ibn Saud's inactivity throughout the remainder of the war was doubtless partly due to his resentment at the favour shown by Britain to his rival, Sherif Husain. He was unable, however, to change sides and join the Turks, because his other rival, Ibn Rasheed, was already their principal ally. He therefore spent the war years, after the death of Shakespear, in consolidating his position at home.

No sooner, however, did the armistice put an end to the First World War than the differences between Sherif Husain and Abdul Aziz Ibn Saud flamed up into open hostility, although both were still allies of Britain and in receipt of British subsidies. Skirmishing and raiding broke out on the border between the Hejaz and Nejed, and in May, 1919, a sherifian army was utterly defeated by a Wahhabi force at Turaba. Ibn Saud did not, however, follow up his victory.

The ten years which had elapsed since Saud Ibn Abdul Aziz Ibn Rasheed came to the throne had passed quietly and even prosperously for the Shammar princedom. But the family seemed unable to escape from the tragic tradition of internecine murder. In 1920, when it might have been hoped that the Rasheed principality might enjoy a calm and even prosperous future, the young Saud Ibn Abdul Aziz was assassinated. The members of the Rasheed family had ridden out with Prince Saud for a picnic and shooting match in the country outside Hail. Abdulla Ibn Telal, great-grandson of the Amir Telal Ibn Rasheed, was of the party. The Amir

Saud, in the course of the shooting match, ventured to mock the bad marksmanship of his cousin Abdulla Ibn Telal. A wave of resentful passion swept over the latter, and swinging suddenly round he shot the Amir Saud dead. Within a few seconds, the murderer was cut down by the slaves of Saud. Thus within two or three minutes, the two most capable possible claimants to the Rasheed throne had been destroyed. Abdulla Ibn Mitab, a weakly youth, succeeded to the princedom.

Just as, in 1887, the internecine struggles of rival Saud claimants had encouraged the great Muhammad Ibn Rasheed to march on Riyadh, so this further butchery between members of the Rasheed family decided Abdul Aziz Ibn Saud to seize the opportunity finally to eliminate the rival dynasty by marching on Hail.

His decision to do so may also have been the result of developments in other parts of the Middle East. For Sherif (now proclaimed King) Husain of the Hejaz was hostile to him on the west, while Husain's third son, Feisal, was about to be made King of Iraq. It will be recollected that the sherifian family had been friendly with Ibn Rasheed. Perhaps Ibn Saud may have thought that a league consisting of the Hejaz, Ibn Rasheed and Iraq would be too strong for him, and that it would be wise to eliminate the Rasheeds before such an alliance could be formed.

Whatever may have been his motives, he decided, in the spring of 1921, to march on Hail. Although he had hitherto contented himself with the semi-religious title of the Imam, in June, 1921, he was proclaimed sultan of Nejed. In July, 1921, he took command in person in the campaign against the Rasheeds. Even with the enemy at the gates, the young members of the dynasty could not sink their differences. Muhammad Ibn Telal, the brother of Abdulla Ibn Telal, the murderer of the Amir Saud, rose against Abdulla Ibn Mitab, who fled from Hail, took refuge with Ibn Saud, and was imprisoned in Riyadh. After a few weeks of desultory operations, Muhammad Ibn Telal surrendered on November 2nd, 1921, and was likewise transported to captivity at Riyadh. The Rasheed dynasty came to an end, after nearly ninety years. Ibn Saud once more became the sole ruler of Nejed, one hundred and three years after the end of the first Wahhabi empire, when Abdulla Ibn Saud surrendered to Ibrahim Pasha, the son of Muhammad Ali Pasha, in September, 1818.

*   *   *   *   *

In November, 1921, therefore, the Wahhabi state suddenly became the neighbour of Iraq. The Hejaz, Trans-Jordan and Iraq, in the same year, all received sherifian rulers. Sherif Husain was King of the Hejaz, his second son Abdulla was Amir of Trans-

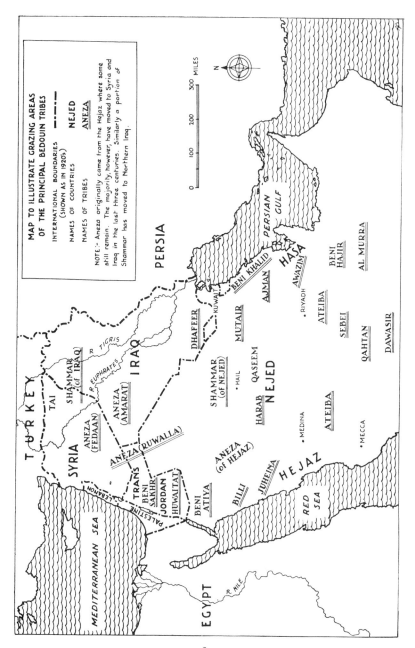

MAP TO ILLUSTRATE GRAZING AREAS
OF THE PRINCIPAL BEDOUIN TRIBES

INTERNATIONAL BOUNDARIES ━━━━━
(SHOWN AS IN 1920s)

NAMES OF COUNTRIES   NEJED

NAMES OF TRIBES   ANEZA

NOTE:- Aneza originally came from the Hejaz where some
still remain. The majority, however, have moved to Syria and
Iraq in the last three centuries. Similarly a portion of
Shammar has moved to Northern Iraq.

0   100   200   300   MILES

N

PERSIA

TURKEY

TAI

SHAMMAR
(of IRAQ)

R. TIGRIS

R. EUPHRATES

IRAQ

ANEZA
(FEDAAN)

ANEZA
(AMARAT)

SYRIA

ANEZA (RUWALLA)

DHAFFER

KUWAIT

BENI KHALID

AJMAN

AWAZIM

HASA

BENI
HAJIR

AL MURRA

MUTAIR

• RIYADH

ATEIBA

SEBEI

DAWASIR

QAHTAN

SHAMMAR
(of NEJED)

• HAIL

QASEEM

NEJED

HARAB

PERSIAN
GULF

TRANS

BENI
SAKHR

JORDAN
HUWAITAT

BENI
ATIYA

ANEZA
(of HEJAZ)

• MEDINA

ATEIBA

PALESTINE

LEBANON

BILLI

JUHEINA

HEJAZ

• MECCA

RED
SEA

MEDITERRANEAN SEA

EGYPT

R. NILE

61

Jordan, and his third son, Feisal, was crowned King of Iraq. Thus Ibn Saud saw himself, as he thought, hemmed in by enemies. In reality this was not the case. King Husain in the Hejaz was, it was true, entirely free to do as he wished, but both Trans-Jordan and Iraq were British mandates. Moreover, the people of these two countries were but little interested in events in Central Arabia, and Iraq was emerging from the confusion of the First World War which had been followed in 1920 by internal revolts and disturbances.

Meanwhile a large part of the Shammar tribe, the followers of the Rasheeds, had abandoned Nejed, and had taken refuge in the Jezira, the area between the Tigris and Euphrates north of Baghdad, whither another branch of the tribe had emigrated from Nejed several generations earlier.[1]

The British Government was anxious to ensure the general pacification of Arabia, and for that purpose sought to persuade Ibn Saud to enter into treaty relations with Iraq. A conference for this purpose was opened at Muhammarah on the Shatt al Arab in the spring of 1922. Sir Percy Cox, the British High Commissioner in Iraq, presided over the negotiations, which were conducted by representatives of Iraq and Nejed.

To the British Government, it appeared obvious that the first step in a settlement between two neighbouring states was to define the boundary which separated their territories. Such a proposal was entirely new to the Nejdis and was viewed by them with profound suspicion. International boundaries had never been heard of in Arabia. For four centuries, the whole area had been vaguely considered to form part of the Ottoman Empire. It is true that for a great part of that time the different provinces had been virtually independent of the Sublime Porte in Istanbul, but such a situation had, even so, never led to the establishment of frontiers in Central Arabia. In practice, the Baghdad administration had never made any attempt to extend its control into the desert to a distance of more than two or three miles from the Euphrates.

The Nejed delegates were far more vividly aware than were the Iraqis or the British that the very existence of nomadic tribes depended on their power to migrate and graze freely. So fickle was the desert rainfall that, in some years, the greater part of Nejed might be afflicted with drought. In such cases, it was essential for the very survival of the Nejed tribes that they be able to move northwards towards Iraq or Syria in search of some desert area where rain had fallen. Conversely the northern tribes might at times be obliged to migrate for a whole season to Nejed. To draw a hard and fast frontier across the desert wastes seemed to the Nejdis to threaten the very existence of those tribes which, as we have seen, constituted a

[1] See tribal map on previous page.

great part of Ibn Saud's armed forces. As a result, the Nejed delegation categorically refused to fix any frontier with Iraq. The Treaty of Muhammarah between Nejed and Iraq was signed on 5th May, 1922, but in it there was no reference to a frontier. The allegiance of the tribes was, however, decided. The Muntifiq, Dhafeer and Amarat (the Iraq division of the great Aneza tribe) were allotted to Iraq, while Shammar of Nejed were recognized as subjects of that country.

Abdul Aziz Ibn Saud refused to ratify the Muhammarah Treaty, even in the form to which his delegates had agreed. As a result, a personal meeting between him and Sir Percy Cox was arranged at Uqair[1] in the Hasa in November, 1922. Ibn Saud was intensely suspicious of the fact that sherifian rulers had assumed control in the Hejaz, Trans-Jordan and Iraq. Mr. Ameen Rihani, the Lebanese poet, who was present at the conference at Uqair, reports Ibn Saud saying, "The English have surrounded me with enemies." He believed that this encirclement was the result of intrigues which the British were spinning against him.

Abdul Aziz Ibn Saud was very conscious of the history of his ancestors, who had built up the first Wahhabi empire from 1800 to 1818. He claimed as his by right everything which had belonged to the first Wahhabi empire at the time of its maximum extent. His ancestors, he truthfully claimed, had taxed the bedouins as far north as Aleppo. But the first Wahhabi supremacy had lasted for less than a quarter of a century, and had collapsed one hundred and forty years before. The Sauds hardly seemed entitled to claim the dominion exercised by their forebears so long ago. Ibn Saud bitterly opposed any land frontier but was prepared to make a concession in the direction of defining the allegiance of the tribes, though this also he opposed. Obviously the more fluid the situation, the easier would it be for him to expand, as and when opportunity offered.

For five days, Ibn Saud and the Iraqi representatives argued with one another without any apparent likelihood of their reaching agreement. On the sixth day, Sir Percy Cox intervened. By the use of his personality, he persuaded both sides to accept a land frontier drawn by himself. Iraq was given a considerable area of desert, being approximately the grazing areas of the Amarat Aneza and the Dhafeer, the two bedouin tribes which had been recognized as Iraqi subjects. A diamond shaped area, which contained a number of perennial wells on the frontier, was made neutral. In it, both governments (not, curiously enough, the tribes of both sides) were to enjoy equal rights. The nature of those rights was not defined. The agreements were embodied in two documents known as the

[1] See map on page 53.

Uqair protocols, which were signed at Uqair on 2nd December, 1922, and appended to the Muhammarah Treaty. Protocol No. 1 defined the frontier between Iraq and Nejed. The whole length of the border lay in complete desert. The text of the protocol bears witness to the anxieties felt by Ibn Saud on the subject of free grazing for his tribes. The wording of Article 2 stated that, as many of the wells fell within the Iraq boundaries, the Iraq Government pledged itself not to interfere with Nejed tribes which might wish to use them. The conditions of nomad life rendered such an agreement essential, but the remarkable fact about the article in question was that the Nejed Government undertook no corresponding obligation in regard to Iraq tribes, for whom it was no less vital. The omission can only be explained by the ignorance of the Iraq and British Governments of the conditions of nomad life.

Article 3 contained a provision that the two governments would not use the wells situated in the vicinity of the border for any military purpose, such as building forts by them, neither would they concentrate troops in their vicinity. As a result of the Uqair meeting, both King Feisal of Iraq, and Abdul Aziz Ibn Saud, sultan of Nejed, ratified the Muhammarah Treaty and the two Uqair protocols. For the first time in history, the deserts of Arabia were divided by frontiers marked on maps.

The diplomatic skill of Sir Percy Cox seemed to have enabled the British Government to take a long step forward in their efforts to ensure peace between the Arab countries. The unremitting efforts exerted by the British to avoid friction between the different Arab Governments is worthy of note, if only because they have been so constantly accused since then of fomenting discord and obstructing Arab unity. Britain believed that peace between the various states was in her interest and the historical facts prove that she laboured untiringly to establish it.

Chronological Table of Sauds and Rasheeds

Date	Sauds	Date	Rasheeds
1747–65	Muhammad Ibn Saud. Friend of Muhammad Ibn Abdul Wahhab the Reformer.		
1765–1803	Abdul Aziz Ibn Saud, assassinated by a Persian.		
1803–14	Saud Ibn Saud the Wahhabi.		
1814–18	Abdulla Ibn Saud, conquered by Ibrahim Pasha and beheaded in Istanbul.		
1818–34	Egyptian period. Nejed in confusion.		
1834–67	Feisal Ibn Saud.	1835–47	Abdulla Ibn Rasheed, a retainer of Feisal Ibn Saud, made governor of Hail.
1867–89	Civil war between Abdulla and Saud, sons of Feisal Ibn Saud.	1847–68	Telal Ibn Rasheed.
		1868–72	Struggle between rival Rasheed claimants.
1889–1902	No Saud ruler.	1872–97	Muhammad Ibn Rasheed sole ruler of all Nejed.
1902–53	Abdul Aziz Ibn Saud.	1897–1906	Abdul Aziz Ibn Rasheed.
		1906–7	Mitab Ibn Abdul Aziz Ibn Rashid (murdered).
		1907–1909	Sultan Ibn Hamood (murdered). Saud Ibn Hamood (murdered).
1921 onwards	Ibn Saud sole ruler.		
1953	Saud Ibn Saud present ruler.	1909–1920	Saud Ibn Abdul Aziz Ibn Rasheed (murdered).
		1920–21	Abdulla Ibn Mitab Ibn Rasheed (fled to Ibn Saud).
		1921	Muhammad Ibn Telal Ibn Rasheed (captured by Ibn Saud).
		1921	End of Rasheed dynasty.

III

Sadoon and Suwait

The hand of the princes and the rulers hath been chief in this trespass.
Ezra ix. 2

Wounded in their pride, the Arabs of Iraq evinced from the first a turbulent, seditious, anarchical, and, in a word, a very Arab spirit. The province soon became a focus for political firebrands—the haunt of brigands and assassins.   DOZY, *The Moslems in Spain*

Hemmed in as they were by lands ruled by historic dynasties, their deserts and their valour ever kept out the invader and from the days of remote antiquity . . . hardly anything was known of this secluded people save that they existed, and that no one attacked them with impunity.   STANLEY LANE-POOLE

III

SADOON AND SUWAIT

I SERVED in France throughout the First World War. In July, 1920, however, I was posted to Iraq as a regular army officer, and landed in Basra at the end of September. Disturbances had been going on for several months, and a number of Iraq tribes had rebelled against the authority of an administration which aspired really to govern the country in a manner which their former rulers, the Turks, had scarcely attempted.

In 1921, after the rebellion, Iraq was the scene of a new experiment, unprecedented in the world, the employment of air forces in place of ground troops for internal security duties. In theory, air forces possessed great advantages over soldiers in a country largely inhabited by armed tribes, and almost entirely lacking in roads. The Egyptians and the Turks had, for example, found it almost impossible to operate with troops in the desert, owing to the difficulties of communications and supply. In Iraq, the same problems arose not only in the desert but also in the roadless marsh areas or in the mountains of Kurdistan.

In face of these difficulties, the idea of using aircraft to overcome the problem of great distances and bad communications appeared extremely tempting. For aircraft could remain concentrated in one great central cantonment, and could take action in a few hours against a hostile tribe, in spite of hundreds of miles of intervening marshes, mountains or waterless deserts. The war, the enthusiasts claimed, could literally be finished in time to be home for tea, if not indeed for lunch.

But one difficulty remained to be overcome. When ground forces moved against an enemy, they acquired information as they advanced. Friendly tribes and villages sent deputations to meet the column and demonstrate their loyalty. Hostile communities fired on the troops. There was rarely much difficulty in knowing who was a friend and who an enemy. In the case of aircraft, however, the reverse was likely to be the case. Air forces, arriving over a target area from a remote cantonment hundreds of miles away, would see below them a country dotted with villages, flocks or tents. How were they to be certain which of them was hostile and which friendly? Moreover, the very fact that the air forces lived together in a central cantonment would result in their being ignorant of the country and the people, and consequently unable to interpret intelligently what they observed on the ground. Lack of intelligence seemed, therefore, likely to provide one of the chief obstacles to the successful use of air forces for internal security.

The system devised to deal with this problem involved the creation of a number of posts for officers in outside districts. These officers were to play the rôle of military attachés, with political officers or governors in charge of districts. It was their duty to familiarize themselves with the district to which they were accredited in such a manner that, should air operations suddenly be required, they would be enabled to make such arrangements as were necessary to ensure that aircraft found their correct targets.

The Air Staff found some difficulty in discovering R.A.F. officers with the desire or the qualifications to fill these posts. My attempts to learn Arabic being known, I was offered a position of this kind on the Air Staff, although I was an army officer. As I was already greatly attracted to the people of Iraq, I accepted the appointment and was posted to the Muntifiq district, the headquarters of which was at Nasiriya on the Lower Euphrates. I arrived there in April, 1922.

In the eighteenth and nineteenth centuries, the Muntifiq had consisted of a large tribal confederation, which had been forged into a single princedom by the noble Sadoon family. Two centuries before, Turkish control over Iraq had been extremely precarious and often extended for only a few miles outside Baghdad. The remainder of the country was ruled by Arab princes, who were virtually independent. These local amirs waged war against one another and not infrequently against the Sultan's wali, or viceroy, in Baghdad.

The Sadoon, the amirs of the Muntifiq, were among the greatest of these semi-independent princes. During the second half of the nineteenth century, however, the Ottoman Empire determined to modernize itself, and, in the process, to reduce Iraq to the status of a regularly administered province. To achieve this end, the authorities decided that the first step must be to destroy the power of the Arab princely houses. Unfortunately the Turks did not possess the resources to subjugate and subsequently to administer the remote and warlike province of Iraq. The Ottoman government accordingly set to work to destroy the power of the Arab princes by intrigue.

Jealousy is perhaps the besetting sin of the Arab character. Ambition which, when possessed in moderation, produces a legitimate desire for advancement, can, if unrestricted, degenerate into an insensate hatred of all competitors. The Turks took advantage of this Arab weakness. A junior member of each ruling family was given Turkish support in asserting a claim to the leadership. The rightful prince, resentful at the bestowal of government favours on

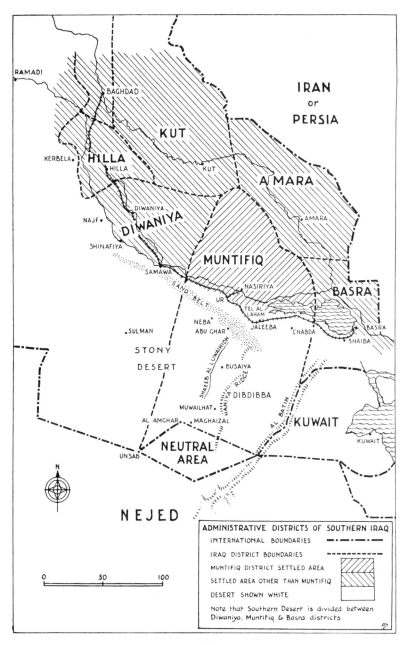

RAMADI

BAGHDAD

KERBELA

HILLA

HILLA

NAJF

KUT

KUT

IRAN
or
PERSIA

A MARA

DIWANIYA

DIWANIYA

SHINAFIYA

AMARA

SAMAWA

SAND BELT

UR

MUNTIFIQ

NASIRIYA

TEL AL
LAHAM

BASRA

SULMAN

NEBA
ABU GHAR

JALEEBA

CHABDA

BASRA

SHAIBA

STONY

DESERT

SHAEEB AL LUWAIHITH

BUSAIYA

HANIN RIDGE

DIBDIBBA

AL BATIN

MUWAILHAT

AL AMGHAR

MAGHAIZAL

KUWAIT

KUWAIT

UN SAB

NEUTRAL
AREA

N

N E J E D

ADMINISTRATIVE DISTRICTS OF SOUTHERN IRAQ

INTERNATIONAL BOUNDARIES

IRAQ DISTRICT BOUNDARIES

MUNTIFIQ DISTRICT SETTLED AREA

SETTLED AREA OTHER THAN MUNTIFIQ

DESERT SHOWN WHITE.

Note that Southern Desert is divided between
Diwaniya, Muntifiq & Basra districts.

0   50   100

his subordinate, would endeavour to suppress the upstart, and soon the clan would be split by civil war.

The great Sadoon family, the rulers of the Muntifiq tribal confederation, were in this manner reduced to impotence. As a result, the Turks succeeded in establishing a military cantonment at Nasiriya, in the Muntifiq country. Sadoon Ibn Sadoon, claiming to be chief of the Muntifiq but outlawed by the Turks, built a castle at Abu Ghar in the desert, whither the Turks could not—or did not trouble to—pursue him.

The principal bedouin tribe in the area was the Dhafeer who, under their shaikh Ibn Suwait, sometimes moved down to the Euphrates in summer. They spent the winter, however, a hundred and fifty to two hundred miles to the south, on the fringes of Nejed. Here they passed beyond the jurisdiction of the Turks and the Sadoon alike and came into the sphere of the then ruling prince of Nejed, Ibn Saud or Ibn Rasheed. The Dhafeer were accustomed to control their own foreign policy, and to negotiate as seemed best to them with neighbouring princes, such as the Shaikh of Kuwait or Ibn Rasheed, though they were probably willing to acknowledge the vague suzerainty of the Sadoon on the Euphrates.

But respect for a noble house, exercised at a distance by a tribe wandering freely in the desert, was a very different matter from submission to a haughty prince in their midst. When Sadoon Ibn Sadoon, trying to keep out of the way of the Turks, joined the Dhafeer in the desert, a clash between him and their shaikh, Ibn Suwait, became inevitable. Sadoon employed, to establish his authority over the Dhafeer, the same methods which the Turks had used to weaken his own family—he allied himself with a minor shaikh of the tribe and supported him against Ibn Suwait for the post of paramount shaikh. Not only so, but he invited Ibn Rasheed to raid the Dhafeer in order to weaken him. Such methods certainly injured the Dhafeer, but they also raised such opposition to Sadoon that the desert became too hot for him. Having fled to the desert to escape the Turks, he was obliged to return to the settled area and surrender to them, to save himself from the resentment of the Dhafeer. A man of turbulent character and immense courage and energy, his arrogance had entirely deprived him of friends. He was deported by the Ottoman Government to Aleppo, where he died not long afterwards.

When the First World War broke out, the Muntifiq were in this state of chaos. The Turks had established a firm grip on their cantonment at Nasiriya, but their control over the local tribes was precarious, and their influence in the desert almost non-existent. When the British landed in Basra and advanced up the railway line towards Nasiriya, Ibn Rasheed declared for the Turks, as also did

Ajami, the son of Sadoon Ibn Sadoon. The Dhafeer retired into the desert and kept out of trouble.

After the war came the 1920 Iraq disturbances, which had been the immediate cause of my posting to Iraq. In 1921, the first Iraq Government had been formed and the Amir Feisal had been crowned king. Ajami Pasha Ibn Sadoon took refuge in Anatolia with the Turks. Ibn Saud, as already related, had meanwhile become the immediate southern neighbour of Iraq.

When the 1920 rebellion petered out and the first Iraq Government was formed, a certain Yusuf Ibn Sadoon conceived the idea of becoming a power in the desert, as his father and grandfather had tried to be. Scion of a line of princes, though with neither followers nor cash, he hastened to Baghdad in the autumn of 1921 to offer his services. The government, persuaded by his arguments or impressed by his lineage, fell in with his plans. He was allotted a salary, and was instructed to raise a desert camel force at the government's expense, and to recruit bedouins for the purpose. Yusuf returned to the Muntifiq in high glee.

Almost the only bedouins available for recruitment, however, were the Dhafeer, whose own shaikh, Hamood Ibn Suwait, was doubtless intentionally by-passed by Yusuf owing to the old family rivalry. By their inept action, the government had made a collision between Yusuf Ibn Sadoon and Hamood Ibn Suwait inevitable. For the moment, however, Yusuf, supported by government money and weapons, was in the ascendant. Hamood left for Nejed to complain to Ibn Saud, whose recent victory over Ibn Rasheed had made him lord of all Central Arabia. The Dhafeer were in reality in a most unfortunate position. Their summer camps and their market towns were along the Euphrates, completely controlled by the Iraq Government, but their winter grazing grounds were a hundred and fifty miles out in the desert, fully exposed to attack by Ibn Saud. Any jealousy or hostility between Iraq and Ibn Saud exposed the Dhafeer to the resentment of one side or the other, if not of both.

Meanwhile Ibn Saud's tribes arrived unexpectedly, fell upon and nearly exterminated Yusuf's camel corps. Having alienated Hamood Ibn Suwait by supporting Yusuf Ibn Sadoon, the Iraq Government, in May, 1922, abandoned their support for Yusuf as suddenly as they had offered it to him the year before. His pay was cut off and he was ordered immediately to disband the desert camel corps, which he had just raised under government orders. Having spent the summer of 1922 in Baghdad vainly seeking redress, Yusuf in his turn left for Central Arabia in a rage. By these strokes of policy, the Iraq Government had succeeded in alienating both the possible leaders of its southern desert, just at the moment when Ibn Saud, flushed with victory, became their neighbour.

For two hundred years, the Sadoon had been a family of princes of social status almost equal to that of the Sauds. When Yusuf Ibn Sadoon therefore visited Ibn Saud, the latter gave him a semi-royal reception and entertained him handsomely in Riyadh. Meanwhile Hamood Ibn Suwait had returned to Iraq, and was camping once more with his tribe, the Dhafeer.

Yusuf, however, failed to obtain employment with Ibn Saud. It had been rumoured that he had hoped to be given a force with which to raid the enemies of Ibn Saud. Eventually, in the early summer of 1922, he left Riyadh, suitably laden with gifts, and set his face for Iraq. But the strongest passion in Yusuf's soul was hatred of Ibn Suwait, shaikh of the Dhafeer, the tribe which had revolted against his father and his grandfather.

The winter of 1922–3 had passed quietly in the southern desert of Iraq and, when Yusuf returned from his visit, he found many of Ibn Saud's tribes grazing their flocks peacefully near the Iraq frontier. These Yusuf attempted to persuade to join him in a raid on the Dhafeer, claiming to have been instructed to do so by Ibn Saud himself. Most of the principal shaikhs refused, but he succeeded in collecting some two hundred bedouins, chiefly of the Mutair tribe, including a number of minor tribal leaders, who were attracted by the prospect of loot. With this force, he suddenly fell upon an encampment of the Dhafeer at Chabda,[1] fifty miles west of Basra, and drove off large numbers of their camels.

The Dhafeer, who saw on the heads of their attackers the white turbans of the Ikhwan, and had of course no idea that this was only their old enemy Yusuf, fled precipitately and took refuge on the edge of the date gardens, only some four miles from Nasiriya, soon after my first arrival in that town.

It so happened that the day after the arrival of the Dhafeer victims in the date palm gardens, I was out riding myself some twenty miles south-east of Nasiriya close to the railway line. I was accompanied by Ali al Yunis, my servant, and by a Shammar boy from Hail, an orphan refugee whose father had been killed in the Wahhabi attack on that town. His name was Ambarak—Blessed—and he was one of the frail, slender and gentle type of youth, which is sometimes found in Nejed. Nearing Tel al Laham we perceived, floating in the mirage, what appeared to be a flock of camels. It was high noon in summer in lower Iraq and the air was like a dancing flaming furnace. Unaware that any bedouins were camped near by, we turned our horses' heads and cantered over to investigate. A dip lay between us and the figures whom we had seen moving indistinctly in the mirage. As we cantered forward into the depression, we lost

[1] There is no ch- sound in correct Arabic and this word should be Kabda. Amongst the local tribes, however, it is universally pronounced Chabda.

them from sight. When we topped the rise the other side of the dip, and saw them once more, they were only some four hundred yards away, and we noticed, with some apprehension, that the camels were not a herd peacefully grazing, but that they consisted of some two hundred riding camels, all saddled up, the sure signs of a raiding party. We could still, being on horses, have turned and galloped away, for a camel has no turn of speed compared to a horse, and we could not see any horses with the party. We had, however, obviously already been seen, and I could not help feeling that there would be something undignified in flight, especially as we were between the railway line and the river, and only twenty miles from the district headquarters. The presence of a serious bedouin raiding party at such a place seemed to me incredible. I felt that there must be some other explanation, and was curious to know it. As we drew closer, we noticed a small white tent, pitched in the centre of the group of grazing camels, and beside it, a long pole stuck into the ground, round which was furled what was obviously a war banner.

We could see large groups of men sitting and lying on the ground, and, as we came closer, Ambarak suddenly hissed to me in a loud whisper, "They're Ikhwan! Look at their *imamas*!" To the initiated, the Ikhwan were unmistakable, but even to the ignorant, there were obvious characteristics about them. Of these the most conspicuous was that they discarded the piece of rope with which most tribesmen kept their headgear in place, and wore in its place a white cotton turban called an *imama*. In addition, they clipped their moustaches short but let their beards grow long. The Prophet himself was reported by tradition to have kept his moustache cut short and the Wahhabis were determined to imitate him. For the Ikhwan were like the Pharisees, who strained at a gnat but swallowed a camel. They religiously clipped their moustaches but massacred their fellow Muslims.

I knew little of bedouins at that time and still less of the Ikhwan, though I had heard that they killed every male on whom they could lay hands if he was not one of them. I was unarmed, Ali al Yunis had a pistol and Ambarak a rifle slung on his back, a somewhat inadequate armament for our situation. However, we were now committed to our course, for good or ill, so pulling our horses back to a walk and closing in knee to knee, we rode boldly through the grazing camels and the groups of Ikhwan to the tent. Who should come forth as we dismounted, wearing a large white *imama*, but—Yusuf Ibn Sadoon, bland and smiling! I had never seen Yusuf before, but his typically Sadoon clothing, accent and appearance (in spite of the *imama*) enabled me at once to guess his identity.

He, of course, imagined that I had come to negotiate with him on the part of the government, although I hastened to assure him of the contrary. I nevertheless expressed (tactfully, in view of our situation) my surprise at his actions and advised him to report to the government in Nasiriya. Meanwhile Ambarak, who was a Shammari, as already mentioned, and who had no love for the Ikhwan, was near to creating, outside the tent, an incident which might have cost us our lives. A group of the turbaned raiders had collected round him and Ali. One of the Ikhwan was expatiating on how they could slaughter and flay all the Iraqis whenever they wished: "But do not be afraid," he added. "We are not going to hurt you now. We are only looking for the Dhafeer at present."

Ambarak's eyes suddenly flashed and his nostrils dilated. "We should pile your dead bodies one on top of the other like dogs," he cried.

Hands flew to daggers, rifle bolts rattled, and the hasty intervention of Yusuf alone saved us from an awkward moment.

As we rode away, the Ikhwan broke into loud cries of *"La illah ill' Allah! La illah ill' Allah!*—There is no god but God! There is no god but God!"—as if to call down the vengeance of outraged heaven on the presence of us heathen in their bivouac. We rode away at a walk through their midst, knee to knee, talking with apparent unconcern, but no sooner did we cross a low ridge and lose the raiders from sight than we clapped our legs to our horses and galloped for Nasiriya.

The arrival of a raiding party of the dreaded Ikhwan almost to the Euphrates, within a few miles of Nasiriya, caused some astonishment and even alarm. Indeed it revealed how open and undefended was the desert frontier of Iraq. If Yusuf and two hundred men could cross the railway unperceived, so could the Ikhwan war banners with two thousand.

The authorities in Nasiriya, engrossed in the administration of a large province, covered with towns, villages and tribes, were by no means clear as to the cause of the trouble in the desert. They decided to despatch simultaneous summonses to Hamood Ibn Suwait and Yusuf Ibn Sadoon, ordering both in peremptory terms to report themselves immediately to Nasiriya.

Now the year before, the Baghdad Government had summoned Hamood Ibn Suwait to the capital, but before he went, he had requested and received an assurance that he would not be imprisoned. When he reached Baghdad, however, a number of complaints had been brought against him by persons who claimed to have been raided or plundered by the Dhafeer in previous years—even in Turkish times. As the government had, however, promised not to imprison him, he succeeded in eluding the complainants.

In the present instance, he was of course the aggrieved party, the Dhafeer having been the victims of Yusuf's attack. Hamood, how-

ever, remembering the old complaints, asked once more for a promise that he would not be imprisoned if he came to Nasiriya. It should
also be remembered that the Turks, who had left only five years
earlier, had a reputation for kidnapping tribal shaikhs and for transporting them to die in exile at Istanbul or Aleppo. The local authorities in Nasiriya, however, were outraged at the idea of a tribal
shaikh endeavouring to impose conditions on the government. To
condescend to give a promise, they considered, would be derogatory
to the prestige of the administration. The promise was peremptorily
refused. The authorities in practice had no intention of bringing up
the old claims against the Dhafeer, and they desired only to obtain
from Hamood the true facts regarding Yusuf's raid upon his tribe.
Thus they could easily have reassured him, had their conception of
their dignity permitted such a course. But unfortunately it did not,
and a curt order was returned telling him to give himself up forthwith and without conditions, failing which drastic action would be
taken. Bedouins, like wild animals, were timid and suspicious of
government and often needed to be coaxed and humoured. Meanwhile, aircraft were instructed to stand by to bomb the Dhafeer,
although the latter were the plaintiffs in the case.

A similar summons to report to Nasiriya had been sent to Yusuf,
who indeed had more reason than Hamood to be apprehensive,
for he had just raided and looted an Iraqi camp, with a force of
cut-throats whom he had raised in a foreign country. He, also,
refused to obey the government summons, and moved out into the
desert as though to return to Nejed. The Nasiriya authorities
accordingly asked for him to be bombed likewise. Their contribution
to the solution of this bitter Sadoon-Suwait feud—now so many
years old—was impartially to bomb both sides.

This policy had, in reality, one great advantage. It could be
carried out without it being necessary for the civil officials concerned
to leave their office chairs, above which large electric fans were
coolly revolving. In Iraq, with the temperature at 120° Fahrenheit
in the shade, this was a consideration of some importance. On one
and the same morning, therefore, four aircraft from Shaiba bombed
Yusuf's raiders near Chabda, while four others were to land and
refuel at Nasiriya in order to bomb Hamood Ibn Suwait. When the
aircraft arrived at Nasiriya to land, however, a complication arose,
because the Dhafeer camels were grazing on the aerodrome. Bombing operations were particularly complicated when the "enemy"
insisted on wandering about on the bombers' own airfield. Meanwhile, however, Hamood had thought of another idea.

About four miles from Nasiriya lived a certain Menshed al
Hubaiyib, shaikh of a small riverain tribe called the Ghazzi. But
though his tribe was unimportant, Menshed was a delightful per-

sonality. Moreover, he had been a member of the first Constituent Assembly of Iraq, in Baghdad. Hamood moved his tent and pitched it against the wall of Menshed's mud-brick house—henceforward to bomb Hamood was to bomb Menshed, which was impossible.

Shaikh Menshed rode into Nasiriya to intercede for Hamood, who, as he rightly pointed out, was the aggrieved party and had done nothing wrong. His efforts, however, were fruitless. Matters had now reached a deadlock, but some days later a few bombs were dropped on some scattered tents of the Dhafeer a few miles away. The owners of the tents knew nothing of the whole affair, and were unaware that Hamood Ibn Suwait was in trouble with the government. Eventually Hamood, giving up hope of success through Menshed's mediation, abandoned his family and his tribe and rode away on his camel with only two followers, vanishing into the desert. His nephew and cousin reported to Nasiriya to receive the orders of the government. Hamood was proclaimed an outlaw.

Yusuf Ibn Sadoon, having been duly bombed, made the best of his way back towards Nejed. On the way, however, he met a bedouin coming from Central Arabia, who told him that Ibn Saud was greatly enraged at his unauthorized raid, and that a force of camelmen had been despatched to apprehend him and bring him to Riyadh in chains. Pursued by both the Nejed and Iraq Governments, he decided to return to the latter. He rode in alone from the desert, boarded the train unnoticed at a small railway station and travelled straight to Baghdad, where he gave himself up and begged for mercy. Not only was he granted a free pardon, but he was told that any of the Ikhwan who had raided with him would be given sanctuary and permitted to live in Iraq, should Ibn Saud send a force against them.

Now Ibn Saud wished to punish them for raiding Iraq, and for the Iraq Government to afford them sanctuary from Ibn Saud's authority was unwise. This was to be one of the causes for the frontier warfare which was to continue on and off for the next seven years. A few days later, Yusuf Ibn Sadoon arrived in Nasiriya from Baghdad, pardoned, honoured and admitted once more to favour. From thence he sent to the Ikhwan who had raided with him, and who were now being pursued by Ibn Saud for their breach of discipline. In response to his invitation, they took refuge in Iraq, and came to camp near Nasiriya, where they discarded their white *imamas*, pronounced the religion of the Wahhabis to be sheer hypocrisy and declared themselves devotedly loyal to Iraq.

Thus the raiders, all of whom except Yusuf himself were foreigners, now enjoyed the favour of the Iraq Government, while the Dhafeer, an Iraq tribe who had been the victims of the raid, were in disgrace, and their leader, Hamood Ibn Suwait, was a solitary outlaw in the desert. Truly the revolutions of Fortune's wheel in the Southern Desert were remarkable. The government, however, had not yet finished venting its resentment against Hamood—resentment principally caused, it must be admitted, by Yusuf, who was a descendant of princes, a man of politics and familiar with courts. Hamood was but a poor illiterate nomad, who feared the unfamiliar atmosphere of cities and government offices.

There was a lesser shaikh of the Dhafeer by the name of Lizzam aba Dhra', or Lizzam of the Forearm. (The appellation was a family name, presumably referring to the strength of some remote ancestor). Lizzam was one of those rare phenomena, a fat bedouin, though how he succeeded in being so none could tell, for he was as poor as a church mouse. He was also dirty.

Personally I always liked Lizzam, who was a humorous old scoundrel. The Arabs have a pleasant way, when they promise to do something, of adding *"Ala rasi"*, on my head or on my eye. I can still never avoid laughing when I think of old Lizzam (he must have been in his sixties), sitting on the floor of his tent in his dirty shirt and ragged cloak, while I lectured him on the prevention of raiding. When I had finished, he looked at me with perfect solemnity saying:

"I would walk on my nose to carry out your orders," at the same time tapping that rather bulbous feature with his forefinger.

On another occasion, when his followers had committed some peculiarly outrageous highway robbery, he exceeded himself in his protestations of devotion. Tearing off the greasy kerchief which covered his matted locks, he cried loudly to all and sundry in his tent:

"You are witnesses, O men! I want to buy a sun helmet! You see I am an Englishman! *Terani rejul Inglezi!*"

At this moment, the government suddenly issued a statement to the effect that old Lizzam had been appointed paramount shaikh of the Dhafeer. The Ottomans had, as we have seen, extensively practised the policy of destroying the tribal system by setting up rival shaikhs, and now the Iraq Government, although ostensibly Arab, was trying to do the same. Even so, however, the Turks had been more skilful. Amongst Arabs, supreme importance is not attached to primogeniture. If a tribal shaikh dies, and his son is not considered capable, his brother or cousin may become the leader, but the successor must be of the family. The government could have found other members of the Suwait to replace Hamood, but it was impossible to appoint as his successor a man who was not a member of the chief's family.

So extraordinary a tale of mismanagement should not, however, cause too sweeping a denunciation of the officials in Baghdad or in

Nasiriya. The fault lay a good deal with the system, according to which an official charged with the administration of a large and densely populated district was made responsible, in addition, for some 15,000 square miles of desert, inhabited by wandering nomads. The area in question was at the time almost completely unexplored, and the tribes living in it were but vaguely known. It was as if the Lord Mayor of London, busy with the affairs of a great city, had been made at the same time responsible for navigation and fishing rights in the North Sea. He would never have had time to go there, and might well have accepted the advice of the first well-spoken stranger he met who claimed to be an expert on the area. In the Southern Desert, it was Yusuf's ambition to appoint himself to the post of government adviser on desert affairs.

IV

First Steps in the Desert

Not for delectations sweet;
Not the cushion and the slipper, not the peaceful and the studious;
Not the riches safe and palling, not for us the tame enjoyment,
  Pioneers! O Pioneers!

Do the feasters gluttonous feast?
Do the corpulent sleepers sleep? have they lock'd and bolted doors?
Still be ours the diet hard, and the blanket on the ground,
  Pioneers! O Pioneers.
Walt Whitman

FIRST STEPS IN THE DESERT

A WEEK or two after Lizzam had been declared shaikh, an urgent message from him arrived in Nasiriya, borne by a ragged bedouin on a camel. He complained that a section of the Dhafeer, the Juwasim, was about to attack him, and he requested official support. This situation was somewhat embarrassing, for the government had, only a few days earlier, declared him to be paramount chief of the whole tribe. As a result, the authorities were unwilling to see him exterminated by his supposed followers. Nobody knew where the tribes were camped, the desert was unexplored and no maps existed. Once a tribe moved away from the Euphrates, it vanished into space and was scarcely heard of again by the government until it returned to the banks of the river, six months or a year later.

Aircraft in those days, as now, were supposed to land and take off only from regular aerodromes. A few weeks before, however, we had tried some experiments in landing on open strips of flat desert, chosen in flight from the air and without previous reconnaissance on the ground. Could this be done regularly, it was obvious that air control would be immensely facilitated, for, in that case, before air forces interfered to quell any disturbance, it would be possible for an aircraft to land in the open country near the troubled area, a procedure which would give an opportunity for an intelligence officer to cross-question the inhabitants and obtain the latest news of the situation. Such an operation was not without risks, firstly because it was difficult to ensure from the air that the ground was really flat enough to land on safely. Secondly, it might well be that the inhabitants on whom such a landing was made might prove to be hostile and open fire on the machine before it could take off again.

In spite of these risks, however, the method seemed to be well worth trying, for, as was explained in the previous chapter, the problem of how to obtain information of a changing situation and of how to identify friend from foe, appeared to be the principal obstacle to the employment of aircraft for internal security in tribal areas, where loyal and hostile tribes might be camped side by side or even intermixed.

It occurred to me that Lizzam's complaint against the Juwasim might provide an opportunity to practise these new tactics. I accordingly volunteered to fly out into the desert, land on the tribes and ascertain what was happening. The local government officials accepted my suggestion with alacrity.

Two De Havilland 9A's (more commonly called ninaks— pronounced nine-aks) were on Nasiriya aerodrome. Squadron-Leader Grenfell was ready to help. I climbed into the rear cockpit of his aircraft and we roared into the air.

We headed south-west and, as we crossed the railway line, the vast beige-coloured desert stretched out beneath and before us like an unending featureless sea. After flying for some forty minutes, we noticed beneath us a few small black specks which proved to be tents. They were obviously shepherds, not the Dhafeer who were a bedouin camel tribe. Donkeys could be seen grazing near the tents, which were of the small size which shepherds were obliged to use, their donkeys being unable to transport the great tents which the bedouins loaded upon their camels.

As we had no idea where we were or where Lizzam might be camped, I asked Grenfell to land, to enable us to find out our location from the shepherds. The task of choosing a level strip of desert, and of holding our breath as we touched down, occupied our full attention for several minutes. When eventually the aircraft came to a standstill and I climbed out and walked over a low rise to the tents, I was just in time to see their panic-stricken inhabitants running madly away, throwing occasional terrified glances over their shoulders at the grounded aircraft. The six or seven tiny tents, each scarcely bigger than a double bed, were completely deserted.

I set off in pursuit at a run. In front three women were in full flight. In spite of their long black skirts, which reached to the ground, they were running like athletes and I was unable to overtake them. Then, further to the right, I noticed a middle-aged man, half clad in rags, whose speed of flight was reduced by the fact that he was carrying a baby and dragging another toddler by the hand. I gained ground on him rapidly, until, casting a terrified look at me over his shoulder, he realized that escape was impossible. Suddenly turning, he ran towards me, and endeavoured to cast himself at my feet—still clutching the children—and crying in an indescribably pathetic manner, "Mercy! Mercy! Babies. Babies." Then straightening up, he made a desperate effort to kiss my nose and cheeks.

Returning his kisses to reassure him, in spite of his remarkably prickly growth of beard, I told him that all was well, put my arm round his shoulders and took his little toddling girl by the hand. No matter what I did, it took me some ten minutes to restore the old man's confidence, whereupon we began walking back slowly towards the deserted tents while other figures commenced to return from here and there, watching us cautiously from a distance. Having discussed a number of indifferent subjects in order to calm his fears,

I at length enquired, in a casual tone, where Lizzam and his Dhafeer were camped. He named a place, but I had never heard of it and there was no map. Eventually I asked him to point in the direction of the bedouin camp and took a compass bearing along his arm. Wandering for months in succession over the undulating wastes of the desert, I have often found nomads to possess an extremely reliable sense of direction, enabling them to point accurately towards distant places.

Bidding my new friend an affectionate farewell and kissing the babies as a further proof of governmental benevolence, I returned to the aircraft, gave the compass bearing to the pilot, and we took off again. After another fifteen minutes flying, we sighted a large bedouin encampment, surrounded by flocks of grazing camels. Circling above the camp, I could see a number of armed tribesmen sitting on the ground in a wide circle before the shaikh's great tent. Close to them, three unfurled war banners, their staffs planted in the ground, were waving in the wind, while horses and riding camels, ready saddled, surrounded the tent on every side. The whole scene had the appearance of a war party, perhaps holding a final conference before setting out on an expedition. There seemed to be little doubt that this camp belonged to one or other of the prospective combatants, but whether they were Lizzam's followers or his rivals, the Juwasim, I could not decide. I had no personal knowledge of the Dhafeer at that time, but the authorities in Nasiriya had told us that Lizzam's people were friendly but that the Juwasim might well be hostile. The Dhafeer were believed in Nasiriya to be all cut-throats and outlaws, and indeed the wildness of the shepherds on whom we had first landed did not convey the impression that any of the tribes of the desert were likely to receive us with cordiality.

The problem was whether to land on this warlike encampment or not. An aeroplane on the ground is a somewhat vulnerable target and, landing on unknown terrain, the machine might easily be damaged and leave us at the mercy of these armed tribesmen. We flew round and round for some minutes, hoping that the tribesmen would either shoot at us, or wave in a friendly manner, but they remained seated and motionless. I scribbled a note, "Land here, please," and passed it over to Squadron-Leader Grenfell.

The ground appeared from the air to be level enough but just as we touched it, we realized that it actually consisted of low waves and undulations of soft sand. The machine shot over one of these, dropped with a bump into a hollow, struck a bush, dipped one wing into the ground, swung round sharply at right angles and finally stopped a few feet from a sand dune. The whole incident had occupied only two or three agonized seconds, during which the aircraft bumped, lurched, and tore through bushes, while I clung with both hands to my seat. What was worse was that Grenfell, in the anguish of the moment, had stopped the engine. It normally required the pilot and three other men to start up a ninak. Aircraft in those days had no self-starters and three men were necessary to swing the propeller round until the engine fired. So here we were, our engine stopped, no one to help us restart it and the ground too rough to enable the second aircraft to land beside us, while three hundred yards away was a bedouin camp, with a large party of tribesmen apparently on the war path.

The first thing was to re-start our engine, which by a surprising piece of good fortune we succeeded in doing—unless indeed our somewhat precarious situation lent the two of us the strength of four. With one eye on the camp, from which at any moment a crowd of tribesmen might advance against us, I ran to seek a more level piece of ground which promised a possible take-off. Having found one, the problem was how to manoeuvre the aircraft to it, threading out way through bushes and between sand dunes. The difficulty in taxi-ing an aircraft on the ground lies in the fact that it cannot go backwards. It can move forwards only, and, in the case of a single-engined aircraft like a ninak, it needs a wide sweep in which to turn. To dodge in and out of bushes, and make right-angle turns round sand dunes, it was necessary for someone to hold back one or other wing tip. I ran to the port wing, Grenfell gave a burst of engine, and the machine swung round to the left. "Other wing tip," he yelled from the cockpit above the roar of the engine, and I ran as fast as I could round the front, making a detour to avoid the whirling airscrew. The aircraft taxied forward a few yards, then the pilot, craning his neck to see the ground in front, roared, "Hold back starboard wing tip!" I dug my feet desperately into the sand, set my teeth and pushed with all my might against the leading edge of the wing. Another burst of engine and she swung round the end of an awkward sand dune. The engine had blown up a little sandstorm of our own, and our eyes, ears and clothes were full of it. At last, when I was almost at the end of my strength, we manoeuvred out of the dunes and faced upwind along a strip of hard gravel. The engine was ticking over and the sand cloud we had stirred up was settling. The second aircraft still circled menacingly overhead. Just at this moment, we saw a dozen horsemen galloping towards us. I ascertained afterwards that the tribesmen had been as alarmed as we were when the aircraft suddenly descended upon their sand dunes. They spent fifteen minutes arguing as to what action they would take, thereby giving us just enough time to manoeuvre our machine through the sand and the bushes.

The horsemen proved to be the "hostile" Juwasim, who however appeared after all to be amicable. They complained of the tyranny of

Lizzam, who, they said, was camped only four miles away and was about to attack them. Their warlike preparations were purely defensive! Eventually the shaikh of the Juwasim agreed to furl his war banners, strike camp and move some miles away from Lizzam, so that a clash between the two sections would be unlikely.

With the affair thus satisfactorily terminated, we flew back to Nasiriya. What might possibly have developed into a tribal battle, with dead and wounded, had been averted in about three hours of flying time.

This little incident created a deep impression amongst all the nomad tribes of the area, who had always been accustomed to regard the government as operating only along the river bank and in the towns and villages of the settled area.

* * * * *

Piqued by this first success and anxious to know more about the desert tribes, concerning which Nasiriya could tell me so little, I decided to attempt a little voyage of discovery of my own.

The only map of Central Arabia available in those days was of the scale of one over a million. There were scarcely any names or physical features marked on it, but across the desert ran a few dotted lines—the routes followed by the great explorers of Arabia: Wallin 1848, Huber 1881, Blunt 1879, Leachman 1912. No one who has not experienced it can imagine the passion aroused by those far blue horizons of the desert and by the knowledge that no European had ever seen what lay beyond them. The map was a blank. What valleys, what ridges, what wells, what tribes lay there? Nobody could tell me.

I succeeded in hiring four camels. One for myself, one for Ali al Yunis, my servant, one for a Dhafeeri escort and one for a man of Shammar. I was in some apprehension lest air headquarters refuse their sanction to my proposed expedition. At first, however, not only did they not oppose it, but they suggested that an air reconnaissance should visit my party twice daily. The R.A.F. had apparently become interested in our experiment of landing in the desert. An air reconnaissance twice daily had its advantages and its disadvantages. It was gratifying to feel that air headquarters thought we were doing valuable work and wished to encourage us, but the plan had the drawback that I could be recalled at any moment. I had not told them, moreover, that I proposed to go right down to the Nejed frontier—the authorities would probably try to stop me when I was only half way to the border, lest I be the cause of an incident with Ibn Saud.

We started out one morning in January, 1924, from Tel al Laham station, and rode for some three hours over slightly rolling desert, thickly covered with small shrubs about twelve to eighteen inches high.[1] Then we entered a belt of high sand dunes stretching to right and left as far as the eye could see. This belt of dunes, I ascertained, extended a distance of one hundred and fifty miles from Shinafiya to Shagra, parallel to the Euphrates and at an average distance of perhaps ten or twelve miles from the river. It thus formed a kind of barrier, shutting off the river area with its palm gardens and sedentary or semi-sedentary tribes, the railway, the government and all its works, from the open desert, the country belonging to the nomads, stretching away many hundreds of miles to the Red Sea and the Indian Ocean. The sand belt itself was in places as much as five or six miles wide, with sand dunes fifty feet high. This strip was the only sandy area in all the vast deserts within the Iraq frontiers, the remainder consisting of rolling steppes, which, after the winter rains, became clothed in fresh grass and at times, in years of good rainfall, with carpets of wild flowers. Every year in April, however, the hot sun would wither the grass, which thus became hay without being cut, and provided good "dry grazing" all through the summer. In Europe, the grass of hay meadows, if not cut, will die and turn rank and sodden in the rain, but in Arabia, when the grass is at its maximum height, the rainfall suddenly ceases, providing animals with natural hay, as it were "on the stalk".

The first night of our journey was spent as guests in the tent of Lizzam of the Forearm, the new "government" shaikh, who was camped in the sand belt. As an instrument by means of which the government could control the Dhafeer, Lizzam was not a success. The tribe had moved southward to the Nejed frontier with Hamood Ibn Suwait. Lizzam was afraid to follow them, lest they vent their resentment on him for his usurpation. In the desert, Hamood, though outlawed by the government, held undisputed sway.

The sand belt was far from being the inhospitable waste so often visualized by Europeans. The dunes gave pleasant shelter, and ample firewood, a consideration of importance to tribesmen (and tribes-women, for to collect firewood is a woman's duty). Lounging round the camp fire drinking coffee was the bedouin's principal recreation and plentiful firewood enabled him to indulge it at his pleasure. Moreover, scantily clad in a cotton shirt and cloak as he usually was, the winter nights in the open desert could be cold enough to make a fire almost a necessity. Another not negligible advantage to the poor bedouin of camping in sand was that it was soft to lie on. No nomad could of course carry a bed, and many had no mattresses, but lay on a threadbare carpet on the stony ground. To such, to sleep in a sand dune was almost a luxury. Admittedly, however, the sand belt was less enjoyable if a strong wind were blowing and the

[1] See map on page 71.

sand rose up to fill eyes, mouth, clothes and food alike. In such circumstances there was no course but to be miserable until the wind dropped.

Leaving Lizzam's tent at dawn next morning, we topped the last sand dune as the sun shot its first pale rays over the open country, and we saw before us a small gravelly plain, in the centre of which crumbled a ruined castle. It was Abu Ghar, once the stronghold of the great Sadoon Ibn Sadoon, who, like Hamood Ibn Suwait today, had in his day also been outlawed by the government. Nevertheless he had for a time lived in independence, a little king in the desert, until his own high-handed ways raised the nomads in rebellion against him.

Sadoon had called in Ibn Rasheed to help him to subjugate the Dhafeer to his will and a battle had been fought on the slopes of Abu Ajaj, a giant sand dune down which we were actually riding. The sun was gilding the peaks and ridges of the rocky desert before us, the winter air was as sharp and fresh as iced wine, the cramped life of towns lay behind us, and before us extended the vast desert, the land of the free. Our two bedouins burst spontaneously into song, that wild, loud singing of the desert tribes. Our camels caught the infection and padded down the long sandy slope at a swinging trot.

There is some wild attraction about the unending blue distances of the desert. A nomadic tribesman, in those unsophisticated days, would be silent and gloomy in the streets of a town. Often he would roll little plugs of rag and stuff them up his nostrils to save himself from what he considered to be the evil odours of these crowded hives of humanity. To mount and ride out with him would at first give a man the impression of having acquired but a morose and gloomy companion. But once the last habitation and the final ploughed field had been passed, and only the vast undulating plains lay all around, the bedouin would cast off his gloom. Tickling his camel with his little crooked riding stick, he would dash off in a wild trot, his arms outstretched but slightly bent at the elbow, in a manner which, with his little stick in his right hand, would suggest a maestro about to conduct an orchestra. Bumping up and down as his camel raced along, he would burst into some wild *hijeini*, or camel-riding song, telling of deeds of war or desert life. His brown cloak would slip from his shoulders, his kerchief would fly from his head, exposing his long black hair, arranged in tight plaits, somewhat reminiscent of a Victorian landlady in curling pins. To the stranger's amazement, his erstwhile morose companion would burst out laughing, and call out cheerfully, "Have you ever heard of Ibn Ali's raid on Aneza?" or, "Do you know what Ibn Mijlad said on the day of the snow?" This intoxication of the vast wilderness now seized upon my two companions, as we raced over the undulating waves of sand towards the ruined fortress.

Three ninaks landed on us at Abu Ghar and then took off again for Nasiriya, covering us in a cloud of gritty dust as they taxied away. In the afternoon we rode on past some rocky hills, where we found a group of shepherd tents of the Budoor, with whom we passed the night. The desert traveller, when he sighted a camp, would choose the tent at which he meant to dismount. If there were a shaikh of some standing in the camp, his tent would be the largest, and would probably be pitched slightly in front of the others, so that guests might come to it across open desert, instead of having to thread their way between the tents and over the tent ropes of the camp. The shaikh's tent could usually be identified by the number of men sitting in it and drinking his coffee, for it was the guest room and club of the camp, as well as the home of the leader. His family and women lived in one half of the tent, which was divided by a curtained partition from the side allotted to the men. The bedouin traveller would not approach from the end in which the family lived, for the front of the tent was usually open and it would have been ill manners for a stranger to ride past in front of the women or to glance at them. He would therefore make a wide detour and approach the tent from the men's end. Couching his camel a few yards away, he would wrap his cloak decorously around himself, walk in a slow and dignified manner up to the group of men seated round the fire and say, "Peace be upon you." To remove the saddle bags from the camel and carry them into the tent was a sign that the guest proposed to spend the night. Perhaps he might be modest and leave the saddle bags on his camel, although it was already nearly sunset. Then the host would call to his fellow tribesmen: "*Hat al gesh ya ayyal!*—Bring in the kit, boys!"—an invitation to the guest to stay the night.

In little groups of poor shepherds such as that on which we had chanced, there might well be no shaikh and no large tent, though the head of the group might make coffee—the sign of leadership— for the men of the camp gathered in the tent of the coffee-maker. "Pounding coffee" was the sign of being a man of substance. If one asked after some boy he had once known, the answer might be: "He has done very well in life. Now he pounds coffee."

We carried our saddle bags into the largest tent of the group, heaped them on the floor and then returned to our camels. Hobbling them by tying their two forelegs together, we turned them loose to graze, for, although camels could eat as they walked along, he who would have them keep in good condition during a long journey was wise to allow them a few hours every day to graze at will. The shepherds soon gathered in the tent of their leader to hear the news brought by the visitors, and were greatly amazed to see an officer who had come riding on a camel. Such an experience had never happened to them before. "When I saw the long tassels on the saddles I thought it was some prince of the Sadoon," said one of them. "There are no Sadoon any more now," said another, "but I thought that it might be Ibn Suwait." Behind the curtain of the tent, the host could be heard arguing with his wife about the preparation of the dinner, greatly to the secret scorn of our two aristocratic bedouin guides, who regarded such an audible consultation as unseemly.

Next morning, we set out once more to the south, leaving on our right the dry rocky water course of Shaeeb al Luwaihidh. The whole surface of the shelving desert was intersected by innumerable stony beds of dry streams called *shaeebs*, in which water flowed for only three or four days a year. If a bedouin heard that rain had fallen in the desert, he would stop all the travellers coming from that direction and ask: "How was the rain? Did the earth flow?" "Ay, by Allah," the answer would come. "The Luwaihidh flowed." After each flow, the passing water would leave numerous pools in the rocky beds of these water courses, and at these the tribes would drink and water their flocks.

At about half-past ten, the aircraft appeared once more in the sky, but at first the pilots seemed unable to see us. We hastily broke down the little shrubs around us and lit a bonfire, of which the smoke soon drew their attention. They flew towards us and began to circle round over our heads. As I was watching the leader, who was obviously looking for a place to land, I heard the Arabs suddenly call in alarm, "Allah! Allah! Allah!" I looked quickly round and was just in time to see one machine, spinning nose downwards, strike the ground, throwing up a cloud of dust. We left our camels and ran as fast as we could to the wreckage. The aircraft was smashed to pieces, but had not caught fire. The pilot was lying on the wingtip, still breathing but unconscious. The observer, with a great wound in his head, was already dead. With the help of my three Arabs, I lifted the pilot off the wing, laid him on his back on the ground, and slipped a pillow under his head. I knew him well and had often myself flown as his observer. The flight commander, Flight-Lieutenant Jenkins, had landed on the desert near by, and, after a hasty consultation, we decided that he would fly to Basra and bring a doctor. He thought he would be back in two hours. His machine roared off the ground, throwing up a cloud of dust as it took off, and gradually the sound of his engine grew fainter and fainter. My three Arabs were sitting fifty yards away, talking in whispers. The silence of the desert descended upon us once more, and I found myself sitting alone in that vast rolling waste, with the head of a dying man on my lap. Soon he opened his eyes and muttered: "For God's sake, give me water," but then seemed to lose consciousness again. We had no water with us, but meanwhile two shepherd horsemen of the Budoor tribe had ridden up. They lighted cigarettes, stared at us insolently and one said to the other, "He's a deader." I asked them where Busaiya wells were, thinking that they must be close by, but one of them merely waved his hand to the west without troubling to answer. I besought them to fetch some water in my water-bottle, for they could easily have cantered over to the wells on horseback in a few minutes. But one of them merely replied casually, "We're busy," and they galloped away together. The government certainly did not seem welcome to the tribes of the desert. It seemed to me remarkable, however, that the shepherds like the Budoor seemed more hostile than the reputedly wilder bedouins. A few minutes later the pilot died in my arms without recovering consciousness. At about one o'clock, two aircraft returned bringing the doctor. There was nothing left for them to do, except to remove the instruments and guns from the aircraft. Meanwhile several men of the Juwasim section of the Dhafeer had gathered round us.

Shaken by this incident and continually apprehensive lest I be recalled before I could visit the frontier area, I told the flight commander not to come out to look for me again. I also was careful not to tell him where I was going, a step more likely to be effective than my instructions to him not to return. It was a thousand to one against aircraft finding four camelmen in fifteen thousand square miles of unmapped desert, dotted here and there with Arab camps and grazing flocks. I hoped by this means to find time for the work which I proposed to do. Meanwhile Haleis Ibn Ufeisan, one of the shaikhs of the Juwasim, had arrived and had invited us to pass the night in his tent. As it was already afternoon, I accepted and we sadly remounted our camels. The Juwasim were the same section of the Dhafeer on whom we had so successfully landed three weeks before, when their war banners were unfurled and they were preparing to attack Lizzam. Their second experience of aircraft in the desert was unfortunately not so calculated to raise government prestige as the first had been.

We found the threadbare carpets already spread on the ground round Haleis' coffee fire. Tea was a rare luxury among bedouins, and hence, though to produce our own food would have been an insult, we did not scruple to place our little kettle on the fire. Meanwhile our good host, loudly exclaiming that this was indeed a most blessed hour, busied himself with the roasting and pounding of the coffee beans. In the economy of the Arab tent, cooking was of course a female occupation and was done in the women's half of the tent, but making tea and coffee was a duty which fell to the men, and was carried out in the men's portion. Tea was a comparatively modern innovation, but the making of coffee amounted almost to an ancient ritual. The fire was first lit or revived, in a small hearth scooped in the gravelly surface of the desert and then the fresh coffee beans were shaken out of a soft leather bag into a special frying pan. The beans were then roasted over the fire in this pan. When the process was completed, the roasted beans were dropped into a brass pestle and pounded to powder with a mortar of the same material. (In Syria the pestle and mortar were sometimes made of hardwood.) Pounding coffee was an art which had to be learnt. The pounder not only crushed the coffee beans, but between each blow and the next, he struck the pestle against the sides of the mortar, the more expert by this means succeeding in beating a regular rhythm. The bell-like tones of the mortar proclaimed that the shaikh was making coffee, and thereby invited all and sundry to come and partake of it. Thus the ringing of the mortar was a sign of the hospitality of its owner.

Soon the sun sank in a scarlet glory, fading across the sky through orange and yellow to mauve in the east. Straight columns of smoke rose from the black tents pitched near by. In the distance the calls of the herdsmen were faintly audible as they led their slow flocks of camels back towards the tents, where the fires of the camp began to wink at them in the growing dusk. Every herdsman had his own style of call, which was known to the camels which followed him. He himself would ride ahead on an old veteran of the herd, herself a leader as much as the man who rode her. The cries of the herdsmen carried far across the desert in the still evening air—"*Yo-o-o-a. Yo-o-o-a. Yo-o-o-a,*" sometimes alternated with a series of short quick cries which sounded like "Up. Up. Up."

Then four men staggered round the corner of the curtain which veiled the women's part of the tent, carrying a great copper tray, laden with rice and surmounted by the traditional sheep, slaughtered three hours earlier to welcome us as guests. According to the bedouin custom, the tray was deposited on the ground, three or four yards in front of the tent, while our host Haleis busied himself pouring hot gravy over the steaming mess, and calling for water to wash our hands. Finally he stood up, straightening his back after bending so long over the dish, and gave us the invitation *tafadhdhalu* —"Do us the honour." We four guests rose to our feet, walked forward, sat down by the great dish, rolled back our right sleeves from our wrists and, piously exclaiming "In the name of God", plunged our right hands into the rice.

Bedouins were extremely particular to observe the niceties of their manners at meals. It is true that they ate with their hands, a greasy process sometimes considered revolting by more nicely civilized persons, but they were careful to follow their code of manners intended to put the guest at his ease. Thus if one man had eaten enough but saw that the others were still hungry, he would continue to eat slowly, taking small mouthfuls. Were he to stop eating altogether, his companions might feel embarrassed and be obliged also to stop eating. The bedouins were, for the same reason, particular that all the men sitting round the dish rose together. If good manners consist in taking the trouble to place others at their ease, then these unsophisticated tribesmen had good manners. Curiously enough, in the much more civilized villages of Palestine and Syria, this convention was often not observed and individuals rose and walked away when they had eaten enough, thereby possibly putting to shame those who wished to eat more. Among some bedouins, particularly the tribe of Aneza, the dish was placed for the guests some yards in front of the tent, so that the hosts might not embarrass the guests by seeming to watch them eating.

In due course we rose from the dish, exclaiming as we did so, "May God reward the host." Right hands (for the left is never used for eating) inevitably became greasy when used in place of spoons and forks, and much washing, pouring of water and soaping was necessary after a meal. But with the poor nomad, water was often the most precious of commodities. When there was not enough of it to drink, it could scarcely be used for washing. In such a case, the guests were fain to rub their hands clean on the end of the tent.

The comfort derived from a good meal is one of the distressing facts of our human composition, to such at least as hold the superiority of the spirit over the clay. Stretched round the camp fire, our aching limbs at ease, and comfortably filled with hot rice and mutton, we began to take a less tragic view of even that harrowing day. We sat long over the embers of our fire, talking of desert life with that genial bearded circle.

Finally we rose and, walking out a few yards into the desert, I lay down, rolled in my cloak, to sleep. But exhausted though I was, sleep refused to come. I lay looking up at the bright stars. My mind was full of new experiences. Although these people were, in some ways, so addicted to violence and bloodshed, although there were lice in their clothes and they ate with their hands there was something about them which attracted me. Was it just simplicity—an utter lack of sophistication?

The nomads of the desert were poor—desperately poor according to the modern standards of the West. Yet they were unaware of any desire to be richer, and they had no ambition to change their mode of life, for they were not aware that it was inferior to that of any other race or comminuty—on the contrary, they believed themselves to be the élite of the human race. To persons brought up in a materialist civilization, not to wish to be rich indicated a despicable poverty of spirit. Such people, Europeans might declare, were perhaps incapable of keeping up with modern progress. Inferior breeds of this kind could only be left to die out.

Yet to know these people was to realize that they were full of spirit, pride, courage and initiative. They were backward only in that they had not absorbed the dogma that the acquisition of money was the principal object of life. They were potentially capable of adopting such a viewpoint, as a result of contact with civilization, but when I knew them, the circumstances of their lives had isolated them from the infection of such ideas. They were even unaware that the rich, the educated or the civilized were superior to them and they greeted all strangers with equal frankness and cordiality. They were completely unconscious of those fears which year by year more and more bedevil human relations—the fear of being thought inferior. The great attraction which they exercised on the occasional Europeans who met them lay in the fact that they lived in a different world, which was neither class-conscious nor race-conscious, and so suffered neither from the aggressiveness nor from the alternative servility of those communities whose members were constantly obsessed by doubts as to their own value in comparison with the other groups with which they came in contact. A complete lack of self-consciousness—to be perfectly natural, as we say—was one of the most attractive of human qualities. The bedouins thirty or forty years ago were unaware of the existence of class or race inequalities. As a result, they unconsciously treated all men as equals, without any mental embarrassments or reservations.

Even that very day, a bearded and ragged ruffian seated in the tent, striking the ground in front of him with his cane for emphasis, had shouted at me: "O man. What is the use of your government? They do not defend their subjects."

Was it this straightforward and open frankness which constituted their charm?

V

The Ikhwan Refugees

The arms and the deserts of the bedouins are not only the safeguards of their freedom ... Their service in the field was speedy and vigorous; but their friendship was venal, their faith inconstant, their enmity capricious: it was an easier task to excite than to disarm these roving bedouins.   GIBBON, *Decline and Fall of the Roman Empire*

They had the right of deciding their private feuds by an appeal to arms; a right of which they liberally availed themselves. They also claimed the privilege when aggrieved of publicly renouncing their allegiance to their sovereign and of enlisting under the banners of his enemy.   PRESCOTT, *Ferdinand and Isabella*

In that desert dwell many of the Arabians, who are called bedouins, who are people full of all evil conditions, having no houses but tents ... and under these they sleep and dwell ... and they are strong and warlike men. They care not for their lives, and therefore they fear not the sultan, nor any other prince. They wrap their heads and necks with a great quantity of white linen cloth; and they are right felonious and foul and of a curséd nature.   SIR JOHN MANDEVILLE (1322)

The reader is invited to refer to the map on page 71 for place names in the following chapter.

V

THE IKHWAN REFUGEES

WE set out next morning from the tents of the hospitable Juwasim. The necks, forearms and quarters of our camels had been daubed with red streaks, from the blood of the sheep which had been slaughtered the night before for our entertainment. Amongst bedouins, this custom is intended to illustrate the generous hospitality of the night's host. It also brings him credit, for as the camel-riders journey on, those whom they meet see the red stripes on their camels and say, "Where did you come from today?" The bedouin is fantastically hospitable, but he does not believe in the gospel precept of the need to do his alms in secret.

We travelled south, following the line of the Haniya Ridge. The Dibdibba is a rolling plateau of sandy gravelly soil, thickly covered with low shrubs. On the east it falls away into the long shallow Batin depression, a valley running from Central Arabia to Basra. On the west, the plateau drops to the bed of the Shaeeb al Luwaihidh, which runs north and south. Looking eastwards from the Luwaihidh, the shelving edge of the Dibdibba plateau looks like a long ridge and this long slope is called the Haniya. On the west of the dry water course of the Luwaihidh, the ground changes in character. Limestone comes to the surface, in a great area of rock-strewn country known as Al Hajara or the Stony Desert.

In the evening, we reached a camp of shepherds at Muwailhat. During the day, we had been joined by a bedouin boy, whom we had overtaken walking alone across the open desert. He said that he had come from Iraq (that is, the river area) and that he was looking for the Dhafeer. He had set out to walk the intervening one hundred and twenty miles of desert, carrying neither food nor water, but trusting to the hospitality of the camps of wandering nomads. Salih al Maadhadi, our Shammari escort, was for warning him off, saying that to allow a penniless stranger to join our party was to invite the theft of one of our camels the next night. But the boy looked honest and I insisted on his being allowed to join us. Fortunately he did not betray our confidence, or I should never have heard the last of it, for Salih was one of those people who always know best. No sooner had we dismounted at the shepherd tents than our new friend hobbled our camels and drove them off to graze, after first enquiring of the shepherds if they had seen near their tents any green *arfaj*, a little shrub much relished by camels.

99

He seemed grateful for our company and anxious to please, and indeed he was fortunate to be with us, as the companionship of such distinguished travellers meant for him a tray of hot mutton and rice for dinner every night.

Next day before noon, we saw on the ridges ahead of us, those tiny, dark, moving specks which the desert traveller or raider soon learns to look for—grazing camels. By noon, we were riding through the great herds of animals which showed that we were near the main camps of the Dhafeer. A little wizened grey-haired old man rode up to us and called in the stentorian voice of the great open wastes: "Peace be upon you."

Amid the ever-moving nomad camps of this great wilderness, always seeking better pasture and constantly on the alert for robbers or raiding parties, every passing stranger or traveller had to submit to cross-questioning. To obtain early news of tribal movements or of the intentions of raiding parties might be to the bedouin literally as much as his life was worth.

"Peace be upon you. What is the news?" said the little old man, tapping his camel on the neck with his cane, to align it with our own, so that we could ride on, side by side.

"God welcome the travellers," he continued, obviously wishing to say the polite thing before beginning his catechism.

"*Min ain entum jai-een?* Where are you coming from?

"What Arabs did you see on the way?

"What was the grazing like?

"Has it rained in the river area?

"Did you find any rain pools?

"Is Lizzam going to move out to the desert?"

Answering or parrying his questions as best we could, we commenced our own, as soon as we could slip in a word.

"Where is Ibn Suwait?

"Where are the Dhafeer?

"Where are Shammar?

"What news of the Ikhwan?

"How is the grazing?"

Ibn Suwait, he told us, was but a few miles ahead near Maghaizal. Our new friend was Jali Ibn Juraiyid, head of the Katheer section of the Dhafeer, once a famous raider and desert guide. At his saddle hung a *jerbua* or kangaroo rat, a delicacy much valued by bedouins, though its likeness to an ordinary rat acts as a deterrent to the squeamish.

"By God," said the old man, "I should not have allowed you to pass without tasting salt, but my people are on the move."

Though I was desirous of meeting Hamood Ibn Suwait, my position was somewhat delicate, for he had been officially declared an outlaw, though here in the desert he was quite openly the ruling shaikh at the head of his tribe. As an officer I felt that I could not deliberately seek out the company of an outlaw. Luckily, however, the first Dhafeer tent we encountered was that of Ajami, a distant cousin of Hamood. We decided to halt here for lunch. I was most anxious to meet the tribe which had everywhere in Nasiriya been described as a gang of bandits and cut-throats, but which scarcely any government official had ever seen, much less mingled with or known.

Ajami was a typical Central Arabian bedouin, small, slim, cat-like, and of sallow complexion with a sparse black beard. He hastened to spread the best carpet with his own hands, and soon we were sitting round a fire, at which a negro slave was roasting a fresh brew of coffee. It was of course impossible to escape the customary sheep, and eventually the copper tray appeared laden with its mutton and rice, over which, to do us special honour, had been emptied bowl after bowl of oil, butter and sugar. Even as I ate, Ajami kept pouring soft sugar from a bag on to my mutton. To my expostulations, he replied only by pouring yet more rapidly, and calling in a loud voice: "Welcome! The blesséd hour! A welcome to you!"

When we resumed our seats in the coffee circle after lunch, we saw three camel riders approaching the tent from across the desert. Their long swinging tassels and gaily coloured saddle bags proclaimed them to be persons of importance. It was none other than the outlaw Hamood. He was a man of middle height, perhaps some forty-five years old, with rather ugly features, a large mouth and a scanty beard. He was said to be sufficiently adroit in the politics of the desert, and as the chief shaikh of a bedouin tribe, he could scarcely be otherwise. At any rate, his outlawry by the government had produced no diminution of loyalty on the part of his tribesmen. But he was essentially a bedouin, born and bred to the desert, to raids, to tribute, to patriarchy, to chivalry, hospitality, largesse— in a word, to the old social order. He could never understand the new dispensation—civilian officials, courts of justice, punctual payment of taxes, and regular office hours. Above all, perhaps, he did not realize (as did his adversaries) that the new way in which men fought their enemies was to slander them in the ears of the government, or if he realized it, he was incapable of making use of his knowledge. The old bedouins, and those amongst whom he had grown up, were no saints. They thought nothing of robbing, looting or killing, but like the men of so many communities which live in an atmosphere of violence, they were remarkably straightforward. Neither Hamood, nor a single man in the whole Dhafeer tribe, could read or write. Hamood employed as his clerk a townsman, who sold his letters to his enemies behind his back.

It is a disconcerting thought, in view of the strong modern tendency in the West to regard the use of violence as the supreme crime, that so many eras of violence have produced such fine types of men. The establishment of public security by some overruling power transfers the leadership from the simple, the brave and the honest to the clever, the crooked and the deceitful. Perhaps in the long run, the abolition of violence produces a higher morality, nobler ideals and more spiritual service, but it only too often occurs that the immediate result of the abandonment of physical force is a lowering of moral standards.

The bedouin dialect differed much from that of the towns. Since 1924, an increasing intermixture of the nomad and settled population in northern Arabia has tended to reduce the differences, but they are even now still considerable. The bedouin in the 1920's was the freest and the most democratic of men. He used no titles and he said what he meant, without beating about the bush. Though extremely proud of his race, he was usually regardless of appearances, and some of the most important men among them were often clad in ragged dirty shirts, like their own herdsmen.

To the Turkish or Iraqi official, accustomed to the "Your honours" and "Your excellencies", the flattering compliments and expressions of devotion used in the towns, the free speech of the bedouin often appeared to be insolence, the raggedness and dirt of his clothing a sign of savagery. With this must be remembered the psychology of the young nationalists, their mortification at the weakness of their countries and their desire to emulate the West. Convinced that education had given Europe her supremacy, they desired it with a passionate longing, which so dominated their minds that to be uneducated seemed to them the most base and despicable of human conditions. It was perhaps natural that, in these circumstances, they confused the qualities of men with their accomplishments. Tribesmen were uneducated, and therefore enemies of progress, and must be smashed. It rarely seemed to occur to them that tribesmen could be educated as well as any other community and that, if that were done, their hardihood and endurance would make them in many ways valuable citizens. As a result of these beliefs and prejudices, the new ruling classes in the northern Arab countries tended to regard their own tribes with a feeling approaching aversion.

Truth to tell, to confuse ragged clothing with moral debasement was not the prerogative of Middle Eastern nationalists. Twenty years later, I was once accompanied by an American press correspondent on a visit to a poor bedouin camp. Everybody of course stood up when we entered the tent, but after we were seated, whenever another bedouin came in, those near by stood up to offer him their seats. It was an everyday scene in any tent in Arabia. After we had left the camp, my companion could no longer contain himself. "I would not have believed," he cried, "that people dressed in rags could be so courteous."

Anxious to be out of hearing of the company in Ajami's tent, Hamood asked me to speak with him outside. This indeed was the only way to secure a private conversation amongst tribesmen living in open tents. We sat together on the ground thirty yards away. He earnestly declared his desire to be reconciled to the government, stating that, although Ibn Saud would welcome him, he could not leave Iraq for Nejed or elsewhere, because his tribe depended on Iraqi markets, both for the sale of their livestock and for the purchase of their supplies. He complained bitterly of the treatment which he had received from the government of Iraq, especially at his outlawry and the attempt to set up Lizzam as his rival. He rightly claimed that he had done nothing wrong, but on the contrary had been raided by the Ikhwan under Yusuf Ibn Sadoon, who was now in favour with the government once more. Everything he said was true. My own situation, however, was somewhat difficult, for I had no powers and little, if any, influence with the government, being merely a British military intelligence officer. All I could do was to promise to repeat Hamood's words to the authorities. Finally he pointed out that he dared not report to the government without safe conduct, knowing that his enemies had the ear of the authorities, to whom they had doubtless described him as a villain and a traitor. If he were to give himself up, he feared that he would be straightway thrown into prison, without trial and without a hearing. His fears were not unfounded, and indeed such action by the government (in Ottoman days at least) had been all too frequent in the past. In fact the persecutions of his enemies were to follow him to his grave, and to pursue his tribe even after his death. The manner in which the government mishandled the Dhafeer may seem almost incredible. It can only be explained by the fact that bedouins in those days lived in a world entirely distinct from that of officialdom. The government had no knowledge of, and little interest in, the affairs of desert tribes and were therefore to a great extent ignorant of the facts.

In spite of Ajami's urgent entreaties that we stay for the night, we remounted our camels at three o'clock in the afternoon and set out towards Al Amghar, where Hamdan Ibn Tawala, a shaikh of Shammar, was said to be camped. Those of Ibn Rasheed's tribes who had remained in Nejed after the fall of the dynasty, had, of course, become Nejed subjects, but the majority had not joined the Wahhabi sect with any great enthusiasm, and they continued to buy their supplies from Iraq. Having once emerged from the camps and grazing flocks of the Dhafeer, however, we travelled on and on without seeing any sign of life. The vast, rolling desert stretched before us, clothed in its sage green shrubs, and melting away into blue ridges in the distance. When the sun set, there was in front and all around us, nothing but silence and an empty landscape, and we seemed likely to spend a cold and cheerless night in the open. Just as dusk was falling, however, we caught sight of the twinkle of a distant camp fire. Our dreary spirits rose once more at the prospect of dinner and company, and we kicked our camels into a round trot. On the slopes of a low ridge overlooking the wells of Al Amghar, we found six small tents of the Aslam division of Shammar. We reached the wells at Al Amghar, lying in a deep depression some four miles long, early the next morning, but only to find that Ibn Tawala had moved away to the south. Such is the uncertainty of desert travel, especially in winter and spring with the nomad camps constantly on the move. Much as I should have liked to meet a member of so famous a family as the Tawala, I had already been absent for six days and was practically playing truant, since I gave the aircraft the slip after the crash. I hesitated to wander further south, especially as we were already in the Neutral Area and nearing the Saudi border which I could not cross.

In Al Amghar we sighted a camp of shepherds, but endeavoured to pass them by, being anxious to cover more distance before halting. All the men of the camp, we could see, seemed to be collected in one tent. As we passed, however, one of them ran towards us waving his cloak and calling out: "Do us the honour. Lunch is ready." We accordingly tapped our camels on the neck with our canes, turned towards the little group of tents and dismounted, but without taking the bags off our saddles. The shepherds spent the summer on the banks of the Euphrates, where their flocks grazed as best they could in the stubble after harvest or on the coarse grass along the edge of the marshes. By autumn the sheep were weak and thin. As soon as the first rains fell and the fresh green grass sprang up in the desert, the shepherds loaded their little tents on donkeys and hastened out. Soon the sheep began to improve in condition, and eventually milk would appear in the camps. Cows could not, of course, live in the desert, and sheep and goats provided milk, butter and oil. As the milk became more plentiful, some of it was churned into butter. This was the sign of spring and prosperity.

"What is the grazing like?" a traveller would enquire.

"*Al Arab yakhadhun*—the Arabs are churning," would be a sufficient reply.

When this happy season came, the families in a shepherd camp would each in its turn kill a fat sheep, and invite all their neighbours in the camp to join in the thanksgiving feast which they called "*dhikr Allah*"—"remembering God." It was such a lunch as this to which we had been invited and delicious it was—fat, tender mutton on a mountain of rice, with bowls of butter and butter milk.

The only other European traveller who had visited the portion of the desert which we had crossed seemed to have been Leachman, and he had used the same route as we on our way south—the Shaeeb al Luwaihidh. This indeed was the normal route from the Muntifiq to Nejed, passing as it did from well to well. I decided to return by the Stony Desert, which, to the best of my knowledge, had never before been crossed by a European. We entered an area of limestone cliffs and escarpments, some of them one hundred and fifty to two hundred feet high. The ground was strewn with grey rocks and beds of black flints, and was divided by ridges and rocky crags, between which lay sheltered hollows, bright with lawns of green grass, over which nibbled flocks of grazing sheep. We called on Shirshab Ibn Zuwaid, shaikh of the shepherd tribe of the Budoor, and on through several scattered camps of the tribe. Few things can convey a greater sense of homeliness and comfort than to cross mile after mile of empty desert and then to round a rocky promontory and to come suddenly upon a bright green hollow in the hills, to find sheep grazing on the short fresh grass, and see half a dozen little tents, thin columns of blue smoke rising from their fires, and a group of girls cutting the low shrubs for firewood. The pleasures of life depend upon contrast. Weary camel riders, who perhaps passed the previous night in the open without dinner and afraid to light a fire for fear of raiders, will laugh and call to one another, "What luck! A host!"

As we passed through the Budoor camps coming from the direction of Nejed, the shepherds ran after us to ask anxiously what news there was of the Ikhwan. When they knew me to be an officer, they pressed me urgently to tell them what were the relations between the government and Ibn Saud, and why we did not protect our subjects from massacre, when they were grazing in their own country.

Soon after midday we had left all the shepherds' camps behind us and we rode on northwards for seemingly endless hours over a rolling gravelly plain, with no sign of life in sight, except for an occasional bustard or a distant gazelle, which started away from us, sometimes cantering, sometimes giving great standing bounds, all four feet together. The sun was already setting, and we were still travelling wearily over this bleak plain, which, worst of all, seemed to produce no shrubs with which we might even light a fire. The prospect of a cold cheerless night, and a dinner of dry bread, depressed our flagging spirits. Then Salih Maadhadi rode on ahead of us to a slight hillock for a last look round before sunset, and shouted back to us that he thought he saw sheep. We trotted down a narrow

valley and, rounding a rocky spur, came upon a small party of
shepherds, three men and four women, driving some twelve laden
donkeys. A few sheep grazed near by. For some unexplained reason,
shepherds in the Muntifiq moved camp in the evening but bedouins
in the morning. The little group upon whom we had chanced were
about to pitch camp, and soon erected two tiny tents, each perhaps
ten feet long by five feet wide. Then one of the men unrolled a
ragged strip of carpet and called to us: "Welcome! Welcome!
God give you strength. Do us the honour."

A woman brought a bundle of twigs and roots, while our host
scooped a hole in the ground with an axe, and in a few moments
our kettle was on the fire. So desperately poor did our shepherds
appear that I suggested to our two bedouins that we contribute our
slender supply of oil and flour to the dinner. But whether they
desired to conserve our provisions for themselves or really feared to
offend our hosts, they whispered back to me that such a course was
impossible. I made the most of my cup of tea, expecting little for
dinner. But in spite of all, two hours later our hosts staggered from
the tent with a big dish piled high with rice and surmounted by a
whole sheep, though the owners of the tent seemed to possess only
fifteen such sheep altogether. With many apologies for the insuf-
ficiency of the meal, the simple shepherds invited us to the dinner
which had cost them about one-twentieth of all their worldly goods.
To form some estimate of the hospitality of these poor Arabs, let
my reader calculate the total value of all his worldly assets, and
consider how he would like to spend a twentieth part of them to
provide a single meal for four complete strangers.

The tiny tents were occupied by four women, six babies and six
lambs, the latter tied by a cord round their necks to a little picket
rope. We decided to sleep outside in the open desert, wrapped in our
cloaks, but just as we were preparing, our hosts came over to us and
insisted on spreading their ragged carpets beneath us. It was not
until my three Arabs were asleep that I realized that these two pieces
of carpet were the only bedding of the two families. Dressed only in
cotton shirts and too cold to sleep without their tattered rugs, they
spent the night crouching over the embers of their fire.

Next day we reached Nasiriya by a long march of about sixty
miles, through Neba and Ur. At Nasiriya I found that I had indeed
been recalled four days before and that aircraft had been sent to
search for me in vain. Had I not eluded them, my journey would
have been cut short soon after the crash. The next few days were
busily employed sketching out my route and adding many fresh
names to the map. A new edition of the one over a million map,
Basra sheet, was issued shortly afterwards embodying my new
topographical information, and on it my track was marked in a

dotted line, like those of the early explorers: Huber 1881, Leachman 1912, Glubb 1924. For three years I fancied myself to be one of the Arabian explorers. Then in 1927, when war broke out with the Ikhwan, troops, police and aircraft poured into the desert. Survey observations were taken, and the map was covered with names. The routes of explorers were omitted from subsequent editions. So I was indeed the last of the explorers, like one born out of due time. Thenceforward the internal combustion engine was to assume the task of the exploration of the desert.

Soon afterwards the Iraq Government was obliged to give safe conduct to Hamood Ibn Suwait, a step which it might have taken the previous summer, thereby avoiding many months of confusion, not to say injustice, and a permanent legacy of estrangement between the bedouins and the civil authorities.

*   *   *   *   *

We left Yusuf Ibn Sadoon at the end of the summer of 1923, pardoned for his raid on the Dhafeer and authorized to bring into Iraq the Ikhwan tribesmen who had joined him in that enterprise. These individuals were not indeed very numerous, but included a number of well-known names, chiefly the younger sons or cousins of shaikhly families. The more obscure bedouins who had joined in the raid had presumably succeeded in evading detection and punishment by Ibn Saud. The most important of the so-called Ikhwan refugees were Ali Abu Shuwairibat and Shuraiyan Ibn Lami, both of the Mutair tribe, Feihan al Dhuweibi of Harab and Naif Ibn Humaid of Ateiba. This little band formed a useful addition to the forces of Yusuf Ibn Sadoon, in his struggle to oppose the influence of the Dhafeer. Even so, he was far outnumbered by the latter and could not venture into the desert, much less take the offensive.

Many of these Ikhwan refugees who gathered round Yusuf had fled from Nejed in such haste to avoid arrest by Ibn Saud that they had left their families, tents and flocks behind them. In Iraq they found themselves destitute. Yusuf had no money to give them. In such circumstances, the only resource of a bedouin was to raid. The Dhafeer would perhaps have been their most natural victims, had they not been too near and too strong. They could have retaliated at once too forcibly. The alternative course was for them to raid into Nejed, an enterprise facilitated by the fact that it was their native land, with every stick and stone of which they were familiar. Accordingly small parties of the refugees set out to steal camels from Nejed.

In order to appreciate this situation, it is necessary to bear in mind the nature of such half-bedouin states as those of Ibn Saud and Ibn Rasheed. These princes, in those days, maintained no standing armies, because their revenues were insufficient. They accordingly relied upon levies from their subjects to defend their country, to invade that of their neighbours, or to suppress sedition. The greater part of these levies were from the bedouin tribes, which, therefore, were not merely to the prince an aggregate of taxpayers or subjects, but divisions in his army. The bedouins were perhaps the most mobile men on earth. All that they possessed in the world could be loaded on their camels and, in order to live, they required nothing but a stretch of desert on which their flocks could graze. As a result, a bedouin tribe, if it were dissatisfied with the ruler of the country, need not attempt rebellion. More often than not, it simply loaded its possessions on its camels and transferred its allegiance to another ruler.

With so fickle an army to depend upon, the Arab prince's chief anxiety was lest his tribes desert him and join his rivals. At the same time, his principal ambition and occupation was to seduce the tribes of his neighbours. The tribes themselves freely employed the threat of desertion to check any signs of despotism on the part of their rulers. Thus Central Arabian politics, in the days before oil or other sources of revenue were discovered, frequently resolved themselves into the mutual seduction of each other's tribes by rival princes, even while the latter were nominally at peace with one another. The present world situation, with Russia endeavouring to win the friendship of Asia and Africa and create trouble between them and the West, is, on a larger scale, not dissimilar.

In the case of the Ikhwan refugees, Ibn Saud had sent a force to punish some of his subjects for raiding into Iraq, whereupon the offenders had taken refuge in the latter country, where he could not reach them. Not only so, but from their asylum in Iraq they had set out to raid their former friends in Nejed. The grant of asylum by Iraq was both unwise and discreditable, as events were to show, but it was not quite so outrageous an action as would appear to those unfamiliar with the Arabian scene of those days.

The Iraq Government, it must be admitted, was completely indifferent to bedouins, tribes and deserts, and lived in another world, but King Feisal had been brought up as an Arab prince of the old régime. While these incidents were occurring in Iraq, raiding and counter-raiding were in process on the frontier between Nejed and the Hejaz. The king doubtless did not believe that Ibn Saud had sought to punish his men for raiding Iraq out of any affection for that country, but because he was about to attack King Feisal's father, old King Husain, in the Hejaz. He therefore did not wish to be committed to trouble on the Iraq frontier until he had finished with King Husain. By corollary, King Feisal wished to make trouble on the Iraq frontier, in order to relieve the pressure on his father.

Reference has already been made to the difficulties which arose from the creation of fixed territorial frontiers in the great deserts. In Turkish times, the government had rarely attempted to extend its influence to a distance of more than two or three miles from the river bank. If the Uqair protocols had not been negotiated, such a situation would have repeated itself. The Ikhwan would have established their sway up to a line only a few miles from the river bank. In practice therefore there would still have been a *de facto* frontier, but it would have been three or four miles from the Euphrates instead of one hundred and fifty.

This had indeed been the situation during the first Wahhabi period from 1800 to 1812. It resulted, as we have seen, in unending attacks, not only on the tribes of Iraq but on all the Euphrates towns from Kerbela to Basra. If the Wahhabis had been a little more daring, it might have resulted in a massacre in Baghdad, similar to that which actually occurred at Kerbela. In addition, the railway now ran in the desert from Samawa to Basra, and we have already seen that Yusuf Ibn Sadoon and his Ikhwan accomplices had found no difficulty in raiding across it.

It may also be noted that, in 1800, the wali of Baghdad exercised little more than a nominal jurisdiction over the Iraq tribes and was certainly unable to extort regular taxes from them. Thus the tribes, contributing nothing to the Baghdad administration, could not reasonably claim its protection. In 1922, however, the Iraq Government aspired to collect full legal taxes from its tribes and thus was in honour bound to protect them.

While, therefore, it is possible to appreciate Ibn Saud's dislike of fixed frontiers, it is difficult to think of any alternative arrangement between countries under modern conditions. It is true, however, that the existence of nomadism calls for freedom of movement across frontiers for the flocks of the nomads. It was not, however, the imposition of fixed frontiers on the nomads which gave rise to the troubles which were to follow. The eight years of hostilities which were to ensue may perhaps be attributed to two causes, firstly, the fanaticism of the Ikhwan and secondly, the hostility and mistrust between the Saud and sherifian families.

The Ikhwan refugees were thus pawns in the power politics between the sherifs and the Saud family. The victims of this rivalry were to be, as this narrative will show, the poor shepherds of Iraq, who had shown us such simple and generous hospitality on our little desert expedition.

On 1st March, 1924, I obtained leave of absence for two months and left Nasiriya. A few days later, Feisal al Duweesh, the chief of the Mutair tribe, with a large force of Ikhwan, fell upon the Iraq shepherds near Unsab, at the west end of the Neutral Area, on the Iraqi side of the border. Warning had been received, even by the

Iraq Government, that a raid was imminent, and aircraft patrols had been sent out daily to reconnoitre. The R.A.F., having taken the first step towards operating in the desert when they contacted me on my trip in January, were prepared now to extend their flights to the Nejed frontier. But their operations were not as yet conducted on any plan and they were ignorant of the country and the tribes. To search thirty thousand square miles of country for two or three thousand raiders was hopeless, when the aircraft had no idea where to look. Meanwhile the Iraq tribes were scattered helplessly all over the desert, so that the Ikhwan had a wide choice of objectives.

The aircraft having missed the raiders, the first information that a raid had taken place was received several days later, when the fugitives reached the Euphrates. The victims were the Beni Salama and Al Yaajeeb, both shepherd tribes from between Samawa and Shinafiya. Several hundred Iraqis were killed, thousands of sheep were looted, together with many donkeys and tents, not to mention clothing, money, foodstuffs and other property.

The air operations in March and April, 1924, completely failed to protect the Iraq tribes, yet they showed that both the R.A.F. and the Iraq Government were at last beginning to realize that some form of action was necessary. To a limited extent, they also served to provide experience, or at least to show that desert raiders were not an easy target to find. Perhaps the principal lesson to be learnt was that the most crying need was to obtain more intelligence. Success could not be expected as long as the authorities remained in complete ignorance of bedouin affairs and of events in the desert. In precisely the same manner, a century and a quarter earlier, the Wahhabis had been able to surprise Kerbela, and to cause panic alternately in Baghdad and in Damascus, by their sudden and unexpected appearances near those cities. Intelligence cannot be relied upon to come to him who waits, unless he goes to seek it. In other words, to remain in touch with events hundreds of miles out in the desert, the government would have to go there; unfortunately the officials and officers of the government regarded a tour of duty in the desert not only with aversion but with positive alarm.

There could be no doubt that Ibn Saud had sanctioned this savage raid to show his resentment at the action of Iraq in affording asylum to the Ikhwan refugees, but to the official protests he replied that he had been unaware of the fact that the Ikhwan intended to raid. When he had protested against the pilfering raids by the Ikhwan refugees, the Iraq Government had replied in the same manner—truthfully in their case, for they had no knowledge whatever of what took place in the desert. As a result, the mutual exchange of accusations led to no result.

VI

Gift Hollow

Now indeed the marauding spirit of the bedouin was in unison with the militant spirit of Islam. The cry of plunder and of conquest reverberated throughout the land and was answered eagerly. The movement began naturally with the tribes in the north ... whose restless spirit led them over the frontier.

Sir William Muir, *Annals of the Early Caliphate*

They came up ... as grasshoppers for multitude; for both they and their camels were without number; and they entered into the land to destroy it. *Judges* vi. 5

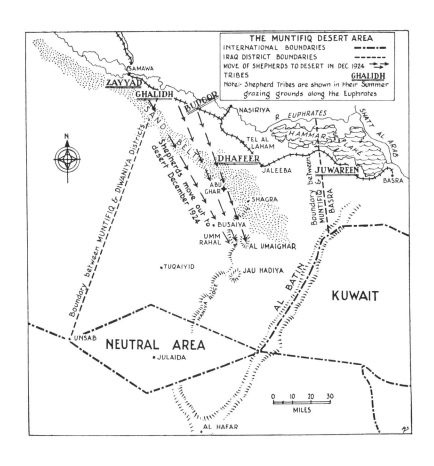

GIFT HOLLOW

MEANWHILE the Ikhwan refugees, camped under the auspices of Yusuf Ibn Sadoon, were continuing their lucrative policy of camel stealing from Nejed. The British Government were the principal losers in prestige as a result of this anarchy. The fact that no apparent attempt was being made to check the activities of the refugees had caused Ibn Saud deep resentment, while the increasingly frequent raids by the Ikhwan had alarmed all the tribes of the Syrian and Iraq deserts. It was generally known that Ibn Saud was in treaty relations with the British Government. The prestige of Britain was still high, both owing to the memory of her victory over the Turks in the First World War, and also to her more recent suppression of the rebellion in Iraq in 1920. The tribes were all firmly convinced that the British could immediately prevent Ikhwan raids if they so desired. Their failure to do so was attributed by the tribes to politics. "In order to keep both Nejed and Iraq weak," they said, "the English wish them to fight one another." Such an explanation seemed to them obvious, accustomed as they had been to long years of Ottoman government. Divide and rule had always been a fundamental principle of the policy of the local Turkish officials.[1] Arabs indeed have always found it difficult to believe in the inefficiency of the British Government. When the policy of Britain seems most inept, the Arabs attribute to it an even more than usual degree of tortuous subtlety.

As the autumn of 1924 advanced, and the time once more drew near when the tribes would be compelled to move into the desert, anxiety grew both amongst shepherds and bedouins. In Samawa the Zayyad, in Nasiriya the Budoor and Juwareen besieged the offices of the government to know what steps were to be taken for their protection. The reply usually returned to them—"If God wills, all will be well"—failed signally to satisfy them.

I also joined the shepherds in their chorus of protests. I endeavoured to urge on the authorities the necessity for preparation, in so far at least as studying the problem and the terrain was concerned. I suggested the appointment of an officer whose sole duty it would be to collect information, and to obtain prior warning of intended raids. In the case of the larger Ikhwan attacks, the tribesmen in

---

[1] May I emphasize that in my remarks about the Turks I refer only to the old Ottoman Empire, and not to modern Turkey.

Nejed necessarily took a number of days to collect beneath their war banners. Information could therefore usually be obtained some days before the raid actually arrived, though the exact objective might still be unknown. In past years, the Iraq tribes had often received information in advance, though the government usually remained in ignorance, because it was not anybody's duty to find out.

To transmit the information from the desert to the government was, however, by no means easy. The Iraq tribes moved to a distance of about one hundred and fifty to two hundred miles from the Euphrates, on which lay all the government posts. Thus even if the tribes received warning when they were far out in the desert, they could not transmit the alarm to the government. I therefore suggested the establishment of a post equipped with wireless at Sadoon's old ruined fort at Abu Ghar.

To these suggestions, air headquarters replied by appointing me as the officer responsible for collecting information on the subject of raids, relieving me at the same time of all other duties. Agreement was refused to any other organization or precautionary measures, or to the discussion and formulation of plans. As a half measure, however, a section of armoured cars was instructed to carry out a reconnaissance in the southern desert, visiting Lusuf, Sulman and Abu Ghar.[1]

This operation did no harm as a small scale exploration, but it was of little use for the immediate need of the moment. Any organization, however small, which could have been permanent, and could have served as a basis to experiment with and to build upon, would have been preferable. To drive out into the desert with a convoy of cars, and then to drive back again so that the troops could return to Baghdad in time for Christmas, scarcely seemed to me to be an adequate way of defending the frontier. A raid was not likely to take place precisely on the day on which the armoured cars were in the field. Writing at the time, I likened this reconnaissance to driving a fire brigade round the town on the chance of finding a house on fire, but, having failed to do so, sending all the firemen away on a holiday on the grounds that there was no work for them.

Scarcely had the armoured cars returned to their bases for Christmas than I received news in Nasiriya that the Ikhwan tribe of Mutair, under Feisal al Duweesh, were preparing to raid. The Dhafeer under the leadership of the (in tribal matters at least) astute Hamood, had not moved out into the desert. Being, moreover, a camel tribe, they had closer connections with Central Arabia than had the shepherds and received better information. Anticipating fresh Ikhwan raids and massacres, the majority of them were still camped on the railway near Tel al Laham, although their herds were

[1] See map on page 141.

suffering from the lack of grazing. Unfortunately, however, while no rain had as yet fallen on the river or railway area, there had been heavy rain storms in the desert, south of the line Sulman–Busaiya,[1] and the shepherds had hastened to move their camps to where the young green grass promised new life to their sheep, thin from the summer heats on the Euphrates. I immediately passed on my information to air headquarters, but the Christmas holidays were about to begin.

While not refusing to take action should a raid occur, headquarters were politely incredulous, requested further confirmation, asked for more details, delayed and postponed. Meanwhile the Ghalidh tribe, and part of the Zayyad and Budoor, all shepherds, were camped at Jau Hadiya,[2] a small basin-like depression just east of the Haniya ridge, and eighty miles south of Tel al Laham.

Jau Hadiya may be translated Gift Hollow, and the origin of the name was not without interest. Soon after the notorious Sadoon had established himself at Abu Ghar, having been outlawed by the Turks, he organized a great raid across the desert against the Ruwalla. Shepherds and bedouins alike followed his banner, for it was before the time of his quarrel with the Dhafeer. The latter were great desert raiders, but perhaps Sadoon and the shepherds lacked experience. Suffice it to say that the Ruwalla were completely victorious, and the defeated Sadoon arrived back with the somewhat demoralized remnants of his force. No sooner did the returning raiders reach their camps than they received a warning that Ibn Saud was advancing to attack them. It must have been soon after the young Abdul Aziz had seized Riyadh, and while Ibn Rasheed was still the ruler of the greater part of Nejed.

Sadoon was undaunted by this new danger. He rode round the tribes in person, urging, imploring, admonishing them to rally in defence. The raiders were encountered in this very place and were completely defeated. In fact so easy a victory did Sadoon win that the site of the battle was named Gift Hollow. Such are the vicissitudes of life. Now one alone of Ibn Saud's many tribes was sufficient to send all the Iraq tribes flying in panic. This change of fortune, it seemed to me, was due to leadership—on the Nejed side, the superb leadership of Abdul Aziz Ibn Saud, on that of the Iraqis, the absence of any leader and the obvious indifference of the authorities. I could almost regret that the turbulent Sadoon was with us no more.

Despairing of any rapid action by the government, I visited Hamood Ibn Suwait at Tel al Laham, and hired a camel rider from him to take a note from me to the shepherds at Jau Hadiya, warning

---

[1] For these places, see map on page 71.
[2] See map on page 124 for ensuing events.

them to retire, because the Ikhwan were about to raid. The letter
being brought by a retainer of Hamood, the shepherds conceived
the idea that the whole affair was a conspiracy. The Dhafeer, they
suspected, wished the shepherds to retire, in order that the bedouins
could then slip in and occupy the best grazing. Such is the tortuous
nature of the Arab mind, always quick to attribute the worst motives
to the actions of others. In reality, however, the wish was father to
the thought. The desert behind them as far as the Euphrates had
missed the first rains, and was still brown and dusty. The country
from Umm Rahal to Jau Hadiya was already clothed in bright green
grass. Every day spent in such grazing meant more milk and butter,
and more and stronger lambs. Surely, they thought, these warnings
must be lies.

As soon as I received news that the shepherds had neglected my
warning, I determined to go out myself and bring them back. I
was not really responsible for their safety—I was merely a military
intelligence officer, and the civil government was in control until
the R.A.F. were called in. But I had begun to know and feel for
these people, and it was obvious that if I did not do something, no
one else would. I accordingly sent word to Hamood to have camels
ready for me on the morning of 23rd December, 1924. Early on that
day, I drove out by car from Nasiriya to the Dhafeer tents at
Tel al Laham. Although Hamood had replied to my message, saying
that the camels would be ready, yet when I arrived no camels were
to be seen. This was indeed an invariable though maddening quality
of tribesmen. When asked to supply anything, they replied that it
was ready when required. But when it was actually asked for, it
took two days to appear, or perhaps it did not exist at all. The
present instance was no exception. The camels, Hamood explained,
had been driven out grazing, the men who were to accompany me
were away, they had not been certain that I really would come,
and, in any case (with a hospitable smile), "Tomorrow is as good as
today and in the meanwhile we can enjoy your company." There
was nothing for it but to curb my impatience, spend the day smoking
and gossiping round the coffee fire in Hamood's tent, and make
certain that all was ready for the morrow. Though we did not know
it then, the day's delay was to prove providential.

In the evening I discovered that Hamood had warned forty
camelmen to accompany me. The desert was dangerous, he
explained, and the Ikhwan might be out raiding. Besides which, he
added, no person of my importance could travel with dignity without
an escort. My pocket, however, did not permit me to enjoy such
state, for I realized that each of the forty camelmen would require
a gratuity at the end of the trip. I therefore persuaded Hamood to
reduce them to four, namely Rumi Ibn Suwait, the brother of Ajami,

Shareeda Ibn Jendel and Ghunaim Ibn Shuwaish, both Dhafeeris, and a negro "slave" called Ali. In addition I hired two camels, one for myself and one for my servant, Ali al Yunis.

The sun was already high when we eventually rode out of the Dhafeer camp, crossed the railway and set our faces for the south. It was one of those clear, sparkling winter days in the desert, a cloudless sky, cool bright air, a mild warm sun and, before us, a horizon as wide as the sea. The bedouins soon broke into song as we tapped our camels with our canes and set off at a trot. The camel trotting song is one of the commonest of the bedouin forms of verse and every desert dweller possesses a long repertoire of them. Shareeda had brought a hawk on the croup of his camel and a greyhound trotting at heel, in the hope that we might put up a hare or a bustard. Towards evening, we reached some camps of the Dhafeer in the sand dunes north-west of Abu Ghar, and we dismounted at a tent where we saw a circle of men sitting round the fire and heard the ring of the coffee mortar. Snugly hidden in a hollow between two high dunes, the fire shed a warm ruddy glow inside the tent, contrasting strongly with the vast blackness and silence of the desert night. In front of the tent, a pile of brushwood broken from the tall feathery *ghidha* bushes, which in the sand belt grow higher than a man, promised cheerful light and warmth for the night. Outside the circle of faces lighted by the fire, the couched camels chewed the cud beneath the bright desert stars. As we half sat and half reclined in the soft sand, leaning our elbows on our camel saddles, watching for our kettle to boil on the embers, I remembered that it was Christmas Eve.

We were away early the next morning, for bedouins do not breakfast, and topping the last dunes of the sand belt, looked far away over the blue ridges of the desert. We proposed to spend the night with the most southerly of the shepherd tribes at Jau Hadiya, and to persuade them to strike camp and fall back the next day, as far as Shagra at least, until some reply or decision could be obtained from the government.

From the dunes in the direction of Shagra, two bedouin horsemen appeared and galloped down upon us, their long white shirts flying and their bare legs hanging down on either side of the pads on which they rode. They wheeled round us at a gallop before they could pull up, and cried that they had heard firing in the stillness of the dawn from the direction of Umm Rahal. They proved to be men of the Ikhwan refugees, some of whom were camped at Shagra. We were heading for Umm Rahal, and after hearing their report, we halted frequently to scan the country ahead of us with field glasses. On our left, the long blue line of the Haniya ridge bounded our view. Straight ahead of us lay rolling desert, already shimmering in the warm sunny air. Towards the middle of the morning, we saw a dark patch moving southwards along the Haniya ridge. It seemed to be a herd of shepherd donkeys. They were much nearer than we were to Umm Rahal, and as they seemed to be moving unconcernedly towards the south, we concluded that there could be no truth in the story told us by the two horsemen. Such alarms were, in those days, of frequent occurrence in the desert.

At midday, we reached the foot of the Haniya ridge below Umm Rahal, and decided to halt, both to break our own fast and to allow our camels half an hour to graze. Choosing the dry bed of a little water course on the slope of the ridge, we dismounted in it for shelter, for the wind was chilly though the sun was warm. Then we quickly cut down and stacked a heap of bushes and lit a fire, round which we warmed our hands. The camels were hobbled and turned loose, and our breakfast of bread, dates and cold meat was laid out on a saddle cloth. Except for the sighing of the wind, the blue desert hills lay apparently silent and deserted.

Half an hour later, we remounted and breasted the steep slope of the Haniya. In ten minutes we topped the rise, and as we crossed the ridge, an animated picture suddenly appeared before us. At this point, Al Umaigher, a depression some four miles long and a mile wide, ran parallel to the Haniya and east of it. As a result, the Haniya became in fact a ridge on both sides, instead of, as elsewhere, merely the western face of the Dibdibba plateau. The Umaigher depression below us was now full of countless flocks of sheep and herds of donkeys, all moving northwards. Here and there horsemen were galloping and men running, apparently urging on the flocks at greater speed. A whole shepherd nation seemed to be moving northwards, the entire face of the desert being covered as if by swarms of ants.

As we paused on the skyline on top of the Haniya ridge, this scene at first conveyed no particular significance to my mind. But the bedouins understood at once and appreciated its meaning. "These people are in flight," said Shareeda. "Something must have happened."

As we could hear no sound of firing, we at first thought that our appearance had alarmed the shepherds, who might possibly have already been nervous after our previous warnings to them of the imminence of a raid. Knowing that no bedouins were camped near them, the sight of us, six camel riders topping the skyline, might, we thought, have stampeded them. We were so completely taken aback at coming suddenly over the ridge on to this scene of chaos, that I, for one, was unable to think sufficiently quickly.

We had scarcely had time to exchange these thoughts when a bullet whistled over our heads, then another and another. We could see that the shepherds nearest to us had paused in their flight, run towards us a few yards, taken up firing positions and were opening fire on us. Our bedouins slipped off their cloaks and waved them above their heads, but with no effect. The bullets came thicker and faster. As the nearest shepherds were only some six hundred yards away, the situation was becoming unpleasant. "Down into that *shaeeb*," called Rumi Ibn Suwait.

We tapped our camels sharply with our canes, trotted rapidly down the slope and dropped into a little sandy water course, where we couched our camels and slipped off their backs. Here we were out of sight, though the bullets still continued to flip past overhead. "Whit—Whit—Whit." We crawled on our stomachs and peered over the sandy bank of the water course.

We were still under the impression that the shepherds had mistaken us for possible raiders and had panicked. "Shoot first and ask questions afterwards" was, in those days, the desert rule. As the bullets continued to whistle just over our heads, we abused the shepherds, laughed loudly (but perhaps a little nervously) and lit our cigarettes. "May Allah take all shepherds," said Shareeda Ibn Jendel as the bullets flicked past. "They do not even know how to shoot."

"Would you have them hit us?" enquired Rumi Ibn Suwait, who seemed to be unable to appreciate the humour of being shot at by the shepherds whom we had come out to save.

Meanwhile we decided to send Ali, the negro slave, to inform the shepherds of our identity. We told him to follow down the little valley in which we were crouching, and in which he would be invisible to them, and then to make a wide detour and come up to them from another direction. We watched him crawl down the bed of the dry water course and then emerge running on the plain below. Waving his cloak above his head, he made for the man nearest to him, who happened to be driving a flock of sheep. The shepherd, however, on perceiving him, threw off most of his clothes, abandoned the sheep and fled incontinently, pursued in vain by our emissary.

"May they all be for hell fire!" exclaimed Shareeda in disgust.

Eventually, however, the negro met and spoke to a man on a horse, who galloped back apparently to warn the others. Gradually the firing ceased, and remounting our camels we kicked them into a trot down the shrub-covered slope.

VII

A Happy Christmas

The Wahabys have established it as a fundamental rule to kill all their enemies found in arms ... It is this practice which makes the Wahaby name so dreaded. Whenever bedouin camps are attacked, the same circumstances occur; all who are taken with arms are unmercifully put to death. This savage custom has inspired the Wahabys with a ferocious fanaticism that makes them dreadful to their adversaries. BURCKHARDT, *History of The Wahabys* (1831)

To what excesses do men rush for the sake of religion, to whose precepts they pay so little regard. JEAN DE LA BRUYÈRE

> Alas! what boots it with incessant care
> To tend the homely, slighted, shepherd's trade ...?
> Fame is the spur that the clear spirit doth raise ...
> To scorn delights and live laborious days;
> But the fair guerdon when we hope to find,
> And think to burst out into sudden blaze,
> Comes the blind Fury with th' abhorrèd shears
> And slits the thin-spun life.
>
> MILTON, *Lycidas*

CHAPTER VII

A HAPPY CHRISTMAS

ALTHOUGH the shepherds had now been informed of our identity, the moving masses of sheep, donkeys, and men showed no signs of checking their flight. As we reached the level bed of the Umaigher depression, we were surrounded by a group of men, some on foot and some mounted, their faces wild with terror and excitement. All shouted together, some pausing for a second only as they ran past, others pushing up to us and jostling our camels or seizing the reins.

"The Ikhwan! The Ikhwan! *Kone! Kone!* A battle! A battle! The Ikhwan!" were all we could distinguish. Then others, seeing me in uniform, cried out, "Where is the government now? Why don't they save us? Oh officer! Have you brought help? The Ikhwan! The Ikhwan!"

The babel was indescribable. I myself was still incredulous, but no consecutive narrative could be obtained from the panic-stricken mob.

Pushing our camels, almost by brute force, through the crowd surrounding us, we seized upon one or two men on the fringes of the human stream which was flowing past us, and demanded to know what had happened. "We are the Uwailiyeen section of the Budoor tribe," replied one of them, who seemed to be in possession of part at least of his wits. "The Ghalidh and the Zayyad were camped to the south of us in Jau Hadiya. Soon after dawn this morning, a horseman galloped into our camp and told us that they had been attacked by a great force. Everyone in his tribe was killed—he only escaped. He saw with his own eyes two green and one red war banner. They have been pursuing us all day. Oh officer! The Ikhwan!"

He dashed away after a flock of sheep before we could cross-question him further, crying as he ran, "Drive on, drive on. O God help us! O God protect us!"

"This is the Duweesh," said Shareeda decisively, after listening to the man's story.

"Are you sure?" I said. "Perhaps two sections of shepherds have fought one another, and these people heard the firing and panicked."

But my own bedouins were already catching the infection. "Oh sir," they called, "the Ikhwan! Let us flee. It is the Ikhwan."

I was undecided what to do. Headquarters were always com-

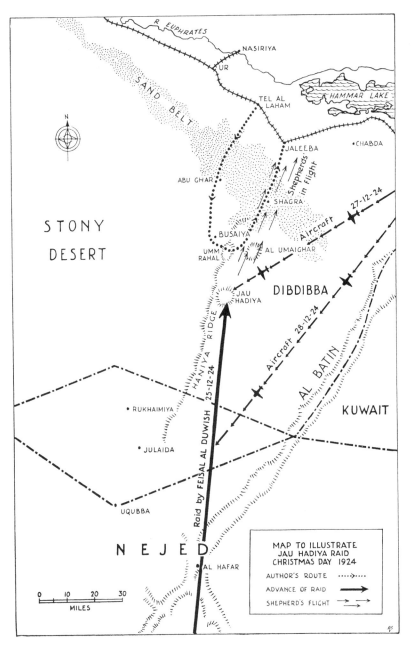

R. EUPHRATES

NASIRIYA

UR

TEL AL LAHAM

HAMMAR LAKE

SAND BELT

JALEEBA

• CHABDA

N

Shepherds in Flight

ABU GHAR

SHAGRA

27-12-24

STONY

Aircraft

BUSAIYA

DESERT

DIBDIBBA

UMM RAHAL

AL UMAIGHAR

JAU SHADIYA

HANIYA RIDGE

Aircraft 28-12-24

AL BATIN

KUWAIT

• RUKHAIMIYA

25-12-24

• JULAIDA

Raid by FEISAL AL DUWISH

UQUBBA

NEJED

• AL HAFAR

MAP TO ILLUSTRATE
JAU HADIYA RAID
CHRISTMAS DAY 1924

AUTHOR'S ROUTE ....
ADVANCE OF RAID ——▶
SHEPHERD'S FLIGHT ⇉⇉

0   10   20   30
MILES

plaining about scares and false alarms. To ride in from the desert and report an Ikhwan raid, when it was in reality only a brawl between two tribes of shepherds, would make us all look fools. There did not, on the other hand, seem to be much good sitting still on the backs of our camels while the stream of terror-stricken fugitives flowed past us. If the Ikhwan had really raided the shepherds, resistance would be out of the question. There would probably be two or three thousand raiders, while we were only six men. I was unarmed, the four bedouins were already very nervous; only my man Ali al Yunis seemed cool and self-possessed. The shepherds were out of their senses from terror.

In the bed of the Umaigher depression in which we were standing, our view was restricted. The end of the depression was closed by a low ridge about a mile to the south of us. I ordered Ali, the negro, to trot back up the Haniya slope down which we had come. Perhaps, on higher ground, he would be able to see over the southern ridge and tell us what was happening beyond it.

A few minutes later, a crackle of rifle fire to the south made us suddenly turn our heads. The last of the shepherd flocks were driving towards us down the slope which closed the end of our valley. Suddenly a long line of camelmen topped the ridge, and urged their camels to full speed in pursuit of the retreating flocks. Those in the centre of the line then stopped, slipped from the backs of their camels, and opened a rapid rifle fire on the fleeing shepherds and flocks. On either flank, the camelmen continued to ride forward at full speed, in order to outflank and cut off a portion of the fugitives. The shepherds, who were on foot, abandoned their flocks, throwing off their cloaks, and fled towards us as fast as they could run. Some fell under the rifle fire of the raiders, others ran wildly on. Meanwhile other fugitives still streamed past us, throwing terrified glances over their shoulders. Some of them began to abandon their flocks all round us, and to fly on foot. An anguished cry went up, as they saw the camelmen pouring down the slope behind them. "Here they are! *Jaona!* They are on us! O God save us!"

This seemed to settle the question that an Ikhwan raid was actually in progress. I couched my camel and dismounting took my message pad from my saddle bag and wrote out two messages. One was a telegram addressed to air headquarters, Baghdad, and reported that the Iraq tribes had been heavily raided that morning by the Ikhwan, and that fighting was still in progress near Umm Rahal. I requested the immediate despatch of aircraft to the site. I looked at my watch. It was five o'clock in the evening. The second message was a note to the station master at Jaleeba, asking him to despatch the telegram urgently, clearing all other traffic off the telegraph line. I gave both notes to Ghunaim Ibn Shuwaish, who seemed to be the

most frightened of our party. I told him to ride at full speed for
Jaleeba station, never halting until he had handed in the messages.
Nothing loath, he set out northwards at a flying trot, whacking his
camel with his cane.

Meanwhile my bedouins were becoming more and more anxious.
They were in anguish at seeing my camel couched and myself dis-
mounted. "Sir, get mounted quickly! *Irkab, irkab.* Mount! Mount!
They are on us."

The advancing camelmen were now about one thousand yards
away from us. If they had ridden straight at us, they would have
been on us in a few minutes, but they lost time rounding up the
flocks and killing the shepherds. Just then Ali, the negro, whom I
had sent up the slope, returned at full speed, racing down the hill on
his camel. He reported breathlessly that a large body of camelmen
with war banners unfurled was passing east of us, doubtless with the
intention of cutting off our retreat to the north. "Come, sir, let us
flee! Mount quickly. The Ikhwan will cut us off. Quickly!"

There was nothing to be gained by remaining where we were, so I
climbed on to my camel and we joined the stream of fugitives going
north. Ali al Yunis, I noticed, had a revolver and a rifle. I called on
him to give me the revolver, which had six rounds in it. A revolver is
not much good in the desert, but it might be better than nothing.
Suddenly I remembered that in England it was Christmas Day.

It was tragic to pass through the innumerable little companies of
donkeys, laden with the humble belongings of the shepherds, a
couple of cooking pots, a few little bags of rice or dates, a goat skin
filled with water, and the rolled up tent. The convoys of donkeys
were urged on by the women, running bare-footed behind them,
frantic with fear, many carrying babies at the breast, pushing and
beating their tiny donkeys, constantly glancing over their shoulders
and moaning: "O Ali, Thy protection! O Husain! O God save us!"[1]

To be overtaken by those camelmen meant not only the loss of
everything they owned in the world, but death to their fathers,
husbands, brothers and sons. It was said that the Ikhwan would
snatch babies from their mothers' breasts to see if they were boys or
girls. If the former their throats were cut and the little bleeding
bodies thrown down; if they were girls they were returned to their
mothers.

We rode for some distance at a walking pace—the pursuing
camelmen seemed again to have delayed to round up more sheep.
There was nothing we could do to help the fugitives, but I was

---

[1] The shepherds were Shiahs, who made a practice of calling upon the names of "saints"
for protection. Ali was the son-in-law of the Prophet Muhammad; Husain was the son of
Ali. To the Wahhabis this practice was anathema, being a form of *shirek* or association
of human beings with God.

instinctively loath to appear to run away and leave them, as the speed of our camels would have enabled us to do. As a result we moved at their pace in the midst of the terrified throng, borne along as it were in the stream. Eventually, however, we decided to push on at a trot. Dusk was already falling. I felt ashamed to desert these poor fugitives to be massacred, but now it seemed that those who were still left would probably escape under cover of darkness. The most important thing was to carry information to a telegraph office, and Jaleeba was sixty miles away. Soon we were driving our camels forward at their best pace towards Shagra.

As we climbed up the first dunes of the sandbelt, we again met some horsemen of the Ikhwan refugees, now greatly excited, galloping round one another in circles, with loud warlike cries, bareheaded, with their long hair flying in the wind. I commented somewhat bitterly on the warlike evolutions of these scoundrels, who were still about eight miles from the nearest enemy. Moreover, they themselves were largely responsible for these massacres of our shepherds, owing to the friction between Iraq and Nejed caused by their camel robberies across the border. It was already dark when we reached their tents at Shagra, and found Feihan al Dhuweibi, of a shaikhly family of the Harab tribe, who was one of the leaders of the Ikhwan refugees.

The camel which I was riding, my bedouin companions told me, was the property of a poor Dhafeeri widow, whose husband had died six months before. Hamood had arranged for me to hire her camel, because the woman was in need of the money which I would pay for its hire. But the result of the camel being the property of a widow was that it had not been regularly ridden. Having spent the summer grazing on the banks of the Euphrates, it was soft and in poor condition, and was showing signs of exhaustion. We were still about forty miles from Jaleeba, which I was determined to reach that night, with a view to sending telegrams to the R.A.F. calling for aircraft to attack the raiders the next day. I was able, however, to get a mare from Feihan al Dhuweibi for myself and another for Shareeda Ibn Jendel, and decided to gallop the remaining forty miles to Jaleeba during the night. Rumi Ibn Suwait promised to take the camels and the remainder of the men back to Hamood's camp.

The mare lent to me was Feihan's own, a lovely little chestnut Arab thoroughbred. She was obviously the pride of the family, for she had a collar of blue beads round her neck against the evil eye, with a little bell hanging from it, which tinkled as she galloped. Shareeda had a less well bred grey mare. The bedouins ride only on a pad, made of canvas stuffed with wool and without stirrups. Usually they do not use a bit or reins, but only a halter and a single piece of rope. Thus equipped, Shareeda and I set out immediately, without waiting for food or drink. It was pitch dark, with an over-cast sky, as we started at a hand gallop for Jaleeba. The first eight miles lay across the sand belt, with loose sand above the horses' fetlocks, up and down steep dunes covered with high bushes. The little chestnut mare galloped strongly without wavering. Those who have only ridden with our English impedimenta of snaffles and curbs and reins may find it difficult to believe that "hands" are as necessary, and equally effective, when galloping a well bred horse with only a rope to hold her. It was a joy to feel her striding so keenly beneath me, yet so light to my hand on the rope.

It was an inky black night, with low trailing clouds and a strong wind with violent gusts. Soon it began to rain. I watched as long as I could the fading light which marked the west, behind the ragged clouds. Then it also vanished and we seemed to be shut in all around by a thick wall of darkness.

At last we felt, from the horses' stride, that we were out of the sand, and on to hard gravelly desert. The mare still galloped steadily on. As I was unable even to see the ground beneath her feet, I left every-thing to her.

We had been riding for perhaps two or three hours and I guessed that we must be within seven or eight miles of Jaleeba, when a call from Shareeda behind me made me pull up. His mare, he said, was done for, and could gallop no more. She had stopped short and refused to go on. We had ridden for perhaps thirty miles, eight miles of it through soft sand, without a rest. Shareeda jumped off his mare and started to walk, driving her in front of him. I should have ridden on, but I was uncertain whether alone I could find Jaleeba in such intense darkness over featureless desert. As a result we decided to remain together, which meant that our pace was reduced to a walk, although my mare could still have galloped.

It was now raining in torrents. The wind seemed to me to be blowing first from our right and then from our left. "Shareeda," I said, "are you sure that you know where we are?" "Certain," he replied, and struggled on against the howling wind, now dragging the grey mare behind him by her head rope.

I was shivering with cold and soaked to the skin. My back ached. I thought it must be about eleven o'clock and we had been on the move for seventeen hours, with no food but a piece of cold meat, which we had eaten at midday before we came upon the scene of battle. Suddenly I noticed that the wind seemed to be behind us — hitherto it had been on my left cheek.

"Shareeda," I shouted again, above the howling blasts, "are you sure that you know the way?"

"I think so," he called back, a little less confidently than before.

We battled on in silence. The rain was still falling in buckets. It ran down my face, my back and my legs in streams. After a little time, during which the wind seemed at first to be behind us and then in our faces, I tried again.

"Shareeda," I said. "Are you really sure that you can find Jaleeba?"

"If God wills we shall find it," he replied.

I realized that this was tantamount to a confession that he had lost his bearings. He stooped down and felt the ground with his hands for the night was still as black as pitch.

"This is the soil of Jaleeba," he said. "We are quite near it, but I cannot be sure what direction it is in."

There was nothing for it but to halt until dawn. I guessed it must be between eleven and twelve at night, but it was too dark to see my watch. We sat down on the ground, holding the headropes of our horses, who turned their tails to the wind and stood miserably with heads lowered. It was still raining in icy torrents.

For interminable hours I crouched shivering with my knees up to my chin, occasionally dropping into a doze only to wake up again stiff with cold. Before dawn the rain stopped and it became a little lighter. Though I was wearing a khaki serge uniform and a heavy Arab sheepskin cloak, I was bitterly, almost unbearably, cold. A few yards away I could see Shareeda curled up fast asleep, although he had nothing on but a cotton shirt and a thin cloak. I thought to myself that I had imagined bedouins to be hardy in bearing the glaring heat of the summer, but I had not visualized that they could, as appeared to be the case, bear cold also with indifference. So fast asleep was he, that three times the headrope of his mare slipped out of his hands and I had to rise and stagger after her. Fortunately she was too cold and tired to stray far.

Such was my Christmas night of 1924.

At last dawn appeared and then daylight. The desert seemed to stretch all around us, uniform and featureless. Shareeda was still asleep, and I was obliged to rouse him. As soon as I touched him, he jumped to his feet, suddenly wide awake. He glanced around and then pointed to the north-west. "Jaleeba," he said, "is over there and quite close to us."

His mare was too stiff and exhausted to be ridden. Leaving him to drag her along by her head rope, I climbed stiffly on to the chestnut mare and set out at a canter in the direction which he had indicated. A mile farther on, topping a slight rise in the ground, I saw before me, and about half a mile away, the raised water tank and corrugated iron sheds of Jaleeba station. I must have looked a curious sight as I arrived at a hand gallop from the desert, soaked to the skin and plastered with mud, on my bedraggled and shivering mare.

Ghunaim Ibn Shuwaish, with my two messages, had not yet

arrived. Five minutes later, the railway operator was tapping out a "clear the line" telegram to Baghdad, asking for the immediate despatch of aircraft from Shaiba[1] to attack the raiders. Mr. Anthony, the Madrasi station master, soon produced a cup of hot tea, followed by a steaming plate of curry and rice. I had eaten scarcely anything for thirty-six hours. I had barely finished the curry and rice when I fell asleep.

But there was still no peace. Telegrams began to come in. Firstly one from air headquarters in Baghdad, ordering 84 Squadron in Shaiba to leave at once, pick me up at Jaleeba and pursue the raiders. Then one from the squadron that they were bombing up their aircraft. Then another from the squadron to say that the weather was unfit for flying. Then yet another that they were about to start. The sky had cleared, but it was cold and raw and blowing a gale. In the corrugated iron station shed of Jaleeba, I sat shivering in my soaking clothes. "Why on earth did not they go out direct and attack the raiders," I thought, "instead of wasting time coming to fetch me?" I had reported the map location of the enemy.

A silence followed with no more telegrams. By one o'clock I was fuming with impatience. I sent a telegram direct to the squadron, asking them not to call for me, but to fly straight out to Umm Rahal, and if the raiders were not there, to follow southwards down the Haniya ridge till they found them. Daylight was already getting short. At three o'clock in the afternoon, a message came from Shaiba to say that three ninaks had left there for Jaleeba, to bring me to Shaiba, with a view to operating against the raiders the next day. The day had been wasted, with a full-scale Ikhwan raid only sixty-five miles from Jaleeba.

By this time, in spite of the night's torrential rain, the high wind, blowing from the west down the sand belt, had raised a sandstorm. The air was full of flying stinging particles of sand, and it was impossible to see more than a few hundred yards—indeed extremely precarious weather for flying in those early days. Finally a single aeroplane arrived at Jaleeba. One had made a forced landing on the way and a second had landed beside it to help it—a chapter of accidents. Shortly before dark, I arrived at Shaiba in a single machine, in spite of a dense sandstorm.

There fresh misfortunes overtook us. The annual troopship was due to sail from Basra the next day. R.A.F. personnel served for only two years in Iraq, so that half the squadron was leaving the next day and being replaced by an equal number of new arrivals. Thus they would be only at half strength for flying. The two machines which had forced-landed on the way to Jaleeba did not return that night, with the result that they and their pilots were *hors de combat* also. At

[1] Shaiba camp was twenty miles west of Basra. See map on page 71.

least, however, I found at Shaiba dry clothes, a bath, dinner and a bed to sleep in.

Next morning, 27th December, 1924, we set out, but with the only three aircraft available. Between Umm Rahal and Jau Hadiya, we soon saw signs of the battle. Dead horses, human corpses and debris strewed the face of the desert. After circling low over the scene of the raid, we turned south and, with the Haniya ridge just on our right, we followed the probable line of retreat of the raiders. Not many minutes later, the pilot pointed to something ahead, and, pulling up the nose of the aircraft, he began to climb higher. Straining my eyes, I could just distinguish here and there a number of tiny figures, like microscopic ants. A few minutes more and we were above them. Over an area of perhaps three miles by two, the whole desert was covered with scattered camelmen, some riding in twos or threes together, others driving flocks of sheep or herds of donkeys.

Bombing so scattered a target was disappointing. It was difficult to record any hits with certainty. The puffs of smoke and dust from the bursting bombs were plainly visible but seemed to include no direct hits. In practice the splinters from the bombs, scattering all round the burst, probably caused casualties, but it was impossible from the air to see how many. If only we had had more aircraft or, better still, a ground force which could have dashed in and recovered the loot!

The bombing, however, did seem to cause something of a panic, for the camel-riders could be seen galloping in all directions. The sheep, suddenly abandoned, bunched together in excited groups, facing outwards as though to repel a ground attack, but undecided what this new terror could be. It was obvious that, as soon as the aircraft broke off the action, the raiders would round up the looted flocks once more and continue their march—and it was possession of the loot which signified victory.

When we returned to Shaiba, it was too late for another raid on the same day. Something, however, had been accomplished. We had been unlucky in my having lost the way to Jaleeba on Christmas night. If I had reached the station, which was actually only a mile and a half from where we were crouching in the rain, the telegrams would have reached Baghdad and Shaiba before midnight. We had again been unfortunate in the fact that there had been a gale and a sandstorm on 26th December, and also in the coincidence that the squadron was at only half strength on 27th December, the one day of the year when this happened. On the other hand, we had been lucky that I had arrived on the scene on the very day of the battle. Had I not been there, the first news of the raid would have been obtained three days later, when the exhausted survivors arrived at Jaleeba. In that case, the raiders would have escaped scot free. But

I knew that my greatest stroke of good fortune was that Hamood Ibn Suwait had not prepared our camels on 23rd December, as I had asked him to do. Had he punctually complied with my request, we should have been sleeping in the tents of the Ghalidh tribe on the morning of Christmas Day, in the very camp from which only a single horseman had escaped alive.

We subsequently ascertained that the raiders had passed as miserable a time as I did, in the cold wind and torrential rain of Christmas night. As a result, they had halted the whole of the next day at Umm Rahal, to rest and dry their clothes. The idea that they would be bombed or pursued had not entered their heads, with the result that they took their time without anxiety. We also received definite information that Feisal al Duweesh in person had been leading the raid.

The next day, 28th December, 1924, the whole squadron went out, and overtook the raiders, luckily a few miles north of the Nejed frontier, which aircraft were forbidden to cross. Meanwhile I returned to Jaleeba, and from thence, for one day only, to Nasiriya, being anxious to return as quickly as I could to Jaleeba to help the shepherd victims of the battle.

*   *   *   *   *

Attention has often been drawn to the manner in which British officers, scattered in the four corners of the world, have laboured with joyful and loving enthusiasm for some community in the midst of which their duties have placed them. Gurkhas, Sikhs, Malayans, Nigerians—innumerable races have evoked this affectionate devotion in sympathetic British officers. My experiences on Christmas Day, 1924, had stirred me deeply. The terror of the women in their flight, the anguish depicted in the faces of the children, the miserable donkeys laden with the few pathetic possessions of the shepherd families—all these and much else had both aroused my compassion and made me boil with indignation that such misery could be inflicted on human beings who relied for their protection on the government of which I was a servant. With youthful passion, I vowed that I would devote all my energies to put an end to such abominations.

VIII

Winter at Abu Ghar

While he was yet speaking there came also another, and said, "The Chaldeans made out three bands, and fell upon the camels, and have carried them away, yea, and slain the servants with the edge of the sword; and I only am escaped alone to tell thee."   *Job* i. 17

In famine he shall redeem thee from death: and in war from the power of the sword . . . neither shalt thou be afraid of destruction when it cometh. At destruction and famine thou shalt laugh: neither shalt thou be afraid. . . .   *Job* v. 20-22

Friends are much better tried in bad fortune than in good.
ARISTOTLE

He who loses wealth loses much; he who loses a friend loses more, but he who loses his courage loses all.   CERVANTES

The best way of worshipping God is in allaying the distress of the times.   ABU AL FADHL

VIII

WINTER AT ABU GHAR

WHEN I arrived back in Nasiriya, I found Guy Moore waiting for me. Moore was the Intelligence Special Service officer for the Diwaniya district, my next-door neighbour in the same job. He was a regular Flight-Lieutenant in the R.A.F. and had flown in the First World War, but he had now become so interested in Arabs that he had given up flying—for the present at least. According to the unpractical system then in force, the slice of the desert which included Sulman and Shebicha was part of the Diwaniya district, and, as the R.A.F. worked according to the administrative boundaries, Moore was responsible for this sector of the Southern Desert.[1] It was a system against which we fought for years, for we believed that the desert was a world in itself, and should have been a separate district.

We sat in my little house in Nasiriya, discussing my experiences in the Ikhwan raid. There was a knock on the door and a boy handed in a telegram addressed to Moore and written in Arabic. It was from his servant, whom he had left in Samawa, and it read: "Ikhwan raided shepherds and fugitives arrived in Samawa."

What could this mean? It was impossible for the fugitives of the Jau Hadiya raid to have reached Samawa—they had not yet arrived at Jaleeba. Could this be another raid? I immediately sent a telegram to the Qaimaqam—or sub-district officer—of Samawa, asking for details, only to receive the reply, "No fugitives arrived Samawa. Ikhwan raided shepherds at Jau Hadiya." The news of the Duweesh's raid, we thought, had doubtless been transmitted to Samawa by trains passing through Jaleeba station. The arrival of fugitives in Samawa was a mistake on the part of the servant. However, Guy Moore decided to call at Samawa next day, pick up his servant and find out why he had reported that fugitives had arrived there. I myself returned to Jaleeba.

On reaching Samawa, Moore found fugitives there from the Zayyad, who stated that they had been raided four days earlier at Sulman—that was on 26th December, the day after the Duweesh's raid at Jau Hadiya. Pursuit of the raiders four days after the battle seemed to be hopeless, as the Nejed frontier was only eighty miles from Sulman. Air headquarters, however, sent three aircraft down to Samawa to fly Guy Moore to Sulman to obtain confirmation and

[1] See map on page 71 for district boundaries.

fuller details. Flying southwards from Samawa, the reconnaissance saw a few scattered human beings walking in the desert, at a point some miles north of Sulman, and landed beside them. They proved to be exhausted women survivors of the raid, trying to reach Samawa on foot. They confirmed that the Zayyad had been heavily raided at Sulman by Muhsin al Firrem, a shaikh of the Ikhwan tribe of Harab, adding that the raiders were still camped at the wells at Sulman. The aircraft immediately flew on, and there—in the bed of the deep Sulman depression—were rows and rows of tents, surrounded by thousands of grazing camels, and great numbers of the sheep and donkeys looted from the Iraq shepherds. Never before or since did an Ikhwan raid offer such a target—and the three aircraft were all unarmed! They flew harmlessly round above the concentrated mass of raiders and then turned back to Samawa.

The Ikhwan, it appeared, supremely contemptuous alike of the Iraq tribes and their government, had camped for four days on the site of their victory, feasting on the captured sheep and other supplies, and resting in the mild winter sunshine. The following day, fresh aircraft from Baghdad arrived at Samawa, and succeeded in overtaking and bombing the raiders twice, before they crossed the Nejed frontier. But they were scattered over the face of the desert and on the move, as the Duweesh had been when we overtook him.

Four days later again, a fresh stream of exhausted women reached the Euphrates at Shinafiya. They were of the Yaajeeb and Beni Salama tribes, and reported that they had been raided near Shebicha by Meshari Ibn Busaiyis of Mutair, with a mixed following of Ikhwan from different tribes.

Along the whole length of the Nejed frontier from Basra to near Nejef the shattered and terrified remains of the Iraq shepherd tribes arrived back in panic and confusion on the banks of the Euphrates. In these three heavy inroads, several hundred Iraqis had been massacred, and many thousands of sheep had been looted, not to mention donkeys, tents, clothing, food, utensils and money. It was a devastating blow.

Meanwhile, on 30th December, I had returned to Jaleeba. The desert round the station buildings was now crowded by a mass of tents, flocks, donkeys and shepherds who had fled back in alarm to the fancied security of the railway. On the station platform sat huddled groups of women and children, many half-naked, exhausted and weak from lack of food. They were the women survivors of the Ghalidh and Zayyad camps which had been raided. All their male relatives had been killed. They maintained day and night a continuous and nerve-racking sound of wailing and sobbing—"Rachel weeping for her children, and will not be comforted because they are not." A week ago, they had been mothers, wives and sisters in

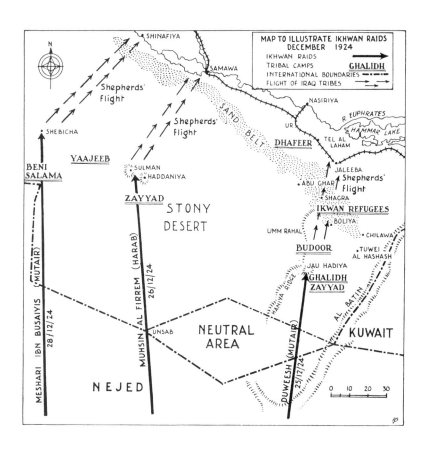

MAP TO ILLUSTRATE IKHWAN RAIDS
DECEMBER 1924
IKHWAN RAIDS
TRIBAL CAMPS   **GHALIDH**
INTERNATIONAL BOUNDARIES ·—··—··—
FLIGHT OF IRAQ TRIBES ⇉⇉⇉

N

SHINAFIYA

Shepherds'
Flight

SAMAWA

SAND BELT

NASIRIYA

R. EUPHRATES

UR

HAMMAR LAKE

·SHEBICHA

Shepherds'
Flight

DHAFEER

TEL AL
LAHAM

YAAJEEB

·SULMAN

JALEEBA

Shepherds'
flight

·ABU GHAR

**BENI
SALAMA**

·HADDANIYA

·SHAGRA

ZAYYAD

STONY
DESERT

IKWAN REFUGEES

·BOLIYA·

UMM RAHAL

·CHILAWA

BUDOOR

·TUWEI
AL HASHASH

JAU HADIYA

**GHALIDH
ZAYYAD**

NEUTRAL
AREA

UNSAB

KUWAIT

NEJED

0   10   20   30

contented little shepherd families. Now they were orphaned, widowed, half-naked and utterly destitute. The Ikhwan despoiled women of their outer garments and jewellery, but I cannot remember ever hearing a complaint of rape or assault—a remarkable example of self restraint in this one direction, on the part of a people so savage and ruthless in killing and looting.

I spent two weary days arranging for the evacuation of these pitiful convoys of women and female children by train to Nasiriya and Samawa, where they would scatter among the settled villages and be taken in and fed. The ever-tender Arab humanity will always take pity on the poor and the destitute, and admit them without question or hesitation into their tents and houses.

I found the attitude of the rank and file of the shepherd tribesmen to be not only resentful, but even hostile. Government, they were convinced—and especially the British—could stop all this wanton massacre and misery if it so desired. The majority believed that some unscrupulous policital motive led the authorities to connive at, and even perhaps to encourage, the massacre of their own tribes. It was only a few years since the Ottoman Government had encouraged civil war in the Muntifiq. As a result, sneers, mutterings and black looks followed me, as I moved up and down the station platform or among the groups of shepherds gathered round the wells outside the station buildings.

Meanwhile the government had woken up with a rude shock. My proposal to establish a post at Abu Ghar, to which previously no reply had been received, was immediately sanctioned. The first problem was how to transport the troops and then how to supply them, for the sand belt lay between Abu Ghar and the railway line. I accordingly set out one morning from Jaleeba in a Ford van to endeavour to find a route through the sand dunes. The first ten or twelve miles from Jaleeba consisted of flat desert with a gravelly surface, liberally sprinkled with small bushes some eighteen inches to two feet high. Then we came in sight of the long line of sand dunes, stretching across the horizon from right to left. We cruised up and down the edge of the sand belt trying to find a gap, but all in vain. Here and there, by accident, we crossed small ridges of sand, running out into the gravelly plain. We seemed to skim over them without trouble. Cautiously we drove a little farther into the sand—and found ourselves sailing over the low dunes with all the exhilaration of a scenic railway. The fact that light cars can travel with impunity over great seas of sand is now a commonplace, but in 1925 we had not yet dreamed that it would be possible. Wide expanses of sand form a superficial crust over which light vehicles with large tyres can drive as easily as over a smooth concrete surface. It is true that, if this crust be once broken, the vehicle can sink even to its axle, and may be difficult to extract, but with the right type of car and an experienced driver, little trouble is encountered. If large numbers of vehicles travel by the same route, however, the surface crust may be broken, and then many of them will sink in.

All this experience was still in front of us in January, 1925. Half an hour later we reached Abu Ghar, having, to our own amazement, crossed the whole sand belt. Two hours later we were back at Jaleeba station, excitedly drafting telegrams to tell Baghdad that our little Ford had crossed the sand belt and that troops at Abu Ghar could be rationed and supplied by motor transport, without resort to caravans of baggage camels. Early in January, 1925, a company of infantry of the Iraq Army reached Abu Ghar, occupied the ruined fort of the old robber baron Sadoon, and erected a wireless station. With a little party of four Arab retainers, four riding camels and three tents, I established my own headquarters at Abu Ghar also. The tribes, which after the Ikhwan raids, had fled to the railway line, ventured out once more as far as Shagra and Abu Ghar.

There was, however, still no system of obtaining intelligence of possible raids from Nejed, no organization of patrols or pickets, and, worst of all, no control over our own tribes, who regarded us with mistrust rather than loyalty. Even, therefore, if we received news of an impending raid, our own tribes disbelieved our warnings. They themselves lived in a nerve-racking condition, alternately fleeing in panic from vague rumours of raids, and advancing dangerously far forward, inspired by the courage of despair in their search for fresh grazing.

Nature allied herself to the Ikhwan in the destruction of the Iraq tribes during that terrible winter. While the desert was capable of producing in winter by far the best, and indeed the only, grazing for sheep and camels, yet sufficient rainfall was necessary and this rain was often variable and local. Here and there, patches of desert which had been soaked by early rainstorms in the autumn would be already clothed with fresh green grass in December. Other less fortunate areas might remain throughout the whole winter and spring as brown and bare as in midsummer. By a disastrous coincidence, the early rains that year had missed the area round Shagra and Abu Ghar, which was therefore entirely lacking in grazing. From Umm Rahal to the Nejed frontier, however, the virgin grass was standing six inches high, none daring to camp in it. Not only so, but January brought a spell of most exceptionally cold weather, with hard frosts every night. Animals with plenty of fresh grazing could resist the cold, but the half-starving camels and sheep were too debilitated to endure hardship. Every morning, the ground in front of the black tents was strewn with the corpses of sheep, goats and camels, and although grazing was nowhere obtainable, the unfortunate tribes were obliged to move camp almost daily to escape the decaying bodies of their own animals. Each deserted camp site presented the appearance of a battlefield, littered with the dead bodies of animals. The Iraq tribes, crowded for safety into the constricted area round Abu Ghar and Shagra, endured almost as heavy losses in livestock from cold and starvation in January and February, 1925, as they had suffered in the three great Ikhwan raids of December, 1924. Meanwhile the Nejed tribes, secure from reprisals or counter-attack, were scattered along both sides of the frontier, enjoying excellent grazing and water.

*   *   *   *   *

With few means of transport and no men at my disposal, and being still to a great extent ignorant of the tribes and the desert, it was all that I could do to maintain close touch with the tribes immediately round Abu Ghar. Meanwhile I had been made nominally responsible for the whole front, a distance of three hundred miles, from Basra to the Wadi al Khirr with the title of Special Service Officer, Ikhwan Defence. Indeed the pooling of intelligence along the whole front was essential, but I had no means of ground transport except camels, and Abu Ghar was the only wireless station in the whole desert. Fortunately, however, Guy Moore was posted to Samawa with a flight of three aircraft, with which he was able to carry out reconnaissances in the Stony Desert.

Already in this sector a new situation had arisen. One Draiwal Ibn Khalawi, a minor shaikh of the Zayyad shepherds, had collected a number of adherents from that tribe, and had set out secretly for Hail. Convinced that the British and Iraq Governments were encouraging the Nejdis to massacre them—or at least that they would not protect them—they had thrown themselves on the mercy of Ibn Musaad, the Governor of Hail and a cousin of Ibn Saud. Ibn Musaad had received the shepherd deputation with cordiality, and with the hospitality and generosity characteristic of the old Arab state, and had promised them immunity from Ikhwan raids. He had instructed them to camp on the frontier at Jumaima, and had sent tax collectors to tax their flocks. Fortified by the promises of that protection, which the British and the Iraqis were unable or unwilling to afford them, these shepherds camped on the frontier in fresh green grass, and willingly paid tribute to the Nejed Government.

To the paper protests of the Iraq and British Governments, Ibn Saud replied that the Ikhwan raids in December had been contrary to his orders. The offenders, however, the great Ikhwan chiefs like Feisal al Duweesh and Muhsin al Firrem, were not only not punished, but remained apparently in high favour. At the same time, the terror inspired amongst the Iraq tribes caused an increasing

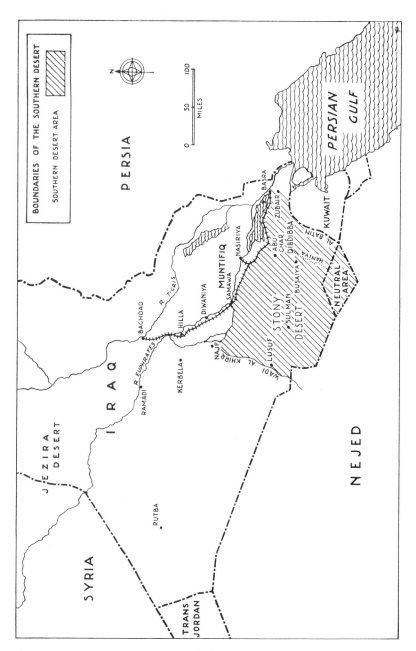

BOUNDARIES OF THE SOUTHERN DESERT

SOUTHERN DESERT AREA

N

100

50

MILES

0

PERSIA

PERSIAN GULF

BASRA

ZUBAIR

ABU
GHAR

DIBDIBBA

NASIRIYA

MUNTIFIQ

AL BATIN

KUWAIT

HANIYA

SAMAWA

DIWANIYA

STONY

SULMAN

BUSAIYA

NEUTRAL
AREA

R. TIGRIS

BAGHDAD

HILLA

DESERT

LUSUF

KERBELA

NAJF

WADI AL KHIRR

R. EUPHRATES

RAMADI

IRAQ

NEJED

JEZIRA
DESERT

RUTBA

SYRIA

TRANS
JORDAN

number of the latter voluntarily to pay taxes to Nejed to secure immunity from Ikhwan raids, thereby increasing Ibn Saud's revenues. If the raids were in reality contrary to his orders, it was remarkable that such tribes as had paid money to his tax collectors (not to the raiding tribal chiefs) were thenceforth immune from attack.

At other times, it is true, the Nejed Government endeavoured to set the "raids" by the Ikhwan refugees against the raids by the Duweesh and Muhsin al Firrem, and to cry quits. The Iraq and British Governments had informed Ibn Saud that raids by the Ikhwan refugees were contrary to their orders—which was quite true. Ibn Saud replied that the raids by Feisal al Duweesh and Muhsin al Firrem were against his orders—which was not true. But at the same time, Feisal I was the King of Iraq, and he and his family were the bitter enemies of the Saudi dynasty. Doubtless Ibn Saud was convinced that King Feisal was encouraging Ikhwan refugee raids into Nejed, though the Iraq Government was denying the fact. Perhaps Ibn Saud said to himself, "Feisal is encouraging raids into Nejed and then denying it. I will encourage raids into Iraq and deny it."

But whatever may have been the diplomatic subtleties employed, we in Iraq suffered under a severe handicap. Whereas, at that time, tribal raiding and the seduction of foreign tribes was the principal sphere of Saudi foreign policy, to the Iraq Government (if not to King Feisal) it was an irritating irrelevance. Bent on transferring their country into a modern state, the Iraq Government regarded tribes and tribal raiding with aversion and resentment. They disliked their own bedouins almost as much as they did those of Ibn Saud, and desired a plague on all their houses.

Our second disability was scarcely more than a matter of words —yet words are responsible for so many misunderstandings and distortions of human thought. The refugees "raided" Nejed, the Ikhwan "raided" Iraq—to the outside observer, there was no difference. But whereas the refugees set out in parties of eight or ten to steal a dozen camels by stealth, the Ikhwan "raid" was two or three thousand strong, with war banners, and massacred several hundred people. The imprudence of the Iraq Government in allowing so much latitude to the refugees can be easily appreciated, for in so doing they provided an excuse for continual massacres of their own subjects.

In 1925, moreover, Britain was still the almost undisputed arbiter of the fates of Nejed and Iraq alike. To her both sides addressed their shrill complaints. Ibn Saud complained of Iraqi "raids" into Nejed (in fact the pilfering expeditions of the Ikhwan refugees). Iraq complained of "raids" from Nejed. How could Whitehall appreciate the difference, especially when Ibn Saud's complaints were usually the more vociferous?

The final anomaly of the situation was that both the refugees and the Ikhwan were camel-riding nomads, to whom the desert was their native element, and who, to some extent at least, could take care of themselves. But the Iraq shepherds, whose transport was by donkey and who were unable to move far or fast owing to their flocks of sheep, were utterly helpless against bedouins, and all the savage Ikhwan reprisals fell upon them.

The Iraq tribes were never for one moment in doubt that Ibn Saud himself had ordered the raids of December, 1924. Meanwhile, seeing him still on friendly terms with Britain, they assumed that the latter was in collusion with him.

During January, 1925, the air was full of rumours of further impending raids. Feisal al Duweesh was said to have sworn that he would exterminate the post at Abu Ghar. I had then little knowledge of the Ikhwan, and their fame seemed to me to be almost as terrible as it did to the Iraq tribes. In February, however, reports were received from Nejed that strict orders had been circulated by Ibn Saud that no further raids on Iraq were to be carried out for the present. All travellers from Nejed were unanimous in the opinion that raiding was most unlikely after the issue of such a prohibition.

Meanwhile on the frontier of the Hejaz, Ibn Saud was already engaged in a full war with King Husain and had recently captured Mecca.[1] On 6th January, 1925, he opened the siege of Jidda.[2] King Husain had largely alienated the loyalty of the people of the Hejaz by his arbitrary and despotic ways, and Ibn Saud's successes were due more to disaffection in the subjects of the sherifian ruler than to military victories. By January, 1925, it was obvious that nothing could prevent him from annexing the Hejaz to Nejed, except the intervention of a Great Power from outside. The employment of British aircraft against the Ikhwan raiders in Iraq had alarmed Ibn Saud. At a time when everything was going so well for him in the Hejaz, it would be most unfortunate if he were to provoke British hostility. Moreover the Hejaz at the moment presented a sufficient outlet for the warlike energies of the Ikhwan and at the same time promised ample loot.

Throughout January, frequent aircraft patrols reconnoitred the desert in front of Abu Ghar. The majority came from Shaiba in the morning, landed at Abu Ghar and picked me up, and then carried out their reconnaissance. On the homeward journey, they landed me again at Abu Ghar before returning to Shaiba. During this period our system of desert air tactics was further elaborated. We had already gone a long way since our first landing on the Juwasim

[1] See map on page 40.   [2] Jidda is the port of Mecca, see map on page 49.

fourteen months before. In the past, aircraft had been sent out to search thirty thousand square miles of desert daily, on no particular plan. Experience had shown such methods to be hopeless, so it was obviously necessary to work out some more logical system.

Warning of an impending raid was often received a fortnight or more before the actual attack took place. Under such circumstances, we suggested, an alarm period should be declared, during which an air reconnaissance would be flown daily. But there was no necessity for the daily reconnaissance to fly aimlessly about the desert. It was obvious that the raiders, whenever they came, would raid an Iraq tribe. Their attack would normally be delivered at dawn, both to facilitate surprise and to allow as much daylight as possible in which to round up the loot. If, therefore, during alarm periods, all the advanced Iraq camps were visited by morning air patrols every day, it should in theory be possible to ensure that aircraft intervened within the first few hours of the battle. While the first onslaught could not be prevented, and many Iraqi lives would probably be lost before the aircraft arrived, yet at least it should be possible to make fairly sure of intervening during the same day. It might even be possible to teach the raiders a lesson which would make them hesitate to raid again.

This method, however, required certain other measures to render it effective. Firstly, it was necessary always to know exactly where all the leading Iraq tribes were camped, so that, in the event of an alarm, they could be patrolled forthwith. It was no easy task to be constantly aware of the locations of all the leading camps, in view of the vast number of nomadic sections always moving to and fro in an area nearly as large as England. This task occupied much of my time and thought that winter at Abu Ghar. In the end, it was only executed with partial success, by employing a few bedouin retainers who rode round the camps by camel. In addition, I had now received a Ford car which had been allotted to me, and in which I was constantly on the move across the desert, when I was not needed to accompany an air reconnaissance. The third method which I employed to obtain news of tribal movements was to open a guest tent close to my own camp, behind a low sand dune some three hundred yards from Abu Ghar fort. My two or three retainers were active in intercepting travellers or passing camel-riders who came near to Abu Ghar, and in inviting them to coffee, a meal or a night's rest and a good exchange of gossip, thereby daily checking the reports of the locations of the ever-moving tribes.

*   *   *   *   *

I do not think that I was very actively controlled by religious motives at this stage of my life. Yet perhaps my intense human interest in and affection for the Arabs by whom I was surrounded, may, in a broader sense, have been akin to religion. "He that loveth not his brother, whom he has seen, how can he love God whom he has not seen?" St. John asks us. Possibly the reverse may also be true— he that loves his brothers, has in him, perhaps unconsciously, something of the love of God. "When we love, we live less in ourselves than in that which we love; and the more we love, the more we establish our life beyond ourselves . . . We do not always feel when we love . . . But we know that we want to love; and to want to love is to love."[1] The last sentence perhaps gives us the key to this quotation. For love thus interpreted is not a passion, still less a sickly sentimentality, but a resolution. Rather is it a determination to help, serve and sympathize with all men, the humility to realize that neither we personally, nor our class, race or nation, can claim a self-satisfied superiority—a selfless devotion to our brothers, as wide as the human race itself.

Yet the brothers by whom I was surrounded were all Muslims, though I do not think that I ever had any inclination to become a Muslim myself. The bedouins around me were unhesitating believers in God, unassailed by dogmatic or metaphysical doubts. The name of God was unceasingly on their lips. "If God wills"; "Praise God"; "God keep you"; "God bless you"—such phrases were mingled in almost every sentence. Rain was God's mercy, food was His grace. Every argument ended with the statement that God alone was all-knowing. Most of them repeated their prayers meticulously five times a day—usually I imagine automatically and without thought. Yet prayers repeated even inattentively do something to impress the mind with the existence of another world beyond the world of sense. In the sacred month of Ramadhan, they fasted with scrupulous care. During that month, Muslims could neither eat nor drink nor smoke, from before dawn until sunset. The Muslim months were those of the moon. Twelve such months were approximately eleven days shorter than our year of three hundred and sixty-five days. Thus Ramadhan fell every year about eleven days earlier, in reference to our year. If, for example, Ramadhan were this year to begin on 1st January, next year it would commence on 20th December and the year after that on the ninth. When the month of fasting fell in summer, it was peculiarly trying to such persons as were obliged to be all day beneath the scorching Arabian sun. The long day from first dawn to sunset without so much as a drink of water, could be a real affliction.

Ramadhan was always an embarrassment to persons who did not fast, for the Arabs would insist on preparing the usual vast meal for such a guest, even though he were the only man who could eat it.

[1] Charles de Foucauld.

In 1925, Ramadhan fell, I think, in April. I was virtually living with the Dhafeer at the time and I fasted with them for the complete month. I did not do this from directly religious motives, but on the principle which constrains an officer to limit his kit to the same weight as that of the men under his command. He is ashamed to take privileges denied to his comrades. When fasting, Muslims were woken up just before dawn to take a last meal, or at least a long final drink, before facing the weary hours which divided them from sun-set. I can still vividly remember being woken, when lying in the sand dunes near Shagra, and seeing leaning over me the lined old face and thin straggly beard of my host of the night, Hamdan Ibn Dhuweihi. "Sit up, sit up," he was saying, shaking me by the shoulder. "Here is your *sahoor*,"[1] holding in his hand an enormous bowl of frothy camel's milk. "Sit up. Dawn will soon appear."

* * * * *

One of the first problems we encountered in working out our desert tactics was how to train pilots to find their way in the desert. In the 1920's, very few of the modern aids to air navigation existed. The ninak carried a magnetic compass. Beyond that the pilot had to find his way by looking at the ground. It was extremely difficult for pilots to become really expert in desert lore, because they changed every two years.

Though the surface of the desert seen from the ground was undulating and diversified, much of it from the air looked like a flat brown sea, remarkably deficient in landmarks when seen from above. Thus even if a raid had been located and other aircraft bases in-formed by wireless, it was exceedingly doubtful whether many pilots would be able to find their way to the site.

Flying over long distances is a most monotonous occupation. In those days, the cockpit was open to the air, and pilot and observer were obliged to wear flying suits, helmets and goggles. Both were strapped in. Had I not been so, there were many occasions on which I should have been shot out of the aircraft. There was no means of intercommunication between pilot and observer in the ninak, except scribbling little notes and passing them backwards and forwards.

It is difficult, thirty-five years later, to imagine how precarious was flying in the desert in 1925. Forced landings were the rule rather than the exception. These long flights were particularly trying to the nerves, because in those days we did not know the desert intimately. Flying over the desert was indeed not unlike flying over the sea. Sometimes, on long patrols, we would fly for two hours or more, without ever recognizing a known landmark. The worst was that, if a

---

[1] *Sahoor* was the name given to the last food or drink eaten before dawn. "Breakfast" of course was literally the meal eaten at sunset at the end of the day's fast.

machine forced-landed, it was not certain that it could be found again, and a slow death from thirst a hundred and fifty miles out in the desert was not a pleasant prospect.

Sometimes we suffered more acute but less prolonged anxieties. I flew with Flight-Lieutenant Jenkins, a flight commander in 84 Squadron, more than with anyone else at this time. One day we landed on a small shepherd camp, situated in a narrow rocky wadi west of Shebicha. We talked to the shepherds and when we had obtained the information which we wanted, we turned the machine to face down the narrow water course for the take-off. We found ourselves enclosed on both sides of the valley by rocky cliffs about thirty feet high. The floor of the little *shaeeb* was a good deal obstructed by low shrubs and rocks. Some two hundred and fifty yards away, the valley made an almost ninety-degree turn to the left, still between its thirty-foot cliffs on either side, with the result that one of these cliffs stood facing us at the bend, closing the bottom of our two hundred and fifty yards runway. A ninak, however, was supposed to take off in two hundred yards, and so we climbed into our cockpit and "Jenks" opened up the throttle. When we had run about fifty yards, the port tyre burst, presumably on a sharp rock, the machine swung to the left, crashed over a high thorn bush and lost half its speed. A few yards on, the other tyre burst, causing a violent lurch to the right. We were now travelling on two flat tyres and making straight for the cliff which was facing us. For a matter of seconds, "Jenks" was faced with the alternative—if he switched off should we stop before running into the cliff?; if he gave her full throttle would we gain sufficient speed to enable us to clear it? For a moment, I clutched my seat, then he pulled back the stick and she took off, flying straight at that rock face. There was a crash, the aircraft staggered—for an instant I thought that all was over—then we were flying on about thirty feet above the ground. Our undercarriage had just hit a heap of stones at the top of the cliff. Had we been twelve inches lower, we should both have been killed. It was one of those occasions on which you have no time to be afraid, but your heart seems to cease beating when the danger is already past.

We climbed to about a thousand feet and then Jenks passed me a note, "Can you see if our wheels are still on?"[1] I craned over the side as far as my harness would allow me. I could see the port wheel, which was still on, though it looked as if it might be buckled. The wheel on the starboard side was invisible from the rear cockpit. I passed a note to that effect to Jenks, who nodded his head. As we came in to land, he passed me a note to say, "Hang on when we touch down. Not sure how much of undercarriage is still with us,"—but by his skill we landed on one wheel without turning over.

[1] In those days aircraft did not have retracting under-carriages.

Landing at Abu Ghar, after four, five or six hours' flying, I would walk with singing head and deafened ears to my little tent, humbly enough furnished with two small carpets, a camel saddle and a packing case. I was still only half-way through the day's work. A cup of tea and a smoke, and then for the news. Sirhan, the brother of Shirshab Ibn Zuwaid, Shaikh of the Budoor, was in our guest tent and must be seen.

"Good evening, Sirhan. How are you? God keep you.

"Where are your people?

"How is the grazing?

"Who is camped near you? Where are the Dhafeer? . . ."

It was largely by such methods that we, to some extent at least, were able to keep in touch with the never-ending nomad moves. Then the guest, in his turn, wished to know the news.

"How is our government? Will she now protect us?

"What are her relations with Ibn Saud?

"What news have you of the Ikhwan?

"Can we move to Umm Rahal? There is good spring grass there. Our sheep are dead. By God, men who had a hundred sheep, now have only ten or fifteen. Some have only the herdsman's stick in their hands, the sole remains of all their flocks."

If I said that they might move forward, and they were subsequently raided, their blood would be upon my head, and it might even be said that I had betrayed them intentionally. If I said that they must not move forward, their flocks would continue to die for lack of grazing and it would again be my fault, for not protecting the tribes where they could graze.

Baghdad had comfortably instructed me to notify the tribes that if they moved further forward, we could not be responsible for their safety, but it was not possible to escape the issue by such means. The shepherds replied that Umm Rahal was two days' march north of the Nejed frontier. Why, they enquired, did they pay taxes to the government, if not in order to be safe within their own frontier? The safety of people who paid taxes to Ibn Saud was guaranteed by him, they pointed out.

When I wrote all this to Baghdad, they replied that they regretted that they could not protect the tribes further forward but that the fact must be recognized as unavoidable. This was more easily written in a memorandum in a headquarter office than explained to a group of unfortunate tribesmen whose flocks were dying of starvation twenty miles from rich green grass.

Such were my feelings during that cold, weary and exhausting winter. To be perpetually cold is depressing to morale. Engrossed in my parochial worries, and faced with the constant heckling of the unfortunate tribesmen, I did not perhaps sufficiently allow for the many other problems and difficulties facing the higher authorities — disturbances in Kurdistan, the dispute with Turkey over Mosul, and successive political crises in Iraq. The young usually think that they know best, and I was no exception.

But the fact that the central government was unavoidably over-burdened with other troubles did not render any easier the task of helping and controlling the Iraq tribes, or of explaining away to them what they regarded as the criminal indifference of the government to their interests. For what to the officials in Baghdad was a regrettable but irremediable situation was life and death to the shepherds. Many of them had lost brothers, sons or fathers, massacred by the Ikhwan in recent raids, while the survivors were now faced with starvation by the destruction of their flocks from hunger. Why could not the government send a force only twenty-five miles further forward and thereby enable them to camp in those green pastures, now lying virgin south of Umm Rahal? In the latter half of February and in March, the situation improved somewhat. Later rains and the warm spring sun brought out some grass and wild flowers in the Shagra and Chilawa[1] areas. Reports from Nejed indicated that Ibn Saud's strict orders against further raiding for the time being had produced considerable effect on the Ikhwan.

Meanwhile my little camp at Abu Ghar had grown. I had pitched my tents some four hundred yards from the old fort, where the Iraq army garrison was established. It was impossible for me to camp inside the barbed wire which surrounded the fort, owing to the number of tribesmen who came and went to my camp. The army would not of course admit civilians inside the wire. We, however, encouraged all and sundry to stop at our guest tent, in order that we might pick up their news.

The mechanism of hospitality was comparatively simple. A few strips of locally-made woollen rugs were spread on the floor of the guest tent. In the centre, a fire of twigs smouldered, with five or six tall coffee pots standing in the embers. Behind the guest tent, in a tiny tent with only one pole, sat a widowed lady of uncertain age, whom we had hired as a cook. At midday, the guests were served with a bowl of dates and a few "pancakes" of unleavened bread, or perhaps a dish of rice and oil. In spring time, bowls of butter and milk would transform the dry and dusty dates into a delicious banquet. The evening meal was not dissimilar to that served at midday, unless a distinguished guest were present, in which case we killed a sheep. By these simple means, we succeeded, without prohibitive expense, in keeping open house, and the guest tent of Abu Hunaik became a frequent port of call for travellers.

I had been nicknamed Abu Hunaik by the Arabs almost as soon

[1] See map on page 137.

as I arrived in Iraq and the name has survived until today. I had been wounded in the face at the Battle of Arras in 1917 and as a result part of my lower jaw was missing. Hunaik in Arabic means "little jaw". The Arabs, especially tribesmen, make great play with diminutives. Curiously enough, they form diminutives, not as in most other languages by adding an additional syllable to the end of a word (as for example in maisonette) but by inserting the syllable—*ai*[1]—in the middle of the word. Thus to apply the same method to English words, the word for a little girl would be gir*ai*l, or for a small garden, gar*ai*den. In the same manner, *hanak* being the lower jaw, *hunaik* meant a little jaw.

*   *   *   *   *

I had not been long with my little group of tents at Abu Ghar when one day a large black bedouin tent appeared beside them. It proved to belong to Sulman al Ghawwal, a prominent man of the Dhafeer. Once prosperous and respected, he had fallen on hard times, like so many of his fellow tribesmen, as a result of Ikhwan raids and consequent bad grazing, and most of his camels were dead. In the happy way of the bedouin, he simply joined us. When I came in one evening, I found his tent pitched beside mine. He came up to me, held out his hand and said, "*Ya taweel al amr*—O long of life, I have camped beside you."

Sulman was tall, with regular features and a small black beard, and the quiet and decorous manners of the best bedouins. Reserved, rather inclined to be shy, but very intelligent, he was perhaps about thirty-five years old. He sported a scarlet ziboon, the long cloth coat worn over the white Arab "night-shirt" and under the brown cloak. This striking garment had been a gift from Ibn Saud, whom he had visited in the company of Hamood Ibn Suwait, in the year of Yusuf Ibn Sadoon's camel corps.[2] Sulman's tent was divided in half by a broad curtain, leaving the larger space free for guests and the ceremony of coffee making. He was useful in our camp, because passing bedouins would call at his tent for coffee and give him the news, which he retailed to me in the evening. When I threw myself down in my tent on returning from an air patrol, I would soon hear a discreet cough outside, and Sulman would appear with his brass coffee pot in his right hand, and a nest of little cups in his left.

"May God make your evening prosperous," he would say, handing me one of his little cups, containing about a tablespoonful of his special brew—for the Arab tribes drink coffee as we drink a liqueur.

When I had ceremoniously drunk the three little cups prescribed by tradition, I would say, "What is the news today, Sulman?"

[1] *ai* pronounced as in tail, snail.   [2] See page 73.

It was of course precisely for this question that he had been waiting. Putting down the coffee pot and the cups, he would sit on the ground in the door of my tent. News in the desert is a precious and much-sought-after prize, and he who obtains it, naturally likes to dawdle over it, relishing each item, morsel by morsel.

"By Allah, I see nothing today worth repeating," he would begin. Then after a pause, which was calculated to whet the appetite of the listener, he would continue, in a casual voice: "Hamed Ibn Jedaan had coffee with us today. He had come from Ibn Suwait."

"What news had he got?" I would ask, showing a suitably intelligent interest.

But Sulman was not yet ready to satisfy my anxiety. "By Allah," he would reply, shaking his head disapprovingly, "in these days news is plentiful, but one cannot believe most of it. Truth is dead and falsehood reigns in his stead."

But it seemed to me time to elicit a few real facts, instead of philosophical disquisitions on the degeneration of morals. "Where is Ibn Suwait?" I would ask.

"Hamood is at Al Boliya."

"Where are the Dhafeer?"

"By Allah, Ibn Dhuweihi is at Chilawa with Ibn Agab, and the Araif are at Tuwei al Hashash."

"What is their ground like?" (meaning the grazing).

"They don't speak ill of it. The *arfaj* is green, and there is *nussi* [a coarse grass] in the hollows south of Chilawa."

"Where is Lizzam?" ... and so on, through the long list of bedouin and shepherd chiefs and sections.

Then we would turn to a new subject. "Has anybody come to them from above?" (Nejed is a high plateau shelving down towards the Euphrates and the Persian Gulf.)

"By Allah, they say that a man of Ibn Tawala's came from Nejed on the way to Zubair[1] and he slept a night with the Dhafeer."

"What did he say?"

But Sulman did not quite approve of this high-pressure way of eliciting information which should suffice to supply several hours of polite conversation. "One would not have a man repeat everything he hears said," he replied sententiously. "A man should report that which he sees with his eyes, not that which he hears with his ears. They say—they say. Many are those who say...."

"That is understood," I interrupted, "but what did he say, even if it be unreliable?"

"The Shammari said," he answered, "that he had heard that the

---

[1] Zubair was twenty miles south-west of Basra and the chief desert port and market in the area. See map on page 158.

Duweesh has sworn that he will drive the infidels from the desert, until he waters his horses in the Euphrates."

"The people of Nejed talk too much," I commented. "He would do better to talk after he has done it, not before."

"God is all-knowing," remarked Sulman, condemning by implication the inaccuracy of men.

"What else do they say?"

"By Allah, they say that messengers from Ibn Saud are visiting the Ikhwan, saying 'Beware, beware, he who would raid the tribes of the government. The surrender of all his property will not save his neck. Let no man say that he is not warned.' "

"Good," I said. "Where is Ibn Tawala camped?" and so on and on once more.

Bedouins were often curiously reticent in repeating their news, especially to outsiders, although to obtain it was one of the principal occupations of their half-idle lives. To extract it from them required a good deal of patience and an intimate knowledge of them and their affairs. They failed to comprehend modern "hustle", or the idea that time was money. To condense all that they had to say into a minimum number of words and then retire was not their method.

"Haste," says the Arab proverb, "is of the devil, but deliberation proceeds from the Merciful One."

It was not until some two years later that I discovered that a little romance had been in progress in my camp during these early spring days. Sulman's tent was some fifty yards from ours, and my retainers frequently sat with him round his coffee fire. Amongst bedouins, women were little secluded, and in fact seclusion to a tent-dwelling people would be difficult if not impossible. In all except the richest tents, moreover, the women were busy all day long.

For a man in those days to accost a woman in the streets of an Arab town to ask the way would have been an unheard-of scandal, and a townswoman thus addressed would have cowered on the ground and screamed. But the desert traveller, when approaching a strange camp, would often encounter a bedouin woman far from the tents, cutting the little desert shrubs with a chopper, for firewood.

"God strengthen thee, O girl," the man would call, reining in his camel. And she would stand up and face him, and answer readily, "You're welcome."

"Who are these Arabs?"

"This is Ibn Suwait," she might answer, with perfect self-possession.

In addition to collecting firewood, the women frequently helped with the camels, fed the mare, milked the sheep, and loaded up the kit when moving camp. Though certainly not as free as Englishwomen are today, they were perhaps freer than the latter were a hundred years ago.

Under these conditions, one of my retainers rashly fell in love with Sulman's wife. Though she had already borne two children, she was probably still little over twenty. She, however, resolutely refused to be unfaithful to her husband, and the two lovers were fain to content themselves with mutual oaths of fidelity. She continued to care for her household, her children and her husband, as she conceived it to be her duty to do, and in a manner with which the most scandalous tongue could find no fault. In a tented community, conjugal strife is difficult to conceal.

Two years later, when I was in Nasiriya, she arrived one day before my door, driving a gaunt camel on which lay poor Sulman in a litter. She sent in a message to me by one of the men to say that her husband was ill. I hired a room for them in the town, and sent for the doctor, but Sulman died a few days later of tuberculosis. His wife attended him with unfaltering devotion until he was laid in the grave. After the lapse of a decent period of mourning, the two lovers at last were married.

Not all bedouin women were so faithful or so scrupulous in their conjugal relations, but the custom which prescribed death to an adultress naturally caused careful concealment of any infidelity. The disgrace of a woman's immorality fell on her own family, not on her husband. The latter would often be satisfied to put away an unfaithful wife. Her father, or perhaps more often her brother, would then kill her.

It there were one characteristic more than another which distinguished the Arabs, it was dignity or decorum. They would never make a noise or play the buffoon, except in the most intimate company. Nor would an Arab ever laugh loudly. (Tradition relates that the Prophet Muhammad never laughed—he only smiled.) In the same manner, the bedouin strictly shunned any display of sexual affection in public, even if legitimate. I have seen young men returning from long journeys or raids, perhaps after an absence of weeks or months, meet their wives in front of their tents. But although perhaps devoted to one another, they would show no sign of it in public. After the exchange of a few verbal enquiries, as it might be between friends, the man might walk over to the shaikh's tent for coffee. Only later, in the privacy of the curtained portion of the tent, would he kiss his wife and daughters. But such customs were only a convention and did not necessarily signify a lack of affection.

When the legitimate emotions were thus restrained, it is only to be expected that anything in the nature of illegitimate love was most strictly suppressed. Openly immoral women were unknown in bedouin tribes. But, as perhaps may be the case in most societies, secret unfaithfulness in wives was not as rare as it might be. Bedouin women moved freely about the camp, and thus any erotic indiscretions committed would probably be kept within a small family circle. Only when strangers were present was it thought unbecoming for women to be seen or heard.

Sometimes when travelling by camel in Arab dress, I have dismounted at a small bedouin tent to find that all the men were out. A woman or even a young girl would come forward to welcome the guests, spreading a carpet for us to sit on, and bringing milk, dates and bread for our refreshment. Some would even seat themselves and exchange the news. But as soon as my identity as an Englishman was revealed, they vanished. A curtain was hastily rigged across the middle of the tent, and thenceforward our requirements would be pushed through to us underneath the curtain by an invisible hand. Later on, amongst certain tribes which came to know me well personally, these precautions were at times once more relaxed, though chiefly by older women. These would now and again appear round the curtain to say good morning, to thank me for helping their sons, or to cry from the fullness of their hearts: "Save us from the Ikhwan." But if any men were present, they would usually say laughingly, "That's all right, Auntie. The officer understands." Then the old lady would disappear behind the curtain again, still chattering and calling out: "May God bless him and his government. Without them we could not live. We should all have been killed by the Ikhwan. May God prolong his life!"

Bedouins were the only community in Iraq who still retained at least the tradition of romantic love. In other communities, which no longer lived in tents, the seclusion of women in houses had destroyed courtship—though not necessarily immorality.

IX

Sorties in the Stony Desert

The ferocious bedouins, the terror of the desert, embrace without
enquiry or hesitation, the stranger who dares to confide in their
honour and to enter their tent. His treatment is kind and respectful;
he shares the wealth or the poverty of his host; and, after a needful
repose, he is dismissed on his way, with thanks, with blessings, and
perhaps with gifts . . . The heroic acts that could deserve the public
applause, must have surpassed the narrow measure of discretion and
experience . . . The freedom of his countrymen disdained the laws of
justice; they proudly indulged the spontaneous impulse of pity and
benevolence.   GIBBON, *Decline and Fall of the Roman Empire*

The firmest friendships have been formed in mutual adversity: iron
is most strongly united in the fiercest flame.   CALEB COLTON

I labour for peace but when I speak unto them thereof, they make
them ready for battle.   *Psalm* cxx. 7

IX

SORTIES IN THE STONY DESERT

THE easing of the tension in February and March, 1925, consequent on the dissemination of Ibn Saud's orders against raiding, on the moral effect of the occupation of Abu Ghar, on our constant air patrols, and on the growth of the new grass in the Abu Ghar-Shagra area, enabled us to relax our vigilance. I was thus able to leave Abu Ghar, where I had hitherto been tied to the wireless set and ever ready on the landing ground to accompany air patrols. I took advantage of the opportunity before the advent of summer dried up most of the desert watering places, to explore a little more of that great arid country of which we still knew so little.

The first of these expeditions was over the Stony Desert to Sulman, across one hundred miles of unexplored country. Guy Moore, who, with a flight of aircraft had been patrolling the Stony Desert while I was at Abu Ghar, had landed several times at Sulman, but it, and the area between it and Abu Ghar, had not as yet been explored on the ground.

Some tents of the Zayyad, encouraged by Guy Moore's air patrols from Samawa, had in February ventured out to Sulman, where the grazing was good. I set out from Abu Ghar one clear, sunny, fresh spring morning, such an intoxicating morning as perhaps only the desert in winter can produce. But times had changed. We no longer started on our expeditions tapping our camels into a cheerful trot, the tassels on our saddles swinging and our bedouins intoning one of their innumerable trotting songs. This time we set out in a Ford car, which lurched over stones and bushes leaving in its wake a slowly drifting cloud of dust. The Stony Desert, which began at Abu Ghar, rose slowly towards the south-west, though the rise was imperceptible to the eye, until at Jumaima it reached one thousand four hundred feet, Abu Ghar being only one hundred and sixty feet above sea level.

At sunset we were still in a desolate waste of rocky hills. To light a fire seemed inadvisable for fear of attracting raiders and we spent a dreary evening amid the cold grey rocks, after eating a piece of dry bread each.

Day dawned cold and silvery on these dark limestone slopes. Soon we were stopped short by a steep drop, almost a precipice, strewn with great boulders. We followed the bed of a little winding wadi, when suddenly, at a bend in our narrow valley, we came upon

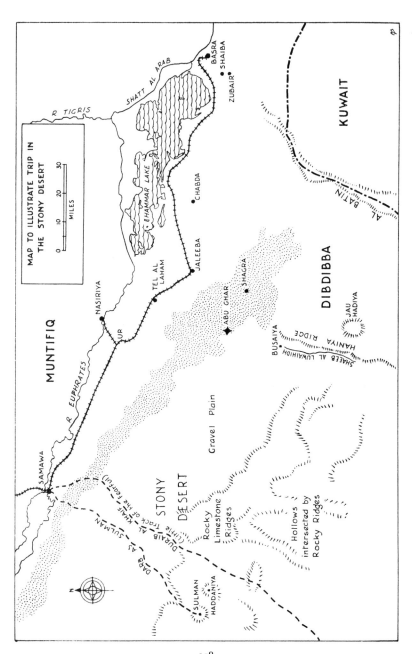

MAP TO ILLUSTRATE TRIP IN
THE STONY DESERT

MILES
0 10 20 30

R TIGRIS

SHATT AL ARAB

BASRA
SHAIBA
ZUBAIR

KUWAIT

HAMMAR LAKE

CHABDA

AL BATIN

JALEEBA

NASIRIYA

MUNTIFIQ

TEL AL
LAHAM

UR

SHAGRA

ABU GHAR

DIBDIBBA

BUSAIYA

SHAEEB AL LUWAIHIDH

HANIYA RIDGE

JAU
HADIYA

R EUPHRATES

SAMAWA

Gravel Plain

STONY

DESERT

Rocky
Limestone
Ridges

Hollows
intersected by
Rocky Ridges

DARB AS SULMAN

DURAIB AL KHAIL
(little track of the fearful)

N

SULMAN
HADDANIYA

158

a scene which, in a flash, changed our silent anxiety into laughing pleasure. Before us lay a wide basin-like hollow, surrounded on three sides by low rocky hills, and backed on the west by a high and precipitous ridge. The bed of the hollow was a bright metallic green, and was dotted with black shepherd tents, from which columns of grey smoke were rising slowly into the pale blue winter sky. Flocks of sheep and donkeys were grazing peacefully here and there and figures could be seen strolling leisurely from tent to tent. The barking of a dog and the occasional call of a shepherd came to us clearly on the crisp morning air. A shepherd girl came running towards us, in pursuit of a runaway lamb. After our dinnerless night and my unexpressed but none the less worrying anxiety about tyres, petrol and water, this quiet pastoral scene seemed to me one of the loveliest on which I had ever gazed.

Soon we had dismounted at the largest tent, amid smiling expressions of welcome and much running and scurrying to lay out the best carpet. The fire was blown into a flame, our kettle was pushed into the cinders and we sat round warming our hands, answering the eager questions of the poor but friendly shepherds. The tent belonged to Auda al Hasan,[1] the shaikh of one of the sections of the Zayyad.

Three hours later we were making up for our fast of the previous day round a huge dish of rice and mutton, running over with milk and butter.

We set out again soon after midday, the shepherds pointing out to us the direction of the wells of Sulman. At sunset we found another section of the Zayyad, with whom we passed the night. They were to move camp the next day, so we trekked with them, amid the little groups of donkeys, on which their tents, supplies and chattels were loaded. In the afternoon our hosts pitched their camp at Haddaniya[2] a deep valley a mile broad and two miles long, shut in all round by cliffs about one hundred and fifty feet high. It lay about twelve miles east of Sulman.

Before leaving Abu Ghar, I had taken the precaution to arrange with the R.A.F. that an air patrol would bring me more petrol to Haddaniya. Accordingly the next morning we chose an open piece of desert on which the aircraft might land, but we waited till evening in vain. It was, however, a glorious day of warm sunshine, with fleecy white clouds drifting slowly across a pale blue sky and it passed pleasantly enough in the tents of the shepherds. The contrast between the bright green of the sheltered grassy hollows and the grey limestone crags surrounding them, the clear freshness of the

[1] The names of the shepherd tribesmen in this and other descriptions have been changed, as many of these men may still be alive.
[2] See map opposite.

desert air and the peaceful shepherd camps made the Stony Desert on that quiet day of early spring a veritable Arcadia.

The next day, however, as there was still no sign of the aircraft, I decided to try to reach Samawa. I calculated that I had just enough petrol to get there, although not enough to enable me to return to Abu Ghar. Kadhim al Hamza, the shaikh of the section with which we were camped, insisted upon accompanying us, claiming that, as our host, he was responsible for our safety. It would be a disgrace if anything happened to us while his salt was still in our stomachs.

The following day we set out on our return journey to Sulman. Although I had obtained five completely new tyres in Samawa, in addition to a supply of petrol, it took us the whole day to cover the eighty miles from Samawa to Sulman, owing to innumerable tyre bursts in the Stony Desert. It was already dark when we reached the lip of the escarpment, which ran round the deep Sulman depression. We had left the Zayyad camp the day before at Haddaniya, but Kadhim had agreed with his brother Abbas to move to Sulman during our absence. As, however, we lurched slowly down the escarpment, the Sulman depression lay before us in inky darkness, with no glimmer of a camp fire to cheer us. Kadhim became anxious. "What can have happened to them?" he kept repeating. The uncertainties and dangers of desert life were always so near to those whose lot was cast in those precarious wastes.

We stopped, descended from the car, switched off the engine, held our breath and listened. Perhaps we might hear the barking of a dog or human voices in the camp, but in the darkness the silence was so intense, so utter, that the ear could identify no sound at all. Nowhere is there a deeper silence than on a still night in the empty desert. We decided to drive to the wells to see if anyone had watered there, and if so, to endeavour to follow the tracks of their flocks leading from the wells to their camp.

We drove at a walking pace over the rough ground, strewn with boulders and dotted with small shrubs, in the bed of the Sulman depression. Our headlights lit up a space of desert in front of us, while on either side the darkness shut us in, producing the impression of two immensely high black walls—or sometimes I imagined it like an avenue leading to some great house in England and lined on either side with giant black trees. Suddenly the figure of a man ran into the lighted space in front of the car. He raised the skirt of his cloak and waved it to us. We drew up and he came towards us, shading his eyes from the headlights. It was Abbas, the younger brother of Kadhim, a boy of only eighteen or twenty, his long corkscrew curls framing his face and falling to his breast.

"Welcome to the travellers," he called cheerfully, and then as

Lieutenant-General Sir John Bogot Glubb

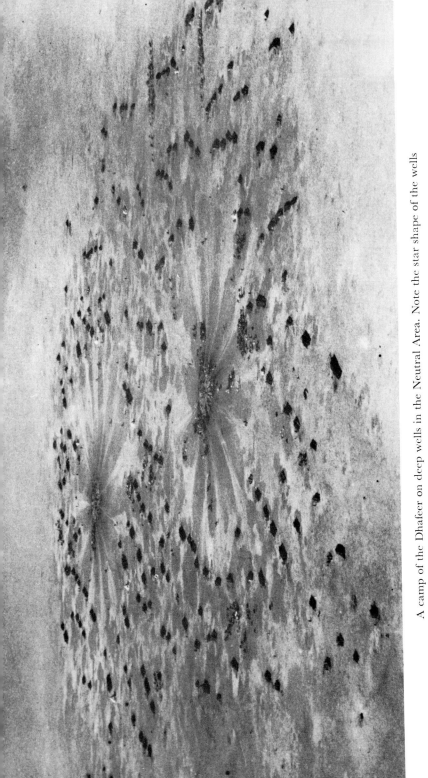

A camp of the Dhafeer on deep wells in the Neutral Area. Note the star shape of the wells

The fort at Busaiya (see page 197)

The Iraq Army established in the ruins of Sadoon's old fort at Abu Ghar. In the middle distance is my own camp, consisting of two white and three black tents

Three Southern Desert Camel Corps vans mounting Lewis guns

Desert Camel Police on the move

Feisal al Duweesh
A photograph of a sketch made by Sqdn.-Ldr. Stewart, R.A.F., at Shaiba, Iraq, in 1929

The meeting of the Arab kings on H.M.S. *Lupin*. Seated: (left to right) Air Vice-Marshal Sir R. Brooke Popham, Air Officer Commanding Iraq; The Captain of *Lupin*; Sir Francis Humphreys, British High Commissioner in Iraq; King Feisal I; King Abdul Aziz Ibn Saud; Naji Beg as Suwaidi Prime Minister of Iraq (see page 343)

he came up to the car, "Peace be upon you. Where have you been?" he added. "We were anxious about you."

"And we were anxious about you," said Kadhim with his little wry smile. "Where are you camped?"

Abbas stepped on to the running board of the car and answered, "Drive on and I will show you."

We drove for perhaps another two hundred yards and then, rounding a spur of the cliffs which had been imperceptible in the darkness, we looked up a small tributary valley, in which stood a scattered line of shepherds' tents. In front of each, by the warm glow of the camp fires, the sheep could be seen couched, closely packed together. In the headlights of the car, we could see the long grass interspersed with bright flowers.

When we examined the Ford the next morning we found that the five new tyres which we had obtained in Samawa were already cut to ribbons and beyond repair. There was nothing for it but for me to remain with the hospitable Zayyad while a shepherd horseman rode across eighty miles of desert back to Samawa, with a note from me asking for the despatch of five more tyres. There followed several days during which I was utterly cut off from the world, but they were not time wasted. I was deeply affected by the kindness of these poor shepherds. I had six years more to serve in the Southern Desert and throughout that time I received nothing but the most loyal and personal friendship and co-operation from the Zayyad, whom I learned to know so well during this stay in their tents. A more simple, honest and courageous little man than Kadhim I never met, in any country or of any race.

Eventually an aircraft landed at Sulman and delivered five new tyres to me, enabling us thereby to bid goodbye to our good hosts and to set off once more for Abu Ghar. We arrived there at last but again with no tyres and we were indeed obliged to finish our trip crawling along at a walking pace, with our blankets wrapped round the front wheels. These vicissitudes will convey some idea of the rockiness of the Stony Desert. We had covered four hundred and fifty miles and had used fifteen tyres in the process.

*   *   *   *   *

When the Iraq tribes had first been scattered and decimated by the Ikhwan raids in December, and had then been crowded round Abu Ghar while their flocks died of cold and starvation, the Ikhwan refugees, had moved to the area between Chabda and Zubair.[1] From there, with renewed energy, they embarked on a series of petty robberies in Nejed. They consisted of only twenty or thirty families, which, to a government ignorant of the desert, were not

[1] See map on page 158.

easy to find in the vast spaces of the wilderness in which camped thousands of Iraqi tents. The Iraq Government, at that time, did not employ one single civil official or policeman in the desert. Their only representatives were the company of infantry which was holding the fort at Abu Ghar, and none of whom ever went outside the perimeter. Whenever I visited Abu Ghar, the Arab officers hastened to cross-question me on the subject of the tribes. British aircraft patrolled the desert, but were not able to keep intimate touch with our own tribes. As a result, most of these petty Ikhwan refugee "raids", averaging probably only about ten men, passed unnoticed by the Iraqi authorities.

Their activities, however, were most injurious to Iraq. The damage which they inflicted on Nejed was negligible. Operating in such small parties, they rarely looted any number of camels worth mentioning, and, acting of course by stealth, they never inflicted casualties or caused fear. At the same time, however, they provoked Ibn Saud's resentment and provided him with an excuse.

Actually, at this time, no Iraq tribe was raiding the Ikhwan, though a few individuals might now and again join one of the refugee parties. The reason for this was obvious. Safe grazing was essential to the livelihood of the Iraq tribes. The activities of twenty or thirty families of refugees from Nejed were carelessly allowed to create doubt of the good faith of both the British and Iraq Governments.

Fortunately, in March, 1925, the Ikhwan refugees decided to try a grand united raid into Nejed. They succeeded in mustering forty-five men, their full manpower, by far the largest raiding party which they had ever put in the field. Even more fortunately, an aircraft patrol located the raiders approaching the Nejed frontier and reported the fact.

I had often protested against the refugee raids, but my reports had merely evoked requests that I produce proof of my charges. The air reconnaissance report was accepted as independent confirmation of my previous statements, and the refugee chiefs were summoned to Nasiriya. I was called in to confront them, in the presence of the civil authorities, and to prove my charges of raiding into Nejed. Although they denied all the accusations, I was able to produce sufficient details to convince the civil government that my statements were true.

As a result, a decision was made to remove them, bag and baggage, to the Ramadi district, on the Euphrates west of Baghdad,[1] a task carried out during the following summer, at considerable expense and with no little labour, under the supervision of Guy Moore. Thirty tents are not always easy to find in a desert waste the size of

[1] For Ramadi, see map on page 141.

England—for it was three hundred and ninety miles from Basra to Ramadi through the desert, about the distance from London to Edinburgh. For nearly two months, in the blazing heat of summer, the little convoy was herded from well to well, until they were eventually handed over to Fahad Ibn Hadhdal, the Shaikh of the Aneza tribe in Iraq, who promised to prevent them from giving any more trouble.

With the surprising faculty for changing sides of which the bedouins were capable, the refugees immediately addressed letters to Ibn Saud asking for pardon—a request which was instantly granted, for his sole concern was to show his other tribes that it was no use their attempting to escape to Iraq to evade his authority. In the course of the ensuing year, all the refugees, with the exception of four tents, slipped back to Nejed, where they rejoined the Ikhwan in raiding Iraq.

*   *   *   *   *

The winter grazing season closed, in April, 1925, in an unexpected atmosphere of peace and security in the Southern Desert. On the one hand, reports from Nejed that Ibn Saud had really forbidden raids on Iraq and, on the other, the fact that the Iraq Government was really tackling the problem of the Ikhwan refugees, created a feeling of optimism in complete contrast to the despair which had been prevalent the previous December.

The Iraq army garrison was withdrawn from Abu Ghar in April, 1925. The R.A.F. intelligence staff was unavoidably reduced during the leave season, while I myself left for a three months' holiday in Europe. Tribesmen and officials alike congratulated themselves on the establishment of peace on the tempestuous frontiers of Nejed. The Dhafeer were no less confident and, in spite of the government evacuation of Abu Ghar, they remained camped in the vicinity of the fort, while their herds of camels grazed far afield in the valleys of the Stony Desert.

In winter, when rainpools collected in the desert valleys, the bedouin camps could move frequently, drinking from these scattered pools, and the camels could find virgin grazing almost daily. In such circumstances, the herds could graze all day within a mile or two of the tents, to which they could return every evening at sunset. But in summer the casual rainpools were dry and the camps were pitched round the mouths of the rare permanent wells, perhaps for many consecutive weeks.

The deep wells were one of the mysteries of the Southern Desert. In some slight hollow in the bare undulating desert, with no visible source of water for hundreds of miles around, a well mouth, some ten or twelve feet in diameter, would open in the ground. Perhaps three hundred feet below the surface, the well would be filled with inexhaustible supplies of water. Often the shaft would be cut through strata of live rock, on which the chisel marks could still be seen. Nobody knew when these wells had been dug, a process which must have taken many years, with perhaps two or three men at a time working away with hammer and chisel, hundreds of feet underground, then loading the stone chips into leather buckets, to be hauled up by ropes to the surface. How, perhaps thousands of years ago, did these early engineers know where to dig for water which was only to be found two or three hundred feet below? Did they dig dozens of such wells, abandoning those in which they failed to find water? If so, all trace of the failures had long ago disappeared.

The bedouins hauled the water up in huge leather buckets, the weight of which, combined with that of three hundred feet of rope, would be more than could conveniently be drawn up by hand. So for these deep wells, they used draft camels. (The bedouins for some reason or other spoke of a well as being "long" not deep— perhaps they considered it on the basis of the length of rope required to reach the water. Thus deep wells were called "longs"—al tuwal.)

Each group of herdsmen brought a little trestle with a pulley, which they fixed at the mouth of the well. The leather bucket (perhaps a whole bullock-skin) was lowered down the well, the rope passing over the pulley. The free end of the rope was then attached to a harnessed camel, standing by the well-mouth and ridden by a man. When the bucket had dropped into the water and filled, the man rode the camel away from the well, thereby hauling on the rope and drawing the bucket up to the surface, where two other men were standing by the pulley-trestle, ready to meet the bucket and tip it into a channel which ran into the trough used for watering the camels. They then dropped the empty bucket into the well again, the camel rider rode back to the well mouth, thereby relaxing the rope and allowing the bucket to fall into the water again.

As the camel walked away and back again, it beat a path leading away from the mouth of the well. Meanwhile, however, there might be six or eight trestles and pulleys arranged around the well-mouth at the same time and thus an equal number of camels going back and forth hauling up the buckets. Thus the well made on the ground a pattern like a wheel, the well-mouth being the hub, the paths of the hauling camels radiating from it like spokes. Such wells were conspicuous from the air. The R.A.F., using a different comparison, named them star wells.

When a bedouin camp was pitched around it, the mouth of a long well often presented an animated scene. Herds of camels would come up to the troughs, pushing and grunting and stretching their long necks downwards. Groups of bareheaded young men, their skirts tucked up to knee-length like kilts, seized the huge leather buckets as they came up to ground level and tipped the sparkling water into the troughs. The draught camels strode up to the well and away again, in a continual coming and going of hauling and slacking off.

It was among bedouins a woman's duty to bring water to the tent for domestic use. Groups of young girls, carrying their empty goatskins, stood round the well-mouth, awaiting a chance to fill them when the buckets came up. And as they toiled, the young men sang "sea-shanties" of the desert to ease their work:

> O well, if but thine eyes could see,
> The black-eyed maid who stands by thee!
> Slim as a young gazelle is she.

When many tribes camped round a long well, the grazing was soon eaten down for a radius of many miles round the wells and the camel herds were obliged to go farther and farther afield in order to find bushes or grass. Camels could endure three, four or five nights without water, a fact which enabled them to travel twenty or thirty miles from the wells in search of grazing. The herds would sleep out in the desert during this time with their herdsmen, who would take a small bag of flour or dates with them, or in some cases would live almost solely on the milk of their camels. On the third, fourth or fifth evening—or however many it might be—the herds returned to water at the well, slept a night in the camp and then set out once more.

When the camels were grazing at so great a distance from their camp, they constituted an easy prey for raiders, the herdsmen being too few in numbers to defend them when the fighting men of the tribe remained in the tents. Sometimes, if a specific raid warning had been received, an escort would accompany the herds to their grazing grounds. But the idle and fickle bedouins soon tired of so monotonous a task in the pitiless summer heats so far from their tents, and if no raid came they returned to the camp.

The Dhafeer camels were grazing in this manner when, on 22nd June, 1925, the Ikhwan suddenly appeared in the form of a large raiding party of Mutair under Ali Ibn Ashwan. They fell upon the Dhafeer herds, killed the herdsmen and drove off one thousand seven hundred camels belonging to the Araif[1] section of the tribe. The alarm was long in reaching the distant camps and the Dhafeer pursuers, though they mounted in haste and gave chase, failed to overtake the triumphant raiders.

[1] Araif is pronounced as in the English word 'safe', not as in 'strife'.

This blow fell like a thunderbolt on the Iraqi nomads. Their despair at the catastrophe was all the greater owing to their previous confidence in the prospects of peace. There seemed for the moment to be no more talk of government indifference or complicity with the raiders. The British, it was said among the tribes, had done their best to ensure adequate defence and to bring pressure to bear on Ibn Saud. Obviously the task was beyond their powers. The Ikhwan were invincible, indifferent alike to threats or to any force which the government could send against them.

The Araif section had lost almost all their herds. They were obliged to beg or borrow camels to transport their families and belongings to the banks of the Euphrates, where the provisions still remaining in their tents would serve to keep them alive for a few weeks.

Such incidents had of course always occurred in the desert. In former times, however, a tribe overtaken by such a misfortune would engage in intensive raiding activity and, before the autumn, would have looted from some other tribe enough camels to enable it to buy food for the winter. When raiding was uncontrolled, camels were always in circulation in this manner. The bedouin was never without hope. Even if he were unfortunate enough to lose all his herds, he could gradually restore his fortunes by his own efforts. Government intervention had upset the natural balance of this system, for it was not as yet strong enough entirely to prevent raiding, but it intervened to prevent the victims of a raid from recouping their losses by counter raids. This was exactly what occurred in this instance.

The Iraq Government, indignant at this outrage after Ibn Saud's promises in the spring, informed the victims that the Ikhwan would be obliged to restore their camels and, at the same time, gave strict orders to the Dhafeer not to raid back. As the government rightly emphasized, counter raids would only produce further Ikhwan raids. For eight or ten weeks, the Araif remained quiescent. As winter drew nearer, however, their hopes of restitution grew weaker, their food stocks fell lower and lower and the season for the annual sales of their camels was almost upon them. The prospect of starvation confronted them. One raiding party after another slipped away to endeavour, by raiding Shammar, Aneza, or the Ikhwan, to provide food for their families during the approaching winter.

The British Government had been a good deal alarmed by the Ikhwan raids into Iraq during the previous winter and had accordingly despatched a British mission to the Hejaz under Sir Gilbert Clayton, to negotiate with Ibn Saud. Hostilities were still in progress in the Hejaz between the sherifs and Ibn Saud, but the mission passed safely through the sherifian and Saudi lines. A conference was held at Bahra, on the road between Jidda and Mecca, and resulted in the conclusion of the Bahra Agreement, which was signed on 1st November, 1925. In Article 1 of this new instrument, both governments agreed to impose severe punishment on raiders. In Articles 2, 3 and 4, both governments undertook not to encourage the tribes subject to the other party to migrate to their territory or to offer them gifts or bribes to do so. As has already been explained, the mutual seduction of each other's tribes was one of the principal political activities of Arabian princes.

It was not so much the actual terms of the Bahra Agreement which were important, but rather the fact that negotiations had taken place and that a fresh agreement had been signed. It was hoped that this outward evidence of good will would be sufficient to put an end to such outrages as had occurred in the past.

Thus when the new grazing season drew near and I returned from leave in the autumn of 1925, the prospects for the coming winter seemed both promising and ominous. On a high level, the chances of peace seemed to be good. The great majority of the Ikhwan were mobilized for the war in the Hejaz where Ibn Saud was still besieging Jidda. The Bahra Agreement promised a new era of co-operation between Iraq and Nejed. But on the local level, nothing more had been heard of the return of the Dhafeer camels looted by Ali Ibn Ashwan, and the victims, the Araif, were busily raiding to recoup their fortunes, thereby providing the Ikhwan with the excuse for more inroads into Iraq in retaliation. It was the same vicious circle which had always bedevilled attempts to stop raiding. Although the Ikhwan refugees had been disposed of, the Araif had taken their places.

Another event which occurred in the summer of 1925 was the disappearance of Hamood Ibn Suwait, who developed acute peritonitis as a result of tuberculosis. He was conveyed to hospital in Baghdad, where he lingered for a few months and then died. He was the only man who might have led the Dhafeer through the stormy years which still lay ahead. With his death, the last of the once famous Dhafeer chieftains perished.

When, with the approach of winter, hopes of the return of the camels looted by Ibn Ashwan began to fade, the Iraq shepherds looked forward with apprehension to yet another season of loot and slaughter. Some of the Zayyad had decided that government was a broken reed, and early in the autumn they despatched secret messengers to Hail, craving permission from the governor, Ibn Musaad, to enter Ikhwan territory, pay taxes to Nejed and to place themselves under Ibn Saud's protection.

As the tribes began to move out in December, Abu Ghar was re-occupied by the Iraq army and the wireless station was re-installed. The tribes, however, refused to be reassured and remained timidly camped near the fort. The vacillating shaikhs of the shepherd tribes called almost daily upon the government, asking whether or not their immunity from Ikhwan raids could be guaranteed.

Hamood Ibn Suwait had left only an infant son, by the name of Naif.[1] His cousin Ajami seemed to be the most prominent man remaining, and the Dhafeer began to look to him as a leader. But Ajami, warned by the fate of Hamood, was determined not to be shaikh, for fear of involving himself with the government. The tradition, dating from Turkish times, of seizing and imprisoning the shaikh whenever a tribe was accused of a crime, had weakened government control. No one wished to be shaikh and the government had no means of controlling tribes other than through such chiefs. It had been difficult enough to control the ever-moving mass of Iraqi nomadic tribes the previous winter. If now the Dhafeer were to relapse into chaos without a leader, the task of defence would be even further complicated. I visited Ajami in the desert in the hope of persuading him to agree to be the official chief of his tribe. We sat on the ground by a group of little shrubs a hundred yards from the tent. I admitted that Hamood had been unfortunate but offered myself to take Ajami into Nasiriya and introduce him to the Mutassarrif, the Arab governor of the province.

All was in vain. "I cannot get on with the government," was all that he would say. "I am not a man for governments." Frustrated, I relapsed into silence. We sat cross-legged on the dusty surface of the desert, staring at the far blue horizon. A man passed us riding a camel, and shouted in the loud voice of the open spaces, "*As salaam aleikum*"—peace be on you.

Ajami reached out his hand and broke a twig off one of the little shrubs beside us. Holding it up between his finger and thumb, he said quietly, "By God and by the life of this twig, I will not betray you or leave you, as long as you are in your present employment in this our country." (Shrubs and grass, the nourishment of their flocks, are the very life of bedouins. They have names for each of the unending variety of their bushes and herbs. To swear by a blade of grass or a twig must be a custom far older than Islam.) This was all I could obtain from him. He would work with me in the desert, but never would he go to Nasiriya, much less to Baghdad.

Although the immediate prospects, viewed at government level, seemed to offer the possibility of a quiet season, the tribes obstinately refused to move beyond Abu Ghar. So crowded were the flocks near the fort that it was obvious that the grazing would soon be exhausted and that there would then once again be disastrous losses in livestock, however good the winter rains might be.

I hastened again to visit the Dhafeer, to consult Ajami as to what

[1] Pronounced like the English word 'knife'.

was to be done. Unless they were accompanied by some visible sign of government support, he told me, the tribes would never move out into the desert. They would die of starvation at Abu Ghar sooner than face once more the possibility of massacre. "After all," he said, "if they all pass the winter at Abu Ghar, their sheep and camels will die, but they will not live in daily fear of having their throats cut. If they move into the desert, they believe that they will lose their sheep and camels and their lives as well."

The Iraq Government and the Royal Air Force, however, were not a little elated at the conclusion of the Bahra Agreement. When I reported the fears of the tribesmen, they replied that peace had been established and that consequently no military defensive measures were necessary. We were in a dilemma. The government had lost all interest in the subject, but the tribes would not move out unless accompanied by government forces. I explained the situation frankly to Ajami and asked him what was to be done. "You must come with us yourself," said he. "Only thus will the tribes move out to graze and thereby keep their flocks—and hence themselves—alive." Between us we worked out a plan.

The previous winter, when I had been camped at Abu Ghar, I had picked up a young Shammar negro. The tribes of Arabia were liberally sprinkled with negroes, imported during the centuries from Africa as slaves. The lot of the slave of a prosperous family was perhaps one of the happiest in the bedouin community. He grew up almost as a member of the family, and the little black Africans raced and played among the tents with the children of their owner or, as he was called, their "uncle". The slave's tasks were light, principally the making of coffee and tea in the tent or escorting his "uncle" on a journey. The simple bedouin community frowned on any shaikh of their own blood who dressed in silk or wore gold thread on his cloak, but the great shaikh could legitimately exhibit his wealth and magnificence in his retinue of negroes, gay in coats of many colours and wearing swords of which the scabbards were incased in silver. Even the puritan Ibn Saud, clad only in a cotton shirt and walking with his bare feet in leather sandals, was attended by slaves in scarlet and gold lace. The negro obtained a reflected honour from the fame of his "uncle"; their interest and their glory coincided. His race debarred him from leadership on his own merit, but as the trusted representative of his master he could often lord it over the "free" Arabs.

Unavoidably, however, the rise and fall of noble families or the natural increase of their negroes, often resulted in the existence of slaves whom their masters could no longer afford to support, and who consequently were obliged to earn their living as free men. I have never come across instances of negroes bought or sold among the bedouins. Born and bred in the free society of the tribes, they would doubtless not endure such treatment. The open life of a constantly moving tented community made it as impossible to retain discontented slaves as to keep women confined and veiled. In the cities of Nejed and the Hejaz, slaves were still exposed for sale, sometimes in tragic circumstances. Many former slaves could, however, be met with as free men, owning herds of camels, date gardens or cultivated land.

The bedouins and their negroes had found an interesting *modus vivendi*, which seemed superior to any system devised in Africa or America. For there was no social difference between Arabs and negroes. All lived and ate together, and negroes were often made rulers and governors of provinces in Arabia, representing their masters. Intermarriage only was forbidden.

Hamed al Bilal had been a slave of Shammar—the Aslam division of the tribe were his "uncles" and he had once owned a date garden, camels and sheep in Nejed. But when the Ikhwan conquered Shammar, some negro cousins of his own lodged information against him with the Wahhabis, to the effect that he smoked tobacco and (consequently) was an enemy of God. They hoped by this means to inherit his gardens and animals. Wahhabi-ism, like every other religious tyranny, led sometimes to hypocrisy and tale-bearing. Hamed found himself deprived of all his property, which was allotted to his suddenly orthodox cousins. Persecuted and taunted, he abandoned his home and, loading his tent and a few odds and ends on his sole surviving camel, he set out with his mother and two sisters, a sad little convoy, for Iraq and freedom from persecution. He had hoped to be able to deposit his women-folk in Zubair and to use Iraq as a base from which to raid the Ikhwan, thereby both taking revenge for his ruin and restoring his fortunes. The death of his only camel put an end to these hopes, for no man can raid in the desert without a mount. In the spring of 1925, he drifted to Abu Ghar, where I engaged him to take my riding camels daily to graze, at a wage of £2 a month and his keep. Short, thick-set, as black as night but for a row of shining white teeth, with a woolly black head, he was shy and silent at first—he had never spoken to, perhaps never seen, a European until he came to me at Abu Ghar. But he later developed a sarcastic but genial humour, which often kept the men laughing through the long winter evenings round the camp fires. He eventually adopted me completely as his "uncle" and followed me for many years through thick and thin, with unfailing fidelity.

Such was the man selected by Ajami Ibn Suwait and myself to represent in the Southern Desert the combined dignity of His Britannic Majesty's and the Iraq Governments. He had more wit and character than many senior officials whom I have known.

There being no hope of government forces to accompany the tribes, and no shaikh of their own to lead them, and they being too frightened to move out and graze alone, we decided on a policy of bluff. I gave Ajami a small white army tent and Hamed the slave. Ajami was to find a camel to carry both. Luck and ready wit were to do the rest. In referring to Hamed al Bilal as Hamed the slave, I do not of course wish to suggest that he was employed in any servile capacity. He thought of himself as a tribesman. If asked whence he came, he would have answered "from the Aslam Shammar". He had all his life been as free as any bedouin. In Arabic, however, the word for slave and the word for an African is the same—*abid*. So Hamed al Abid might be interpreted Hamed the African as much as Hamed the slave. Certainly to me Hamed the slave was as much a comrade in arms as a retainer. Equipped with a white tent and Hamed as the embodiment of the government, Ajami struck camp and moved out into the desert. Sensation! The word flew from tent to tent—"Ibn Suwait has moved out." Gradually the camps followed, cautiously, step by step, camping well behind him in order to have time to escape if he were attacked. Leaving their tents and flocks at a safe distance in the rear, the men rode forward to see the shaikh and to find out the news, and lo! a white tent was pitched beside his (the Arab tents are of course all black).

"Whose tent is that?" the visitors would enquire.

"That?" Ajami would say unconcernedly, "Oh, that is the officer's tent. His slave is in it."

The enquirers, incredulous, peeped inside, to see Hamed the slave, cross-legged, impassive, sucking his old pipe (the same pipe that caused his ruin by making him an enemy of God).

"Peace be upon you!" said the enquirers respectfully (for I had bought for Hamed a coat of many colours).

"And peace be upon you," returned Hamed, still impassive.

"Where is the officer?" enquired the visitors, unconvinced.

"*Yebghi yiji hel heen*,"—"He'll be coming along just now," Hamed would say, raising the flap of the tent to look out, as though expecting to see me approaching. The enquirers remounted and cantered back to their camps.

"Well?" asked their fellow tribesmen eagerly. "Where is Ibn Suwait going? Has he news of the Ikhwan?"

"Ibn Suwait has the government with him," they replied. "What need has he to fear? Tomorrow we will move camp and join him."

If only the powers that be could have relented sufficiently to give me a wireless set, the whole situation would have been changed, but the authorities were adamant. The Bahra Treaty meant peace with Ibn Saud, and no commitments in the desert were necessary.

I was not by any means free from anxiety. We had succeeded by a ruse in coaxing the tribes out to where the grazing was good, but this only increased my responsibility. If the Ikhwan were to come and massacre them, I alone would be blamed by all parties. The tribes would return to their old suspicions and be convinced that I had lured them to their death because the British Government was secretly encouraging Ibn Saud. The Baghdad authorities would blame me for not having left all the tribes concentrated between Abu Ghar and the river. (While the Iraq tribes believed that the British were betraying them to Ibn Saud, the latter was equally convinced that His Majesty's Government was treating him unfairly in order to please Iraq.)

Neither British nor Iraqi officials ever seemed to understand the economic basis of nomad life, which was, after all, the key to all our problems. Many people seemed to think that tribes moved into the desert just to give trouble to the government—the same idea had always been present in the minds of the Turks. Yet anyone who lived near to them in these years could not fail to be impressed with their intense fear of massacre and their dread of moving into the desert—but in spite of their terror, they continued to go. Economic necessity forced them to move out into the desert. Fresh spring grass for so many animals could be found in the desert alone. On the quality of the grazing in winter and spring depended the number of lambs which would be born and survive, the quantity of cooking oil which they could make from their butter, the wool clip and the fatness, and consequently the price, of the camels and sheep they would sell to the butchers. The incomes of themselves and their families for the year depended entirely on the grazing they could obtain during the four months from December to April. But not only was their income for that year at stake, for if they were obliged to pass the winter without grazing, half their animals (or perhaps more) might die. In other words, to be unable to scatter in the desert in winter meant no income to live on for the following year, and also a possible loss of half or more than half, of their capital. The Baghdad authorities, whether British or Arab, never seemed to grasp this, with the result that, when the tribes asked for protection, they were apt to reply: "If the tribes are afraid tell them not to go out into the desert this year."

I seem to have spent so much of my life seeing both sides of a question, endeavouring to explain to one nation or group or community, why the other party behave as they do. It is sometimes a thankless task, but it has impressed me deeply with the immense difficulty of seeing other people's points of view—of putting ourselves in the other man's shoes, as the old saying goes. And how few of us try seriously to do so! The greater part of mankind are so narrowly and so complacently satisfied with their own standpoint that it never occurs to them to imagine themselves in other men's positions, or to endeavour to analyse their motives. What a different world it would be if we all did so!

X

The Year of the Tent

Enlarge the place of thy tent and let them stretch forth the curtains of thine habitations: spare not, lengthen thy cords, and strengthen thy stakes . . . Fear not; for thou shalt not be ashamed: neither be thou confounded; for thou shalt not be put to shame.

Isaiah liv. 2, 4

Of all the wonders that I yet have heard,
It seems to me most strange that men should fear;
Seeing that death, a necessary end,
Will come when it will come.

SHAKESPEARE

Cowardice is not synonymous with prudence. It often happens that the better part of discretion is valour. WILLIAM HAZLITT

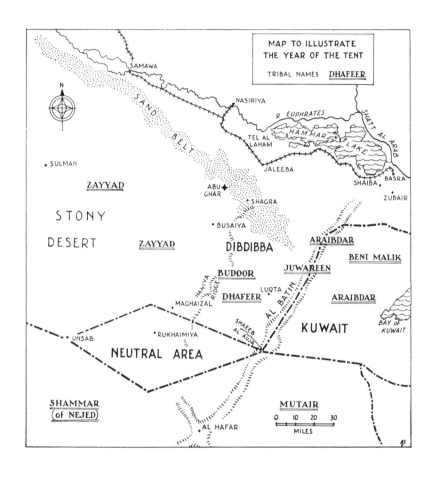

MAP TO ILLUSTRATE
THE YEAR OF THE TENT

TRIBAL NAMES   DHAFEER

X

THE YEAR OF THE TENT

I COULD not myself remain permanently in my tent with Ajami, because air headquarters wanted me to write reports, to answer correspondence and to maintain liaison with civil departments. I was afraid that if I had argued, they would have forbidden me to go to the desert at all. I could accordingly pay only fleeting visits, and in the interval the dignity of government was represented by Hamed the slave.

Ajami and I had agreed that he would move direct to Luqta, where an early rainstorm had left a pool of water, and where the grass was already green and the little desert shrubs were pushing out tiny leaves. As soon as he reached Luqta, I set out in my Ford car to visit him, having meanwhile moved my office and kit once more to Abu Ghar. As I drove southwards, the rolling plain of the Dibdibba north of Luqta was covered with tents, both of the Dhafeer and also of the shepherd tribes of the Budoor and the Juwareen. The most forward tent of all was that of Ajami, and beside it the little white tent with Hamed the slave.

No sooner did I sit down in Ajami's tent, in the wide circle of bearded tribesmen drinking coffee, than an excited conversation, interrupted by my appearance, was resumed. A herdsman had just arrived in haste from the camel flocks grazing a few miles to the south, to report that three unknown camelmen had appeared on a hill top overlooking the grazing herds. On seeing the latter, however, they had quickly turned tail and fled back towards Nejed. Two of the Dhafeer herdsmen had ridden to the hill where the strange riders had been seen and had followed their tracks for some miles. While the tracks showed that the riders had been riding at a walking pace while they were travelling northwards and before they saw the Dhafeer camels, their flight to the south after locating the herds had been at a rapid trot, and they had made no pause in their retreat for as far as the herdsmen had been able to follow them. An examination of the dung of their riding camels, some of which had been found, showed that they had been grazing on dry grass and bushes.

Now the belt of green grass and leafy shrubs where our tribes were camped extended only some thirty miles south of Luqta, beyond which no rain had fallen as yet, and the grass from the previous year was still dry and brown. In the desert, when a party of riders advanced to a hill from which they could see a camp or grazing herds of camels, and, having seen them, they fled back at full speed in the direction from which they came, it was fairly safe to assume that they were hostile, and in all probability the scouts of a raiding party. In this case, the direction of their flight and the food which their camels had been eating seemed to indicate that they came from the Ikhwan tribe of Mutair. The opinion of the majority of the tribal elders was that we should be raided the next morning at dawn by those dreaded Ikhwan war banners. Ajami's tent, with the little white tent, and one or two others, was pitched a few miles south of the rest of the tribes. We should inevitably be the first victims. I called Ajami out of the tent and we went and sat on the ground together, fifty yards away and out of earshot, for a private consultation.

I was sceptical about the chances of our being raided. When the Duweesh had fallen upon the shepherds at Gift Hollow the year before, we had heard rumours of his preparations for a fortnight beforehand. This time we had heard no warning reports. Ibn Saud, although he was still himself away in the Hejaz, had, it appeared, given genuine orders against raiding Iraq. The first Wahhabis, a hundred and twenty years before, had made the mistake of provoking the neighbouring governments too far and had been destroyed as a result. And they had provoked only the Turks and the Egyptians, who invaded Nejed on foot and on horses. Now their neighbours were defended by Britain, who had aircraft with which Central Arabia could be bombed in a few hours. Moreover, Ibn Saud was still fighting the sherifs. British intervention at this stage might reverse the fortunes of war and enable the sherifs to turn the tables on him. He did not seem likely to gain anything by raiding Iraq just at that moment, when he was still at war in the Hejaz.

On the other hand, Feisal al Duweesh had returned from the Hejaz war. It was suggested that Ibn Saud was angry with him. Perhaps, excluded from the Hejaz campaign, he wished to show that he could fight a war on his own. One could not be sure, one way or the other. One thing, however, was obvious. Having once started this bluff about my tent accompanying the tribes, I would be obliged to keep it up. If we ran away now, as the tribe wanted to do, and then no raid materialized, we should have made fools of ourselves and the moral value of the tent would have been lost. There was nothing for it, I decided, but to risk it and stay where we were. Ajami agreed to do whatever I thought best, though he was probably secretly as frightened as I was. I never, I think, felt as afraid during the First World War as I did in the desert. In the Great War I had been surrounded by comrades, my own company first, and then millions of others beyond, all doing the same thing. So many had already passed on ahead of us; we were still alive, at least for the moment, but death seemed less terrible when it meant joining the comrades who had gone before us. But out here I was alone, and moreover the decision rested solely upon me. The tribe said they would follow me in whatever I decided.

Yes, in the desert I was alone. The government was indifferent; it had not ordered me to lead the tribes. To some extent, the tribesmen were now convinced that I was doing my best to help them, but if things went wrong, they would turn against me. In so many of those cold long nights in the desert, when the wind whistled across the open wastes, the great question was "Will they come in the morning?" If they came, we should almost certainly all be killed. We had no power of resistance; a few scattered tents of bedouins who would be charged by a tearing mass of two or three thousand wild riders, who never gave quarter. If a man fell wounded, a bearded scoundrel would kneel on his chest and cut his throat with a knife. It was not war but massacre. To graze our flocks, we were gambling on whether "they" would come or not. The stake was our lives, in cold blood, with a knife on our throats.

After dark, we sent out two scouts on horseback to the south. I had little or no confidence in them. Though bedouins are hardy, courageous and resourceful, there is no discipline in the tribes, and, in their tolerant philosophy, it seems to them but natural that a man should be frightened of death and run away from it. As a result, one can never trust their scouts or patrols, unless he knows them personally. In any case, mounted scouts were of little use. The advancing raiders would be on the look out for them, and should they see them they would give chase hot foot, to prevent their carrying the alarm back to the camp. If the scouts were not overtaken and killed, they would probably reach the camp only a few minutes before the attackers.

Anxious though we were, we had to put a good face on it in public, and we sat long into the night talking, in the circle of wild cloaked figures round the flickering fire in Ajami's tent. Some of them assumed an air of cheerfulness, but there were many anxious hearts around that fire.

"Above all," said Dahloos al Salimi, an old white-bearded Suwaiti, "a truce to hares and bustard in the morning. Any man seeing a hare may grant it life!"

A chance rifle shot at dawn would have stampeded the camps from Luqta to Abu Ghar.

The Dhafeer certainly slept little that night. From dusk to dawn, they continued to load up camels and prepare for flight. Every mare was saddled and bridled, tied up only by her halter, instead of the usual shackles on her feet, that she might be the quicker released and mounted in an alarm.

Hamed, impassive as usual, sucked his old pipe all night, with a rifle across his knees. He amused himself by teasing the new driver of my Ford, a city dweller from Basra, unused to desert alarms. "They will say 'In the name of God' before they cut your throat," Hamed was explaining to the Basrawi, "and that is a great mercy, because it will sanctify your death. Maybe you will go straight to Heaven—that is if you have not been up to any games in Basra."

It is notoriously an ill wind that blows nobody any good, for, thus exhorted, the driver worked all night cleaning and re-cleaning the car. Again and again he took out and polished the sparking plugs and rubbed up all the electrical contacts with sand paper. Never, in more peaceful times, had our old Tin Lizzie enjoyed such a treat. Ahmed was leaving nothing to chance—if that Ford was wanted to start up in a hurry in the morning, he had made up his mind that she would start. The only unworthy doubt which entered my mind was whether Ahmed would remember to pick up Hamed and myself before he left for Basra. Hamed indeed continued to follow him with his taunts.

"Your black horse will need his best legs when the green banners come over the hill," he said, taking his pipe from his mouth and pointing with it at the Ford. "By Allah! the Ikhwan will make short work of you—a heathen with a shaved beard and your pockets full of tobacco and cigarettes."

Long before dawn, Ahmed started up the car—it would be better, he thought, to have her ready warmed up before the green banners came over the hill. In the more distant tents, a panic nearly ensued, for the sudden rumble of the engine was for a moment mistaken for the thunder of galloping hoofs. But those nearer at hand mistook it for aircraft engines, came out of their tents, looked up at the night sky and said: "Abu Hunaik has wirelessed for the aeroplanes to come to our help. May Allah bless and preserve him!"

Day dawned in a misty drizzle, with low trailing clouds, more like a December morning in England than in Arabia. All was still and quiet, except for voices here and there from the black tents looming through the fog and for the occasional bark of a dog. From Ajami's tent, a thin column of smoke told of morning coffee. When it was broad daylight, I suggested a reconnaissance in the Ford down to the Nejed frontier, in order finally to set our fears at rest. We started at about eight o'clock, Ajami, Matiq Ibn Shaaban of the Dhafeer, a man reputed as a desert guide, and myself.

We lurched and rattled through the mist, bumping over or crashing through the low desert shrubs. The Dibdibba, slightly rolling but devoid of conspicuous physical features, stretched interminably on either hand, away into the mist. The rain stopped but the low grey clouds still kept the sun invisible. The grass and bushes were covered with diamond drops. The damp fog allowed a visibility of only a mile or two. Here and there, wisps of white ground mist drifted along the surface of the desert.

We advanced cautiously. We drove across low ground, but whenever we came to a rise we stopped the car before reaching the crest of the ridge. Then one or other of us ran forward on foot, crawled to the skyline, and scoured the country beyond. After travelling thus for about two hours, when we reckoned that we must have covered nearly twenty miles towards the south, we came upon the two horsemen whom we had sent out the night before as scouts, and who reported that they had seen and heard nothing, and were returning to camp. Matiq thought we must be near the Shaeeb al Auja. We decided to push on south a little farther until we reached the great depression of the Batin.

By this time the fog had thinned, and visibility was perhaps two miles or slightly more. We continued to travel on cautiously, advancing from ridge to ridge, taking it in turns to crawl up to the skyline and use the binoculars. When we had been travelling thus for about an hour after seeing the horsemen, it was my turn to scout from the next ridge. The car stopped below the skyline, I ran forward, bending double, and lay down on my face behind a little bush on the summit. When I put the field glasses to my eyes, my heart seemed all of a sudden to stop beating. In a gentle hollow, some two or three miles ahead, I could see through the mist a great number of little moving specks. Though they showed only dimly, on account of the misty atmosphere, they were obviously camels and it seemed to me that they were moving towards us. I signed to Ajami and Matiq to come up beside me. We scanned them in turn, passing the field glasses from one to the other. We crawled cautiously backwards off our ridge, jumped into the car and threaded our way towards the camels by following low ground. Down a dry water course, across a wide shallow hollow and we reached a low hill half a mile nearer to them. If only we could identify them definitely as raiders, we would yet have time to get back and warn our tribes, let them strike their tents and retire towards Abu Ghar with a good start.

All three of us side by side crawled up the next hill. We were closer to them now, but we still could not see if all the camels were saddled —the sign of a raiding party. There were many hundreds of camels, but they seemed to be dispersed and grazing, wandering here and there. A raiding party might well halt in the early morning after a cold night's march, but it seemed unlikely that they would do so only twenty-five miles from our camp, the location of which they must have known from the three scouts, who had been seen the day before by the Dhafeer. We crawled back below the crest of the ridge and held a rapid consultation, each grasping his rifle. In the distance, we had thought that we could see a white speck, like a little tent. Some of the great Ikhwan leaders did carry small tents with them on raids—but again it seemed curious that they should pitch it so near our camp. Ajami suggested that they might be a party of camel merchants from Central Arabia, some of whom, perhaps out hawking for bustard, had the previous day been mistaken by our herdsmen for hostile scouts. We crawled back on to the ridge for a second look. On the right, a small group of camels had separated slightly from the rest. There was a man standing amongst the camels. We decided to stalk this group and then to charge down in the Ford upon the man. If necessary we could kidnap him, throw him into the car, make away, and cross-question him at leisure. Should the whole force prove hostile, we should probably have time to escape before this isolated man could be reinforced by the main body, though in such soft going with many shrubs the Ford could travel at only about ten to fifteen miles an hour. We set off down a series of depressions towards our objective, until we reached the last little valley and we reckoned that the group of camels and the man were just beyond the next ridge. Then grasping our rifles on our knees, with our thumbs on the safety catch, we gave the driver the word. The Ford topped the ridge, bore down at full speed on the solitary herdsman and then pulled up with all brakes. Ajami stepped out of the car, his headcloth wound round his face so that only his eyes were visible. He advanced cautiously, catlike, his rifle muzzle forward towards the enemy. "Peace be upon you," he called. "And on you peace," the stranger replied calmly. To return the greeting meant that they must be friendly. The bedouin's headcloth was also wound round his face, against the cold drifting mist.

"Who are those people over there?" asked Ajami curtly, still holding his rifle ready.

No answer.

"What are those camels and whose is that tent?" he said more sharply, while we fingered our triggers significantly.

"What camels?" answered the stranger.

"Those over there," replied Ajami, nodding towards the herds.

"Why they are your own camels and that is Abu Hunaik's tent," said the man in mild surprise. "Don't you know your own people?"

Ajami pulled his headcloth off his face and smiled sheepishly. "*Nahnu munejjimeen*," he said. "We are star struck. We lost our way in the mist and we have been stalking our own camp!"

*   *   *   *   *

This ludicrous incident relieved the tension in the camp, whither we returned for a late breakfast. Seeing everyone cheerful once more, I decided that it would be safe to leave them for a day. Hearing that some of the Kuwait tribes had crossed the Batin and were camped in Iraq territory, I decided to visit them and left camp in the afternoon, promising to return the next day.

The low clouds and mist had turned to steady rain, and as we bumped across the dreary waste the little streams of water were already trickling down the hollows and forming pools in the dry water courses. Hamed the slave, bedouin-like, could not contain his joy. "Praise be to God!" he kept exclaiming fervently. "The Arabs this year will have their fill of grass and of truffles." (The little truffles of the desert are known in the north as *chimma*, in Nejed as *fugga*.)

The bedouin followers of the shaikh of Kuwait were a motley collection, consisting of sections or families—fugitives, immigrants or retainers—from half the tribes of Arabia. The backbone of the group, however, was from the Ajman tribe of the Hasa. This tribe had provoked the indignation of Ibn Saud in 1916 and a punitive expedition had been sent against them, with the result that many of them had taken refuge in Kuwait. I was genuinely anxious to make the acquaintance of these tribal neighbours of ours, who like ourselves were constantly menaced by raids by the Ikhwan. In former days, in the lifetime of Mubarak[1] Ibn Sobah, Araibdar as they were called, were a powerful tribal group, for the shaikh had regularly attracted bedouins to his territory, and had subsidized them generously, in order to use them to protect his comparatively rich little town from the depredations of his Arabian neighbours. Kuwait even in those days was considered wealthy and prosperous, living on the pearl fisheries in the Persian Gulf.

But Shaikh Ahmed al Jabir, the grandson of Mubarak, seemed to have halted between two opinions. He was not on cordial terms with Ibn Saud but he had neglected to build up his tribes or to seek from Britain the means of defence. The subsidies paid to the tribes by Mubarak Ibn Sobah had been reduced, and many of his former subjects, ruined by Ikhwan raids, had abandoned Kuwait and gone over to Ibn Saud. The unfortunate remnant, too weak to fight, led an uncertain life, continually alarmed by rumours of imminent Ikhwan attacks. Thus, although no political or defensive co-ordination between Iraq and Kuwait had ever been considered (Ibn Sobah was perhaps a little afraid of absorption by his bigger neighbour), yet the tribes themselves, being in the same predicament, could not but observe each other's misfortunes with sympathy.

As in some sort embodying the hope of salvation of the Iraq tribes, I was received by the Kuwaitis with hospitality bordering on enthusiasm. We had found a small group of black tents in the great

[1] The name of Ibn Sobah is so widely known as Mubarak, that I have not changed the common transliteration.

Batin depression. Stopping the car a few hundred yards away, we sent Hamed the slave on foot to ask the whereabouts of Ambarak Ibn Hajruf, who was then the chief of the Kuwait tribes. We purposely stopped at a distance because to halt beside a tent, and then drive on again to find hospitality elsewhere, would have been to put a slight upon the tent owner. But our caution was of no avail, for, pulling up their cloaks over their heads, the men came out of the tent, battling against the wind and the rain, as far as the car. "Peace be upon you," they shouted, their voices blown here and there by the gale.

"And on you peace," we replied. "Who are these Arabs?"

"Your servants, the retainers of Ibn Sobah," they answered. "Alight with your hosts, the night is at hand."

Our excuses were of no avail. The amir,[1] they said, using the Nejed expression in referring to Ibn Hajruf, was camped far away. We could not pass them by and go on elsewhere that night. Our host was Mabkhoot Ibn Mikrad, originally of the Ajman tribe, as was also Ibn Hajruf. These Ajman of Kuwait lived on pay from the Shaikh rather than on the produce of their own flocks. Ibn Sobah kept these "tame" bedouins, as a rich city businessman will keep a farm and a herd of cattle in the country, as a pleasant rural amusement, even if it were to operate at a loss. Compared with the lean and hardy Dhafeer, Araibdar seemed to be living in luxury. New carpets spread the floor of the tent and we were soon seated deep in soft cushions, while a kettle sang on the fire, and—rare luxury indeed in the black tents—a china tea service was laid out on the ground. Two whole sheep, piled high on mountains of rice swimming in oil, were borne in for dinner, but it was the hospitable geniality of Mabkhoot which made the evening so enjoyable. As the Arab proverb goes—"To say welcome is better than to slaughter sheep."

Next morning we moved on to the tent of the amir, Ambarak Ibn Hajruf, to receive no less cordial a welcome. It will be long indeed before I forget the hospitality and the almost courtly politeness of these two old Arabs, neither of whom I was ever to see again. Two years later, Ibn Mikrad, unable any longer passively to endure the constant fear of Ikhwan raids, made his peace with Ibn Saud and went back to the Hasa, while the grey-bearded old Ambarak Ibn Hajruf, staying on in Kuwait territory, was killed in a raid by the Ikhwan.

My old Ford met with a great success with Araibdar, who had never believed that a car could run in the desert. Ahmed the Basrawi, who had recovered his self-confidence since the Ikhwan had

---

[1] In most Arab countries, amir is translated into English as prince, and means a member of a great family. In Nejed it is used as commander. When meeting a party of four or five men in Nejed, one asks for the amir, that is to say the man in command of the party.

not come, explained to a wide circle of admirers that the headlights were a wireless, by means of which I held frequent and intimate consultations with King George in London. It was well on in the afternoon before I could at last break away from such pressing hosts, two more sheep having been sacrificed for our lunch. At last we set out once more, lurching and bumping over the rolling plains of the Dibdibba towards Ajami's tent.

When still several miles from Luqta, we came in sight of distant figures in front of us, apparently all moving rapidly northwards. As we draw nearer, we distinguished many flocks of sheep and herds of camels, shepherd women driving loaded donkeys, and caravans of camels bearing the swaying litters in which bedouin women and children travelled. "*Al Arab hajjeen*," said Hamed, leaning out of the window of the car and peering forward. "The Arabs are in flight."

My heart sank. The alarm must have been true after all, but instead of attacking the camp that first morning, they must have come twenty-four hours later, when we were sleeping with Araibdar. Ajami had doubtless been attacked at dawn and his little camp exterminated, while the remaining camps fled—it was another tragedy like Gift Hollow the year before. Now we could see a few men on horses, stripped to their white shirts, and hung with belts of ammunition, galloping here and there urging on the herds in their flight. We hailed one of them, and yelled to him to know what had happened. His wild hair was hanging over his face, which was convulsed with excitement.

"By Allah, I don't know what happened," he shouted. "The tribes in front of us fled, so we fled also." Then turning to a shepherd girl, he bellowed: "*Y 'Allah ya bint*—come on girl! Drive those donkeys faster!"

A shepherd galloped after us waving his cloak. We stopped, hoping that he might have news.

"I am your servant, Haj Annad of the Juwareen," he yelled. "Is it safe for us to camp? We are exhausted with marching. Has there been a battle?"

"We don't know," we shouted back. "Why did you move camp anyhow?"

"The other tribes fled, and we fled too," he called.

"Camp where you are," we bellowed back at the top of our voices—his excited horse would not come within fifty yards of the car. We drove on fuming, partly from anxiety and partly from anger at seeing this panic-stricken crowd.

"May God destroy all shepherds!" said Hamed the slave in an ill-temper.

The Ford seemed quite heroic, racing at full speed towards the south, through this stream of fugitives flying northwards. We were keyed up to an anguish of nervous strain and compressed excitement. The Ford seemed to us to crawl and we danced in our seats, tapped our feet nervously on the floor boards, and peered ahead grasping our rifles. Hamed and Ali al Yunis had stripped to their shirts and were tightening their ammunition belts. I tore off my jacket and sat with my loaded rifle ready. Every moment we expected to see a long line of camelmen in open order appear on the distant plains in front of us, but instead there were only the unending flocks of camels, donkeys, and sheep hurrying past us to the north. The whole plain seemed to be on the move. I had not realized what great numbers of tribes had followed the little white tent out into the desert.

At last we saw in the distance a group of camels carrying the great swaying litters in which only the women of bedouin shaikhs travelled. We steered towards them, hoping to find some shaikh of importance who could tell us what had occurred. A *self*, or advanced guard, of half a dozen men on camels rode in front of the party. We stopped the car and waved to them to come over to us, not wishing to drive up to them and stampede the camels which were carrying the women and children. A man slipped off one of the camels and ran over to us on foot.

"Peace be upon you."

"And on you peace. Who are these Arabs?" we asked.

"It is Hamdan Ibn Dhuweihi," said the man calmly. Here at least were Dhafeer, less panicky than the shepherds.

"What has happened?" I asked, holding my breath with anxiety.

"By Allah," said the bedouin composedly, "nothing has happened. You were away so long that the Arabs became afraid and began to move."

"May God destroy their houses!" we exclaimed fervently, partly in anger and partly in relief. "Where is Ajami?"

"Ajami is in the same place," he answered. "He said he would not move until you came back."

"Drive on," I shouted to Ahmed Basrawi.

"What is your news?" gasped the bedouin, running beside the car. "Is the Duweesh raiding? Shall we camp here? Will Ajami move camp tomorrow? Where have you come from? What is . . .?", his voice faded away behind us.

Now we had passed all the fugitives and were in the open desert, with no living thing to be seen. Eight miles farther on we came in sight of our little white tent. Beside it stood Ajami's large black house of hair, with two other small ones near by. The rest of the desert was empty. Ajami and three other men were sitting in the tent.

"Where is everybody?" I enquired hotly, sitting down by the fire.

"The Arabs were afraid," said Ajami quietly, blowing the fire with a hand bellows preparatory to making a fresh brew of coffee.

I felt driven to despair by this disgraceful episode. There are moments when it is worth while, even essential, to risk a gamble. If we remained where we were, the tribes would gradually move back in a day or two and rejoin us. But if we moved south towards the Ikhwan in the meanwhile, all alone, with our four tents . . . that would show them! Indignation boiled within me.

"They say that the grazing at Rukhaimiya is good," I said to Ajami. "We shall move there tomorrow, just you and I."

"As you like," said Ajami calmly, measuring out the coffee beans into the palm of his hand.

Good little Ajami.

*   *   *   *   *

Next morning, a group of seven men, with a Ford car, four tents and a flock of camels, moved southwards towards Nejed. We camped in virgin grass near Rukhaimiya. Ajami had ordered an old negro of his to ride back northwards on a camel. He gave him careful instructions. He was to accost all the Arabs he met, and ask them if they had seen an old white camel which he had lost. When they cross-questioned him eagerly (as they surely would) as to what had become of Ajami, he was to reply in a voice of unconcern, that Ajami had moved to Rukhaimiya, where the grazing was better.

Three or four days later, odd horsemen and camelmen began, rather shamefaced, to drop in on us at Rukhaimiya. Within a week, we had some two hundred tents of the Dhafeer round us and the shepherds were grouped a few miles farther north.

I was sleeping one night in the little white tent at Rukhaimiya, when suddenly I was woken by a wild galloping of horses. In an instant I was sitting bolt upright and wide awake. For a second my heart stood still—had they come at last? Snatching my rifle I slipped out of the tent and stood outside, my heart beating fast. In the east, the pale light of dawn was beginning to show. The sound of galloping hoofs was growing fainter towards the north. From the south all seemed quiet. Gradually I recovered confidence. Then, after a few minutes' silence, the horses seemed to be returning. They flashed past me—three loose horses dragging their headropes, their tails in the air, snorting with wide-open nostrils. From Ajami's tent a voice called "O Ali! O Ali! Where are you? The horses are loose."

*   *   *   *   *

In the Neutral Area the grazing was splendid. The Arabs began to scrape up the truffles from the gravelly soil. Soon the shepherds were churning butter and inviting one another to the springtime feasts in their tents.

When summer drew near the camps moved slowly back towards

the Euphrates. The great milch camels, each with her calf at foot, were so fat that they seemed hardly able to waddle. The sheep had borne a double toll of lambs. It had been a wonderful grazing season.

With the rearguard moved the little tent and the real hero of the campaign, Hamed the slave. For had it not been for him, sitting in his white tent and stolidly sucking his infidel pipe, none of the tribes would have moved out to the desert at all.

There were no raids; the Ikhwan were still fighting in the Hejaz.

XI

Busaiya

It happens in affairs of state, when the evils that arise have been foreseen, they can be quickly redressed, but when, through not having been foreseen, they have been permitted to grow in a way that every one can see them, there is no longer a remedy. Therefore, the Romans, foreseeing troubles, dealt with them at once, and, even to avoid a war, would not let them come to a head, for they knew that war is not to be avoided, but is only put off to the advantage of others.   MACHIAVELLI, *The Prince*

There is a limit at which forbearance ceases to be a virtue.
                                                    BURKE

The patient and active virtues of a soldier are insensibly nursed in the habits and discipline of a pastoral life.
                GIBBON, *Decline and Fall of the Roman Empire*

XI

BUSAIYA

BOTH the British and the Iraq Governments had been convinced that the conclusion of the Bahra Agreement on 1st November, 1925, would result in peace between Iraq and Nejed. The signature of the Agreement had been followed by the year of the tent, from November, 1925 to April, 1926, which had passed peacefully. Hamed the slave and the little tent had rendered an immense service by offering the Iraq tribes a symbol of government leadership, but we could scarcely claim that they had frightened away the Ikhwan. The tent had, for the first time, suggested to the tribes the possibility of co-operation with the government. But after April, 1926, the government abolished all defensive planning and abandoned the tribes once more to their own devices.

In the autumn of 1926, I resigned my British army commission and was given employment by the Iraq Government as an administrative inspector. I was posted as a civil offical to the provinces of Diwaniya and Hilla, farther up the Euphrates.[1] Throughout the whole of 1927, I was fully employed in the administration of an area as large as six English counties. Revenue, taxation, public works, police, irrigation and tribal land disputes provided me with more than enough work. The desert was quiet and in any case I was far away from it and out of touch with its people.

I have always been grateful for the period which I spent in Iraq, engaged as a civilian in pure administration, a task which, in those countries at least, gave one the best possible insight into the life of the people. I will never forget the happy years I spent in Iraq or the innumerable friends I made among officials, townspeople, cultivators and bedouins alike.

*   *   *   *   *

The Dhafeer had always been unfortunate in their dealings with the Iraq Government, and their situation was worsened by the death of Hamood Ibn Suwait and the refusal of any of his relatives to be official shaikh. The seduction of one another's tribes had, as I have explained, always played a large part in the politics of Arabian princes. The dissatisfaction of the Dhafeer with their treatment in Iraq offered Ibn Saud an opportunity to win them over. He made advances to Ajami, offering pay, gifts and honour if he brought the

[1]See map on page 71.

tribe to Nejed, although such action had been specifically prohibited by the Bahra Agreement, on which the ink was still scarcely dry.

Although I was far away and had no longer any connection with the desert, the Suwait came to see me and to ask my advice. I urged them not to abandon Iraq. Ibn Saud's promises of pay and gifts might appear tempting, I said, but they would always be looked upon as foreigners in Nejed. The Dhafeer, it must be admitted, were in a dilemma. All their interests bound them to Iraq, where they sold their livestock and bought their provisions, but their grazing grounds were exposed to Ikhwan raids, against which the Iraq Government had adopted no effective measures. If I had remained in the desert, I could perhaps have brought Ajami in to the Iraq Government, but now I was far away. The Suwait promised to follow my advice, but when they returned to the desert Ibn Saud's offers became even more tempting. In the summer of 1927, Ajami and about half the Dhafeer went over to Ibn Saud. The tribe was split into two.

Governments grind slowly. When I had been employed as R.A.F. intelligence officer in the desert, I had emphasized the impossibility of exercising control over the tribes without the establishment of government posts in the area. The occupation of Abu Ghar had been temporary and purely military. I pressed for a permanent police post, which would enable the government to enforce public security. Abu Ghar, only forty miles from the railway, was too far back.

It so happened that, just before I left Nasiriya, a large raiding party of Shammar from northern Iraq had on 5th October, 1925, come down through the Iraq deserts west of the Euphrates and, after watering at Busaiya, had looted a great number of camels from the tribes of Kuwait.[1] This affair did not in any way concern the Ikhwan and Ibn Saud, but it greatly reinforced my arguments in favour of permanent police posts in the desert, for here was a tribe living in Iraq, which had plundered the tribes of the friendly state of Kuwait. A glance at the map will show that Busaiya was centrally placed in the Southern Desert. From it, Iraq tribes could be prevented from raiding either Nejed or Kuwait. I accordingly strongly recommended the construction of a police post at the wells of Busaiya. The proposal was sanctioned in February, 1927, four months after I left the Southern Desert.

Meanwhile the news from Nejed was not entirely reassuring. Feisal al Duweesh, it appeared, was already on bad terms with Ibn Saud. The tribe of Ateiba, under its chief Sultan Ibn Humaid, claimed that it, not Ibn Saud, had conquered Taif and Mecca and the tribesmen had become proportionately arrogant. The Ikhwan as a whole were greatly elated by their victorious campaign in the Hejaz and were seeking fresh fields to conquer.

[1] See map on page 195.

Caution had always distinguished the policy of Abdul Aziz Ibn Saud. He had been confident of his power to defeat other Arabian princes, like Ibn Rasheed or the sherifs of Mecca, but he was not prepared to engage in hostilities with Britain. Doubtless he remembered that the arrogance of the first Wahhabis had led to the destruction of their empire in 1818. But unfortunately he had encouraged a revival of fanaticism to assist him in defeating his Arab rivals. The Ikhwan were able to quote against him his own pronouncements of an earlier date. The Iraqis, they claimed, were renegade Muslims, enemies of God, whose lives and property were forfeit to the Ikhwan, the only true believers.

The broad mind and clear intellect of Abdul Aziz Ibn Saud were able to grasp the essentials of a situation, even in countries which might have been expected to be far beyond the range of his experience. He was a model of common sense and prudence. If he encouraged fanaticism, it was to use it as an instrument to achieve his object; he was never himself a fanatic. To a wild and unruly people, however, prudence and common sense offered few attractions. Even in countries politically far more sophisticated than Nejed, experience has proved that violent extremists can always command a following, while the moderate and the wise are coldly regarded. Indeed it is this human peculiarity which is responsible for many of the troubles of our modern world.

It was the towering personality of Abdul Aziz himself which was eventually to bring back moderation to Nejed and that only after a bitter struggle. Any lesser man would have succumbed.

*   *   *   *   *

In September, 1927, a small party of twelve workmen were sent out to Busaiya to construct the police post which I had recommended eighteen months earlier. They were accompanied only by seven policemen. Ibn Saud immediately protested, on the basis of an article in Uqair protocol No. 1 annexed to the Treaty of Muhammarah, signed on 2nd December, 1922. Article 3 read: "The two governments mutually agree not to use the watering places and wells situated in the vicinity of the border for any military purpose, such as building forts on them, and not to concentrate troops in their vicinity."

Ibn Saud's protests were plausible. The Iraqi case was based on the fact that Busaiya was eighty miles from the Nejed border and not in its vicinity. It was, moreover, not a military fort but a police post, to be manned by ten policemen. Yet other considerations made these arguments appear to Ibn Saud less valid than Europeans might consider them. For example, in Nejed, there was no difference between soldiers and police, so that a point which appeared of basic importance to the Iraqis and the British, meant nothing to the king. After all, it is only just over a hundred years since a regular police force was established in Britain. Previous to that time, the army or the militia were the only forces used to prevent civil disturbances. Another essential factor was that the Nejed Government in those days made no use of maps. Thus the exact distance of Busaiya from the border, a point quite obvious in Baghdad and in Whitehall, was less vivid in Riyadh. The differences which arose over Busaiya were therefore perfectly natural and, in normal times, could doubtless have been solved by negotiation.

On the night of 5th/6th November, 1927, however, a party of about fifty Mutair rushed the workmen's tents at Busaiya at midnight. All the workmen and police were massacred with the exception of one policeman who survived, though left by the Ikhwan for dead.

The rudimentary organization which had been created in 1924–5 to deal with Ikhwan raids had been disbanded after the signature of the Bahra Agreement. The massacre did not convince the government that extensive defensive measures were necessary. It was, however, decided to continue with the construction of the post, and on 18th November, Busaiya was reoccupied by workmen and police, with a section of R.A.F. armoured cars as escort.

The Iraq shepherd tribes were meanwhile moving out for the winter grazing season. Two winters passed without Ikhwan raids had reassured them and they moved boldly down to the Nejed frontier. Some, if not all, of them intended to pay taxes to Ibn Saud as soon as they reached the border, to secure immunity—as they thought—from Ikhwan attacks.

Nevertheless, it soon became apparent that more trouble was in store. On 4th December, 1927, a party of four hundred Mutair under Turaiheeb Ibn Shuqair, raided Araibdar some miles northeast of Jahra in Kuwait territory. As a result, on 13th December, Ibn Sobah requested R.A.F. air reconnaissances over Kuwait territory.

On 9th December, a routine air reconnaissance over the neutral area was heavily fired on, one R.A.F. wireless operator being wounded. It later transpired that the aircraft had arrived at the very moment when Feisal al Duweesh was raiding the Ghalidh tribe of shepherds. The aircrews, however, apparently failed to realize what was happening and returned to Shaiba. After two years without raids, there were no pilots with experience of hostilities against the Ikhwan. The Duweesh was therefore able to complete his looting and massacre of the shepherds. Other aircraft returned later in the day, however, and attacked the raiders, who were already moving back southwards towards the Nejed border.

After this partial success, the Duweesh did not return home, but

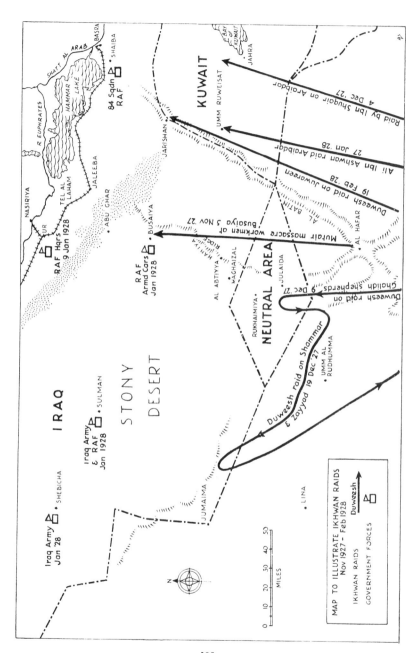

MAP TO ILLUSTRATE IKHWAN RAIDS
Nov 1927 - Feb 1928

IKHWAN RAIDS
GOVERNMENT FORCES

Duweesh

proceeded westwards toward Jumaima, keeping south of the Iraq frontier. On 19th December, he attacked again between Unsab and Jumaima, the victims being the Zayyad and Beni Huchaim shepherds from the Samawa area. The Ikhwan killed forty Iraqis and looted twelve thousand sheep, one thousand five hundred donkeys and one hundred and seven tents.

On this occasion the Ikhwan also raided a camp of Nejed Shammar. Not only were these people subjects of Ibn Saud, but Ibn Saud's own father-in-law, Al Aasi Ibn Shuraim, was in the camp and was obliged to flee for his life. The Iraq shepherds raided in the neutral area on 9th December and also those attacked on the 19th west of Unsab, had all alike moved to the frontier in order to pay taxes to Ibn Saud for their immunity. There could thus be no doubt whatever that these raids were contrary to the king's wishes; indeed they were as much a rebellion against his authority as an attack on Iraq. Reports that many of the Ikhwan were deeply dissatisfied with Ibn Saud's rule had been current for over a year. The Mutair raids were therefore in the nature of throwing down the gauntlet to the king.

Ibn Saud, who had long been absent from Nejed since the conquest of the Hejaz, returned to his capital Riyadh at the end of December. A lull in the Mutair raids ensued, the offenders being in constant expectation that the king would march against them and exact summary vengeance. The tribes still loyal to him were in daily expectation of a summons to arm against Mutair. The king, however, anxious to avoid civil war against his former most enthusiastic supporters, remained apparently passive in Riyadh.

Interpreting Ibn Saud's inaction as weakness, Mutair resumed their activities. On 27th January, 1928, Ali Ibn Ashwan of Mutair with four hundred men, raided Araibdar at Umm Ruweisat, thirty-eight miles west-north-west of Jahra, looting many camels and sheep. On this occasion the retainers of Ibn Sobah distinguished themselves. Giving chase with seventy-five riflemen in twenty-five civilian cars, they overtook the raiders and recovered a portion of the loot.[1] On 29th January, British aircraft located and attacked the retiring raiders near Al Hafar, in Nejed territory. One aircraft forced-landed five miles from the raiders, but another landed beside it and picked up the crew. Next morning, 30th January, the raiders were again overtaken eight miles west of Al Hafar. One aircraft was hit by rifle fire and forced-landed only four hundred yards from the raiders. Flight-Lieutenant J. F. T. Barrett, D.F.C. landed beside the aircraft under heavy rifle fire and picked up the crew, an act of gallantry for which he was awarded the Distinguished Service Order.

On 19th February, the Duweesh with some two thousand five hundred Mutair raided the Juwareen and other Iraq tribes at

[1] Dickson. *Kuwait and her Neighbours.*

Jarishan, only fifty miles from the R.A.F. camp at Shaiba, killing many Iraqis and looting eighteen hundred sheep, and many camels, donkeys, horses and tents. The R.A.F. attacked the raiders on 19th, 20th and 21st February, one aircraft being shot down in flames and the pilot killed.

*　　*　　*　　*　　*

Tribes and government were alike convinced at last that all their dreams of peace had been illusory. The whole machinery of defence had been dispersed, all R.A.F. personnel had changed. Everything had once more to be improvised from nothing and that in a crisis. After the first Ikhwan raids, orders were issued as usual for all tribes to retire behind Busaiya. Those who complied lost their flocks for lack of grazing, those who failed to comply were raided.

On 14th December, 1927, the British Government gave permission for R.A.F. aircraft to pursue Ikhwan raiders across the Nejed frontier. On 16th December, the building of Busaiya post was completed, and the new fort was occupied by a platoon of the Iraq army, Abu Ghar being simultaneously abandoned. On 8th January, the R.A.F. established an operational headquarters at Abraham's old city, Ur of the Chaldees, twelve miles south-west of Nasiriya. Nine aircraft of 55 Squadron with ninaks, and two sections of armoured cars were stationed at Busaiya. Meanwhile a company of the Iraq army was sent to occupy Sulman, where it was supported by nine aircraft of 84 Squadron from Shaiba, and two sections of armoured cars. The remaining aircraft of 55 and 84 Squadrons were held at Shaiba. All Iraq tribes were again warned to withdraw behind the line Busaiya-Sulman, regardless of the fact that there was little grazing there.

Air headquarters, however, claimed quite rightly that they could not be certain of locating advancing raiders, even if the whole area between the frontier and the Busaiya-Sulman line were cleared of tribes. They suggested that a belt of Nejed territory seventy miles wide south of the frontier be also cleared of tribes. The British and Iraq Governments, alarmed by the tempest of raids which had fallen on Iraq and Kuwait and at Ibn Saud's apparent inactivity, sanctioned the proposal.

On 11th January, aircraft flew across the Nejed frontier and dropped the following notices on all tribal encampments seen:

> Feisal al Duweesh and the Mutair tribe have, contrary to the orders of His Majesty the King of Nejed, made war upon the tribes of Iraq. As punishment for this offence, the British and Iraq Governments hereby order that all Nejed tribes must retreat to a distance of four days' march from the Iraq frontier. Any persons who disobey this order will be liable to be attacked from the air without further warning.

This notice was dropped on all tribal camps beyond the Nejed border and as far south as the line Lina-Al Hafar. None of the tribes, however, appeared to make any movement to comply. As a result, orders were issued to drop warning bombs in the vicinity of the camps concerned, in such a manner as not to inflict casualties.

There were no camps of Mutair within seventy miles south of the frontier and, as a result, none of them were affected, although they alone had raided. The only tribe present in considerable numbers in the forbidden zone were the Nejed Shammar, the former followers of Ibn Rasheed, who were not only loyal to Ibn Saud, but had themselves been raided by Mutair on 19th December, as already related. The dropping of warning bombs on Shammar produced an unexpected result. Instead of retiring seventy miles south of the border, they moved into Iraq and asked for asylum.

As a result of this unforeseen development, the attempt to compel Nejed tribes to move back seventy miles from the frontier was abandoned. The R.A.F., however, continued to reconnoitre as far south as Al Hafar and Lina. On 17th February, permission was granted for the R.A.F. to operate in Kuwait territory, and one flight of aircraft and one section of armoured cars were based on Kuwait town. H.M.S. *Emerald* arrived in the bay of Kuwait.

In spite, however, of all these operations, the Duweesh, on 19th February, raided the Iraq tribes at Jarishan, as already mentioned. With aircraft scouring the desert for one hundred and seventy miles to the south of Shaiba, he had reached a point only fifty miles from that place. With remarkable daring, he had crossed a zone one hundred and twenty miles wide, which the R.A.F. was supposed to be covering with continuous reconnaissances. Had he been a little more reckless, he might have reached Shaiba itself.

Air headquarters had evidently over-estimated the ability of aircraft to locate raiders on the ground, even if vast areas of the desert were cleared of camps, thereby condemning our own tribes to starvation. It is only fair to admit that not only was the desert a vast area, but that January and February, 1928, were remarkable for bad weather, especially gales of wind and violent storms, and that the aircraft of the nineteen-twenties had none of the navigational aids available today.

After the Jarishan raid, it was considered that the passive defensive in the desert was ineffective, and it was decided to show Mutair that the R.A.F. could also take the offensive. Orders were issued for a bombing raid on the nearest Mutair settlement at Lusafa.[1] The distance from Shaiba to Lusafa and back was four hundred miles, which was beyond the radius of the aircraft of those days. As a result, a section of armoured cars was sent across the frontier

[1] For Lusafa see map on page 53.

with a convoy of petrol, as far as Al Hafar. On the afternoon of 23rd February, twelve ninaks and three Vickers Victorias landed at Al Hafar, refuelled and spent the night with the armoured cars. This operation was not without risk, for both aircraft and armoured cars were extremely vulnerable in the dark. At dawn on 24th February, the aircraft took off and bombed Lusafa, and a large Mutair bedouin camp twenty miles to the north of it. The pilots reported Lusafa to consist of three wells, one mud fort, about a dozen mud houses and one large tent.

Meanwhile, the plunder and glory won by Mutair and the passivity of Ibn Saud in face of their disregard of his orders, had inspired other Nejed tribes to rebel. Towards the end of February, Sultan Ibn Humaid of Ateiba was reported to have unfurled his war-banners and declared his intention of marching against Iraq. At the same time, he was alleged to have called on all the tribes of Nejed to join in a jehad, or holy war, against the infidels of Iraq.

The rumour of a holy war spread profound alarm in Iraq. All the tribes were even more rigidly swept back behind the line Shebicha-Sulman-Busaiya-Jarishan, where they cowered in terror and their animals died for lack of grazing. Meanwhile, owing to the accidents of rainfall and grazing, the Amarat, the Iraqi division of the great Aneza tribe, had moved south-eastwards, crossing the Wadi al Khirr towards Shebicha, and thereby entering the zone of possible Ikhwan attack. As a result, two companies of the Iraq army occupied Shebicha on 25th March. On the same day a section of R.A.F. armoured cars established itself at Lusuf.[1]

Thus the winter of 1927-8 was as disastrous for the Iraq tribes as had been that of 1924-5. Indeed Iraq and Britain had come perilously close to war with the Ikhwan, if not with Ibn Saud. From the point of view of defence, everything had to be built up afresh from nothing. It was all the tragedy and muddle of 1924 again. If any framework of defence had been maintained after the signing of the Bahra Agreement, the second catastrophe need never have occurred. "Show force and you will never have to use it," is alleged to have been a favourite adage of Marshal Lyautey in Morocco. If the Ikhwan had been able to see that Iraq was ready to defend herself, they might never have rebelled.

While, however, the situation in the Southern Desert seemed the same as it had been three years before, Nejed had entirely changed since the conquest of the Hejaz. During the raids from 1921 to 1925, Ibn Saud had been completely in control of the Ikhwan and himself provided the inspiration for their inroads. Moreover he had had some excuse for the raids of 1924 and 1925. Iraq had, as already explained, given asylum to the refugees and had

[1] For Lusuf, see map on page 141.

not prevented them, nor the Shammar refugees, from stealing camels from Nejed, if indeed she had not encouraged them to do so.

When, however, Ikhwan attacks were renewed in 1927, no such pretexts existed. The Iraq Government had removed the refugees and had prevented Shammar from raiding. It had still not obtained complete control of its nomads, but at any rate no raids had taken place into Nejed. Indeed the erection of the police post at Busaiya, which served as a pretext for the renewal of Ikhwan raids, was intended more to prevent raids by Iraq tribes into Nejed and Kuwait, than to protect Iraq's nomads from Ikhwan attacks. Ibn Saud's demands that the Iraq Government prevent its tribes from stealing, while at the same time objecting to police posts in the desert, were somewhat illogical.

The real change in the situation, however, was that in 1927 Ibn Saud was no longer in complete control. The Ikhwan, as a result of their victories in the Hejaz, were intoxicated with their own strength, and claimed that it was their fighting power which had made Ibn Saud great. They were perfectly aware that they were the backbone of his army and that he possessed no regular forces with which to discipline them. Their real intention after the Hejaz campaign was to overthrow Ibn Saud and to divide the spoils between them. They sought only an excuse to rise in rebellion.

Wahhabi religious feeling was too strong in Nejed to permit the Ikhwan to revolt and thereby divide the "true Muslims" in civil war, merely to enable the Duweesh and Ibn Humaid to seize power. In such a struggle, the oasis dwellers and the other tribes would have rallied to Ibn Saud. By challenging the king on the question of war with Iraq, however, the Ikhwan were able to claim religion on their side. The Iraqis were not Wahhabis and were therefore renegade Muslims, against whom holy war was a duty. It was Ibn Saud who was guilty of religious laxity in being unwilling to engage in hostilities against the enemies of God. Wahhabi public opinion was divided on this point. At least the Nejdis were not prepared to use force to prevent the Ikhwan raiding Iraq.

The king was also in a dilemma in his foreign relations. He was unwilling to confess to other governments that he was no longer in control of his own subjects. Yet to claim that he was still in perfect control would expose him to protests and reproaches, if the Ikhwan raided contrary to his wishes. Busaiya provided him with a useful pretext. He proclaimed loudly that all had been well until the Iraq Government had been guilty of the aggressive action of building a police post in the desert, contrary to the Uqair Protocol. In view of this outrageous breach of faith, he stated that he could not be responsible for any counter-action taken by his subjects.

The contest which followed was in reality a three-cornered one.

The Ikhwan were indirectly rebelling against Ibn Saud. Both claimed Iraq to be the villains of the plot, because both were anxious to win the support of public opinion in Nejed. The Iraq Government protested that it could not control its nomads, as Ibn Saud demanded that it should, if he simultaneously objected to the Iraq police being used in the desert. The net result of these complicated political issues was that, once again, the Iraq shepherd tribes were massacred.

*   *   *   *   *

While these developments were in progress, I was still far away in Diwaniya, where I had been engrossed in the assessment of the taxes on the rice crop. One day, without warning, I received a telegram, informing me that I had been transferred to the Southern Desert, and was to proceed immediately. I left Diwaniya on 2nd March, 1927, to assume my new duties.

Active operations were in full swing. The R.A.F. had established a forward headquarters at Ur, with advanced detachments of armoured cars at Busaiya and Sulman, each with an R.A.F. Special Service Intelligence Officer. Many air reconnaissances were being flown all over the desert. The formation of two small forces of camel police had also been sanctioned, one for the Diwaniya and one for the Muntifiq district. The two forces, however, were based respectively at Ruhba, twenty miles south of Najf, and at Tal al Laham, on the edge of the cultivated area and completely out of touch with the desert. Of these two little forces, twenty men of the Muntifiq and thirty of the Diwaniya group were placed under me for duty. For training and discipline, however, these men were still under their respective commandants of police, a hundred miles away. I could thus order a man to perform a duty, but if he failed to comply, I had no alternative but to write a complaint against him by post to his commandant. My own appointment was that of Administrative Inspector, Southern Desert, but as there was no administration, the title did not enlighten me as to my duties.

When I reached the desert on 2nd March, 1927, Feisal al Duweesh and Mutair were back in their camps and settlements after their raids. The leaders of the Ikhwan revolt against Ibn Saud's authority were the Duweesh and Sultan Ibn Humaid[2] of the Ateiba tribe. Of these, Sultan was perhaps the more powerful, but Feisal was in the fortunate position of living near the frontier of Iraq and thus of being well placed for raiding. Ibn Humaid's country, however, was west of Riyadh, and was consequently separated from the Iraq frontier and from his Mutair allies by the provinces of the Aridh, the Sudair and the Qaseem. If therefore he were to set out for a raid on Iraq

[1] Sometimes called also Sultan Ibn Bijad.

contrary to Ibn Saud's orders, he would leave his home and his herds at the mercy of the king.[1] These circumstances had enabled Mutair to raid with impunity even against Ibn Saud's orders and to win both loot and fame, while Ateiba had achieved nothing. Whether for this reason or because he was by nature more head-strong, Sultan Ibn Humaid had now become more aggressive than the Duweesh, who appeared to hesitate to rebel openly.

*   *   *   *   *

The first problem confronting me on my return to the desert was that of intelligence. In winter Ikhwan raiding parties were several thousand strong. The collection of such a force from scattered tribal camps required time and could not be concealed. Travellers and merchants brought down reports of this mobilization to Sulman, Busaiya, Basra and Kuwait. In the past, as soon as this information was received, the R.A.F. began intensive patrolling and the tribes fled in panic. When nothing happened for ten days or a fortnight, precautions tended to be relaxed, reconnaissances were reduced and the tribes moved out once more in search of grazing. Then one evening a party of exhausted women and children drifted down to the Euphrates, reporting that, five days before, the men of their tribe had been exterminated in an Ikhwan attack at some point eighty or a hundred miles away.

The reason for this procedure was that, during the early stages of the concentration, travellers continued to arrive from Nejed. But once the Ikhwan started on a raid, they were liable to kill every man they met, whether friend or foe. As soon, therefore, as the raid was nearly ready to start, travellers and merchants ceased to move. As a result, no further reports were received for ten or twelve days. This in the past had been interpreted to mean that the first reports had been untrue. In fact it meant the reverse — that the raiders were coming. It seemed obvious to me that it was for this reason that our intelligence failed to locate approaching raiders. Actual scouts, reconnaissance parties, air patrols or other direct visual means were needed. Hitherto the R.A.F. had relied solely on air patrols to locate advancing raiders, a method which had never yet succeeded.

My plan was to organize the Iraq tribes to defend themselves, using the R.A.F. as a supporting arm rather than as the sole defensive weapon. The air staff conception, on the contrary, was exactly the opposite to mine. They regarded the Iraq tribes as a useless crowd of civilians who were apt to obstruct operations. Their first demand was for all the tribes to be swept out of the desert in order to give aircraft a clear field for their operations. The result had been to destroy the tribal herds for lack of grazing. Moreover, the morale

---

[1] See tribal map on page 61.

of the tribes had been undermined by their being always ordered to run away. Yet in the days of Sadoon, these same tribes had defeated Ibn Saud himself at Gift Hollow, as has been already related.

As soon as I could visit the tribes, I arranged for them all to send groups of scouts on horses to a distance of twenty or thirty miles in front of their camps. The Iraqi ministry of the interior willingly allotted me funds to pay these scouts. It was obvious, however, that mechanized patrols would be far more valuable. The ministry was again co-operative, and sent an official into the Baghdad bazaar where, in one morning, he bought, cash down, three Chevrolet one-ton trucks, three Chevrolet vans, one Ford one-ton truck and one Ford vanette. Next day the ministry engaged eight civilian drivers, in whose charge the new vehicles were sent to me in the desert. This really was prompt action. Unfortunately the eight civilian drivers, when told that they were to scout for advancing raiders, resigned as one man and returned to Baghdad. Gradually, one by one, more courageous drivers were discovered. I dismounted my camel police to supply crews for the motor patrols and my plan for ground reconnaissance went, rather spasmodically, into action.

The next task to be undertaken was to bring our own tribes under control and to marshal them where we wanted them, with due regard to their grazing requirements. The R.A.F. had hitherto reconnoitred the vast desert in hour after hour of weary flying, but without any very clear-cut method. The principle which I wished to submit to the air staff was that the Iraq tribes were the objective of the raiders. If therefore we always knew where our tribes were, all the aircraft had to do was to visit our most advanced camps, make sure that they were safe and then examine the ground in front of them. It was waste of time to reconnoitre vast areas of desert where no Iraq tribes were camped, because raiders would obviously not go there.

The work of the R.A.F. would be further reduced if we could group our tribes in certain areas agreed upon. Yet another refinement would be to select a landing strip by the most advanced camps and for air patrols to land there, exchange information and then examine the ground in front of the camps from the air. Such a system, combined with ground screens of car patrols and horsed scouts, would greatly reduce the risk of surprise at a cost of one-third of the flying which the R.A.F. had hitherto done in vain.

These proposals seem simple enough in print, but they were not easy to expound to air headquarters two hundred and fifty miles away over a wireless set which sometimes functioned and at other times did not. It was still less easy to explain them to thousands of suspicious Arabs of many different tribes, spread over an area nearly as large as England.

*   *   *   *   *

Meanwhile Sultan Ibn Humaid of Ateiba had moved out with some twelve war banners, breathing threatenings and slaughter against the enemies of God. Feisal al Duweesh, more cautious and already satiated with loot, excused himself on the grounds of the poor condition of his horses and camels after his December and February raids. Muhsin al Firrem of Harab, a third great Ikhwan tribal chief, whose raid had camped at Sulman in 1924,[1] had declared his loyalty to the king.

Thus Nejed was divided, but neither side had burnt its boats. Emissaries and mediators continued to come and go between Ibn Saud and the rebels. Ibn Humaid was alleged to have invited the king to send one of his sons to lead an Ikhwan force in an attack on Iraq but Ibn Saud was believed to have rejected the suggestion, although he was rumoured to have sent many gifts to Ibn Humaid, including ten thousand Saudi dollars, thirty boxes of ammunition and two hundred camel-loads of rice and dates, accompanied by cordial messages. A Shammar bedouin, however, arriving from Nejed, reported that all Shammar camps beyond the border had moved hastily south-west, in order to be out of the route of an Ikhwan force twelve thousand strong under Ibn Humaid, which was moving up to Jumaima. On 11th March, 1928, a circumstantial report was received from a man of the Dhafeer to the effect that a large force was approaching Rukhaimiya from the south.

On 20th March, it was rumoured that Ibn Musaad, the governor of Hail, had asked Ibn Saud's permission to call out Harab and Shammar, who were still loyal to Ibn Saud, to attack the Duweesh. The king was stated to have refused, on the grounds that he did not want civil war. The next rumour which gained currency, however, was to the effect that Ibn Saud had given permission to Ibn Humaid to raid Iraq if he so wished. The Duweesh was said to have warned Ibn Humaid that he had only received this permission because Ibn Saud hoped that the Iraq Government forces would destroy the raiders and thereby rid him of rebellion.

Throughout March the tension continued. Report followed report, rumour succeeded rumour day after day. Any morning an exhausted fugitive or a panic-stricken horseman might come in to say that Ibn Humaid's twelve war banners had appeared here or there and exterminated several hundred Iraqi families. The strain of anxiety was severe. Amid all these alarms, we toiled day and night to improve our scout screens and to marshal our own tribes where we knew their location and could visit them and check up on their safety. Every day the possibility that the enemy might come the next dawn lent a feverish urgency to our preparations.

On 31st March a report was received to the effect that a great

[1] See page 136.

Ikhwan force with fifteen war banners would water at Lina on 1st
April and would attack our post at Sulman. But meanwhile the
weather in Iraq was already growing hot and the rainwater pools
in the desert were drying up. By the first week in April, any sheep
looted in the Southern Desert would probably have died of thirst
before reaching Nejed. Moreover, the difficulty of watering so large
a raiding force as that which Ibn Humaid was leading, would present
him with an increasing problem. Already Umm al Rudhumma, Lina
and Sulman were probably the only wells on his route large enough.
If he advanced on Sulman and failed to capture it, so that he was
unable to water at the wells, he would have a costly and thirsty
retreat back to Lina.

On 5th April, 1928, a circumstantial report from a traveller, who
reached Kuwait from Nejed, stated that Ibn Humaid had left Jarab
on 24th March with twelve banners to attack Sulman, but had been
overtaken by messengers from Ibn Saud accompanied by Wahhabi
religious leaders and by the son of Feisal al Duweesh. The upshot of
the resulting discussions was not known.

On 7th April, 1928, I signalled an appreciation to the ministry
of the interior and to air headquarters in the following terms:

"If nothing happens in the next ten days further large scale
raids are unlikely. The latter are always accompanied by large
numbers of horses, the watering of which becomes increasingly
difficult as summer approaches. From the middle of April onwards,
the only threat will be from parties of from one to five hundred,
all camelmen, which would raid isolated camps as has been done
in the past.

"I suggest that the present defensive arrangements be maintained for a further ten days. After that if nothing has happened,
I will come to Baghdad to confer on the subject of reduced
defensive measures for the summer."

Thus ended the grazing season of November, 1927, to April, 1928.
It had begun disastrously, with the killing of the workmen at Busaiya,
and a succession of the usual massacres of shepherds. The authorities
had been taken completely unawares. These early catastrophes,
however, sufficed to spur the government to action and by the
middle of April the main outlines of a regular defensive system were
appearing. Moreover, this new technique had, to my mind, the
immense advantage that it gave to the Iraq tribes an active part in
their own defence.

By far the most important success achieved, however, was that
Ibn Humaid did not come. It was true that Ibn Saud did not approve of the raids on Iraq but above all things he wished to avoid a
civil war. If Ibn Humaid had attacked and massacred the Iraq

shepherds and returned laden with spoils, it was unlikely that Ibn Saud would have been in a position to use force against him.

There could be little doubt that Ibn Humaid left his home with the intention of raiding but that the information which he received from Iraq made him hesitate. The tribes were grouped, all approaches were picketed, aircraft were overhead and armoured cars at Sulman and Busaiya. The prospect which confronted him was not as tempting as he had imagined. These circumstances probably accounted for the slowness of his approach. When he was overtaken by messengers from Ibn Saud, the pretext which they provided enabled him to turn back with honour, perhaps also with relief.

On 12th April, I received an urgent signal to report to Baghdad immediately. On my arrival there, I was informed that an Anglo-Iraqi deputation was to go to Jidda forthwith to confer with Ibn Saud. The party was to be led by Sir Gilbert Clayton, who two years before had negotiated the Bahra Agreement. Mr. (later Sir Kinahan) Cornwallis, adviser to the Iraqi ministry of the interior, was to be a member of the delegation and I was to accompany them as desert expert.

XII

The Conference at Jidda

Therefore take heed . . .
How you awake the sleeping sword of war:
We charge you, in the Name of God, take heed:
For never two such kingdoms did contend
Without much fall of blood; whose guiltless drops
Are every one a woe, a sore complaint
'Gainst him whose wrongs give edge unto the swords
That make such waste in brief mortality.

SHAKESPEARE, *King Henry V*

Resolved to die in the last dyke of prevarication.   BURKE

That frankness and boldness of language by which the bedouins have
always been distinguished, widely differing from the ceremonious and
complimentary style usual among other eastern nations in similar
cases.   BURCKHARDT, *History of the Wahabys*

I have found out the art of deceiving diplomats: I speak the truth,
and I am certain they will not believe me.   CAVOUR

No peace was ever won from fate by subterfuge or argument.

RUSKIN

XII

THE CONFERENCE AT JIDDA[1]

CORNWALLIS and I left Baghdad by air on 21st April, 1928, reaching Cairo the same day. Sir Gilbert Clayton arrived on 24th April, accompanied by Guy Moore who had been with us at Samawa in 1925. He had since been posted to England but had come with Clayton as his Arab expert. On 26th April, we travelled to Port Said to embark on the s.s. *Chindwin* for Port Sudan, where we transferred to the sloop H.M.S. *Dahlia* and made a dignified arrival at Jidda on 2nd May, 1928, under the protection of the Royal Navy. Ibn Saud, we were told, had not yet arrived. We were accommodated at Kandara, a villa which was then half a mile outside Jidda and had once been the property of a rich Arab merchant, engaged in business with Malaya and Singapore. I flattered myself, perhaps unduly, on my familiarity with bedouin life. As guests of Ibn Saud, the king of the bedouins, I had anticipated lordly hospitality, with camels and sheep roasted whole and served on immense dishes piled with rice. Few pictures could have been more inaccurate. Kandara was staffed by Berberine waiters from Egypt and, at the expense of the king of the Wahhabis, we were served with free whisky and cigarettes. I was no less surprised when we made the acquaintance of the Nejdi representatives. Instead of being greeted by Saudi princes or notables from leading Nejdi families, we were introduced to the following:

Dr. Abdulla al Damlooji, an Iraqi.
Shaikh Fuad Hamza, a Palestinian of Druze extraction, once a journalist and then a schoolmaster under the Palestine Mandatory government.
Shaikh Hafidh Wahba, an Egyptian lawyer and journalist.
Shaikh Yusuf al Yaseen, a Syrian by origin, who had also commenced his career as a schoolmaster in Palestine.

The atmosphere of Jidda was cosmopolitan, with a flavour of Egypt, and there was a considerable colony of Europeans. There was certainly nothing to suggest Nejed or bedouins.

On 7th May, Ibn Saud arrived at 9 a.m. and received the members of our delegation at 10 a.m. Suddenly Nejed had come. The staircases and passages of the house where he was staying were full of bedouins and negro slaves. A ragged and barefooted bedouin

[1] Jidda is the port of Mecca, see map on page 49.

brought in the coffee, when we were seated. Ibn Saud seemed to be younger than I had anticipated. He wore spectacles at all times. He was extremely smiling and pleasant when talking to Sir Gilbert.

In the evening there was a state dinner at the Jidda municipality, with two hundred guests including many Europeans, though of course without women. Before the meal was served, I went out to look at the seating in order to identify my place. Dinner was laid at long tables on the roof beneath the bright Arabian stars, after the damp and enervating Red Sea heat of Jidda's long day. As I was searching for the card bearing my name, the minister of a certain small country appeared silently and began to examine the seating arrangements at the top table. Finding himself nine places away from the king, he surreptitiously changed his card for that of the minister of another country, who was next but one to Ibn Saud. But at the critical moment an official appeared, the manoeuvre was observed, an undignified altercation ensued and our conspirator was obliged with shame to take the lower seat.

It was curious to see the old king walking barefoot, amid so many diplomats in dinner jackets and patent leather shoes—a contrast which seemed to epitomize the divergence between two such vastly different cultures. One could not but admire the fact that no Nejdis tried to imitate European dress.

On 8th May, Sir Gilbert Clayton was given a private audience with the king, at which the latter explained his viewpoint. Sir Gilbert then put the Iraqi case. Mr. George Antonius, a Christian of Jerusalem who had come with Clayton, acted as interpreter. On 9th May, there was a meeting between Ibn Saud and his four advisers and our full delegation. Before the discussion of business, the king gave us a dissertation on true religion and the sin of *shirek*, or the association of other things with God. He spoke impressively and there could be no doubt that he was perfectly familiar with the tribal and raiding situation. The next day, Sir Gilbert was accorded another private audience with Ibn Saud, at which he told the king that Iraq could not abandon her posts in the desert.

For several days there were no more meetings with the king, but we daily held wearisome hair-splitting discussions with the advisers— Dr. Damlooji, and Shaikhs Fuad Hamza, Hafidh Wahba and Yusuf Yaseen.

I have already frequently emphasized the fact that the politics of Arabian princes under the old dispensation consisted largely of attempts to seduce each other's tribes. They thought in terms of tribes and not of territory, a fact never properly appreciated by European governments or even by the government of Iraq.

In the first Wahhabi period of domination from 1796 to 1815, they had taxed nomadic tribes on the banks of the Euphrates and within sight of the city of Aleppo. They had attacked and looted cities and villages in Syria and Iraq, but they had never claimed to annex any part of the territory of those countries. The bedouin community, in the 1920's as much as in 1800, was a world of its own. The ruler of Nejed regarded himself as the monarch of all bedouins, wherever they might be. This idea of loyalties based on communities, not on territory, had always been familiar to the Middle East. Thus, before the Crimean war, the Czar of Russia had claimed to be the protector of the Orthodox Christians in the Turkish Empire, while Napoleon the Third wished to be recognized as the patron of the Ottoman Catholics. Ibn Saud, aspired, in a not altogether dissimilar manner, to be the patriarchal chief of all bedouins everywhere, regardless of frontiers. Members of the Greek Orthodox or Roman Catholic communities in the Turkish Empire were indisputably Ottoman subjects and yet they were also members of religious communities extending far beyond the frontiers of Ottoman jurisdiction. The Turks of the imperial régime were familiar with such situations. Their broad-minded toleration showed little narrow jealousy of Christians or Jews, and in fact allowed many such communities in their midst to be governed by their own laws and customs. On a somewhat similar principle, the bedouins of Iraq, Syria or Jordan might be subjects of those countries, owing to their geographic location throughout most of the year, yet owe a simultaneous, although ill-defined, allegiance to Ibn Saud, the bedouin king, just as Ottoman Catholics did to the Pope. In the 1920's, Ibn Saud had scarcely emerged from the Turkish era, with which he had long been familiar. Perhaps some such loose relationship was still vaguely present to his mind. Such happy-go-lucky illogical compromises, perhaps unavoidable in the old fashioned multi-national empires of the nineteenth century—Ottoman, Austro-Hungarian or British—were utterly foreign to the tight, jealous little nationalisms of today, and Iraq, Syria and Trans-Jordan were growing up into states of this new type. The old empires receive short shrift from the angry young men, who today form the bulk of the new politicians, fanatically dedicated, each to the independence of his own particular backyard. But the historians of some future age, when this tyranny will be overpast, may perhaps at least accord to the old-fashioned imperial dominions, the credit for the broadness of their tolerance.

Perhaps the conflict between Iraq and Ibn Saud may be illustrated in another and quite a different manner. Every study of the desert brings us back to the simile of the sea. The recent international differences over the extent of territorial waters gives us an alternative form of comparison. The desert had always been as free as the Atlantic Ocean, Iraq and Syria normally limiting their administration to the edge of the cultivation. The ruler of Nejed, however, (be he Ibn Saud or Ibn Rasheed) being the only great "sea power", controlled all deserts, much as the British fleet once dominated the Atlantic, unopposed by such riparian states as Portugal, Spain, Belgium, or Holland.

In 1922, however, Ibn Saud had signed the Treaty of Muhammarah, recognizing international boundaries in the desert. It would have been logical for him to reject the whole principle of dividing up the high desert, just as the north Atlantic states would object to the annexation of half the Atlantic Ocean by the U.S.A.

It is only possible to conjecture why he agreed. His experience had hitherto been limited to dealings with the Ottoman Empire in the desert. The Turks had attached importance to forms, which had no direct application in fact. They delighted in professions of loyalty from Arabian princes, upon whom they thereupon conferred Turkish ranks and appointments, pretending that they were officials and that they administered Turkish provinces. Thus Ibn Saud was appointed quaimaqam or governor of the Turkish province of Nejed, although he was in reality entirely independent. Perhaps he thought that, in the same way, British vanity was flattered by this frontier-drawing, but that in reality no action would result. Moreover, in the past, the ruler of Nejed had automatically dominated all deserts because he alone possessed forces mounted on camels, which could operate there. In 1922 it was not yet obvious that aircraft and motor transport could operate in desert and consequently that the camel had lost its monopoly of mobility. Thus he believed that he in practice would dominate all bedouins, whether he signed the treaty or not.

Although Ibn Saud signed the Muhammarah Treaty of 1922, he continued to act as if nothing had changed. The twentieth-century Wahhabi revival modelled itself consciously on that of a hundred and twenty years before. Confronted only by an Ottoman Empire in chaos, Saud the Wahhabi had made good his claim to be ruler of all the nomads of Arabia, regardless of frontiers. In the 1920's, Abdul Aziz Ibn Saud felt himself to be the heir to the same position. Several times in Jidda we were asked: "Why do you people in Iraq want to control bedouin tribes? Town Arabs do not understand anything about them. Ibn Saud is the king of all nomads."

There was much truth in this contention. The Iraqi mishandling of the Dhafeer, resulting in the transfer of the allegiance of the Suwait to Ibn Saud, was a case in point. All bedouins felt more at home in Ibn Saud's barefooted court than in the offices of Syrian or Iraqi officials. At Jidda a further piquancy was added to Ibn Saud's claim to be the natural ruler of all bedouins, when we discovered that the four Nejdi representatives were not Nejdis and knew little or nothing about the nomads. On more than one occasion, I found myself explaining to them the bedouin way of life. For Nejed was represented by those northern town Arabs whom the Nejdis themselves alleged to understand nothing about nomads.

Ibn Saud's desire to be the ruler of all bedouins provided the key to our problem. The Arabian tribes had always been turbulent and the Ikhwan rebellion with which he was confronted was in the true Arabian tradition. If all the deserts of Arabia accessible to the nomads had been under Ibn Saud's domination, his subjects might have hesitated to rebel, but the fact that other Arab governments also controlled vast areas of desert grazing country might make it possible for unsuccessful rebels to move to Kuwait, Iraq, Syria or Trans-Jordan with impunity—countries which claimed rigid land frontiers which the king's punitive forces were forbidden to cross. The fact that the Ikhwan refugees, who had raided with Yusuf al Sadoon, had actually been given asylum in Iraq touched Ibn Saud on a very tender spot. Although the Iraq Government had taken action against the Ikhwan refugees three years earlier, he continually harped on the subject. Indeed to some extent, it provided him with an excuse for his impotence in face of the Ikhwan rebellion. He was perfectly prepared, he claimed, to punish Feisal al Duweesh, but who, in such an event, was to guarantee that Iraq would not give him asylum also? The excuse was too naïve, for, as we have seen, the king was in reality doubtful of his power to suppress the Ikhwan and hence was desperately anxious to avoid civil war; but it provided his representatives with a good talking point.

The official Nejdi solution to these problems was the conclusion, of an extradition treaty between Iraq and Nejed. It was perhaps to be suspected that the four advisers had suggested this step, which seemed to be in line with the practice of modern states, but quite contrary to old Arab tradition. When such a treaty was concluded, the king said, he would then punish the Ikhwan.

We were instructed to form a sub-committee to draft an extradition treaty. It consisted of Dr. Damlooji, Fuad Hamza and Yusuf Yaseen for Nejed, and Cornwallis, Guy Moore and myself for Iraq. As soon as we began work, we ran into trouble. The Iraq Government, intent on being civilized and democratic, demanded the insertion in the treaty of a clause excluding political offenders. But Ibn Saud was interested only in political offenders, that is, in persons in rebellion against his authority. He was not interested in the extradition of thieves or forgers.

Although the Iraq Government insisted on the political offenders clause in the treaty, it offered to give a separate pledge not to afford asylum to Feisal al Duweesh, should he be punished by the king. This compromise was rejected. We spent endless futile days arguing in our sub-committee over political offenders. Hafidh Wahba, perhaps the most reasonable of the advisers, put his finger on the true seat of most of our difficulties, when he remarked that the real trouble was that the two kings did not trust one another.

He was right. The sherifs had ruled the Hejaz for centuries. Only three years before, Ibn Saud had driven King Husain, the father of King Feisal of Iraq, from the throne of that country. How indeed could we expect King Abdul Aziz and King Feisal to trust one another? The Arab nationalist of today will cry out in indignation at the idea that, in 1928, Iraq was represented by three British officers in negotiations with a "sister" Arab state. Yet, strange as it may seem, the method adopted was the only course possible. So deep in those days was the hatred and mistrust between the two dynasties that no negotiations would have been conceivable without British intervention.

In the course of the discussions in our sub-committee, the Nejdis claimed the Dhafeer to be their subjects, although the tribe had been specifically mentioned by name in the Muhammarah Treaty as being subject to Iraq.

Under the date of 17th May, 1928, I made the following entry in my diary:

"I have rarely been so miserable as in the last two days. Yesterday we again met Ibn Saud. His manner was much changed since our first meetings, and he seemed depressed and bitter. To Clayton he said—'When the English first came to Iraq, I congratulated my people. They were surprised and asked me why. I had always abused the Turks as unbelievers, they said, yet here were people who were even worse, because they were not Muslims at all. I told them that the English were honest, and were my friends. Now I must admit that we have despaired of the English and of their hair-splitting. At Uqair I understood from Cokus[1] that the protocol meant no forts in the desert. Now you say that the wording of the agreement does not mean that. How do I know? I am a bedouin and that was what Cokus told me and I trusted him.'

"It was pathetic to hear such a speech, so obviously sincere, and Clayton's vague reply to the effect that he was sure that friendship would always continue between His Majesty and Britain. 'Though the sun,' he declaimed poetically, 'may one day be obscured by clouds, we know that before long it will shine forth once more.' "

Ibn Saud was intensely suspicious of King Feisal and imagined that the British were intriguing with the sherifs against him. The same evening, at an interview with Clayton, he burst out: "My people may be angry and suspicious of the desert posts in Iraq. You

[1] Sir Percy Cox,

may say that they are fanatical, but I tell you that I am sixty thousand times more fanatical than they."

One of our errors, it seemed to me, was the idea that all "the East" was the same, or even, for that matter, all "Arabs". Bedouins, using the phrase as Ibn Saud used it when he called himself a bedouin, were frank and outspoken, as bluff and hale as the traditional sailor. Perhaps indeed both bedouins and sailors were formed in the same school—the navigation of vast distances across which they battled with the elements. One expects an admiral to be bluff and straightforward, not tortuous or intriguing. Ibn Saud was admiral of the desert seas. His four advisers were of a directly opposite character—subtle and legalistic intellectuals. The king had been told that he had been tricked by the English at Muhammarah and Uqair, and hence that he obviously was not clever enough to deal with them. It was his advisers who reported all our discussions to Ibn Saud, probably indicating to him all the subtle subterfuges which we were attempting to employ and how we had been foiled by their skill. Thus whenever the king was present, he burst forth in tirades against our sophistry. We believed that it was his advisers who were splitting hairs.

I was familiar with the bedouin faculty for openly putting all the cards on the table, and in the king's speeches I recognized the authentic bedouin frankness which I knew so well. Clayton could not be expected to appreciate these differences, and seemed to believe that oriental diplomacy required flowery compliments and a circuitous and courtly approach. Such methods were indeed not entirely out of place with the Syrians and the Egyptians, though they would perhaps have been even more suitable for the Shah of Persia a hundred years earlier.

It is perhaps unjust to blame Clayton for his failure to appreciate the frankness and honesty of bedouin speech and the complete absence of ceremony practised in Nejed. The quotation from Burckhardt at the head of this chapter refers to the negotiations between Tusun Pasha and Abdulla Ibn Saud in 1815. The explorer, who was himself in the Hejaz at the time, explains that the Egyptians employed complimentary phrases, while Abdulla Ibn Saud spoke with guileless frankness. Where the rulers of Egypt misunderstood their man, it would be captious to expect Sir Gilbert to do better.

I was, however, personally entirely convinced that the only way out of our deadlock was for Clayton to tackle Ibn Saud man to man with perfect frankness in a tête-à-tête, though admittedly the necessity of using an interpreter was a serious handicap. The king's advisers were probably strongly opposed to a method of negotiation which would have made their services redundant. Day after day, we fenced with words with the king's subtle representatives, while in the background the old king, like ourselves, raged with impatience at what he considered to be legalistic arguments. Clayton, who was one of the most charming chiefs under whom I have ever worked, patiently allowed me to expose my views to him, but though he listened with unruffled kindness, he did not adopt my solution. It seemed to me that he should have tackled the king directly and given him the main features of the situation something as follows:

"It may be that the king thought King Feisal to be his enemy but he was a constitutional monarch. It was quite impossible for him to drag Iraq into war with Nejed, even had he so desired. On the other hand, Iraq tribes and shepherds had always grazed in the desert. Now these tribes paid taxes to the Iraq Government, which was in return bound to protect them. The trouble with the Ikhwan was that they massacred. It was this indiscriminate killing, rather than the looting of flocks, which had compelled both the British and Iraq Governments to intervene.

"Ibn Saud had frequently complained against Iraq for not preventing the refugee Ikhwan and Shammar from raiding. His charges in this respect had been true, but the reason for the failure of the Iraq Government to live up to its obligations had been that it had no adequate means of controlling its desert. Now it was determined to put an end to raiding once and for all, and posts were being erected for this purpose. It was not logical for Ibn Saud to blame Iraq for not controlling its bedouins, and then to object when it took measures to control them. Any suspicion that the posts were being built for aggressive purposes against Nejed was completely erroneous.

"Both the British and the Iraq Governments were aware that Mutair and Ateiba were giving trouble. We believed that their professed indignation against Iraq was little more than a pretext and that their real object was to overthrow the king himself. Both Britain and Iraq cordially supported Ibn Saud in this struggle. Nejed in anarchy would cause them far more trouble than Nejed ruled by the king. As a result, they were offering a definite guarantee that Iraq would not give asylum to the Duweesh or his allies, if Ibn Saud attempted to bring them to order. Both governments were most desirous that the king emerge victorious."

Such a statement would, I thought, impress Ibn Saud, especially if given to him in a private interview. It would probably not lead to an agreement, because a solution was in reality impossible, as long as the Ikhwan were out of control. But I thought that it would impress the king with its truth and sincerity and would convince him that we knew the real situation and that we were not merely indulging in sophistry.

I was intensely anxious to avoid war and under the effect of these sterile and frustrating negotiations, I made this entry in my diary:

"I am afraid that, if no settlement is reached before next autumn, we shall have a state of war rather than one of spasmodic raiding:

"A war would give rise to considerable bloodshed and expense and would result

(*a*) either in the British Government losing its nerve when serious fighting began and giving way, which would expose Iraq to unending incursions by the Ikhwan, until the nettle was finally grasped, or

(*b*) in the ultimate fall of Ibn Saud and the relapse of Nejed into chaos.

"If our mission leaves now for Baghdad and London, the impression of a rupture will be created. If one or two members of the mission were to remain, their presence might give the impression that conversations were continuing.

"The ultimate compromise might take the following course:

(1) An agreement that section 3 of the Uqair Protocol, prohibiting the erection of forts in the vicinity of the frontier meant a distance of so many miles (perhaps thirty).

(2) An exchange of notes in which Ibn Saud would express the hope that, although Busaiya was outside this distance, Iraq, as a proof of friendship and confidence, would not build there. To this Iraq would reply agreeing to abandon the post at Busaiya.

"In practice the Iraq Government would then re-occupy Abu Ghar. Sulman would, perhaps later on, become the headquarters for the Southern Desert control."

Thus, in order to avoid war, I was in favour of agreeing to Ibn Saud's demand to destroy Busaiya. By reverting to Abu Ghar, we lost twenty-five miles, but I was already thinking out a system of tactics by which mobile camps during the grazing season would be the nucleus of the defence. The desert posts in that case would be merely bases for stores and not tactical defensive positions. From my own point of view, the drawback to such a plan was that the armoured cars belonged to air headquarters, who, I feared, would never consider tribal grazing requirements in locating them. The Iraq Government, on the other hand, would not, or could not, give me enough forces under my command to enable me to organize mobile defensive camps without calling on the R.A.F.

My proposal to find a compromise by abandoning Busaiya was, however, rejected by both the British and the Iraq Governments, as constituting a weak surrender to the Ikhwan, after they had massacred the workmen there.

Ibn Saud's immediate object was, of course, to secure the abandonment of Busaiya, in order that he could return to Nejed with a
diplomatic triumph. He could then say to the rebels: "You tried to
get rid of this post by raiding, even though I advised against such a
course. As you saw, your raids did not produce that result. Now I
have talked to the English and the Iraqis and they have agreed to
demolish Busaiya."

I was anxious to allow the king this success, in order to enable him
to re-establish his control. It is, however, unlikely that my proposals
would have led to final peace, because the Ikhwan were really in
revolt against the king, whose authority they wished to usurp. Moreover I proposed to replace Busaiya by mobile camps and thereby
enable the Iraq Government to exercise control in its own deserts.
This was precisely the outcome which Ibn Saud wished to avoid. For
if the Iraq Government became an efficient power in its own deserts,
he would always be haunted by the fear that his disgruntled subjects
would be able to take refuge in the deserts of Iraq, secure from his
retribution. In one of his candid outbursts, Ibn Saud once said to us,
"I would sooner that the Iraq tribes raided Nejed a thousand times,
than that the Iraq Government build posts in the desert."

Immersed in these problems in 1928, we believed ourselves to be
endeavouring to settle disputes between Iraq and Nejed. Looking
back now, thirty years later, these battles assume a different complexion. The Wahhabi revival, with its fanaticism and its slaughter,
was endeavouring to put the clock back a hundred or a hundred and
fifty years. Already airlines and motor transport roads were crossing
the desert. Unknown to us, the era of oilfields and pipelines was only
a few years ahead. The desert would no longer remain the sole
preserve of the bedouin and his herds. It was not King Feisal or King
Abdul Aziz, it was neither the Ikhwan nor the British, who were
fomenting these conflicts. It was the twentieth century which was
making its entrée into ancient Arabia.

*   *   *   *   *

While the official negotiations thus hung fire, we saw another side
of King Abdul Aziz, which was thereafter more rarely shown to
Europeans. Four years later, I again visited Jidda as a member of a
diplomatic mission. The process of sophistication had made rapid
strides in the interval. A palace had been built and our mission was
accorded only one formal visit to the king, to which we were
escorted by A.D.Cs in European uniforms. In 1928, however, Ibn
Saud was still, to use his own words, a simple bedouin.

In Jidda, the mornings of our stay were devoted to futile argu-
mentation with the king's four advisers. After lunch came the siesta,
for the Red Sea coast is unpleasantly damp and hot, even in April.

But before sunset, in the grateful cool of the evening, Ibn Saud would often visit us in Kandara. His cortège was picturesque. The days of horses and camels had gone but those of armoured cars, machine guns and pseudo-European-uniformed soldiers had not come.

The royal procession consisted of several saloon cars, packed with negro slaves in scarlet and gold. The king travelled in a large limousine, with slaves standing on the running boards on each side, so that they completely blocked the windows. Handgrips had been fixed to the body of the car to enable them to hold on. As soon as the convey stopped before the front door of our villa, a horde of gorge-ously clad negroes carrying silver-mounted swords jumped out of the cars and raced round the house. Some entered by the front door and some by the back, others stationed themselves beneath the windows or scattered over the garden, while one or two apparently especially confidential retainers enquired where the king would sit and carried out a hasty examination of the room. Everything was done with considerable alacrity and efficiency. By the time that the old king had descended from the car and was slowly mounting the steps to our front door (for his eye-sight was very defective), the house had been completely ransacked.

Seated tailor-wise with his legs tucked up beneath him on the sofa in our small living-room, he talked freely and without reserve, passing lightly over religion, and lingering fondly over the beauty of women. The Saud family itself was originally of the Dhana Muslim division of Aneza, but the king did not defend the ladies of the tribe. "Aneza women are ugly," he told us one day, "but the women of Shammar are beautiful and they do not veil."

Clayton enquired why Shammar women did not veil.

"*Shammar ma andehum deen*," replied the king, but without any apparent trace of disapproval in his voice. "Shammar have no religion." The former subjects of Ibn Rasheed had not become enthusiastic Wahhabis.

On the whole, however, Ibn Saud talked mostly of the govern-ment of men. "Government by despotism or by force is not good," he stated on one occasion. "A despotic government may appear to hold its subjects in a band of iron, but, in a crisis or in war, if the iron were to snap, the whole structure falls to pieces. Government by consent is like a thread. A thread is sometimes stronger than iron."

The king expressed strong disapproval of Mussolini's power in Italy. "The rule of Mussolini is bad," he said. "It is a disgrace for a subject to dominate his king."

He derided the order issued by Mustafa Kemal (later Ataturk) that all Turks should wear European hats. "The Turks also have a despotism like the Italians," he declared. "They want to change their hats in order to be like Europeans. But it is best for all nations to adhere to their own religion and customs."

I heard the king on several occasions explain, with considerable candour, why he had been for fifteen years the ally of Britain. "I have nothing in common with the English," he said. "They are strangers to us and Christians. But I need the help of a Great Power and the British are better than the other Powers like France and Italy."

He praised the British, "because," he said, "you find them all over the world, voluntarily serving their king, whereby he may sit quietly at home. There is no compulsion in the English method. *Hadha tayyib*," he repeated twice, "that is good, that is good." Although he had never left Arabia, he showed not only a remarkable knowledge of world affairs, but an amazing power of grasping the essentials—surely the sign of a singularly powerful mind.

One evening a few days before we left Jidda, Guy Moore and I were given a private interview with King Abdul Aziz. Clayton was, I think, a little anxious about this meeting. I had explained all my fears and hopes to him, but he never reproved a rather conceited young man who thought that he knew better than his superiors. He was always kind, considerate and interested when I asked if I could expound my views, but he was not anxious that I should declaim them to Ibn Saud himself. As a result, he asked me to promise not to discuss anything connected with the negotiations in our interview with the king.

Unable therefore to speak of the frontier situation or of the object of our mission, we confined ourselves to bedouin topics—grazing, horses, camels and sheep. With the vanity of youth, I was not averse to showing Ibn Saud how familiar I was with the bedouin dialect and manner of life. Sweet tea was served in small glasses, followed by bitter black coffee. Six or seven small boys, of perhaps eight to ten years of age, were shown in to say goodnight to the old king. Some appeared to be sons or grandsons of his own, others were sons of the Rasheeds, who, since the conquest of Hail, had been living in gilded captivity in Ibn Saud's personal entourage. The king kissed the small boys with patriarchal benevolence, patting them kindly on the head.

There was something extraordinarily impressive about Abdul Aziz Ibn Saud. Physically he stood head and shoulders above the other Arabs, particularly the small and slight Nejdis. There was something paternal about his manner. He almost seemed to radiate benevolence. He practised, at this time at least, all the democratic and patriarchal manners of Arabian tradition and talked freely, as if on equal terms, with high and low alike—and he was a fluent and forceful speaker. He was careful to avoid the appearance of autocracy and at least to observe the form of consultation with notables and religious leaders. His methods would seem strange to those accustomed to European governmental machinery, for he had no civil service, no regular officials and no professional army. There was no system for the decentralization of authority and many points of small detail were referred to him, though we should consider them to be within the competence of junior officials. On the other hand, there was scarcely any official correspondence, with the result that subordinates were not obliged to spend hour after hour and day after day in offices. They could carry out their duties by being out and about among their people. Charlemagne or William the Conqueror probably ruled in a similar manner.

But even while one was under the influence of this immensely powerful and yet apparently benign personality, it was difficult entirely to forget that this man had reached his dominant position by ruthless methods. Certainly from the point of view of the Iraq tribes, it was fear of massacre which drove them to submit to Ibn Saud and to pay him tribute. Moreover the Ikhwan not only killed fighting men, but children and even babies in arms, provided they were males.

We so easily and so conveniently justify our own actions, or we forget the means which we employ and emphasize the worthiness of our ultimate aim. Ibn Saud, an entirely benign patriarch, breathing benevolence and the service of God, employed massacre to rise to power. Perhaps in the same manner, the United States Government, pointing out the elevation of its own ideals over those of other nations, was to drop the first atomic bomb on Hiroshima. I do not believe that either was guilty of hypocrisy. The human mind is a surprising mechanism.

XIII

Hors D'Oeuvre

This attitude of perpetual revolt against every power which seeks to control his freedom is the key to the series of aimless crimes and treacheries which make up the greater part of Arab history . . . This psychology must be borne in mind in the history of all dealings with Arabs. Conquest does not mean control. It is futile to expect that by bestowing on them the blessings of civilization they will be made loyal and obedient subjects.

DE LACY O'LEARY, Arabia before Muhammad

If the Arabian princes abuse their power, they are quickly punished by the desertion of their subjects, who had been accustomed to a mild and parental jurisdiction. Their spirit is free, their steps are unconfined, the desert is open, and the tribes and families are held together, by a mutual and voluntary compact.   GIBBON

They mostly have a democratic government and are much addicted to robbery.   TACITUS

CHAPTER XIII

HORS D'OEUVRE

W E arrived back in Baghdad at the end of May, 1928, after the abortive negotiations at Jidda. I felt frustrated at our failure to reach any agreement with Ibn Saud, especially after appreciating the king's difficulties at close quarters. Nejed was obviously in complete confusion and there was every indication that the 1928-9 grazing season would see an extensive outbreak of Ikhwan raiding, if not of open war with Nejed. We had six months in which to prepare. I began work by endeavouring to do something to improve the desert forces. I had already pointed out to the Iraq Government the waste and inefficiency which resulted from the existing police system. I commanded fifty men and eight vehicles "for duty", while two independent commandants of police at an average distance of one hundred miles away were each responsible for half of the men and vehicles, in so far as recruiting, discipline, pay and administration were concerned. Recruiting was indeed a major consideration. These men were required to scout for advancing raiders and it was essential that they be experienced in all the lore of desert warfare. In several cases, however, the police commandants had sent me marsh Arabs, whose lives had been spent paddling canoes through the vast reed-covered swamps of the lower Euphrates.

My proposals were submitted in April, 1928, before we went to Jidda, but no action was taken on them until 1st September. Thus our five months' possible training period was lost. The British inspector-general of the Iraq police was opposed to the desert force being placed under my command and threatened to refuse all co-operation if this were done. He had minuted my memorandum with the note, "I will have nothing to do with such catch-'em-alivos." This was embarrassing because, although I wanted to recruit and command these men, I had no machinery for keeping accounts or buying uniforms or petrol. I wished the machinery of the Iraq police to do this administration for me.

Eventually on 1st September, 1928, sanction was given for the formation of the Southern Desert Camel Corps, to consist of seventy camelmen and the original eight vehicles, and to be under my command. In March, 1928, when we had originally obtained our eight vehicles, I had strongly urged that they be armed with machine guns. Their rôle of scouting for Ikhwan raiders, I pointed out, was one of extreme danger. In most parts of the theatre of operations, whether in the stony or the bush-covered desert, horsemen could travel considerably faster than one-ton trucks, at least for a short distance. In some areas, men on camels could overtake vehicles. When scouting for raiders, it was essential that the cars be able to approach any persons encountered, and if possible that the car-crews be in a position to cross-question them. If the trucks moved so slowly and were manned by only two or three men with rifles, it was impossible to expect them boldly to approach unknown bodies of men in the desert. If, on the other hand, they retired as soon as they saw a distant party of camel-riders, they might spread a false alarm of raiders, when in reality they had only seen a caravan of merchants. Armed with automatic weapons, however, they could approach boldly and,'if the party proved hostile, a burst of machine-gun fire would cause the enemy to sheer off and enable the vehicles to get clear.

A second reason for my request was that, during the long scorching months of summer, the R.A.F. and the Iraq army disappeared and the Desert Camel Corps would be left to fend for itself. It is true that major Ikhwan forces could likewise not operate in the heat of summer, but raiding parties of one hundred camelmen or more were quite possible. The Desert Force would alone be responsible in summer, for the repulse or pursuit of raiders and the recovery of their loot. Two or three trucks, each containing a few riflemen, would not be adequate to this task.

A copy of my memorandum explaining these reasons for my request for machine guns was submitted to the air officer commanding, from whom it elicited only a marginal pencil note: "I do not agree. I do not want the police to fight." This was only another aspect of the air staff demands that all tribes be removed from the desert to give the R.A.F. elbow room. The air officer commanding made no reply to any of my arguments, but his note was sufficient to postpone the issue of machine guns from March to September, 1928, thereby losing us the five months' period during which we might have trained machine gunners.

In the autumn, the approach of the raiding season and the obvious anarchy in Nejed resulted in more active measures in Baghdad. In September, we received two very ancient Vickers guns and a class of twelve bedouins was sent to Baghdad for training. Then sanction was received for the purchase of four more Ford trucks mounted with machine guns and for two Ford vans fitted with wireless, and for the recruitment of thirty more men to be employed as machine gunners in the trucks. Although, therefore, the five months' delay had deprived us of the opportunity of training our tiny army, yet at the beginning of the grazing season we had obtained sanction for a force, the effect of which on the desert situation was to prove decisive.

At the beginning of the 1928-9 grazing season, therefore, the Southern Desert Camel Corps order of battle was to be as follows:

70 camelmen
30 machine gunners in trucks
 8 miscellaneous vehicles, two of them with Vickers guns
 4 new Ford trucks with Vickers guns
 2 wireless vans.

One disappointment however remained. Although there were hundreds of wireless sets in Iraq, no other department would agree to lend us the two we needed. As a result, two sets were ordered from England and arrived the following year. We were obliged to complete another raiding season, patrolling over more than twenty-five thousand square miles of desert, without any means of communication.

Never before had any attempt been made to train or discipline bedouins. All the Arab governments I knew had accepted as an axiom that bedouins were militarily useless. Yet when our men were sent to be trained in Baghdad as machine gunners, their instructors pronounced them to be above the average of Iraqi recruits in keenness and intelligence.

*   *   *   *   *

Meanwhile the furnace-summer of Iraq was upon us. The shepherds were on the banks of the Euphrates, but the Dhafeer could not go down to the river until September, for fear of the stinging flies which killed their camels. They accordingly camped at Abu Ghar and Busaiya. We were anxious lest some raiding party of two or three hundred camel-riders should arrive from the Ikhwan and round up the Dhafeer camels from their grazing grounds, as had happened to the Araif in 1925.

I accordingly arranged to leave a detachment of our new desert trucks at Busaiya. Each day at dawn a patrol of two or three vehicles was to leave the fort and drive some fifty miles to the south, where it would take up positions on hilltops and remain in observation until sunset, returning to Busaiya after dark. We could not by this means be absolutely certain of intercepting raiders should they come, but we could very greatly reduce the risk. In hard figures, we may have reduced the chances of a successful camel raid by half, but even more important, we reckoned, would be the moral effect. A hundred and fifty or two hundrd miles away in the camps of Mutair or the Ajman, reports would be received, from their spies or from travellers, that vehicle patrols were operating. They would not know the exact times or distances or the precise numbers of vehicles or men. Bedouins rarely dealt in accurate numbers and usually tended to exaggerate, and the reports of our operations which reached the Ikhwan would certainly be magnified. As a result of these factors, it seemed to me that we were probably giving the Dhafeer herds about eighty to eighty-five per cent security. Twenty miles behind our scouting positions they scattered unguarded to graze and wander.

I often accompanied these patrols myself, both to maintain the enthusiasm of the men and to learn in detail how such duties could best be conducted. Leaving Busaiya before sunrise, the atmosphere at first would be cool, the air clear and the vast blue distances of the desert sharply outlined. Perhaps by eight o'clock in the morning, we should have reached the line of our outpost positions, between Al Abtiyya and Maghaizal.[1] The diary of events of the previous twenty-four hours in the desert was written on the surface of the earth in the form of tracks. To the bedouin the tracks of camels soon made a story. He would of course immediately notice the number of camels which had passed, whether they were walking or trotting, whether they were ridden, carrying loads or grazing (a ridden camel went straight, a grazing camel wandered from bush to bush), whether all were fully grown or whether there were young camels, or mothers with calves at foot. So much for the first glance. Then he would follow the tracks, his eyes on the ground. Soon he would find some droppings, which he would eagerly pick up and break between his fingers. The dung dried quickly in the heat of the midday sun in that clear, dry air, but less rapidly at night. The degree of dryness of the dung would tell him how long ago the camel riders had passed. Sometimes undigested pieces of vegetation would enable him to deduce where the camels came from, for he knew the kind of bushes or grass in each area. With wells so scarce in the desert in summer, the direction of march would tell him where the party of riders had come from or towards what well they were moving. If they appeared to be going towards a well in the vicinity, the next step would be to visit that well. It was just possible that the party might be found watering, but, even if the riders had already passed on, the well mouth would always have a tale to tell; for at a well travellers dismount and relax. The number of riders could be checked by the number of human footprints, for all would almost certainly dismount. Perhaps there would be tracks of women or children. Some might have taken the opportunity to eat, throwing away date stones or—if Iraqis—cigarette ends. If they had prayed, as all Muslims should five times a day, then if they were Wahhabis they would have drawn a line (or mosque) on the ground to line up on. If non-Wahhabis, they might have prayed individually. To those who had lived all their lives in local surroundings, such and many other tell-

[1] For Abtiyya and Maghaizal see map on page 238.

tale factors were instantly discernible, so that an exact description of the party could at times be deduced, with a detailed accuracy which, to the uninitiated, would seem almost magical.

Nevertheless these bedouins of southern Iraq were not so skilled in tracking as were Arabs who lived in sandy deserts. Such an area of sand lay on the border between southern Trans-Jordan and the Hejaz. Some years after the time of the present narrative, I slept a night in this country. In the morning, an old Arab remarked that a stranger had ridden through a neighbouring valley during the past night. I innocently enquired how he knew from the tracks that the rider was a stranger. "You recognize people," the old man explained to me patiently, "because they all seem to you to have different faces. In exactly the same way, all camels have different feet. You do not notice this, because you do not spend as much time looking at camels' feet as you do at people's faces. I do—and I know the feet of all the camels near here—the tracks I saw this morning belonged to a camel I do not know."

We were fortunate when we discovered tracks on our patrols, not only because we might overtake the riders and cross-question them, but because they provided a break in the long monotony of the day.

Eventually, as midday approached, we took up our position below some hilltop, or beneath the crest of the Haniya ridge. After posting a sentry with binoculars on the summit above us, we drew our trucks beside one another and prepared to pass three hours of furnace heat as best we could. Little could be done in the way of scouting during these midday hours, because the distance danced and trembled in the mirage. Little shrubs twelve inches high on a ridge a few hundred yards away, were magnified into a flock of gigantic camels, and lakes of silvery water lay gleaming on the parched surface of the desert.

A blanket, stretched between one truck and the next, afforded a few square feet of shade. Alternatively the men crawled under the trucks and lay gazing up at the sump or the backaxle, where the dust lay in a thick crust around the grease nipples. I lay at times with arms and legs outstretched, as though crucified on the surface of the earth, for the touch of an arm on my body was too hot to bear. Sometimes we made coffee or tea, and sat round in a circle sipping it and talking. Then we would lie half-dozing, panting with the heat or refreshed, every now and again, when a breath of air brought a momentary coolness. The metal portions of the trucks were too hot to touch. Dust devils—miniature cyclones swirling the dust in tall corkscrew columns into the air—chased one another across the glaring plain.

Sometimes, lying thus half-gasping for breath, I would picture to myself the long shadows of elm trees falling across a green English meadow on a summer's evening, where the cows stood knee deep in the tall grass, or an Italian mountainside covered with mighty Spanish chestnut trees, between which, far below, could be seen the Lydian laughter of the blue Lake of Garda.[1]

As the sun dropped lower and lower in the sky, our spirits revived. The kettle and teacups were cleared up, our blanket awning came down, and engines were started up. Sunset was the best time of the day for seeing distance and we spent the last two hours of daylight scouting from hilltop to hilltop. When dusk made it impossible any longer to see the hills and plains to the south, we would set off for home on a three-hour bumping and lurching drive back to Busaiya. At last a few distant flickering lights would reveal the fires in the black tents pitched outside the fort, for Busaiya was now manned by the Southern Desert Camel Corps. The heavy doorway swung open, revealing in the courtyard the glow of the coffee fire and a group of rough bearded men sitting on the ground around it. "God give them life! God give them life," called welcoming voices, as the trucks rattled slowly through the gateway. The toils of the long weary day were past.

*   *   *   *   *

Although we were unable to make use of the summer months of 1928 to train our new desert force, I devoted all the time I could to the study of Ikhwan warfare. Under nomadic conditions it was obvious that the party which took the offensive enjoyed an immense advantage. Both the Ikhwan and the Iraq tribes depended on the often sparse desert grazing, which compelled them to scatter far and wide to secure grass for their flocks. As we were (for diplomatic if for no other reasons) debarred from taking the offensive, the Ikhwan herds were able to scatter unguarded as they desired in Nejed, free from any fear of raids from our side. The Iraq tribes, however, were faced with two alternatives—to scatter in search of grazing and be raided and defeated in detail, or to concentrate and suffer losses in their livestock. The greater part of our problem, therefore, lay in the question of how to obtain information. We could allow our tribes to scatter and graze, if we could be certain always of obtaining four or five days' warning of an impending raid, which would give us time to concentrate. How was such prior intelligence to be obtained? I decided to study the question from the Ikhwan angle.

To the Ikhwan, intelligence was also vital. Starting two hundred or more miles from the Iraqi camps, they would have a fair idea where their objective was located. Their attacks, however, always took place at dawn and were preceded by a forced night march of

[1] Tennyson. *Frater ave atque vale.*

sixty miles to insure surprise. It was essential for the raiders to arrive at dawn at the sleeping camps. If daylight broke while the raiders were five miles away, the tribes would see them and take to flight. Thus accurate information and timing were essential to the Ikhwan. All the main principles of war applied as much to desert camel raiders as to European armies—a definite objective, simplicity of plan, offensive action, concentration by the Ikhwan of overwhelming force against the scattered Iraqis, speed of movement and tactical surprise. Their success or failure depended on accurate intelligence.

While the Ikhwan tribesmen were concentrating for attack, they sent spies to Iraq to locate the tribal camps. Some of these spies returned before the raid set out. Others were given rendezvous on the intended line of advance of the raiders.

The raid itself was preceded by a number of strong reconnoitring parties, each consisting perhaps of thirty or forty camelmen. In winter, horsemen would also be included. On approaching the objective, these parties sent out scouts in twos or threes to locate the camps. Such parties would often creep up quite close under cover of darkness and would also count the camp fires. Some of these reconnoitring parties would also be given rendezvous, perhaps one or two days' march short of the objective.

A most valuable device to advancing Ikhwan raiders was to send a spy to sit in the camps which they intended to attack. Assuming a suitable disguise, this man would endeavour to stay in the Iraqi tents as a guest until the day before that fixed for the attack. He would then try to slip away, probably under cover of darkness and meet the advancing raiders at a prearranged rendezvous, a few hours before that chosen for the attack, to inform them of the eleventh-hour dispositions of the camps.

In the past, the only source of intelligence in Iraq had been the cross-questioning of travellers coming from Nejed. If no such people happened to come, the government received no information. Meanwhile we had taken steps to supply a chain of reconnoitring patrols and pickets in front of our tribes. It seemed to me that all that was now necessary was to organize spies, similar to those used by the Ikhwan, to sit in their camps and slip away at night and report to us, as soon as a raid set out. I accordingly set myself to organize such an espionage service.

*   *   *   *   *

Although Nejed was in anarchy, Ibn Saud spent the whole summer in Mecca. He did not return to Nejed until November, 1928. As soon as he arrived in Riyadh, he called a mass meeting of the Ikhwan in the capital to discuss the situation. Meanwhile the Ajman tribe—which had never been enthusiastically loyal to Ibn

Saud—had joined the rebel league of Ateiba and Mutair. Sultan Ibn Humaid of Ateiba, Feisal al Duweesh of Mutair and Dhaidan Ibn Hithlain, chief of the Ajman, refused to obey the king's summons, but the Duweesh sent his eldest son Azaiyiz. Without the attendance of the rebels, nothing could be done to effect a compromise.

The king's position was extremely insecure. Apart from the rebel tribes, many other Ikhwan leaders were playing with both sides, and, while complying with Ibn Saud's summons, were also in correspondence with the rebels. As has already been emphasized, Ibn Saud had no force which he could use to coerce the rebels, except the other tribes or the oasis-dwellers. At this stage, neither of these groups had any particular quarrel with the rebels and indeed many were in sympathy with them. The king was therefore powerless to coerce the tribal leaders, who had refused to obey his summons. His only device, for the moment, was to employ the methods so often used by the Turks in the past, namely to sow dissension in the disloyal tribes. He sent for other shaikhs of Ateiba and Mutair, potential rivals of Ibn Humaid and the Duweesh, gave them money and endeavoured to create a split in the rebel ranks.

Before this policy could bear fruit, however, the rebels assembled their followers, unfurled their war banners and proclaimed their intention of raiding Iraq, whether Ibn Saud liked it or not. In fact, the rebels had already agreed among themselves to divide Ibn Saud's dominions between them. Feisal al Duweesh was to be the ruler of Nejed, Sultan Ibn Humaid was to govern the Hejaz and Dhaidan Ibn Hithlain of the Ajman was to receive the Hasa. Their success depended on the still uncertain attitude of the other Nejed tribes. To proclaim their rebellion against Ibn Saud might have caused the rest of Nejed to rally to the king. To announce their determination to fight against the heathen Iraqis—a plain religious duty which Ibn Saud was trying to avoid—might win them the sympathy of all good Wahhabis.

A series of major Ikhwan raids on Iraq appeared imminent, but before the campaign opened the British Government made a last attempt to pour oil on the troubled waters. It suggested arbitration between Ibn Saud and Iraq, as to whether or not Iraqi desert posts should be abolished. I protested strongly against this proposal.

I had myself, when at Jidda, suggested the demolition of Busaiya as a concession to Ibn Saud, but my proposal had been rejected as a weak surrender. My intention had been to give the king an apparent victory, in order to strengthen his hand against the rebels, but I proposed to use Abu Ghar and Sulman instead. Now His Majesty's Government was suggesting arbitration over the principle of Iraq having any desert posts at all. If we were defeated at arbitration on this point, only anarchy would ensue. The Iraq Government would abandon the attempt to control its deserts and the rebel Ikhwan would raid down to the banks of the Euphrates.

The British Government seemed to have failed to appreciate that the nature of the struggle had changed. We were witnessing a contest for power between Ibn Saud and the Ikhwan. If the latter were able to raid the Iraq tribes successfully, they would return in triumph and overthrow the king. If they failed to raid, their prestige would fall and Ibn Saud would win. Thus it was essential for the king's survival that the rebel raids should fail. Yet the British proposed arbitration on the question whether Iraq should abandon the desert altogether, thereby leaving the triumphant Ikhwan to destroy Ibn Saud. In practice, however, the time for negotiation was past, for the war banners were already unfurled.

To some extent, the fluctuations of policy in London represented conflicting schools of thought. Ever since the First World War, British official opinion had been divided between those who desired to support Ibn Saud and those who favoured the sherifian family. The conquest of the Hejaz by the Wahhabis had provided the supporters of Ibn Saud with a gratifying opportunity to say, "We told you so." Now in their eyes, the pro-sherifian party were repeating their former error and were "backing King Feisal". They accordingly protested loudly and pressed for the withdrawal of the R.A.F. and a conciliatory attitude to Ibn Saud. They did not realize that the only way to save Ibn Saud was to defeat the rebels.

Baghdad likewise was divided. King Feisal himself could not but sympathize with the rebels. If Ibn Saud were overthrown, the sherifs might conceivably win back the Hejaz. The Iraqi ministers, on the other hand, regarded the whole affair as a troublesome sideshow, involving a number of uncivilized tribes in whom they were not interested. The result of these divisions of opinion in Baghdad and London was that we sometimes felt ourselves supported while, at others, for reasons unknown to us, government help would suddenly be cut down.

The news from Nejed made it essential for us to agree on a plan of campaign. Early in November, 1928, I went to Baghdad to make the final arrangements with the Iraq Government and the R.A.F. For the first time, the air staff agreed to commence desert air patrols as soon as the Iraq tribes moved out. The procedure in the past had been for no air reconnaissances to take place until a series of savage Ikhwan raids had been delivered, whereupon every aircraft and pilot was used until the personnel were exhausted and the machines due for overhaul. This year the R.A.F. agreed to commence flying from the beginning, but to carry out only a moderate number of patrols for specific objects.

The Iraq army likewise came nobly to our assistance and promised to send a motor machine gun company to the Southern Desert. The plan agreed upon was that a detachment of this company, the greater part of the new Southern Desert Camel Corps and myself, should constitute a mobile force which would accompany the largest possible concentration of Iraq tribes moving down to the frontier.

Having made these arrangements in Baghdad, I called a meeting of the nomad tribal leaders in Samawa. The Dhafeer bedouins and shepherds of the Juwareen, Budoor, Zayyad, Beni Salama, Yajeeb, Ghalidh and other smaller groups were all assembled. This gathering warmed my heart in one direction at least. Only three or four years before, the tribes had regarded us with resentment and distrust. Many of them, suspecting us of some tortuous treachery, had endeavoured in the past to communicate secretly with Ibn Saud and to purchase his protection by paying taxes to Nejed. But this year, all doubts of our sincerity had vanished. Our tribes were completely convinced of our honesty and were anxious to co-operate with us whole-heartedly. All the tribal leaders reported punctually to Samawa, engaged in a full and frank discussion and pledged themselves to move with us, camp under our directions and stand to offer battle if we so ordered.

All agreed that there was no grazing north of the line Busaiya to Sulman. The Dhafeer claimed that they would have to move at least as far as Tuqaiyid and preferably to the Neutral Area. Thus it was obvious that once we moved into the desert we should in actual practice be obliged to move forward immediately to the actual frontier, on the other side of which the enemy were already gathering under their war banners. We thus threw down the gauntlet to the dreaded Ikhwan, advancing deliberately in the midst of our tribes, straight for the enemy. For many years, no Arab force had ever moved towards the Ikhwan or offered them battle.

The R.A.F. commenced operations at the same moment. The moral effect of air activity was very great. It is true that the majority of air patrols saw nothing and pilots were inclined to be bored and to doubt the value of their efforts. It was not always easy to persuade them that, although they had seen nothing, a great many Arabs had seen them. Would-be Ikhwan raiders were apprehensive of aircraft and they took great trouble to collect reports regarding air patrols. Our own tribes also observed the air reconnaissances with considerable attention. Moreover enemy spies were frequently in our camps and the news that aircraft were operating regularly soon reached the Ikhwan. While, however, the moral effect of air patrols was great, their practical value was small. Even if aircrews were to see some movement on the ground, their knowledge of Arabs and the desert was insufficient to enable them to tell friend from foe, or a raiding party from a tribe moving camp.

At this critical juncture, when for the first time the Iraqi forces, the tribes and the R.A.F. were working in perfect co-operation, the British Government was seized by a fit of caution. The previous winter, after the massacre of Busaiya and a series of Ikhwan raids, permission had been given for the R.A.F. to cross the frontier. Now with all the Ikhwan rebels moving out apparently for a grand offensive, we were notified that aircraft were not to approach within twenty miles of the frontier. Never before had such a restriction been imposed. We had always flown up to the frontier though we had not crossed it. As our tribes were already on the frontier, the result of this restriction from London was that aircraft were henceforth employed in reconnoitring the desert behind us and our tribes.

This prohibition, like the offer of arbitration, was intended to be a gesture of conciliation to Ibn Saud, due perhaps to the efforts of the pro-Saud party in the councils of Whitehall. His Majesty's Government still did not seem to have realized that the Ikhwan were about to raid us, contrary to Ibn Saud's orders. The only help which we could give to the king was to defeat the raiders. If we were to succeed in doing so, the waverers in Nejed would rally to him and enable him to overthrow the rebels. Ironically enough, the British Government's "gesture of conciliation" to Ibn Saud might well have led to his undoing, by enabling the rebels to raid us successfully.

At the beginning of December, 1928, we camped at Maghaizal. The grazing had been good once we had passed Tuqaiyid, as the Dhafeer had foreseen. Early autumn rainstorms had passed over this area and soaked the ground, before any rain fell at Busaiya or Abu Ghar. The young grass was therefore already above ground, imparting a pale green colour to the surface of the hollows and valleys of the desert.

A curious and unforeseen development had now occurred. In the past, tribal confederations had often moved across the desert to war under the leadership of some great tribal chief, like Sadoon Ibn Sadoon. But the Turks in their last years and the Iraq Government after them—whether by accident or intentionally—had destroyed tribal chiefs. If the Sadoon had fallen the Suwait should have replaced them but they also had disappeared. As a result, the Southern Desert was now peopled by many and various tribes and sections, each acting as it thought best, without leadership or co-ordinating authority.

In the desert, war or no war, the business of grazing had to be carried on as usual. Where many tribes were moving in a great concentration ready for war, some central authority was needed to choose the grazing areas and tell each group where to camp. I unexpectedly found myself in the rôle of the tribal chief, deciding when to move camp, choosing the next grazing grounds and apportioning areas to different sections, with due regard to the grazing and watering needs of camels, sheep and donkeys. No such tribal operations had been attempted in the Southern Desert since the days of the great Sadoon. I could not but smile at an incongruous fate which had allowed the mantle of that splendid old bandit to fall upon the ridiculous shoulders of a little European driving a rattling Ford car.

Arab nomads measured the rate of growth of new winter grass by the animals which could eat it. When the first tiny green blades appeared on the surface of the desert they would say, "The ground is alive." At the next stage the sheep abandoned the twigs of the desert shrubs and began to nibble the young grass shoots. "*Al naaja tataasha*, the ewe can dine," the Arabs would say. Soon the sheep could obtain their fill of young grass and the shepherds would say happily, "The ewe is satisfied." A further period was required before the mare was also proclaimed as satisfied. The camel was the last to be able to graze and could only do so when the grass was long enough to be caught by his big lips. The requirements of the camel also represented two stages, "The camel dines" and "The camel is satisfied"—a happy state rarely attained until the month of March. When we reached the Neutral Area in December, the ewes were able to dine.

*   *   *   *   *

No sooner did we camp at Maghaizal with the camel corps and a detachment of the Iraq army than the tribes poured past us and scattered far and wide in the Neutral Area. We patrolled their camps all day in our cars but we were not allowed to enter Nejed and consequently we could no longer picket the desert in front of them. Meanwhile, however, I had built up the first skeleton of an espionage system and we were obliged to rely on our spies who, we hoped, were sitting in the camps of the Ikhwan.

On the evening of 16th December, 1928, one of these men arrived in our bivouac at sunset flogging his exhausted camel along at top speed. I was sitting in my tiny tent, when a discreet cough without announced the presence of Hamed the slave. A second later his black face was thrust in at the door of the tent and he announced in a stage whisper—"A man has come from the Ikhwan." For a second my heart stood still and then I told Hamed to show him in.

"*Khair in sha Allah*," I said in no little anxiety, "Good news if God wills."

"Mutair are raiding," said the bedouin curtly.

The grand offensive by Mutair, the Ajman and Ateiba still hung fire, he explained, but meanwhile a minor shaikh of Mutair had thought to make a name for himself and acquire both fame and loot by carrying out a little raid of his own, until such time as the great leaders made up their minds. Menahi Ibn Ashwan had accordingly set out at the head of a hundred camelmen. He knew that we and many Iraq tribes were camped in the Neutral Area and as far north as Tuqaiyid, so he had decided to move south of the frontier until he reached the vicinity of Jumaima and to seek some unprotected shepherd tribe in that area. "I saw the raid watering at Al Hafar yesterday evening," said our informer.

I called in some trusted old bedouins and then men of the camel corps, one after another, and consulted each in turn. We calculated the marches from Al Hafar to Jumaima. We reckoned that the raiders would pass Umm al Rudhumma that night. The consensus of opinion was that they would reach Jumaima on the morning of 19th December.

Jumaima was a masonry cistern on the track known as the Darab Zubaida. Thirteen centuries ago, the Prophet Muhammad taught his followers that a pilgrimage to Mecca was incumbent on all good Muslims who were able to accomplish it. For one thousand three hundred years, vast caravans of pilgrims had flowed across the deserts of Arabia once every year to the Holy City and the soft pads of their camels had scarred the surface of the wilderness into great highways worn by the tread of myriads of men and animals. Of all these great pilgrim tracks, perhaps the most important led from Nejef in Iraq to Hail, Medina and Mecca. To facilitate the passage of the pilgrims to the Holy Cities was a work worthy of pious Muslims.

Haroon al Rasheed had been the khalif in Baghdad during the Golden Age of the Abbaside dynasty—the Augustus, the Louis XIV of his day. Tradition related that his wife, the Lady Zubaida, had undertaken the pious task of providing cisterns of water for the use of the pilgrimage, the whole way from Nejef to Hail. Jumaima was one of these immense masonry-lined tanks, filled from a great desert catchment area. Her benevolence had been commemorated in the name ever since applied to the Nejef pilgrim route—the road of Zubaida. A thousand years after the death of the Lady Zubaida many of the cisterns which she had built had fallen in ruin or were blocked with rubble, but Jumaima still held water and provided a camping ground and a watering place for the wanderers or the raiders of the desert, if no longer for the pilgrims. It was at this time-honoured site that we decided to seek an encounter with Menahi Ibn Ashwan.

Here indeed was a chance. This was the very first time that we had ever received accurate prior information of an Ikhwan raid. It had only been possible because we had camped so far forward

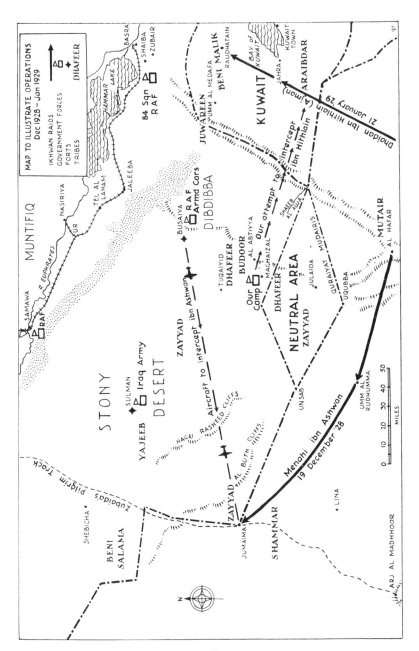

MAP TO ILLUSTRATE OPERATIONS
Dec 1928 – Jan 1929

IKHWAN RAIDS
GOVERNMENT FORCES
FORTS
TRIBES   DHAFEER

and so near the enemy. But would the R.A.F. believe us? Would they ask for further confirmation and meanwhile refuse aircraft? I crouched on the ground in my tiny tent, putting a long signal into cypher. I thought it best to visit Jumaima on the morning of 18th December, to see if there were any shepherds in the area. They had been told to remain near Sulman, where the grazing for the moment was adequate. There was also the possibility that Ibn Ashwan might travel faster than we had calculated. I asked for air patrols, with guns and bombs, on the mornings of 18th and 19th December. To my great relief, the reply came detailing three ninaks for each reconnaissance.

Early on the morning of 18th December, I climbed into the cockpit of the leading ninak at Busaiya and we took off, rising slowly over the rocky and jagged surface of the Stony Desert. At length we came to the edge of that grey rock-strewn area and dropped over the line of cliffs of Hakai Rasheed. A few miles of flat beige-coloured plain, with pale green hollows here and there where the new grass was showing, then over the second long escarpment of Al Butn, a few more miles of plain, then the Darab Zubaida track coming in from the north, and we were circling over the Lady Zubaida's great pilgrim reservoir at Jumaima. No living thing seemed to be in sight. The vast empty desert appeared to extend limitless in every direction. Then about two or three miles away, in a green hollow, I thought that I could see a few black specks. I tapped the pilot on the shoulder and pointed. He looked, nodded his head and turned in a steep bank. I stood up in the rear cockpit straining my eyes. Yes, there was a wisp of grey smoke. As, losing height, we neared the green hollow, we saw a little camp of about ten shepherd tents. Donkeys were grazing by the tents and a few flocks of sheep wheeled in alarm as the aircraft roared overhead. I tapped the pilot on the shoulder again and pointed to the ground. We landed on a gravelly strip, a hundred yards from the tents

An old man with a grey beard hurried towards us, followed by three or four others. I climbed out of the cockpit. The other two ninaks continued to circle overhead. "Who are these Arabs?" I asked the old man.

"The Zayyad, the Zayyad," he answered. "I am Haj Hamdan Ibn Jendeel."

"What are you doing here?" I enquired in assumed indignation. "Were you not told to remain near Sulman?"

"What could we do?" answered the old man deprecatingly. "Look at the grass here. In a day or two we shall be churning butter."

"You cannot churn butter if your throats are cut," I said severely.

Their faces fell and they suddenly looked anxious. "Why?" they enquired. "Has anything happened? Where are the Ikhwan?"

I told them the whole story of Menahi Ibn Ashwan and his hundred camelmen

"*Allahu akbar!* Great God!" exclaimed one of the younger men. "Only yesterday two camelmen passed our camp and asked for a drink of milk. We were suspicious of them at the time."

"Without doubt they were spies for Ibn Ashwan," I said.

The old man cried excitedly: "Here, boys, tell the women to round up those donkeys and start loading up."

"Take it easy," I interrupted, "and I'll tell you what to do. They will not attack in daylight today. Anyhow send out two scouts on horses to keep a look-out until sunset. Then light your fires and cook your dinners. The raiders will probably have scouts out to watch for your fires and make certain you are still in position. Then when it is quite dark, pack up and go for your lives and don't stop walking till you get to Sulman. And next time, obey the orders you get from the government."

"But why cannot we flee now?" asked Haj Hamdan anxiously.

"Because I want Ibn Ashwan to attack this valley tomorrow morning," I said. "I want him to see your camp fires tonight, so that he will attack at dawn. But we, not you, will be here to meet him."

Haj Hamdan stroked his beard. "True," he answered thoughtfully. "May God give you success. We will do as you order."

The ninak was still ticking over. I climbed into the cockpit.

"Goodbye, goodbye," I called. "May God preserve you."

"In His safe keeping," they shouted back.

I pulled down my goggles, the pilot opened up the throttle, the machine dashed forward at increasing speed, a trail of dust arose behind us, and in a few minutes, we were skimming over the Butn cliffs, heading for Busaiya.

When we took off again at dawn the next morning, I had explained the situation to the pilots and told them what I had said to the shepherds. Once more we flew high over the Stony Desert, then over the first line of cliffs, the Hakai Rasheed, and the second, the Butn. We had agreed to make straight for the green hollow, where the shepherd camp had been the day before. I strained my eyes ahead . . . yes, there seemed to be specks . . . two were moving . . . could it be? . . . sure enough, where yesterday the shepherd camp had been, a hundred camels were grazing. I could scarcely believe my eyes. Could it really be as easy as that? Had my little plan worked so perfectly?

But I had doubts. We circled round. There were a hundred camels all right, but no men were visible. No, there were two men, but there should have been a hundred. This was not a flock of grazing camels because there were no small ones. All were fully grown.

But the road of Zubaida ran past this hollow. Could it be a caravan, perhaps of Shammar, going down to buy supplies in Nejef? Or perhaps a merchant, travelling across the desert to sell this flock of camels in Palestine or Egypt? I sat down in the rear cockpit and scribbled a note to the pilot, saying that I could not be certain that they were raiders and asking him to fly lower and lower and to notice if they fired on us. I passed the note over to the front cockpit. The pilot read it, nodded his head and pushed the nose of the aircraft downwards.

At two thousand feet it was impossible to see enough detail. We circled round and round over the green grass hollow, while I leant over the side of the cockpit, straining my eyes to see. Nobody fired at us. The two men whom I had seen a few minutes before had vanished. We should have to come low enough to distinguish whether the camels had pack saddles or riding saddles on their backs.

Lower and lower we circled. We must be below a thousand feet now. The other two aircraft were still circling above us at two thousand feet. The very absence of men seemed to me suspicious. If they had been friendly and we had shown such interest in them, would they not have stood up and waved? The pilot pulled up the nose of the aircraft. Perhaps he thought we had come low enough. I patted his shoulder and pointed downwards. He pushed her nose down again and flew round another turn. We came roaring in over the camels at about five hundred feet and as I leant over the side, I saw clearly that every camel had a riding saddle on its back. It was Ibn Ashwan and no mistake. I tapped the pilot on the shoulder again and gave him the thumbs up sign. Then, to make quite certain, I sat down in the cockpit and wrote on a slip of paper—"Raiders. Shoot."

The pilot looked at my slip, then pulled up the nose and began to gain height. We flew straight away from them, climbing upwards. I wondered whether the raiders were heaving sighs of relief, thinking that we were satisfied and were flying away. The pilot rubbed his goggles with his gloved finger, looked at his bomb sights and fiddled with his front gun. When we were about a mile or more away, he banked steeply and we flew back towards the target at two thousand feet. The camels were still moving here and there—not a man was visible. I hung over the side as we came up to the target, saw the camels appear from under the bottom wing and then the first stick of bombs dropping away below us.

Suddenly spurts of dust shot up in the green hollow. In an instant, the whole scene was transformed. There was suddenly a man on every camel, each riding at full speed in a different direction. Never in my life have I seen so miraculous a change. The men, wrapped in their brown cloaks, must have been crouching motionless near their camels. By the time the second aircraft came over to attack, there was no target left, only individual camelmen riding madly towards every point of the compass.

When we had dropped our bombs, we came round again to use our front gun. A small group of men had collected in one place. A man seemed to be on the ground. Three others dismounted and ran towards him, pulling their camels behind them by their head-ropes. The pilot put the nose of the machine down into a dive. Now I could see over his head and over the engine. The little group of men and camels was straight in our sights. "Tat-tat-tat-tat" went the gun, the dust flicked up on the ground all around the little party. "Tat-tat-tat-tat". The ground was coming up towards us fast. Then we pulled out, the horizon wheeled around, for an instant the sky seemed to be beneath us and the world above and we climbed away in a steep turn.

I banged the pilot on the back in my excitement and showed thumbs up. He waved a hand in the air, we banked again and down went the nose: "Tat-tat-tat-tat."

I do not know how many times we dived. At last the aircraft pulled up in a straight steady climb. The pilot pointed to his gun and shrugged his shoulders—no more ammunition. We watched one of the other machines doing a final dive on a fleeing camel-rider and then the two other aircraft turned to follow us home. A few specks could still be seen here and there, speeding across the desert— some of them were already several miles away.

I sat down again in my cockpit and wrote the pilot another note: "What a show! That'll teach them." He turned over the paper and wrote on the back, "Pity the whole squadron was not with us."

Thus ended the raid of Menahi Ibn Ashwan. It was the first complete success achieved by our new methods, and formed an exhilarating little hors d'oeuvre to the decisive struggle which lay before us.

XIV

Couch and Hobble

The use of arms, which is at all times honourable to the brave, now offers the only safety even to cowards ... Since then all hopes of mercy are vain, at length assume courage, both you to whom safety and you to whom glory is dear ... Not only then are we to reflect that death with honour is preferable to life with ignominy, but to remember that security and glory are seated in the same place. Even to fall in this extremist verge of earth and of nature cannot be thought an inglorious fate.   TACITUS,. *Agricola*

O Lord, in Thee have I trusted: let me never be confounded.
Te Deum

> If evils come not, then our fears are vain;
> And if they do, fear but augments the pain.
> SIR THOMAS MORE

CHAPTER XIV

COUCH AND HOBBLE

THE defeat of Ibn Ashwan's raid produced a profound moral effect on the Ikhwan, exactly at the moment when they were preparing their grand offensive against Iraq. If we had missed the raiders and they had returned laden with plunder and driving flocks of sheep before them, the outcome of the season's operations might have been different. If the Ikhwan, exhilarated by this first success, had simultaneously raided Iraq at several different places, we could not have been everywhere at once. Some of the raiders would have been successful. Had they returned in triumph from raiding the "infidel" Iraqis, more Nejed tribes would have joined them, Ibn Saud might have been overwhelmed and American companies might never—or not for many years—have secured a concession to prospect for oil in Arabia.

We also were encouraged by the Ibn Ashwan affair. It seemed to me to confirm my theory that, if we moved out with our tribes and lived with them, we could obtain sufficiently accurate intelligence to enable us to meet Ikhwan raids before they attacked our tribes, an exploit never achieved before.

At the end of December, we were camped at Maghaizal, with many Iraq tribes in front of us in the Neutral Area. We could not camp with them because, owing to one of those trying diplomatic restrictions which made reasonable operations almost impossible, the Desert Camel Corps and I were allowed to enter the Neutral Area, but the Iraq Army Machine Gun company was forbidden to do so. Moreover the R.A.F. were forbidden to approach within twenty miles of the frontier, though when we camped at Maghaizal, they were given permission to land on us there. They were, however, forbidden to fly south of Maghaizal, with the result that the arm which was supposed to reconnoitre for the enemy, could only do so behind us.

At the same time, the nomadic portion of Mutair (for some had settled in the Ikhwan colonies) were camped between the Neutral Area and Al Hafar, only a few miles from our camps. The Nejdis, through their spies, had discovered that aircraft were not flying along the frontier and that the police cars did not cross it. The proximity of the Mutair camps, although it greatly increased our anxieties, was in some ways an advantage, for it helped us to insinuate spies into the Ikhwan tribes. It was no easy task to procure such spies, who perforce had to be men who could pass themselves off as Ikhwan among these suspicious fanatics. Moreover only very brave men would undertake the task for, were they to fall under suspicion, their throats would be cut without a moment's hesitation.

Meanwhile, ample confirmation had been received that the rebel Ikhwan had unfurled their war banners all along the frontier. On the west, Sultan Ibn Humaid with Ateiba was coming up through the Qaseem.[1] In the centre, the Duweesh was concentrating, while on the east the Ajman, under Dhaidan Ibn Hithlain, were advancing from the Hasa.

Our force was not sufficient to enable us to divide it and to offer battle south of Sulman, as well as near the Neutral Area. We were accordingly obliged to prevent the tribes in the Stony Desert from moving far in front of Sulman, where an Iraq army garrison had joined the detachment of the Desert Corps. Fortunately, however, the grazing in the Tuqaiyid area was excellent, enabling the Zayyad to incline to the east of their normal grazing grounds and join us. Soon, as they gained confidence, they also moved past us to the Neutral Area and up to Unsab. The presence of a government camp at Maghaizal enabled many different Iraq tribes to camp near to one another where grazing was good, without fear of quarrels and fights between them, such as might otherwise have occurred.

On the eastern flank, many Iraq shepherds, notably the Juwareen and Beni Malik tribes, had crossed the Batin into Kuwait territory. The Shaikh of Kuwait, Ahmed Ibn Sobah, had taken no defensive measures to protect his tribes and his relations with Ibn Saud were somewhat strained. The British Government was bound by treaty to come to his assistance if he were attacked, but he had made no request for such support. As a result, both British and Iraq forces were forbidden to enter or fly over Kuwait territory. As, however, the Ikhwan preparations became increasingly menacing, Ibn Sobah was reported to have communicated direct with the rebels, seeking an assurance that he and his tribes would be immune from their raids.

From our point of view this situation was most unsatisfactory. We did not know whether any agreement reached between the Shaikh of Kuwait and the Ikhwan would or would not afford immunity to the Iraq shepherds camped within the borders of Kuwait. I accordingly sent orders to the Juwareen and Beni Malik to cross the Batin westwards into Iraq territory. All the Juwareen and some of Beni Malik complied, but part of the latter tribe disregarded the order. The grazing in Kuwait territory was excellent and their sheep were daily growing visibly fatter. The shepherds accordingly visited Ibn Sobah, offered to pay him taxes and begged to be allowed to place themselves under his protection.

[1] See map on page 61.

At dawn on 21st January, 1929, Dhaidan Ibn Hithlain with the Ajman, accompanied by part of Mutair, fell upon Beni Malik at Raudhatain, massacring the men and looting all their property and flocks. Our police cars and R.A.F. armoured cars were only a few miles away, while 84 Squadron R.A.F. at Shaiba were within twenty minutes' flight of the scene of the battle, but we all had strict orders not to cross the Kuwait border. We signalled frantically for permission. If only we were allowed to move, here was the perfect opportunity to teach the Ikhwan a lesson, which might put an end to raiding for ever. Great as was the moral effect of aircraft, they could not give really decisive results against scattered camelmen in the vast spaces of the desert. Moreover, although the raiders often panicked while aircraft were overhead, as soon as the machines flew away, they returned and collected the loot. Only a ground force could produce a crushing Ikhwan defeat and recover the plundered Iraqi flocks. Now, for the first time, a ground force found itself ideally placed to overtake and engage a large Ikhwan raid.[1]

The whole affair had to be referred to London. For three days we fumed and fretted, lined up on the Kuwait frontier in the Batin, all limbered up for battle. On the third day we obtained permission to enter Kuwait territory, on condition we did not cross into Nejed. We raced across the border, picked up the tracks of the retreating raiders, and followed them, only to find that the Ikhwan had re-crossed the Kuwait-Nejed frontier with all their plunder a few hours earlier. For three days they had been within easy reach of us, travelling at a leisurely pace driving vast numbers of Iraqi sheep across a flat plain, ideal for the operations of fighting vehicles.

The moral effect of this disaster was most unfortunate. The growing confidence of the Iraq tribes was once more rudely shattered, while the spirit of the Ikhwan, perplexed by the defeat of Ibn Ashwan, was raised once more to a state of intense excitement and elation. It was nevertheless interesting to notice that the enemy seemed to be giving a wide berth to our concentration at Maghaizal, Ibn Ashwan having made for Jumaima and Ibn Hithlain for Kuwait.

Nobody of course remembered that I had warned Beni Malik and told them to return to Iraq, nor that, by placing themselves under the protection of Ibn Sobah, they had virtually freed Iraq from responsibility for defending them. To the tribes, and indeed to the world at large, Iraq had once again failed to protect her subjects.

Meanwhile the conference of notables called by Ibn Saud at Riyadh had dispersed without achieving any useful purpose. The king remained passively in the capital, while the country was in chaos. It became apparent that Ibn Saud did not intend to take

[1] See map on page 238.

any action against the Duweesh, Ibn Humaid or Ibn Hithlain, who had refused to obey his summons. Released thus from any apprehension of royal punitive measures, the Ikhwan prepared for action, free to concentrate all their forces for their grand offensive against Iraq.

*   *   *   *   *

I have already explained that nomad warfare is almost entirely offensive. The unwieldy nature of great herds of animals and the native impatience of the Arabs make the passive defensive peculiarly difficult and uncongenial to them. On investigation, however, I discovered that a technique of defensive tactics did exist, though it was rarely used, and I decided to employ it.

Napoleon's aphorism that an army marches on its stomach did not apply to nomad defensive campaigns. Rations for the personnel offered no problem; a tribal family could live for weeks on a sack of dates and a sack of flour, carried on a camel or on two donkeys. The ruling factors in nomad warfare were grazing and water. The tribesman's wealth consisted perhaps in fifteen camels or in thirty or forty head of sheep and it was surprising how quickly these animals died when they had nothing to eat. It was useless, therefore, for the bedouin commander to order his tribes to a certain area in accordance with a strategic plan, unless there were adequate grazing and water there to support their animals. Otherwise they would either refuse point blank or groups of families would sneak away unseen in search of better grazing grounds. It was this constant necessity for dispersion in search of grazing which made the nomads such an easy target for raiders. Bedouin armies marched on the stomachs of their animals.

Were it possible, however, to concentrate the tribes, a tactical method for establishing a defensive position did exist. According to this technique, the various tribes camped side by side in a long line, all the tents of each tribe being grouped together. Sometimes the tents were pitched in rows so close to one another that the tent ropes crossed, forming an obstacle impassable to horse or camel riders. At times, the herds were brought in between the rows of tents, the camels being made to kneel and then hobbled so that they could not rise. This formation, as impenetrable to a mounted charge as were the British squares at Waterloo, was known as a manakh, or couching, and the process of making it was called "to couch and hobble", referring of course to the camels. Strong as such a solid mass of tents and animals was against a charge, it meant that the herds could neither eat nor drink. It would be possible to hold it for twenty-four hours, perhaps at a pinch for forty-eight, but no longer.

The problem for the bedouin commander, therefore, was to allow his tribes to scatter and graze until the very last moment and then to collect them, couch and hobble, only a few hours before the enemy's attack. To be able to carry out such an operation successfully obviously required extremely accurate intelligence of the enemy's movements, calm nerves on the part of the commander who would see his forces still scattered far and wide although the enemy was advancing, and strict obedience on the part of the tribes. If the commander were really to delay the order to concentrate until the last moment, any tribe which stopped to argue would be lost. On the other hand, if the commander gave the order to couch and hobble, the tribes complied and no enemy came, the tribes would never obey the same leader again. In spite of the many difficulties involved, however, there appeared to be no alternative. I consequently spent a great part of the months of December and January, visiting the tribal camps and explaining the situation to the tribal chiefs, in the hope of securing their co-operation should a defensive concentration prove necessary.

Another problem to be considered was how to employ the desert force and the Iraq army. If the tribes were to form up in line of battle, our little force could either camp separately or be located in the centre of the position. It was tempting to consider keeping the cars out of the main position, waiting until the enemy delivered his wild charge into the camps, when we could appear in our vehicles on his flank and rear. In practice, however, we decided that such a course would be impossible to carry out, for if the cars stayed out of the defensive position, the tribes would suspect treachery. We would be compelled therefore to occupy a position in the line with the tribes.

For this purpose, I proposed to bring the desert force and the Iraq army into a selected position, where the machine guns would be unshipped and dug in. The whole bivouac would then be surrounded by a light barbed wire fence, and the tribes instructed to camp on either side of this central strong point. I visualized that, if the Ikhwan delivered a mounted charge against such a position, they would probably swing off to right and left and attack the tribes, by-passing our little redoubt. There would be good prospects of obtaining enfilade fire on them while they passed us. If then our own tribes took to flight pursued by the Ikhwan, we should have to load up our guns on the trucks and sally forth. This would divide our force, because our stores, petrol, the Iraq army wireless set and other impedimenta were in the redoubt and must be defended. Thus only half our force could take the field. The R.A.F. had stationed their armoured cars at Busaiya. I begged them to allow a section of these armoured cars to join us. If they had done so, they, with the Desert Corps cars, would have formed an ideal force to sally out to the counter-attack and our plan could scarcely have failed to lead to a great victory. But the R.A.F. would have nothing to do with my tribal tactics and replied that their armoured cars could not assist us. At the same time, I received an order that only four Iraq army machine guns were to remain with us. The rest of the Motor Machine Gun Company was to concentrate at Busaiya. I was informed that more than four machine guns so far forward might be interpreted by Ibn Saud as military aggression. In the Jidda negotiations, the king had based his arguments on Article 3 of the Uqair protocol, in which both governments had agreed not "to concentrate troops" in the vicinity of the border. The Iraq Government had replied that the men to occupy Busaiya and other desert positions were "police" and not "troops". It accordingly was unwilling now to use the Iraq army. I, on the contrary, pointed out that ten thousand Ikhwan were marching on us in the full panoply of desert warfare and could reasonably be considered to be Nejdi "troops". The presence of an additional hundred men of the Iraq army was, I claimed, in these circumstances justifiable.

The British and Iraq Governments did not appear to me to have appreciated that the worst that could happen, from Ibn Saud's point of view, would be that the Ikhwan raid us successfully. Although active hostilities were in progress, the authorities were still principally concerned with the nice interpretation of treaties. It was illogical so to weaken us as to risk a defeat, with the idea of appeasing the king, whose interests, in reality, were the same as our own. We were reduced to four Vickers guns from the Iraq army; the R.A.F. refused to allow their armoured cars to join us and aircraft were reconnoitring behind us. My whole plan to use the Iraq tribes to defend themselves with government support seemed crazy to the Royal Air Force and the Iraq army. Nevertheless I was not only convinced that it was right but I was now committed to it and withdrawal was impossible. Virtually I was preparing for my war, while the commanders of the regular forces were preparing for theirs. The two plans had little in common. Indeed, even if we had been attacked, I was uncertain whether the powers that be would come to our aid except with aircraft.

Meanwhile the Iraq tribes were scattered from Kuwait to the Wadi al Khirr, while reports and rumours poured in daily, all to the effect that innumerable hosts of Ikhwan with war banners were advancing upon us from every direction. I was now imminently faced with the responsibility which, truth to tell, I had volunteered to undertake. I realized that I had thrown down the gauntlet to the Ikhwan and that it appeared to be certain that we should be attacked. More than once, alone amidst the nomad tribes in the vast spaces of the desert, I shivered with nervousness in the chill evening air as I crouched in my tiny tent, and the great empty desert grew dark. Would my spies across the border be able to slip away in time to warn us? Or would that torrent of screaming horse and camelmen in the grey light of dawn be our first notification that the Ikhwan had come?

It was at such a moment of doubt and uncertainty, at dusk on 15th February, 1929, that one of the camel police put his head into my tent and announced in ominous terms, "A man has come from the Ikhwan." It was one of my most reliable spies. He had ridden, he claimed, straight from Mutair, travelling day and night, without even dismounting to eat, drink or rest. The Duweesh, he stated, had started two days before with ten war banners and was marching northwards.

"Where is he going?" I enquired.

"*Yebghik ent,*" the bedouin answered laconically. "He wants to get you yourself."

I called on the most experienced of the police camelmen to cross-question the informer, but all his answers appeared perfectly circumstantial. There seemed to be little doubt that the day of decision was upon us. The spy also told us that Sultan Ibn Humaid was to raid the Jumaima area on the same day as the Duweesh would attack us.

"Well," I said to my bedouin councillors, "what do we do now?"

"It is for you to give the order, O long of life," they replied quietly.

As a "general", I was in an unenviable position. Of all the forces in the field on our side, only the bedouin police of the camel corps were actually under my command, though on them I now placed complete and utter reliance. The very dangers of our situation had already made us brothers. The tribes might, or might not, do as I told them, and there was no penalty which I could inflict on those who refused to obey me. The four guns of the Iraq army were not under my orders, although we co-operated well. The R.A.F., though they were in reality our only powerful weapon, might well be even more difficult.

As we finished our conference, the men were just carrying in the tray, laden with rice, which I and they were to share for dinner. With an air of assumed indifference, we decided that the Duweesh could wait until dinner was finished. It so happened that Lizzam aba Dhra',[1] who was safely camped near the armoured cars and the Iraq army at Busaiya, had ridden forward that day to pay us a visit. When he heard the news, he shouted loudly for his riding camel. "Have dinner before you go," the men called to him, half banteringly; "you'll fight all the better on a full stomach." "Pity to lose your last meal on earth," said another with a grin. "You may not be in a position to want any breakfast tomorrow morning."

[1] See page 79.

But the old man was in no mood for joking. He climbed on to his camel and set out for Busaiya, flogging it along at a fast trot with his cane.

No sooner was dinner over than we set to work in earnest, for there was much to be done. We calculated that the Duweesh would attack us at dawn on 19th February, so we had three days in which to round up all our tribes and draw up our line of battle. I had already chosen the position where we meant to fight. It was a few miles to the north-east, at a place called Al Abtiyya. Two hours after receipt of the spy's report we sent the police cars out in all directions to warn our tribes that the Duweesh was coming and to tell them to concentrate at Al Abtiyya.

I had considered four factors in choosing Al Abtiyya. Firstly, it was the most northerly point at which there was good grazing, which was essential when concentrating so many herds in a small area. Secondly, water for a large tribal concentration was even more necessary, and there were fortunately good pools of rainwater near by. Thirdly, the ground was open and therefore suitable for the armoured cars, which we hoped would join us. Finally, Al Abtiyya was a little farther back from the frontier than Maghaizal, and, as we were not allowed to cross the border, this gave us slightly more room in which to locate the advancing raiders.

After a forced march of nearly forty-eight hours, the last of our tribes from the Neutral Area passed our camp at Maghaizal on the evening of 17th February. This rapid retirement of about forty-five miles in as many hours, involved considerable hardship for the shepherds, most of whom, including the women and children, performed it on foot, many of them carrying infants or young lambs, for the whole distance. It was impossible for us to move forward and cover their retreat, because the Iraq army was, for diplomatic reasons, forbidden to enter the Neutral Area, and all the police cars had been dispersed to warn and rally the tribes.

As they streamed past our camp, the weary and footsore shepherds presented a pitiable sight. Unaware of the diplomatic shackles which hampered us, they attributed our immobility to cowardice, while they had been fleeing hot-foot from Julaida and Uqubba. As the exhausted Zayyad women passed us, dragging their weary limbs after forty hours or more of walking, they hurled bitter taunts at our little group of police and soldiers. As soon as the last of the tribes had passed us, we ourselves moved back after them to Al Abtiyya.

On the morning of 17th February, we had already marked out our battle position and some of the men had set to work to dig the trenches for our little redoubt. We decided to draw up the Zayyad on our right and the Dhafeer on our left. I drove round all the chiefs in the vicinity, urging the tribes to rally, to concentrate round the government forces and to show the world their mettle. "Backs to the wall is the order of the day," I wrote in my diary.

I had obtained some rifles and a supply of ammunition from the Iraq Government and, in the evening, as the weary tribes pitched their tents in their allotted positions, we made an issue of rifles and ammunition to the tribesmen.

As the men returned in the police cars from rallying the tribes, their faces and clothes white with dust, we called upon them for a further and more dangerous effort. We organized patrols to go out daily from Al Abtiyya to Shaeeb al Auja on the east, to Quraiyat Mudairis and to Uqubba. We were still slightly too near the frontier to be certain of locating the enemy the night before his attack. The Ikhwan could cover sixty miles in their forced night march and still attack at dawn. From Al Abtiyya to Shaeeb al Auja was forty-five miles, to Quraiyat Mudairis forty, to Uqubba fifty-five.[1] Thus we could not be certain that our frontier patrols would see the advancing banners before dark. There was, however, a chance that they might or alternatively that they might encounter an enemy scouting party. Three patrols left our camp every morning at half-past seven, and travelled down to the frontier, deliberately searching every fold of the ground and scanning the wide expanses of the desert with field-glasses from the summit of every hill. The main body of the raiders would not be encountered in broad daylight. At this stage, the patrolling cars were looking for enemy scouts or reconnoitring parties, or for casual stragglers who might have news. At midday the patrols reached the frontier and lay there, on some convenient hilltop until after dark.

Raiders normally had their evening meal in the late afternoon and started just before sunset on their last long night march. It was possible that our pickets might catch a glimpse of the masses of camel-riders approaching the frontier, just before dark. As soon as complete darkness had set in, they returned as rapidly as possible to Al Abtiyya to report.

If, however, the frontier patrols had failed to see the raiders, the latter might have crossed the frontier just after dark. In this case, we calculated, they might be surprised by the dawn a few miles before they reached our camp. We accordingly arranged for two vehicles to carry out a dawn patrol each day. Setting out when the very first pale light began to appear in the east, they were to move cautiously to a position some fifteen miles in front of us. Here, if they saw nothing, they were to remain in observation until the day patrols passed them on their way south.

If the day patrols could only see the raiders at sunset the advantage to us would be immense. We could signal Baghdad before every-

[1] See map on page 238.

one went to bed, and orders could be issued for aircraft and armoured cars to support us at dawn the next morning. If the dawn patrol sighted the enemy, we should at least be able to send off a signal before we were overwhelmed in the noise and passion of the battle. Aircraft might still be in time to help us, though the issue of the battle would be decided before the R.A.F. armoured cars from Busaiya could reach us.

On 18th February, another of my spies came in. He had joined the Duweesh's raiding party and had marched northwards with them for two days, before slipping away at night and riding full speed to join us. He stated quite categorically that the Duweesh with a large force would attack us at dawn on 20th February. The informer's veracity and his accuracy seemed to be beyond question. I accordingly sent a signal to Baghdad, reporting the date of the expected attack and adding that the Al Abtiyya position had been chosen owing to the suitability of the ground for operations by armoured vehicles. I asked that a section of R.A.F. armoured cars from Busaiya be instructed to join us, as an opportunity might well occur to teach the Duweesh a lesson, which he would not forget. No reply was received to this signal, and I remained at Al Abtiyya with the police cars, four Iraq army cars and some forty camelmen of the Southern Desert Camel Corps. The Zayyad were now drawn up in position on our right, the Dhafeer on our left and the Budoor shepherds behind us.

Arab nomads were capable of the most reckless bravery in their wild charges, but on the passive defensive, their ardour was inclined to cool. Accordingly, on 18th and 19th February, we held war dances in our camps, and roused one another with song and dance to fresh martial ardour. The bedouin war dances illustrated the profound differences which distinguished them, culturally and to some extent perhaps racially, from the settled or shepherd Iraqis. The bedouin dances were performed by the men, usually formed up in two long lines, swaying slowly or taking a few paces forward and then a few back. Sometimes one or two men would dance between the lines, swaying rhythmically and gracefully, waving drawn swords above their heads. The shepherds used the same war dance as the settled Iraq tribes and known as the *hosa*. It involved vigorous dancing, and loud full-throated choruses in quick time. Both types included the firing of shots in the air.

On the evening of 18th February, I drove back to Umm al Medafa in Kuwait territory (which I was now permitted to enter but the Iraq army was not), in order to organize the resistance of the Juwareen and Beni Malik. These and other Iraq tribes had been concentrated by us in this area, but I was apprehensive lest they be raided by an easterly column—possibly from Mutair and Ajman

—on the same day as the Duweesh attacked us. I slept with them that night, sitting up late round the camp fire discussing the situation, the probable enemy line of advance and the distribution and posting of their scouts.

I left the camps at Umm al Medafa before dawn. It had rained during the night, the earth was wet and, as the sun rose, every blade of grass and every little twig on the low shrubs was sparkling with diamond drops. The sky had cleared, the air was fresh and intoxicating—it might have been a May morning in England rather than February in the Arabian desert.

As we drove across the rolling plain of the Dibdibba, I wondered if I should find my people still in their camps. The spy's report seemed to be perfectly accurate and according to our time and distance calculations, the attack would come at dawn the next day. Where would I be in twenty-four hours, I wondered. It was eight o'clock. The attack would probably have taken place two hours earlier and the issue would already have been decided.

That morning the vast emptiness of the desert seemed to be more than ordinarily full of meaning. It made the silly fussiness of civilization seem trivial. These tribesmen lived such simple lives, confined to so few elemental things. Their possessions were camels, sheep and a tent. Their food flour, rice and dates. Their clothes a shirt and a cloak. They were daily confronted by life and death, plain and undisguised. No wonder that such conditions bred in them the simplest of religions—one God, Almighty, Conquering, Merciful. The desert indeed had the same effect on me. Yet here was I, probably about to have my throat cut by men who had been affected by the desert, much as I had been affected. They would cut my throat in the name of their religion. But no—that was not really true. Wahhabism had started as a simple return to religion, but now it had degenerated into murder and loot.

All the world, I thought, was like that. Men began with a great idea, but it would then be captured and utilized by the powers of evil, and would soon be transformed into greed and cruelty.

At length we topped the last ridge and there in a wide expanse of open desert lay our little group of white tents and vehicles, the black Arab tents stretching east and west on either side of them and the flocks and herds dotting the plain all around. It looked a peaceful pastoral scene. As I drove into our little camp, our bearded bedouin machine gunners were stripping and cleaning their Vickers guns. There must be no stoppages at dawn tomorrow.

As there was no reply from air headquarters to my signal about the armoured cars, I sent off another cypher message. In the hope of goading the authorities into action, I said that I considered my position at Al Abtiyya unsafe, unless a section of armoured cars could be sent. This time the answer came back almost immediately. It suggested that, if my position were unsafe, I could retire to Busaiya, where the armoured cars were located.

It was, of course, out of the question to abandon the tribes at Al Abtiyya. For four days we had been urging them to stand and fight and, as the Duweesh's attack was expected the next morning, it would be unthinkable for the government forces to run away today. The tribes would have panicked and fled to the Euphrates, the morale of the Ikhwan would have soared and Ibn Saud's position would have been correspondingly weakened. The safety of the Iraq tribes and the future stability of Nejed itself seemed to necessitate our standing firm.

I felt myself not a little aggrieved at the refusal of the authorities to support me, yet, looking back thirty years later, I can now appreciate more justly what they thought. They doubtless regarded me as a conceited young man, roused to enthusiasm by some romantic notion about bedouins. The Iraqi ministry of the interior seemed to desire to support me, and the service commanders had acquiesced, but they had no intention of allowing regular forces to be mixed up in such lunacy. Like the inspector-general of police, they would have nothing to do with "catch 'em alivos". But what really was past endurance was that, having insisted in getting myself mixed up in this foolishness, I was now crying out that my position was unsafe, and trying to drag R.A.F. armoured cars into the precarious situation in which I had placed myself. This the service commanders (perhaps rightly) were determined to resist.

The Duweesh was due to attack at dawn the next day, I thought. If he had not done so by ten o'clock in the morning, it would be safe to fly back to Baghdad, returning the same evening. I accordingly signalled my chiefs, the Iraqi ministry of the interior, asking permission to fly to Baghdad for two hours the following day. Surely I could convince air headquarters that to run away now would be disastrous.

*   *   *   *   *

The remainder of that day, 19th February, 1929, was spent interviewing shaikhs and tribesmen, discussing the morrow's tactics and rehearsing the rôle of the police and the army. We waited anxiously for the return of the day patrols. If the Duweesh were to attack us at dawn the next day, our scouts might see him near the frontier at sunset. It was ten o'clock at night before they came in and reported that they had seen nothing. I lay down, fully dressed in my tent, with my rifle beside me. The hours passed slowly. I dropped off several times to sleep and woke again. Long before dawn, I left my tent and went out in the cool night air. Overhead the stars shone with Arabian brightness. The bark of a dog here and there in the tribal camps alone broke the deep silence of the desert.

Some of the men were already stirring, going over their guns with slightly oily rags. As soon as the first pale light appeared in the blackness of the eastern sky, the dawn patrol set out. I told them to go forward only a mile, and there to stop their engines and listen. If they heard anything, they were to fire red Very lights. Even a few minutes would give us time to send off a signal before the battle broke over us. As soon as it was light enough for them to see, they were to go forward for five miles and lie in observation on the hills. The patrol commander nodded in silence. The men climbed into their vehicles, and settled themselves behind their guns. "God be with you, brothers," said Rimaithan the Anezi quietly, as the trucks drew out into the open through a gap in the wire.

After so many days of waiting, now that the hour had come I did not feel afraid. A feeling of exaltation possessed us. We laughed and joked. I sent messengers along the tribal camps, with cheerful greetings. I myself did not wish to leave the Iraq army wireless set, in case of sudden alarm. I had agreed with the tribes that if we repulsed the Ikhwan, or if aircraft arrived and compelled them to break off the action, every man would mount horse or camel and join in the pursuit.

Hamed the slave arrived with the inevitable coffee pot, soon followed by little glasses of sweet tea. Gradually the light grew. We strained our eyes to the south. The dawn patrol had disappeared. The men in the trenches lit cigarettes and drank coffee. Then for the hundredth time, they took out their oily rags and rubbed over the mechanism of their guns.

At half-past seven, the day patrols went out. An hour later the dawn patrol came back having seen nothing. At ten o'clock, a ninak landed to take me to Baghdad. We agreed to let the flocks go out grazing. The men began to cook a meal.

The Duweesh had not come.

XV

From Jumaima to the Mother of Guns

The bedawin—who, it must be admitted, were little better than brigands on occasion—had greatly scandalized the austere and puritanical citizens, natural enemies of the sons of the desert.

DOZY, *The Moslems in Spain*

XV

FROM JUMAIMA TO THE MOTHER OF GUNS

ON my arrival in Baghdad, I drove straight to air headquarters where I was received by a senior officer. I enquired what action could be taken on my telegram asking for armoured cars, explaining at the same time the impossibility of retiring to Busaiya and abandoning the tribes. "We thought," replied the officer drily, "that if you were as frightened as your telegrams seemed to indicate, you had better run away."

I was young and still hot-tempered. I thanked the speaker, snatched up my hat and left the office. Boiling with internal resentment, I drove back to my aircraft and we took off at once for Al Abtiyya. It was obviously a capital error to have lost my temper in this manner. If I had been older and wiser, I should have swallowed this little gibe and possibly been able to convince air headquarters of the wisdom of my views. They would have taken me home to lunch and we would have parted with sufficient mutual comprehension to enable them to appreciate the significance of my telegrams in future. Boys however, will be boys and the young are rarely patient and tolerant —indeed we are fortunate if we become so, even in our old age.

I had been attached to the R.A.F. for five years and had flown with them for thousands of hours. Indeed my present indignation was not against the R.A.F., to whom I felt a considerable bond of loyalty, but against senior officers, who, I told myself, sat comfortably in Baghdad, indifferent to us bedouins and shepherds, pilots and car crews, daily facing death in the far deserts. Time brings its own nemesis—twenty years later I was myself to pace anxiously up and down an office, envying the young men who, careless of the outcome of the war, were engrossed in the passions of battle, free from the gnawing anxieties which deprived senior officers of their sleep.

It was unfortunate also that, although I had been seconded to the R.A.F. for five years, I had left them two and a half years earlier and all their personnel changed every two years. To the new occupants of the office chairs in air headquarters, I was therefore not one of them, but a rather bumptious civilian. Air officers commanding could scarcely be expected to follow the advice of such a young man, especially on the subject of how to use their forces on active operations. Moreover, they regarded the idea of asking the Iraq tribes to fight with no little scepticism.

Several months later, an officer of air headquarters explained to me the reason for my reception by the staff. There was, he told me, a general feeling of annoyance. It was said that I always thought that I knew best. Some officers wished therefore to punish me for my conceit.

It may well be that their charges were justified. Young people are all too often arrogant, possibly because their outlook is too narrow. I admittedly was entirely engrossed in my own work, which appeared to me to be all-important. I was far indeed from the attainment of "that clear view of human nothingness matched against the perfection of God, which is the sovereign remedy against pride and self-love."[1]

*   *   *   *   *

The next day, we again stood to our arms before dawn, but again the Duweesh did not come.

It will be recollected that the spies who had come in to us at Al Abtiyya to warn us of the advance of the Duweesh, had also informed us that Sultan Ibn Humaid of Ateiba would raid the Jumaima area on the same day as the Duweesh attacked us. Mutair were our neighbours. Their grazing grounds lay next to those of the Dhafeer, and I had been able to find spies who knew them well and were able to live in their midst. But Ateiba lived on the other side of Nejed. Nobody in the Iraqi Southern Desert knew them and I had been unable to find any informers who could visit them and bring us warning of their intentions. Then I was struck by an idea.

At the Jidda meeting in May, 1928, it had been agreed that I was authorized to communicate direct on frontier matters with Abdul Aziz Ibn Musaad, the governor of Hail. In January, 1929, it occurred to me that I might send a camelman to Ibn Musaad with a letter, in which I enquired his views on a number of minor frontier incidents. But before my messenger left, I explained to him that, in the event of his obtaining information of any danger threatening us, he should return instantly to warn us.

This man was in Hail when he heard that Ibn Humaid with his war banners had moved out to attack Iraq. The messenger had been told by Ibn Musaad to wait until the reply to my letter was ready for him to take, but day followed day and no reply was forthcoming. He suspected that he was being intentionally delayed to prevent his bringing us news of events in Nejed. He accordingly slipped away from Hail under cover of darkness and, leaving behind his smart clothes and disguising himself as a ragged bedouin, he rode day and night as fast as he could to bring us warning. He passed, not without risk, within a few miles of Ibn Humaid's force, which

[1] Evelyn Underhill, *Mystics of the Church.*

was then bivouacked at Arj al Madhhoor, about a hundred miles south-west of Jumaima.[1] He reached our camp at Al Abtiyya on 17th February, the day after we had received the report that the Duweesh was advancing against us. He accurately reported the strength and location of Ibn Humaid's force, the largest and the most fanatical of the Ikhwan columns. He gave it as his opinion that Ibn Humaid was making for Lina and that, from there, he would advance on Iraq and cross the frontier at Jumaima. Obviously Ibn Humaid and the Duweesh were synchronizing their movements most carefully.

Shortly before the receipt of this information, I had received a report that the Yaajeeb shepherd tribe had moved forward from Sulman where they had been told to remain and were actually camped at Jumaima, exactly in the path of the advancing war banners. I hastened to Sulman and arranged for the despatch of two police camelmen to order the Yaajeeb to return instantly to Sulman, because the Ikhwan were coming. I returned on the same day to Al Abtiyya, where we were expecting the Duweesh to attack us, only to be informed two days later that the Yaajeeb had refused to move. The grazing at Sulman, they said, was poor while that at Jumaima was excellent.

I was afraid to leave Al Abtiyya, where we were momentarily expecting attack by the Duweesh, but I signalled most urgent orders to Sulman that the Yaajeeb must be withdrawn immediately at whatever cost. Thinking, however, that messengers direct from my camp at Al Abtiyya might carry more conviction than those emanating from Sulman, I also sent two police camelmen direct. For so risky a task, I chose Radhi al Toomi of Shammar and Sulman Ibn Lafi of Aneza. I told them the story of the Yaajeeb and the advance of Sultan Ibn Humaid and emphasized that they simply must make the shepherds move camp immediately. The desert camel police at Sulman also did all that was possible. Two tribesmen on horses were sent at full speed to warn the Yaajeeb again, behind them two police camelmen and then two more police camelmen.

I passed these days and nights in intense anxiety. It is true that it was only a trifling little war. Even Baghdad hardly regarded it as of the first importance. Perhaps the capitals of Europe did not so much as know that it was in progress. The "army" under my command consisted only of ninety bedouin police, in co-operation with a small sub-unit of the Iraq army. The R.A.F. contingent consisted of two squadrons of ninaks and an armoured car company. Compared with the immense issues at stake between the Great Powers today, our tiny war was trivial indeed. Yet to some extent, the responsibilities of an independent commander are always the same. He stands alone

[1] See map on page 238.

to make decisions, which will bring success or disaster to the cause he serves and to the men whom he commands.

In spite of all these successive warnings, the Yaajeeb still refused to move camp. In doing so, however, they were not merely reckless. There were some Shammar camped near by, just south of the frontier near Jumaima, and the shepherds assumed that these bedouins must know what was happening in Nejed and would themselves move away if they knew that the Ikhwan raiders were coming.

Eventually on 20th February, 1929, I signalled to the Iraqi ministry of the interior, asking them to hire three civilian taxis and send them immediately to Sulman. The desert police cars, all of which were fully engaged in patrolling the frontier, were not available. Camel police were put in the three taxis at Sulman and were sent post haste to Jumaima with yet more peremptory orders to the Yaajeeb to retire immediately. At last on 21st February, the day after the Duweesh was expected to attack us at Al Abtiyya, the shepherds complied.

Meanwhile Sultan Ibn Humaid, with three thousand men, had reached Umm Rumah, forty-five miles south-west of Jumaima on 21st February, the day on which the shepherds left the latter place. His scouts captured Abdulla al Daham, a minor shaikh of Shammar in Iraq, and took him back to their leader for cross-questioning. Abdulla, whose throat the Ikhwan were quite ready to cut if he gave them false information, reported to Ibn Humaid the locations of all the tribes in the Jumaima area. These included a number of camps of the Nejed Shammar, Ibn Rasheed's one-time subjects, and a large group of Nejed merchants with flocks of camels, which they were taking to Egypt for sale. He also reported that the Yaajeeb were camped at Jumaima, though in actual fact they had moved that very morning.

Ibn Humaid also asked Abdulla the location of the Iraq frontier and, when the latter told him that it was approximately the line of the Butn, he asked how far the Butn was from Jumaima and whether the frontier was patrolled by aircraft or cars.

The locations given to the Ikhwan by Abdulla al Daham were perfectly accurate, except that he did not know that the Yaajeeb had moved that morning from Jumaima. Neither did he—nor did we—know that a small section of Zayyad, which for the previous month had been camped at Lifiya, south-west of Shebicha, had suddenly moved forward to near Jumaima. It is essential to appreciate the vast size of the desert and the ease with which small groups of tents could wander away and lose touch completely with the world.

On the basis of the information received from Abdulla al Daham, Sultan Ibn Humaid divided his force into three approximately

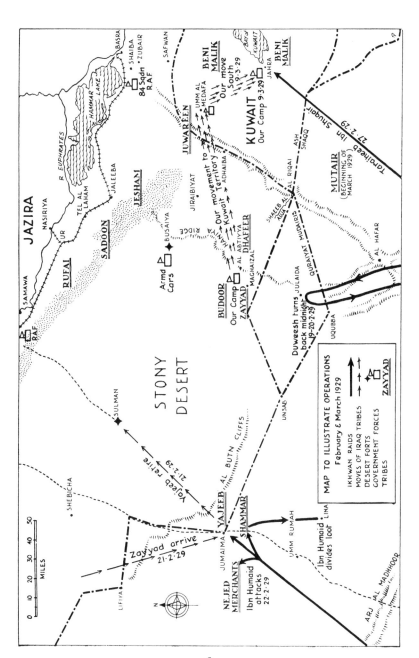

MAP TO ILLUSTRATE OPERATIONS
February & March 1929

IKHWAN RAIDS
MOVES OF IRAQ TRIBES
DESERT FORTS
GOVERNMENT FORCES
TRIBES
ZAYYAD

equal portions. One of these was detailed to attack the Nejed Shammar, while the second raided the Nejdi camel merchants, both groups of victims being subjects of Ibn Saud and camped in Nejed territory. Sultan himself, with a thousand men, decided to fall upon the Yaajeeb at Jumaima. The three attacks were launched simultaneously at dawn on 22nd February, 1929.

Shammar suffered heavily, being totally unprepared and not apparently anticipating that Ibn Humaid would attack the subjects of Ibn Saud. The camel merchants, mostly natives of the Qaseem, were massacred almost to a man. When Ibn Humaid himself reached Jumaima, the Yaajeeb had vanished, having moved camp twenty-four hours earlier, after the visit of the Sulman camel police in the three taxis. His scouts reported to him that they had crossed the Butn, whereat Sultan replied, "If they have crossed the Butn, leave them alone,"—a significant remark in the light of the statement, made to him by Abdulla al Daham, that the Butn was the frontier of Iraq.

The little group of Zayyad shepherds which, unknown to us, had moved from Lifiya to Jumaima, had camped the previous evening near the camel merchants' convoy. They were entirely ignorant of Ibn Humaid's raid, while the Ikhwan themselves were unaware of the arrival of the Zayyad.

It will be remembered that I had also sent two camel men from Al Abtiyya to Jumaima to compel the Yaajeeb to move. They reached Jumaima on the evening of 21st February, the Yaajeeb having moved away northwards that morning. Scouting in the vicinity at sunset, they located the Zayyad, who were just pitching their tents for the night. Radhi and Sulman slept with them that night and explained the situation. The Zayyad agreed to move camp and escape northwards the following morning.

At dawn, the two camelmen left the shepherd camp, intent on finding the Yaajeeb or any other shepherd camps still in the vicinity. Shortly after leaving the Zayyad tents, however, they heard the noise of battle and suddenly, over a ridge, some thirty Ikhwan horsemen galloped down upon them. Escape was impossible. Hastily couching their camels on a low hill, they dismounted, lay on the ground and opened fire. Three days later we found their dead bodies, stripped naked and full of wounds. Beside each body lay a pile of one hundred and fifty empty cartridge cases. They had held the overwhelming numbers of the enemy at bay until each had fired his last round, when, remaining defenceless, they had been over-whelmed. Such was the spirit which inspired the Southern Desert Camel Corps, although the force had been in existence for only a year.

Ibn Humaid did not know of the little camp of Zayyad which had arrived the night before, but some of the raiders who charged through the camp of the merchants came upon the group of shepherd tents by accident. As a result of the fact that the Ikhwan did not know that the Zayyad were in the area, they did not surprise their camp at dawn. Moreover, having been warned by Radhi and Sulman, the shepherds were aware that a raid was imminent, and, hearing shots from the camp of the camel merchants, they realized that a battle was in progress. The Zayyad men and boys accordingly immediately took to flight. When the excited raiders blundered into the shepherds' camp, they found it occupied by women alone. They made a clean sweep of the sheep, donkeys, tents and all their possessions, but they did not interfere with the women and there were no casualties. At least, therefore, our two camelmen, though they lost their own lives, were in time to warn the Zayyad and thereby save them from a massacre. As they ransacked the shepherds' camp, the men of Ateiba taunted the Zayyad women, saying, "Where is your friend Abu Hunaik now? Let him save you from the Muslimeen if he can."

*   *   *   *   *

As already related, the principal Ikhwan rebel chiefs had already, in their plans, divided Ibn Saud's dominions between them. The Duweesh was to be the ruler of Nejed, Ibn Humaid of the Hejaz and Ibn Hithlain of the Hasa. Nida Ibn Nuhaiyir, one of the few Shammar to become a Wahhabi and receive a war banner from Ibn Saud, was said to have been promised that he would be the ruler of Hail. Nida, however, was cautious and waited to declare himself. Eventually, the rebels meeting with indifferent success, he remained loyal to Ibn Saud after all.

The oasis of Jauf consisted of a separate little group of villages, lying surrounded by deserts, half way between the Qaseem and Damascus. It had been conquered by Ibn Saud only seven years before, previous to which it had been controlled for some years by Ibn Shaalan, the powerful chief of the Ruwalla or Syrian Aneza.[1] A restless and discontented young member of the Shaalan family, Ferhan Ibn Mashhoor, had professed Wahhabi-ism, and had now allied himself with the rebels, in return for a promise of the governorship of Jauf.

While the Duweesh and Ibn Humaid were moving up for their grand invasion of Iraq, Ibn Mashhoor with a force of about one hundred and fifty of his own Ruwalla tribesmen—but all wearing white Ikhwan turbans—surprised a camp of Wuld Suleiman near the head of the Wadi Arar in Nejed territory. Wuld Suleiman were a branch of Aneza and hence "cousins" of the Ruwalla, and were

[1] See tribal map on page 61.

likewise a Syrian tribe. The camp comprised some thirty families, all the males of which were savagely massacred and their herds and property looted.

While Ibn Humaid was resting at Lina after his Jumaima raid, Murdhi al Rufidi, a shaikh of the Amarat or Iraq Aneza, also arrived to join him. Murdhi had gone over to Ibn Saud eighteen months earlier and had professed Wahhabi-ism, because he was dissatisfied with the position accorded to him by the Iraq Government. It is interesting to notice that Ibn Saud himself had insisted on the insertion, in the Treaty of Bahra, of an article prohibiting the seduction by one government of the tribes subject to the other. Yet after the conclusion of that treaty, he himself seduced Ajami Ibn Suwait and Murdhi al Rufidi, both leading tribal shaikhs of Iraq.

It had been Murdhi's intention to raid with Ibn Humaid, but, to his intense disappointment, he arrived after the battle, while the men of Ateiba were dividing the loot. Ibn Humaid, however, apparently took pity on him and gave him his blessing, together with a contingent of four hundred Ikhwan of Mutair and Ateiba. Thus reinforced, Murdhi set forth, in the name of religion, seeking whom he could devour. Like the Duweesh and Ibn Humaid, he hesitated to cross the Iraq frontier, but found some fifty tents of Sulubba near Umm Khunsir, in Nejed territory. The Sulubba were a remarkable race of desert tinkers, of unknown, and possibly not Arab origin. They were despised by the Arabs, were unarmed and took no part in desert wars. Thus to attack them was not only a flagrant insult to Ibn Saud, for they were his subjects and camped in his territory, but was also a despicable action according to the old Arab rules of honour—according to any standards indeed, for they were unarmed non-combatants. Nearly all the Sulubba were massacred in cold blood, although they offered no resistance.

Murdhi al Rufidi thereupon joined Ibn Mashhoor and the two, with about eight hundred followers, proceeded towards Jauf at the commencement of March, where for the moment we may leave them.

*   *   *   *   *

In the previous chapter, I related how we had expected the Duweesh to attack us on 20th February and again on the 21st but that he did not come. Three more days passed without news. All the spies whom I had put out with Mutair to warn us of his coming had already come in to report his intention of attacking on 20th February. We were left now without informers. In front of our camp lay an empty no-man's-land, which nobody, anticipating the appearance of the Ikhwan at any moment, was willing to cross. It was a situation which I had not foreseen when I placed my informers amongst the Nejed tribes.

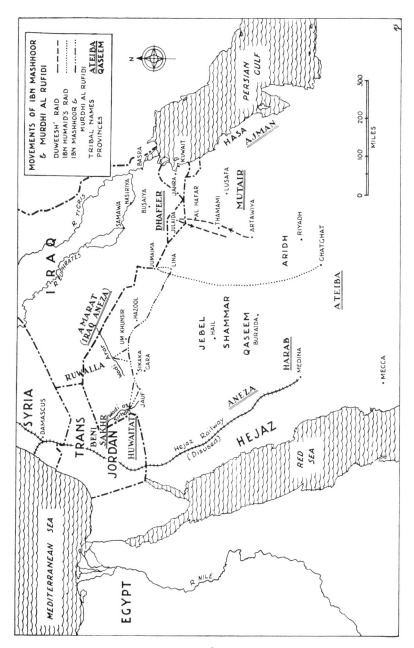

MOVEMENTS OF IBN MASHHOOR & MURDHI AL RUFIDI

DUWEESH' RAID — — —
IBN HUMAID'S RAID ....
IBN MASHHOOR &
MURDHI AL RUFIDI — · — ·
TRIBAL NAMES
PROVINCES

ATEIBA
QASEEM

N

MILES
0   100   200   300

IRAQ

R. TIGRIS
R. EUPHRATES

BASRA

SAMAWA
NASIRIYA
BUSAIYA
JAHRA
KUWAIT

DHAFEER
JULAIDA
AL HAFAR
THAMAMI
LUSAFA

MUTAIR

HASA

AJMAN

PERSIAN GULF

JUMAIMA
LINA

ARTAWIYA
RIYADH
CHATGHAT

ARIDH

ATEIBA

AMARAT
(IRAQ ANEZA)

UM KHUMSIR
HAZOOL

Wadi Araf
RUWALLA

SIKAKA
GARA

JEBEL
SHAMMAR
HAIL
BURAIDA.

QASEEM

HARAB

MEDINA

MECCA

ANEZA

JAUF
Wadi Sirhan

BENI SAKHR
HUWAITAT

TRANS
JORDAN

DAMASCUS

SYRIA

Hejaz Railway
(Disused)

HEJAZ

RED SEA

MEDITERRANEAN SEA

EGYPT

R. NILE

It was not until some days later that we pieced together the story of those days. The Duweesh, it appeared, had fully intended to raid us at dawn on 20th February, as our spies had said. He had advanced to Julaida,[1] only thirty miles from our position, during the first half of the night of 19th-20th February. The remaining distance he intended to cover between midnight and dawn on 20th February. Meanwhile, however, he had taken the precaution of sending a spy to our camps, with orders to slip away during the night of 18th-19th February, and meet him at Julaida on the night of 19th-20th. This spy had been in our camp when we issued the rifles and ammunition to our tribes. He had seen the tribal war dances and had also been within sight when three ninaks landed beside our camp. Then he had slipped away unnoticed and had encountered the Duweesh at Julaida during the night of 19th-20th February.

He reported that we were at Al Abtiyya, that we had received warning of his intended attack and that the Iraq tribes were rallied around us; that the tribes had received a free distribution of arms and ammunition and were prepared to resist attack and that we had with us a large force of aircraft and armoured cars. Fortunately most Nejdis were never clear as to the difference between armoured and armed cars, that is open trucks carrying machine guns.

When the Duweesh had unfurled his war banners at Artawiya, he knew that we were at Maghaizal and that the Iraq tribes were scattered far and wide in front of us in the Neutral Area. He had believed that he could mop up the tribes near the frontier one day at dawn before we could intervene. The efficiency of our spies, who had warned us of his advance, and the speed with which we had brought the tribes back to Al Abtiyya, had foiled him.

In addition to the spy who had met him at Julaida, other scouting parties two days before had examined our camp after dark and had returned to report to the Duweesh. They had seen very many camp fires at night, they said, apparently massed on a front of about three miles, indicating that our tribes were drawn up in line of battle.

A council of war was held at midnight that night on the well of Julaida. The detailed report brought by the spy was corroborated by the account of the camp fires seen by the reconnaissance parties. The Duweesh had many times sworn that he would water his horses in the Euphrates and especially that he would come personally and cut my throat. The argument waxed animated between those lean dark-faced tribesmen with their white Ikhwan turbans, and when at length it ceased, the great and invincible Duweesh gave the order for retreat. "We must be past Uqubba before daylight," he emphasized, "or the armoured cars may come." Fortunately he was not aware that the armoured cars were far away at Busaiya.

[1] See map on page 265.

For nine years, the tribes of Iraq had lived under the shadow of fear. If a passing camel-rider fired a shot at a hare, whole tribes would strike their tents, fleeing in panic, looking over their shoulders, crying, "The Ikhwan, the Ikhwan, they are on us." That night at Julaida the tide turned, and the Duweesh, his war banners and his thousands of warriors, retired pell-mell across the frontier. Only when he was many miles beyond the border did he venture to bivouac in the Batin, above Al Hafar and some eighty miles south of our camp at Al Abtiyya.

It is merely academic now to speculate what would have happened if the Duweesh had decided to accept our challenge and had given the order to advance from Julaida to Al Abtiyya. As he was a little late at Julaida, he would probably not have launched his charge until an hour or more after dawn. Our own dawn patrol might have given us enough warning to enable us to send off signals to the R.A.F. It is possible that aircraft could have been with us an hour or two after the attack. The armoured cars from Busaiya would probably not have arrived for four or five hours, the heavy vehicles moving slowly in the soft shrub-covered desert. But the success or failure of the first Ikhwan charge would probably have been decided in the first hour before help could come. It would appear then that we should have had to fight our battle alone, but had we won or lost, the R.A.F. aircraft certainly, and the armoured cars possibly, would have overtaken the Ikhwan and inflicted casualties.

Thus ended the first phase of the great Ikhwan triple offensive which, under the guise of a holy war, was to have exterminated the "heathen" tribes of Iraq. Ibn Shuqair had not attacked at all. The Duweesh had advanced to within six hours' march of our camp and had hastily recrossed the frontier before day dawned. Ibn Humaid, carefully enquiring the location of the Iraq frontier, had deliberately raided other subjects of Ibn Saud in Nejed territory.

*   *   *   *   *

The position from our point of view was not entirely satisfactory. The Duweesh was camped in the Batin and near him another Mutair force under Turaiheeb Ibn Shuqair. Between us the desert was completely empty. Had they decided to attack us after all, they could have reached us in fifteen hours and we could not possibly receive warning from any intelligence source.

For the moment, however, the most urgent problem was that our tribes could no longer remain concentrated. The grazing around our large camps was exhausted and, what was even more critical, the water was nearly finished in the pools on which we depended. If we remained in our camp, our tribes would scatter once more and we could not prevent their doing so; indeed it seemed more than probable that Mutair themselves were counting on just such a development. Like a cat watching a mouse-hole, they were waiting for some groups of tents to wander away from us down towards the frontier, in order to pounce upon them. I realized that if we remained passive, our "army" would melt away within three or four days. Obviously we must take the initiative and organize the next move.

Only two areas were capable of supporting so many tribes, from the point of view of grazing and water—the Neutral Area and Kuwait territory east of the Batin, where exceptionally heavy rains had fallen. Yet it did not appear possible for us to move to either of these areas, owing to the diplomatic restrictions constantly imposed upon us. It was tempting to consider moving to the Neutral Area, thereby once more throwing down the gauntlet to the Ikhwan. But, although the year before the R.A.F. had bombed Mutair at Lusafa, one hundred and twenty miles inside Nejed, this year they were forbidden to enter or fly over the Neutral Area. The Iraq army were also forbidden to go there. Only I and the camel corps could have camped there. Attractive as such a move would have been as a gesture of defiance, it appeared unnecessarily risky, with the Duweesh and Ibn Shuqair still in the field within one night's march.

In so far as Kuwait territory was concerned, the position was the reverse of that in the Neutral Area. R.A.F. aircraft and armoured cars were allowed to operate in Kuwait but the Iraq army and the Desert Camel Corps were not. By a remarkable piece of diplomatic nicety, I was authorized to enter Kuwait territory by day, but not to sleep there. Our defensive system, involving the R.A.F., the Iraq army and the desert camel police could not therefore, owing to diplomatic restrictions, operate in either of the areas where the tribes could find grazing. In face of this situation, the authorities fell back on their usual proposal—why not withdraw to Busaiya? As there was no grazing in that area, I knew that if we withdrew, the tribes would scatter far and wide and the Duweesh, who was still waiting with his war banners just across the border, would find a helpless victim for a fresh massacre.

I explained all these points in detail in long cypher telegrams which I sent off to Baghdad. At length a compromise was reached. The concentration of all the Iraqi tribes in Kuwait territory east of the Batin was sanctioned. I had visited the area twice on recent day reconnaissances. It had remained virgin since Ibn Hithlain's raid on 21st January, 1929, when all the tribes had fled. Now the grass and the wild flowers were almost knee-deep. Some hollows in the rolling hills looked like an Alpine meadow in May—never before or since have I seen such grazing in a desert. The desert camel police and myself received permission to camp in Kuwait territory, although the Iraq army was still not allowed to cross the border. The four Iraqi machine guns and the wireless set, which had been with us at Al Abtiyya, were, however, to be replaced by a section of R.A.F. armoured cars. This satisfactory arrangement was not reached any too soon, for the drinking water pools at Al Abtiyya were already little more than damp mud.

The authorities having thus agreed to a plan, it remained to convince the tribes. The news of the splendid grazing which we were enjoying had spread to the Euphrates and across it to the Jezira area, extending over to the Tigris. Great numbers of Iraq tribes, who normally did not venture into the Southern Desert at all, had followed us out, tempted by reports that the Ikhwan had been discomfited and that the grass was green. These people camped behind us and devoured the grazing like locusts, making any northward retirement even more impossible.[1] The Dhafeer, the Jesham, the Budoor, the Juwareen, Beni Malik, the Rufai—even some members of the once princely Sadoon—were ready to enter Kuwait under our protection. But the problem was how to convince the Zayyad and Beni Huchaim of Samawa, who had already come so far. The normal winter habitat of these tribes was the Stony Desert, as far south as Jumaima. By rallying to us at Al Abtiyya, they had already come far east of their usual territory. How could I persuade them to come yet farther?

They received with dismay my proposal to move nearly another hundred miles to the east. Their reluctance was not due only to fear of strange new country. We were already at the end of February. The hot weather began in April. However fat the sheep had become, they would then have to travel two hundred and fifty miles back across nearly waterless desert to their summer grazing grounds. Caught by a heat wave on such a march, the sheep might die in hundreds. After prolonged discussions, however, the shaikhs agreed to make the attempt, a course to which they were strongly urged by the ever indomitable Kadhim.

The march in itself presented considerable problems. The Duweesh and Ibn Shuqair were still within striking distance and might endeavour to seize the opportunity as soon as we broke up our defensive position at Al Abtiyya. The distance from our camp to the new position, which we had chosen at Umm al Medafa, was seventy miles and there was no water on the way. Such a march was nothing to camel bedouins, but threatened to be a weary trek for sheep and for tribes which travelled on foot, with their tents and supplies loaded on donkeys.

The Dhafeer, being the most mobile, moved off ahead of the other tribes. I decided to bring up the rear with the Zayyad and Beni

[1] See map on page 265.

Huchaim. My own party consisted of my car, six police trucks and forty camelmen. I could not prevent myself from smiling that spring morning, as I looked out over the vast rolling spaces of the desert all around us, covered with moving flocks of sheep, caravans of laden donkeys driven by women in their long black cotton dresses and men on horseback with their rifles slung on their backs. They seemed to cover the desert as far as the horizon with a moving horde like swarming ants. In the midst of this immense nomadic throng, almost unchanged except for their rifles since the days of Abraham, moved a saloon car containing a solitary Englishman, and followed by a little convoy of trucks and forty camelmen. Never before, I thought, could so incongruous a collection have been seen in the desert, but perhaps we were merely symbolic of the new age which was dawning, when the camel, for thousands of years lord of the desert, was so soon to be eclipsed by the machine.

Our forty camelmen proudly bore with them our new war banner, on which was embroidered in gold thread the verses, "There is no god but God, and victory is near." The authorities in Baghdad had queried the suitability of using Muslim texts, on the grounds that not all the members of our force were Muslims. Perhaps the reference was to myself, but the statement that there was no god but God seemed to me theologically unexceptionable and our hopes that victory was near were rising daily.

The march proved to be a trying experience. The Zayyad were entirely ignorant of the country, and had to be organized, guided and shepherded along by the police camelmen. By a perhaps literally providential dispensation, a heavy fall of rain on the way solved our anxieties over the water crisis. As the rain pelted down and began to trickle over the face of the desert in tiny streamlets, forming little pools in the hollows or beneath the shrubs, the flocks of sheep here and there could be seen stopping, while the sheep lowered their heads to drink from the puddles. The shepherd girls, picking their empty water skins from the loads on the backs of their donkeys, ran laughing and calling to one another wherever a little stream of water was flowing. Then, scooping a hole in the gravelly soil into which the water would run, they squatted on the ground, their left hands holding open the mouth of the skin, while with their right hands, they baled the water—a little muddy perhaps—from the hole in the ground into the mouth of the water skin. When they had filled their water skins, they baled up water with their hands into their own mouths.

Shaim al Jenfawi, a little Shammari who had enlisted with us (as game and loyal a man as any soldier I ever knew) trotted up on his great striding camel, as I sat at the wheel of my car, watching the flocks go past in the driving rain. "Praise be to God for this mercy," he called out to me, spreading out his two hands, palms upwards, and looking up to heaven. "*Kull al arab shereboo*—all the Arabs have drunk."

Throughout this move, each day's march was worked out and instructions were issued to all the tribes as to their movements, almost in military fashion. At last we reached Adhaiba, on the west side of the Batin depression, where water was found in the shallow wells.

When we issued orders for the march for the next day, from Adhaiba to Umm al Medafa, the Zayyad said nothing. Next morning, however, when we moved off to the east, they broke away from our line of march and turned back towards Jiraibiyat, declaring that they would follow us no farther. Somebody, it then transpired, had circulated a rumour to the effect that the Ikhwan were about to attack Basra and that the government was decoying the tribes to Shaiba, in order to use them in the defence of the city.

I have spent the greater part of my life amongst Arabs, often, as during this winter of 1929, without any other Englishmen near me. I have made innumerable Arab friends, some as dear, as intimate and as trusted as any of my own countrymen. But all over the Arab countries I have, from time to time, encountered this maddening tendency to attribute some treacherous and sinister motive to my most sincere efforts to serve them. This inclination to suspect of unworthy and dishonest intentions even their most devoted friends, is one of the least attractive qualities of this otherwise so charming people.

After much patient arguing and explanation, the Zayyad were next day persuaded to rejoin our march.

Our wanderings in the wilderness during the winter of 1928-9 gave me a lasting sympathy for Moses, which I have ever since retained. Surely to lead a nomadic people through the desert was no sinecure. "And all the children of Israel murmured against Moses ... would God we had died in this wilderness! And wherefore hath the Lord brought us unto this land, to fall by the sword, that our wives and our children should be a prey? Were it not better for us to return ... ?"[1]

All complaining, however, was silenced when we reached Umm al Medafa. Here we camped beside a rainpool as large as a lake, lying in a shallow valley in the rolling plains, where the grass and the flowers were almost as luxuriant as an English meadow in June. Soon we were joined by the Dhafeer, the Jesham and the Sadoon, while the Budoor camped a few miles away from us on one side, the Juwareen and Beni Malik on the other. Dispositions were quickly made for defence, after consultations with the chiefs. Then all the

[1] *Numbers* xiv. 2, 3.

tribes held war dances, hurling our defiance at the Duweesh and his allies.

At Umm al Medafa, which appropriately meant the mother of guns, the Nejed-Kuwait frontier lay fifty miles to the south of us. We arranged to picket it with tribal horse and camelmen and to patrol it with police cars from dawn to dark. We were, moreover, only fifty miles from Shaiba, where our good friends 84 Squadron were ready for action. Having a section of R.A.F. armoured cars with us would enable us to communicate direct with the squadron if we were attacked. In such splendid grazing, we were able to assemble, in a small area, a tribal concentration perhaps unprecedented since the days of Thuwaini Ibn Abdulla.[1] With the frontier well covered by our pickets and patrols and the R.A.F. close at hand we could reap the reward of our past labours and anxieties.

I shall always remember that happy month—March, 1929—which I spent in the midst of our joyous and triumphant tribes, knee-deep in grass and flowers. Until that spring time, I had never seen the desert really luxuriantly carpeted with wild flowers. Perhaps the contrast between such a scene and the dusty glare of the flaming Iraqi summer made the grass and the flowers of spring seem all the more beautiful, just as a cloudless morning in England is enhanced by a preceding week of rain. God seems to use these contrasts to draw our attention to the wonderful effects which He has designed. If we look too long at one thing, no matter how beautiful, we cease to see or appreciate it. So He changes it suddenly to some entirely different style, recapturing our wandering attention, that we may "give thanks unto Him for His great glory".

Yet, in a sense, the desert was always beautiful, even the scorching heats of summer, with the far blue ridges dancing in the mirage and the little dry sandy water courses, so clean and virgin, with their fragrant scented shrubs. Just indeed as nature, left to herself, is lovely in all her moods—even the cries of the sea birds through a grey morning mist, the green twilight of the great forests or the innumerable little channels of the Euphrates marshes, shut in by walls of tall reeds, where the great buffaloes stood cooling themselves in the sparkling waters, with only their nostrils showing above the surface. Even in summer, the full furnace heat of the desert afternoon had scarcely passed by, when the air suddenly grew cool. After gasping for breath for several hours, we would feel by contrast a new rush of vitality. The moon and the stars shed a silvery light over the great plains, while every now and again a little breath of cool air whispered through the tiny shrubs.

It may be that, in some future age, the worst indictment of our industrial civilization will be that it went everywhere destroying

[1]See pages 43 and 44.

beauty and substituting man-made ugliness. And, what perhaps is worse, we are proud of this desecration. When we find lovely lands of wide plains, clear air or forest ranges, we call them backward countries and hasten to trample on their beauty, covering them with factories, skyscrapers, oilfields and blocks of concrete flats—the wonders of modern invention, we explain complacently. But who invented the sunrise, or roses, or the sunset glow on the ranges of snow-clad peaks?

XVI

The Day of Sibilla

Men change their rulers willingly, hoping to better themselves, and this hope induces them to take up arms against him who rules: wherein they are deceived, because they afterwards find by experience that they have gone from bad to worse.   MACHIAVELLI, *The Prince*

This day hath made much work for tears in many a mother.
                                                        SHAKESPEARE

XVI

THE DAY OF SIBILLA

WHEN Ibn Humaid left his home at Ghatghat at the end of January, 1929, declaring that he was bent on a holy war against the infidel Iraqis, Ibn Saud was reported to have sent after him urging him to delay action until all the Muslimeen could join him in his pious enterprise—a ruse doubtless to gain time. When Ibn Humaid disregarded this advice, Ibn Saud was alleged to have sent a second messenger after him, informing him that he could raid Iraq if he liked on condition that he did not attack any Nejed tribes. It was doubtful, at this stage, whether Ibn Saud had the power to raise forces in Nejed against the rebels, even if he had so desired. For the tenets of Wahhabi-ism and the duty of holy war against infidels had been diligently inculcated into the people by the king himself and had indeed been instrumental in enabling Ibn Saud to overthrow his Arab rivals, Ibn Rasheed and the sherifs. As long, therefore, as the rebels adhered to their professed intention to carry on the duty of holy war, it was difficult for the king to raise much enthusiasm against them. In fact he himself was in danger of falling under suspicion of having abandoned his religious duty, in pursuit of worldly advantage, by making friends with the infidels. Many indeed may have thought Ibn Humaid and the Duweesh to have been too hasty in throwing down the gauntlet to Ibn Saud, and may have considered that by so doing, they were dividing the Muslimeen. Others, bought to the royal cause by generous gifts, may have been unwilling to abandon the source of these gains until it was plain who was going to win. Others again, chiefs of the same social status as Ibn Humaid and the Duweesh, may have been jealous of their peers aspiring to be their rulers. But it was one thing to sympathize with the royal cause for these or other reasons, and quite a different one to be willing to embark on a fratricidal civil war against Mutair, Ateiba and the Ajman, while they were claiming that their sole ambition was to fulfil the duty of holy war against the infidels.

Ibn Humaid's raid at Jumaima revolutionized this situation. The massacre of the merchants raised a storm of indignation amongst the townspeople of Nejed. The other great bedouin tribes were scarcely less outraged. Shammar had themselves been heavily raided by Ibn Humaid. A section of Aneza—Wuld Suleiman—had been massacred by Ibn Mashhoor, and various sections of Aneza formed a large part of the tribes of the Hejaz. Harab had never joined the rebels and were now loud in their expressions of indignation. Above all, Ibn Humaid's claim to be a true Muslim, while Ibn Saud was a worldly renegade, had been revealed to be complete hypocrisy. When fighting the infidels had appeared to be dangerous, he had raided his fellow Muslimeen instead. The royal cause, which had appeared so precarious only a month before, suddenly enjoyed countrywide support. Ibn Saud, instead of being obliged to urge his followers to rally round him, found himself adjured by them to take strong measures against those who committed such outrages.

The Duweesh was a much more skilful politician than Ibn Humaid. Unable to find an Iraq tribe which he could raid without danger, he bided his time and meanwhile never completely broke off relations with the king. Had the Duweesh been in command, he might have continued almost indefinitely in semi-rebellion, never coming into the open, always professing religious motives, careful not to go far enough in his insubordination to provide Ibn Saud with a pretext for fighting. But no two Arab chiefs can agree for long. Ibn Humaid had no political skill and by his hot-headed rashness was to play into Ibn Saud's hands.

When the news of Ibn Humaid's Jumaima raid reached Ibn Saud, he proceeded to Buraida in the Qaseem, and called out a double levy of the townspeople of Nejed. The latter responded with alacrity, convinced that they could no longer live and trade if the wild bedouins of Ateiba could massacre their merchants with impunity. The king then appealed to all the tribes to join him.

*   *   *   *   *

We left the three principal rebel forces at the end of February, camped south of the Iraq frontier. Ibn Shuqair and the Duweesh were near Al Hafar and had not yet delivered their attack on us. Ibn Humaid divided his plunder between his followers at Lina. He had meanwhile sent spies to ascertain whether Ibn Saud showed any signs of activity. If so, it had been arranged that he and the Duweesh should join forces to confront him. If not, it was believed that he proposed to carry out further raids northwards against Aneza in the Wadian area, west of Kerbela, where there were no Iraqo-British forces.

Meanwhile Taraiheeb Ibn Shuqair had found a safer objective than the main concentration of Iraq tribes. Unknown to us, some thirty tents of Beni Malik shepherds had, at the end of January, moved to Jahra and camped with Araibdar. The cordial relations between Araibdar and the Ikhwan rebels were well known and hence the shepherds thought that to camp with the former would ensure their safety.

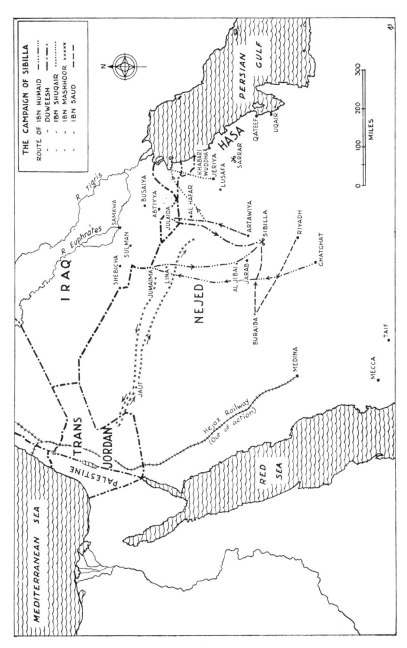

THE CAMPAIGN OF SIBILLA

ROUTE OF IBN HUMAID ·–··–··
    "   "   DUWEESH ········
    "   "   IBN SHUQAIR ·–·–·
    "   "   IBN MASHHOOR ×××××
    "   "   IBN SAUD –––

N

MEDITERRANEAN SEA

PERSIAN GULF

HASA

R. Tigris

R. Euphrates

IRAQ

NEJED

TRANS JORDAN

PALESTINE

RED SEA

SAMAWA
SULMAN
SHEBICHA
JUMAIMA
BUSAIYA
ABTIYYA
JULAIDA
AL HAFAR
KHABARI WUDHA
JERIYA
SARRAR
LUSAFA
QATEEF
UQAIR
LINA
AL JIBAI
JARAB
ARTAWIYA
SIBILLA
RIYADH
CHATGHAT
BURAIDA
MEDINA
MECCA
TAIF
JAUF

Hejaz Railway
(Out of action)

MILES
0   100   200   300

Ibn Shuqair, however, hearing of their presence notified the shaikh of Kuwait that he proposed to raid them, and requested Araibdar to separate from them. This the latter did, leaving the shepherds camped alone near Jahra.[1] Alarmed, Beni Malik fled to Kuwait town, where they pitched their camp not far from the town. They had already paid taxes to Ibn Sobah, who had, by accepting their money, made himself responsible for their safety. Early in March, a force of five hundred Mutair with three war banners, under Ibn Shuqair, Al Fughum and Ibn Lami, attacked these unfortunate shepherds who took refuge beneath the very walls of Kuwait. The shaikh ordered the gates of the town to be closed, so that even the fugitives were denied admittance. The poor shepherds, fighting against nearly twenty to one odds and with their backs literally to the wall, put up a desperate resistance. Nearly all the men—a total of thirty-seven—were massacred, but twenty of the Ikhwan were alleged to have been killed in the attack. If a diversion had been made from the walls of Kuwait, the lives of the victims might have been saved, but such was the terror inspired by the Ikhwan, that not a hand was raised to stay the massacre. Aircraft from 84 Squadron at Shaiba carried out a bombing raid against the retiring raiders the same afternoon. A few of the Ikhwan were killed, as was a considerable number of the looted sheep. Taraiheeb Ibn Shuqair thereupon returned to his home in Jeriya, leaving the Duweesh to fend for himself. This raid took place while we were moving up from Al Abtiyya to Umm al Medafa without a wireless set, for the Iraq army detachment had parted from us, not being permitted to enter Kuwait territory, and we had not yet joined up with the armoured cars who were to replace them. Thus we were out of touch for precisely the forty-eight hours during which this raid took place. I then went down to Kuwait with three police trucks and collected the pathetic survivors of the thirty Beni Malik families, all weeping women and children.

Meanwhile the Duweesh and Ibn Humaid had heard of Ibn Saud's warlike preparations at Buraida, and had joined forces at Jarab about the middle of March.

Ibn Saud had collected a large force in the Qaseem, of which the following were the principal bedouin contingents:

Part of Ateiba, under their chief Abdul Rahman Ibn Rubaiyan, a rival of Ibn Humaid
Meshari Ibn Busaiyis of Mutair who had gone over to Ibn Saud
Dulaim Ibn Barrak, of Hutaim
Most of the Harab tribe
Nearly all the Nejed Shammar

[1] See map on page 265.

Ajami Ibn Suwait with part of the Dhafeer who had gone over to Ibn Saud

A part of Aneza of the Hejaz, Wuld Suleiman (whose relatives had been massacred by Ibn Mashoor), the Faqeer and others

There was in addition a double levy of the townspeople of Nejed.

The rebel force was considerably smaller, consisting principally of the fanatical members of Mutair and Ateiba, who had settled in the Ikhwan colonies. The number of men from other tribes was small, but included Ayyad Ibn Nuhaiyir of Shammar and Muhsin al Dhichri of Harb. On 20th March, the Duweesh sent urgent appeals to the nomadic portions of Mutair to join him, but only a few did so. Ibn Shuqair, Al Fughum and Ibn Lami, as has been stated, had gone home to divide the Beni Malik loot.

The rebels, though outnumbered, were more homogeneous than the king's forces and had long been used to victory. In Ibn Saud's army, however, the townspeople of Nejed, the steadiest fighters in Arabia, were fired with the bitterest indignation at the massacre of their merchants. This act was the greatest of Ibn Humaid's mistakes. Without this blunder, it is doubtful whether Ibn Saud could have faced the rebels in the field. The oases townspeople were to the wilder mounted bedouins somewhat like the London trained-bands in the English civil war, in relation to the dashing individual courage of the undisciplined cavaliers.

About the middle of March, while the king and the rebels were mustering their forces, a sudden and intensive outburst of raiding took place between the Nejed tribes of the opposing factions. Mutair raided Sebei who were loyal to Ibn Saud, and Sebei retaliated in kind. Mutair also looted flocks from Harb—civil war, it was obvious, could no longer be delayed.

When the rebels concentrated their forces to face Ibn Saud's army, the Duweesh, although he had called up some of the nomadic sections of Mutair to support him, asked Ibn Shuqair and Ibn Hithlain of the Ajman to remain at Jeriya and Khabari Wadhha respectively, to protect his rear against an advance by the Saudi governor of the Hasa. In this, he probably committed a major strategic error. The only important battle, from the point of view of the rebels, would be the collision with Ibn Saud which was obviously imminent. If all Mutair and the Ajman had joined the main rebel army before the battle, the ultimate outcome might perhaps have been different.

*   *   *   *   *

From the moment of his arrival in Buraida, Ibn Saud had been in correspondence with the rebel chiefs. The Duweesh was inclined to favour compromise. Azaiyiz, his son, who had sworn loyalty to Ibn Saud three months before in Riyadh, was even more opposed to extreme measures. Ibn Humaid, however, was obdurate, and frequent disputes, often verging on an open breach, took place between him and Azaiyiz al Duweesh.

On 26th March, Azaiyiz al Duweesh and Feisal Ibn Shiblan, a member of the Duweesh family, visited Ibn Saud and requested the despatch of Al Ungari, a leading Wahhabi religious teacher to the rebel camp, to mediate between them and Ibn Saud. Al Ungari was duly sent, but failed to induce Ibn Humaid to agree to refer his differences with Ibn Saud to the arbitrament of a religious court. Ibn Humaid, possibly quite correctly, stated that the offer was obviously a conspiracy, and that it was a foregone conclusion that Ibn Saud's religious friends would pronounce him worthy of death. Indeed Ibn Humaid's Jumaima raid had, in a sense, caused a divergence of interest between him and the Duweesh. For the latter had only raided Iraqis, and could plead religious enthusiasm in his defence. But Ibn Humaid had attacked his brother Muslims, and could hope for no mercy.

Two Shammar shaikhs then came to the rebel camp from the king, with a proposal for a private interview between the latter and Feisal al Duweesh. In spite of the strenuous opposition of Ibn Humaid, Feisal agreed and the meeting actually took place on 27th March, in a tent pitched in front of Ibn Saud's army which had advanced to within about four miles of the rebel camp. Feisal spent the night in this tent with the king, and eventually agreed to endeavour to persuade Ibn Humaid to meet him also. If he refused, the Duweesh was alleged to have promised to separate from him and to retire to his home at Artawiya.

While Feisal al Duweesh was away on his visit to Ibn Saud, Ibn Humaid visited Feisal's son Azaiyiz, and told him that his father had been treacherously kidnapped by the king. Ibn Humaid suggested a night attack, offering to lead the men of Ghatghat against Ibn Saud's own tent. The suggestion was categorically rejected by Azaiyiz. Had he accepted it, the course of history might have been different. The rebels, it is true, were less numerous than Ibn Saud's army, but they were compact and of higher morale. In the confusion of the night, a determined attack might well have succeeded. A large part of Ibn Saud's army consisted of fickle bedouins, many of whom were at the same time in correspondence with the rebels, and who might well have fled pell-mell under a surprise night attack. No two bedouin chiefs, however, can co-operate for long, and divided counsels ruined the rebels' hopes of success.

Ibn Humaid's objective in his proposed night attack had been to kill Ibn Saud himself. So much did the government of Nejed at that time rest upon the personality of the king, that the whole country would have fallen into anarchy had he indeed met his death. The ensuing establishment of the state of Saudi Arabia and the discovery and exploitation of its oil might thereby have been indefinitely postponed, with all the consequences to Western industry and the involvement of the United States in Arabia. It is fantastic today to consider what immense developments in modern history may have hung upon the vacillations of Azaiyiz al Duweesh, an ignorant young bedouin fanatic, on that fateful night in the far-off deserts of Arabia.

The next morning Feisal al Duweesh returned from his visit to Ibn Saud, bringing with him, as gifts from the king, three hundred pounds in golden sovereigns, a handsome new suit of clothes, and two short cavalry carbines, weapons much prized among the bedouins. Ibn Humaid, however, firmly rejected Ibn Saud's blandishments. Some said indeed that the Duweesh did not attempt to persuade him, but reported that he had seen Ibn Saud's army, that they were a motley collection of no fighting value and that there was nothing to fear. What really passed between them, we shall never know.

However this may have been, on the following morning, March 29th, the Duweesh sent a messenger to Ibn Saud, informing him that Ibn Humaid had refused his proposals. As regards his promise to desert his ally in this event and retire to Artawiya, "The Muslimeen," he said, "had refused to be separated from the Muslimeen," —that is to say Mutair from Ateiba. As soon as this message was received, Ibn Saud gave the word for the war banners to be immediately unfurled, and orders were issued to advance against the rebel camp at Sibilla.

The greater part of Ibn Saud's army moved forward on foot, halting frequently to re-adjust their formations. On the right, however, the war banners of Ibn Rubaiyan of Ateiba and Meshari Ibn Busaiyis of Mutair, were mounted. The left wing consisted of the bedouins of Aneza, Shammar and the Dhafeer, also mounted.

The Nejed townsfolk, who were burning to avenge the slaughter of their merchants, were the first to engage their immediate opponents, Ibn Humaid's own comrades, the men of Ghatghat. The latter, equally anxious for the fray, ran forward to meet them. A little later, Harab and Hutaim engaged the settled fanatical Mutair of the colonies of Artawiya and Imbayidh. The mounted bedouins of both sides skirmished on the flanks at a safe distance. Nida Ibn Nuhaiyir of Shammar, who had previously sworn alliance with the rebels but had since joined Ibn Saud's army, manoeuvred on the left flank without engaging at all.

A desperate struggle swayed to and fro for a time, between the Nejed townsmen and the Ateiba of Ghatghat. Two successive attacks by the townspeople were repulsed. On the third attempt, the men of Ghatghat were beginning to give way, when suddenly the war banners of Ibn Rubaiyan and Ibn Busaiyis appeared on their left rear. The rebel army then broke. Some horsemen of Ateiba succeeded in partially covering the retreat of Ibn Humaid. The Mutair of Imbayidh suffered most heavily in the rout, having no horsemen to cover their withdrawal. At this stage, Feisal al Duweesh was shot through the stomach, and was with difficulty carried from the field by a man of Mutair. As the rebel army disintegrated, Saud Ibn Saud,[1] eldest son of the king, with the townspeople of Riyadh and the "manjiya" or royal bodyguard, advanced to complete the victory.

Meanwhile the Mutair nomads had fled incontinently from the field and did not draw rein until they reached their homes at Al Hafar. Ibn Saud's bedouins, who had done little serious fighting, were well to the fore in the pursuit once the victory was won, until they were recalled by horsemen from the king, who halted his army on reaching the rebel camp. In the tents of the Duweesh and Ibn Humaid were found letters from Nida Ibn Nuhaiyir and Jadhayyil Ibn Laghaisam, both chiefs of Shammar, and from other leaders, who had been careful to maintain relations with the fanatics in case they should prove successful.

Next morning a party of six camelmen was sent by the Duweesh to offer his surrender to Ibn Saud. As soon as their coming was reported, orders were given for them to be killed without further parley. Four out of the six were shot in cold blood, in front of the camp. Alarmed at the reception of his emissaries, the Duweesh resorted to the Arab custom of sending "mughattiyat", or veiled women, to sue for mercy. Three women of the Dushan (the plural form of Duweesh—that is the Duweesh family), including a daughter of Feisal himself, set out in camel litters under the care of Feisal Ibn Shiblan, who had loaded his mare with a large bale of grass, and succeeded thereby in mingling unnoticed with Ibn Saud's retainers, who were cutting forage for their horses in front of the camp. By this means, Ibn Shiblan reached Ibn Saud's tent unrecognized and in safety, followed by the women.

On receiving the Duweesh's offer of surrender, Ibn Saud called a grand council of his supporters, and, as was his habit, he first asked the Wahhabi religious teachers to propound what course the word of God prescribed. The religious elders replied that Mutair should be spared further slaughter, but should surrender all loot taken from other Nejed tribes during the previous three years. No mention was made of the surrender of loot taken from Iraq. They were also bound to hand over the means of war, which was to say all horses, riding

_____
[1] Now King Saud.

camels and rifles. Ibn Saud added that Azaiyiz must report to him, but promised that his life would be safe. As for Feisal al Duweesh, he must be handed over unconditionally, alive or dead. The king had said to us at Jidda that arbitrary rule was not to be commended, and indeed, at this stage of his life, he always followed the procedure of consulting the religious leaders in public conference. Doubtless he and they were hand in glove, and he knew in advance the reply which they would give. In spite of this, however, the procedure was skilful, and conciliated his often turbulent subjects.

At the urgent entreaty of Feisal Ibn Shiblan, the king agreed not to enter the Duweesh's own settlement, Artawiya, but to camp outside with his army. Feisal al Duweesh was carried to Ibn Saud's camp on a stretcher, where he was examined by a doctor, who declared him to be at death's door. He was accordingly allowed to return to Artawiya, his son Azaiyiz being detained by the king as a prisoner.

The night after the battle, Ibn Humaid held a conference with the Duweesh, and apparently endeavoured to persuade him to continue the struggle. The Duweesh, however, who was in a state of physical prostration owing to his stomach wound, had no heart for further fighting. Ibn Humaid, collecting his loot, left during the night in a southerly direction.

In this posture we may leave the principal actors in the drama, on March 31st, 1929.

*   *   *   *   *

As already related, Ibn Shuqair with five hundred camelmen had raided thirty tents of Beni Malik on 2nd March beneath the very walls of Kuwait. After the raid, he and his followers returned to their homes at Jeriya to divide the loot. Meanwhile, however, Dhaidan Ibn Hithlain of the Ajman, with his war banner, was camped at Khabari Wadhha, eighty miles south of Kuwait.[1] Throughout the month of March, he continued to proclaim his intention of raiding the Iraq tribes, camped with us only ninety miles north of him, a short distance north and north-west of Jahra. A party of his scouts actually reached a point twenty miles north of Jahra, where they reconnoitred the camp of No. 6 Armoured Car Company at night. Curiously enough, I myself met this party, when I was accompanying a motorized patrol the next morning. I recognized with them a man of Araibdar whom I knew, and who informed me that the party consisted entirely of his relatives. As a result, we allowed them to proceed unmolested. Our position was rendered difficult by the presence of Araibdar around us. They being Kuwait subjects, were officially our allies, but many were in reality, as in this case, helping

[1] See map on page 283.

the Ikhwan rebels—out of fear of being raided themselves rather than from malice against us.

Ibn Hithlain, on receiving the report of these scouts, was alleged to have prepared his plans for a night attack on the armoured car camp, but, at the last moment, a report that Ibn Jiluwi was advancing against him, caused him to abandon his project. Abdulla Ibn Jiluwi, it will be remembered,[1] had been one of the companions of Abdul Aziz Ibn Saud in the desperate *coup-de-main* by which the latter had seized Riyadh from its Rasheedian governor in January, 1902. Now an old man, Abdulla was governor of the Hasa, and his son Fahad was his commander in the field.

During the month of March, a considerable number of Mutair bedouins had camped along the Kuwait-Nejed boundary, chiefly in the vicinity of Ash Shaqq, in order to replenish their supplies by sending caravans into Kuwait. Several collisions occurred between them and car patrols of the Southern Desert Camel Corps, as a result of which Mutair moved away hastily to the south. The desert police cars were daily engaged in patrolling the Kuwait-Nejed frontier, to cover our tribal concentrations in the north. On 8th March, two police cars, each carrying a Lewis gun, fought an animated little action with forty Mutair horsemen, east of Al Riqai, in Kuwait territory. The police cars endeavoured to outflank the party of horsemen, in order to ascertain whether they were the advanced guard of a large raiding party, or whether they were acting independently. In this process, the horsemen, who were suddenly seen to be receiving reinforcements from some broken ground near by, endeavoured to cut off the retreat of the cars, and surround them. The police, however, accepted the challenge, closed in on the horsemen and opened fire with their Lewis guns, killing three Mutairis and wounding others, thereby causing the horsemen to sheer off, opening a line of retreat for the cars. It was just such an incident as I had foreseen the year before, when I asked for automatics for the desert police and the air officer commanding had replied that he did not wish the police to fight. This and other similar skirmishes with the scout cars produced on Mutair a moral effect far out of proportion to the scale of the engagements. It was the first occasion on which the Ikhwan had come into contact on the Iraq frontier with vehicles mounting automatic weapons.

The Ikhwan had, during ten years, acquired the most profound scorn for Iraq and the Iraqis, whom they had come to regard as scarcely capable of even firing a shot in their own defence. The stand made by the tribes at Al Abtiyya, from which the hitherto undefeated Duweesh had turned back dismayed, and the subsequent encounters in which police car patrols had skirmished with the Ikhwan, revealed

[1] See page 55.

a new spirit in Iraq. As is often the case with undisciplined tribes, these incidents became greatly exaggerated and struck terror into Mutair. Before the battle of Sibilla, the rebels were more afraid of us than they were of Ibn Saud.

Indeed the Ikhwan were not the only people who professed contempt for the Iraq tribes. I engaged in some slightly acrimonious correspondence with the authorities in Baghdad on the same subject. The British High Commissioner's office, in a despatch to London of which I was shown a copy, made disparaging remarks on the fear inspired in the Iraq tribes by Ikhwan raids. It was a challenge which, with youthful enthusiasm, I was only too ready to take up. However, even thirty years later, I still feel that these reflections were unjust. Mutair, Harab and Ateiba differed little from Aneza, Shammar or the Dhafeer. But the Ikhwan had been forged into a hitherto invincible weapon, by religious enthusiasm, the magnetic leadership of Abdul Aziz Ibn Saud and a long succession of victories.

As against this, the authorities in Baghdad (whoever they might be at the time) had, for a century or more, regarded the bedouin tribes as their principal enemies, a hostility ardently reciprocated by the tribesmen. The R.A.F., who had done splendid work in the desert, nevertheless contributed to the demoralization of the tribes, by their habit of ordering them to flee and leave the desert empty for the R.A.F. to fight in. Constantly treated as though they were unarmed women and children, and punished for any attempt to raid back, the tribes lost any desire to stand up to their enemies.

Thirty years have elapsed since these old battles were lost and won, but both Britain and America have since then more than once repeated similar errors. The United States announces that she will stand up to Russia and save the Middle East, but she often tends to do so in ways by no means acceptable to the local people. The unconscious assumption in all these instances is that the Arabs do not know what is best for themselves and that only the West can take efficient measures to deal with a critical situation. It is erroneous to attribute this attitude to wicked imperialism. In most cases it is sincere and often indeed profoundly conscientious, but unwittingly it illustrates the unconscious Western conviction that the peoples of the Middle East are incompetent to handle their own affairs, a belief intensely resented by them.

Only the peoples of the Middle East can save their countries from Communism, just as the Dhafeer and the Zayyad proved ultimately the best defenders of their native deserts from the Ikhwan.

*   *   *   *   *

By this time the grazing in the area of Umm al Medafa was no longer what it had been, in view of the large numbers of tribes in the area. On 9th and 10th March we accordingly moved southwards, and my camp remained for the rest of the month at a distance of about five miles north of Jahra.

Early in the month, while the Duweesh was still camped near Al Hafar, a good deal of anxiety was felt. The tribes were kept concentrated as closely as possible, the Zayyad and the Dhafeer being martialled on either side of the little camp containing the police and myself. Frequent rallies, war dances and hosas were held, both to keep up the morale of the tribes and also to impress the world at large. For everything we did was undoubtedly reported to the Ikhwan. *Nemo me impune lacessit* could well have been our motto.

After the middle of March, however, news of the move of Ibn Humaid and the Duweesh to Jarab, and of the preparations made by Ibn Saud, considerably eased our situation. The continued presence of Ibn Hithlain at Khabari Wadhha throughout the month, however, prevented us from relaxing our vigilance. Ibn Hithlain's force was not strong enough to frighten us, but even a tip-and-run raid which made off with our camels or sheep would have served as a sorry close to what had in reality been a triumphant season. Moreover we were too near the Nejed frontier, which we were not allowed to cross, to allow us to make sure of overtaking such raiders

The tribes were happy. The hollows in the rolling surface of the desert were filled with virgin grass, sprinkled with many coloured wild flowers. The camel stores fat in its hump when it finds good grazing, and all day the great herds stood munching, while the humps grew bigger and bigger.

One day Kadhim accompanied me in my car in a reconnaissance down to the Nejed border. As we returned to leave him at his tent, before going to my camp, we passed the sheep flocks of his tribe out grazing. The sheep wheeled and stampeded, jumping up in the air with all four feet, in the rather foolish way sheep will. Their enormous fat tails flapped behind them.[1] "See how the sheep stampede," said Kadhim with his gentle smile. "It is you who did that. Two months ago they were so weak they could scarcely walk. Now they can leap and gallop."

All the desert valleys were filled with grazing flocks and herds. In the small black tents of the shepherds, the women were sitting on the ground, shaking goatskin churns back and forth with the pleasant gurgly sound of butter-making. Young lambs were tied by the leg in the tents or frolicked on the grassy carpet of the hollows. The whole desert presented such peaceful pastoral scenes. The tribes gave lunch parties and invited one another to remember God, while they enjoyed the great dishes of rice and lamb, swimming in butter and oil. The Ikhwan, we heard, had gone off to fight Ibn Saud. "May God

---

[1] Arab sheep store fat in their tails, just as the camels do in their humps.

cause them to vent their evil on one another," one of the Dhafeer remarked to me.

But alas, the spring in Iraq is all too short. Towards the end of March there were several hot days. In April, the grass was already withering. In the hollows it was still green, but on the slopes it was already drying and turning yellow. The Zayyad had more than two hundred miles to walk to get back to their lands round Samawa. There was no use having fattened the sheep, if they were to die of thirst on the way home. Unwillingly our partnership broke up. Day after day, in early April, one tribe after another bade us goodbye. We ourselves began moving northwards towards Safwan.

One day early in April, I was sitting in my tent in the afternoon, when I heard the discreet little cough with which Hamed the slave always announced his presence. "What is it, Hamed?" I called out.

His face peered in at the door of the tent. "Tumeish al Buraichi has come from Ajami," he replied. "He says there has been a great battle between Ibn Saud and the Ikhwan."

Tumeish was standing outside. He was a reliable four-square sort of old man, rather thickset for a bedouin. For privacy, we climbed into my car and sat in the back seat. "Good news, if God wills?" I said enquiringly.

"If God wills, good," he replied.

Then he told me, much as I have related it, the story of the day of Sibilla.

We were a joyous party, with Tumeish and the men of the desert police, as we sat that evening in a circle round the coffee fire, beneath the bright desert stars. The story of Sibilla was repeated again and again, discussed, commented upon and argued. Hamed the slave sat cross-legged by the fire, rising every now and again with the brass coffee pot in his right hand and the pile of tiny cups in his left, to move slowly round the circle pouring a cup for each. At last we rose, yawning, to snatch a little sleep before "stand-to" at dawn. Hamed, who had hitherto been silent, summarized, in a quiet voice, the thought which had been at the back of all our minds: "From now onwards, may God protect us from their evil deeds."

* * * * *

Although nearly all the Ikhwan were still at large, and Ibn Saud was obliged to disband his army after Sibilla (for his levies were of course unpaid), yet the position of the rebels was in reality almost desperate. Their claim to be truer Muslims than the king himself (previously their strongest card) had been completely disproved by their raids against other Nejed subjects. They had been revealed to be merely self-seekers, to supreme power in place of the king. Many tribes in Nejed were only half-hearted in their loyalty to Ibn Saud and would probably have joined the rebels if they had won the battle. But, as the event had proved, the rebels had failed in both directions. They could no longer claim either to be martyrs for religion or to be successful politicians and soldiers with whom it would be wise to come to terms. Moreover, their defeat at Sibilla had caused a final estrangement between Ibn Humaid and the Duweesh. The former had left for his home on the other side of Nejed, and it so happened that the province of Aridh, the most loyal part of the king's dominions, lay between Ateiba and Mutair, with whom Ibn Saud could henceforward deal separately.

Meanwhile, however, we left Dhaidan Ibn Hithlain with his war banner at Khabari Wadhha, eighty miles south of Kuwait, awaiting an opportunity for another raid. After the battle of Sibilla, Fahad Ibn Jiluwi, son of the Governor of the Hasa, set out with a large force against the Ajman. His army was composed of the townsmen of the Hasa with contingents from the southern Nejed tribes of Al Murra, Beni Hajir, the Awazim, Beni Khalid and Sebei.[1]

Meanwhile Ibn Saud endeavoured to employ against Dhaidan Ibn Hithlain the same policy which he had used in January when he encouraged Ibn Rubaiyan of Ateiba as a rival to Ibn Humaid. Now he set up a cousin Dhaidan, Naif Ibn Hithlain, commonly known as Aba al Kilab or the father of the dogs, as a rival to Dhaidan. Naif, with a portion of the Ajman, now moved out with the army of Ibn Jiluwi against Dhaidan, who with his forces, awaited attack at his settlement of Sarrar. An exchange of letters took place. It is not certain whether the letters from Fahad Ibn Jiluwi contained a promise of safe conduct to Dhaidan or not. Anyhow, after this exchange of communications, Dhaidan, with eight horsemen, visited Fahad and dismounted at his tent. After drinking tea and coffee, he was suddenly arrested.

When news of this apparent treachery reached Sarrar, the Ajman advanced to attack Ibn Jiluwi, whereupon the latter gave orders for Dhaidan to be killed instantly. The Ajman attacked Ibn Jiluwi's force at ten o clock the same evening. The numerous bedouins with the army took no part in the ensuing battle. Naif Ibn Hithlain and the Ajman with him decided that blood was thicker than water and joined the attackers, turning on their former commander. Only the townsmen of the Hasa stood firm.

Despairing of victory, Fahad Ibn Jiluwi mounted his mare to flee, but his servant, himself a man of the Ajman, seized his bridle and drew his revolver. To Fahad's cry, "Would you betray your master?" he replied, "I have no master but Ibn Hithlain whom you betrayed," and emptied his revolver into Ibn Jiluwi. With the news of Fahad's death, his half-hearted army disintegrated.

[1] See tribal map on page 61.

Thus, whereas after Sibilla, all rebel resistance seemed to be at an end, the unwise behaviour of Fahad Ibn Jiluwi suddenly resulted in a defeat for the royal cause, and a revival of hope among the rebels.

*   *   *   *   *

We left Ibn Mashhoor and Murdhi al Rufidi, with eight hundred men who were carrying slaughter and robbery through the oases of Jauf.[1] They failed, however, to seize the town, whereupon they moved up the Wadi as Sirhan raided the Huwaitat of Trans-Jordan, with only partial success, and returned and captured the oasis of Sikaka.

Always on the move, with true nomad restlessness, they abandoned Sikaka and moved to the Hazool wells, where they raided some camps of Nejed Shammar, also subjects of Ibn Saud. A force of three hundred camelmen had been sent by Ibn Musaad, the governor of Hail, to intercept them, but found itself outnumbered and defeated, and with difficulty effected a hasty retreat. Meanwhile Ibn Saud had defeated the Duweesh and Ibn Humaid at Sibilla. Ignorant of this disaster to his allies, however, Ibn Mashhoor moved to Lina during the third week in April, and raided further camps of Shammar and Aneza in Nejed, all subjects of Ibn Saud, massacring all the men in true Wahhabi style. Thence he proceeded towards Al Hafar, with the idea of joining the Duweesh.

At Umm al Rudhumma, a force of four hundred Shammar attempted to bar his path, but were repulsed with loss. Striking at all who barred his way, he watered at Shellala, the northernmost of the Bishook group of wells. He had already sent messages on ahead with letters to the Duweesh, announcing his arrival. At Shellala, the messengers returned to him, bearing a letter from the Duweesh informing him of the defeat at Sibilla, and urging him not to come to Artawiya.

The change in the fortunes of the rebels rendered Ibn Mashhoor's position suddenly precarious in the extreme. Himself a native of Syria, he had fought his way across six hundred miles of desert to join the rebels, only to find them already defeated and cowed. Between him and Syria, Shammar, Aneza, the Huwaitat, the people of Jauf and Ibn Musaad's retainers were thirsting for his blood. Moreover, half his strength came from Ateiba, the men whom Ibn Humaid had given him and who now deserted him, and scattered to their homes in Nejed. Accompanied by Murdhi al Rufidi and a remnant of some two hundred followers, he watered at Al Hafar and took refuge in Kuwait territory on 2nd May, 1929.

The Shaikh of Kuwait was in an embarrassing situation in regard

[1] See maps on pages 269 and 283.

to the rebels. He had been in correspondence with them and had possibly wished them well. His object was two-fold. On the one hand, he was himself afraid of being raided by them and even of an attack on the town. Although he might have been able to defend the walls of Kuwait, his tribal retainers, his own flocks, a number of settlements south of the town and at Jahra, and the camps of Araibdar, were exposed to attack. Perhaps, also, as a small independent state, he was alarmed at the rapidly growing power of Ibn Saud, who might well aspire to annex Kuwait to Nejed.

In the last resort, however, Ibn Sobah depended on his treaty with Great Britain to defend his independence, and Britain had promised Ibn Saud, after consultation with Ibn Sobah, that the defeated rebels would not be given asylum in Kuwait. The shaikh found himself in the awkward situation of having either to deny hospitality to the rebels, or of coming into diplomatic conflict with Great Britain, on whom his survival ultimately depended. As soon as Ferhan Ibn Mashhoor camped in Kuwait territory, the British Political Agent was instructed to call on the shaikh and express the hope of His Majesty's Government that he would warn the rebels to leave his territory forthwith. As a result, Ferhan was invited to evacuate Kuwait. He duly undertook to recross the frontier, but was able, before doing so, to replenish his supplies from Kuwait and unostentatiously to leave with Araibdar for safe custody a portion of the camels which he had looted, from the various tribes of Nejed which he had raided.

In May, 1929, the advent of summer put an end to major operations in the desert. A month earlier, after Sibilla, the rebellion had seemed to be at an end. Then the sudden victory of the Ajman over the king's forces in the Hasa had once more revived the spirit of the revolt. The arrival of Ibn Mashhoor had strengthened the morale of the rebels, even if it had brought little addition to their armed strength. Ateiba, it is true, had separated from their fellow rebels, but Mutair, the Ajman and Ibn Mashhoor formed a compact group in close contact with one another.

This was the position when the burning heats of the desert summer postponed further large-scale operations until the return of winter.

XVII

Summer Holidays

Camels, the only substance of the nomads, are the occasion of all their contending.   DOUGHTY, *Travels in Arabia Deserta*

From whence come wars and fightings among you? come they not hence, even of your lusts that war in your members? Ye lust, and have not: ye kill and desire to have, and cannot obtain: ye fight and war, yet ye have not. . . .   *James* iv. 12,

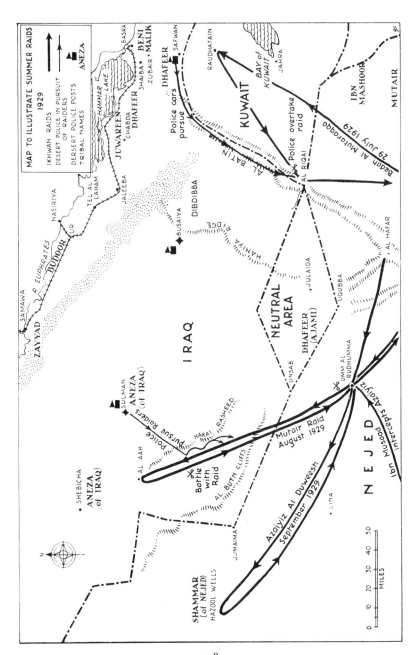

MAP TO ILLUSTRATE SUMMER RAIDS
1929

IKHWAN RAIDS
DESERT POLICE IN PURSUIT
OF RAIDERS
DESERT POLICE POSTS
TRIBAL NAMES
ANEZA

XVII

SUMMER HOLIDAYS

A CHANGE occurred in the leadership of the rebellion during the summer of 1929. Sultan Ibn Humaid, the firebrand who had been principally responsible for the civil war, surrendered to Ibn Saud, who cast him into prison in Riyadh, whence he was destined never to emerge. Meanwhile, however, the defeat of Ibn Jiluwi by the Ajman had revived the rebellion on the east. Naif Ibn Hithlain, with the Ajman, Feisal al Duweesh and Ferhan Ibn Mashhoor, swore loyalty to one another, and remained camped south of Kuwait territory, but able to purchase supplies from the town.

On the side of Ibn Saud, the Governor of Hail, Abdul Aziz Ibn Musaad, was camped at Al Jubai[1] with twelve war banners, while the Amir Saud,[2] went down with a force to the Hasa. Ibn Saud, after attending the pilgrimage at Mecca, returned to Riyadh. Such large concentrations as that of Ibn Musaad were unable to operate in the desert in summer, with the result that the rebellion inevitably dragged on until the following winter.

The bedouins profited by this summer holiday from major operations to indulge in some raiding in their traditional style.

On 1st July, the Ajman and Ibn Mashhoor with a force of one thousand five hundred camelmen attacked the Awazim, a tribe loyal to Ibn Saud, near Al Qateef in the Hasa.[3] The Awazim "couched and hobbled" as we had done at Al Abtiyya and were reported even to have dug trenches, with the result that the attacking Ajman suffered heavy casualties. The battle seemed to be indecisive. Soon after it, however, the Awazim sent messages to the Duweesh and the Shaikh of Kuwait, asking for peace.

Shammar and Ajami Ibn Suwait with part of the Dhafeer were camped from the Neutral Area westwards; Mutair, the Ajman and Ibn Mashhoor were gathered east of the Batin. Between the two groups, small parties of raiders came and went, intent on looting camels from the opposite party. The Dhafeer in Iraq were meanwhile camped from Safwan to Rafaiya and Chabda, with police cars at Safwan patrolling to the south of them.

It was obvious that no major operations could take place until the first winter rains fell in the autumn and thereby made it possible

---

[1] See map on page 283. [2] Now King Saud Ibn Saud.
[3] For Awazim, see map on page 61.

for large forces to operate in the desert. Having therefore taken no leave for three years, and being somewhat worn by the toils and anxieties of the winter, I took advantage of the hot weather to pay a visit to England. Meanwhile the Southern Desert Camel Corps, though so newly formed, was already a veteran unit, with high morale and *esprit de corps*. By some means or other, it had even acquired a nickname, which was already known over half Arabia, though nobody could tell how it originated. "Al Aujan", which could perhaps be freely translated "the crooks", soon became their war cry as well as their nickname, althought it had doubtless been bestowed upon them by their enemies.

While, however, the rank and file of bedouins, principally Mutair, were taking advantage of the chaos to loot each other's camels, Feisal al Duweesh was in profound anxiety. He had but little chance of survival when the winter came, if Ibn Saud could take the field with all his forces against him. From time immemorial, the bedouins in the last resort have retained their freedom, when threatened with domination by a ruler or government, by migrating to some area beyond his jurisdiction. This was now the only course open to the Duweesh. If he and his closest retainers could have found asylum, the rank and file of bedouin Mutair could have made peace with Ibn Saud. Ibn Sobah was, to some extent, sympathetic to the rebel cause, and the Duweesh determined to try what could be done in that direction. On 2nd July, 1929, Azaiyiz al Duweesh secretly visited Kuwait and interviewed Shaikh Ahmed Ibn Sobah.

Meanwhile Ibn Saud, was of course, fully aware of the relations between the rebels and Kuwait. Already in June, he had approached the British Government informing them that, when the winter campaigning season arrived, he would pursue the rebels into Kuwait territory if Ibn Sobah should give them asylum. His Majesty's Government replied that the entry of Ibn Saud's forces into Kuwait would be extremely embarrassing, but that they themselves, with the co-operation of the shaikh, would keep the rebels out. Ibn Sobah meanwhile denied any intention of giving asylum, and claimed that the rebels were not receiving supplies from Kuwait. The shaikh was still indeed in a highly embarrassing situation, for, whatever might be the ultimate outcome of the operations of the following winter, the rebels were during the summer in a position to raid the Kuwait Arabs mercilessly, to reduce them all to penury, and to inflict heavy loss of life. It is unjust to criticize the shaikh's policy, without making allowances for his military weakness.

Meanwhile raiding and counter-raiding between the two tribal groups continued. We had succeeded in organizing the Camel Corps to collate and record its own intelligence at its forts of Shebicha, Sulman and Busaiya, and in the temporary tented post at Safwan.

Here are the entries for three days, taken at random, from the station diary on Nejed intelligence, at the Safwan outpost.

26th June. Muhamad Ibn Hamdan, travelling from Kuwait to Zubair, reported that Ateiba looted many flocks of camels from near Riyadh.

27th June. Ribah Ibn Khushman of Harab, raided Ibn Shuqair near Jeriya, and seized several flocks of Mutair camels. (Informant Zeid Ibn Hamad, coming from Ibn Tawala.)

29th June. Nahar ash Shuraiti of Shammar, camped at Umm al Rudhumma, set out to raid the Ajman.

30th June. The Amir Saud raided Ateiba and seized three hundred camels.

30th June. Al Damir of the Ajman with thirty camelmen raided the Dawasir, and looted a hundred camels. On his return, he captured two caravans on the track between Riyadh and the Hasa.

Thus every day the list of incidents lengthened. A guest tent, in a black house of hair,[1] had been established outside every fort, where visitors and passing travellers were entertained, and where all the news of Arabia was daily discussed. Patrols, moving from camp to camp, collected the information and the rumours circulating among the tribes and carried from tent to tent by the ever restless nomad camel-riders.

On 29th July, 1929, while I was still away on leave, a raiding party of camelmen of Mutair under the leadership of Bedah al Mutaraqqa looted from Raudhatain, in Kuwait territory, two hundred camels belonging to the Iraq tribes camped at Safwan. The herdsmen escaped and reported to the desert police at Safwan on the 30th.

Two Ford trucks mounting Lewis guns gave chase,[2] hoping to overtake the raiders watering at the little well at Al Riqai. The well was in a small, narrow ravine, a tributary valley leading into the great Batin depression. The country around the well was intersected by narrow valleys, tributaries to the little Riqai gorge in the bed of which lay the well. The desert police had once again been forbidden to enter Kuwait territory and thus were unable to go to the scene of the raid and follow the tracks of the retreating enemy. The raiders had a twenty-four hour start on their pursuers. The latter accordingly gambled on the fact that they would water at the well of Riqai and drove there by the most direct route straight down the

---

[1] To the tribes, a tent was the white canvas affair with which Europe is familiar. Their own heavy black tents they called houses of hair.

[2] See map on page 298.

Batin. In the blazing heat of July, the two little commercial trucks
sped along the gravelly bed of the wide depression, the faces of the
men tense with excitement, straining their eyes ahead to catch sight
of any moving figure in the vast empty wastes. On the left, and
parallel to their course, lay the long ridge forming the eastern side
of the Batin depression. At last they saw, breaking through the ridge,
the mouth of the little valley of Al Riqai, dancing in the desert
mirage—yes, sure enough, the well and the broken ground around it
were swarming with camels.

The leader of the patrol was a certain Abdul Kerim al Khushman,
a native of Hail, and once a retainer of the Rasheeds. When the
young Saud Ibn Abdul Aziz Ibn Rasheed was made amir of Hail,
his self-appointed protector Zamil Ibn Subhan had conducted the
affairs of state during his minority. But when Saud grew up, he tired
of the advice of his middle-aged guardian. Zamil was assassinated
and Ibn Khushman was alleged to have been implicated in his
murder. When Hail fell to Ibn Saud in 1921, he took refuge in Iraq.
Abdul Kerim was a quiet, serious man, devotedly loyal to any cause
which he espoused. Indeed it was doubtless loyalty to his Rasheed
patron, rather than a criminal disposition, which involved him in the
murder of Zamil Ibn Subhan. There was, in any case, little of the
remarkable in one murder more or less in Hail.

Now, within rifle shot of the Ikhwan, Ibn Khushman signalled to
the two trucks to stop and himself dismounted. Calling the excited
men around him, he said quietly: "Before we go at them, I want you
all to remember that there is a man in London who will hear how
we behave today. We here are fighting for our lives and to protect
our women. His home and his women are in London, yet for years
he has been fighting for us. Let us not today give him cause to be
ashamed of us."

The men jumped back into their two little trucks. The two Lewis
gunners each clapped a pan of ammunition on his gun. Then
throwing off their headgear, their long black hair flying, their faces
livid with excitement, they roused one another with cries of "Where
are the gallants? Where are the Aujan? *Al Aujan! Wain al Aujan?*"

The two trucks formed up abreast and drove at the raiders. Tat-tat-
tat went the Lewis guns. Soon the bullets were flicking up the dust
among the crowded men and camels. But Mutair were experienced
fighters. Some, mounting their camels, endeavoured to drive the
crowded herds out of the narrow valley. Others, scattering over the
broken spurs of the slope, opened a heavy rifle fire on the cars and
their eight passengers. But the narrowness of the little valley, which
on the one hand made it impossible for the cars to close, on the other
made it difficult for the raiders to drive off the now terrified camels.
Meanwhile the Lewis guns continued to spit and soon the lithe figures

of the raiders could be seen scrambling away up the spurs of the hills, dragging their riding camels behind them. The enemy rifle fire slackened and two bedouin police, rifle in hand, ran forward towards the now abandoned herds. Soon they appeared again, each now clinging to the back of a camel, moving slowly towards the now stationary cars, calling "Yo-a-a! Yo-a-a!" to the slowly following herds. The raiders had vanished.

All the looted camels were recovered. One man of the Camel Corps lay dead in the back of his truck. The Ikhwan had suffered two killed and five wounded. Unfortunately no pursuit of the discomfited enemy was possible, for Al Riqai was almost exactly on the Nejed frontier, which the desert police were strictly forbidden to cross.

*　　*　　*　　*　　*

Four years earlier, I had suggested to the Iraq Government the construction of a desert post at Sulman, to act as depot, store and report centre for the Stony Desert, just as Busaiya was for the Dibdibba. The recommendation had been shelved in 1925, but after the massacre of Busaiya, work was commenced energetically at Sulman also. A large stone fort was constructed, two storeys high, and surrounded by barbed wire entanglements. During the winter, it also was occupied by a garrison of the Iraq army. The establishment of this permanent base at Sulman was of immense advantage to the defence. It will be remembered that in 1924 Muhsin al Firrem of Harab had actually massacred the Iraq shepherds on this very well. The establishment of a fort there had therefore provided a refuge for the shepherds in times of fear, eighty miles south of the Euphrates. But more still was it a centre for the reception and transmission of information and a depot for petrol, oil, ammunition, tyres and spare parts, thereby giving vehicles and aircraft adequate mobility.

Thirty years after the fort was built at Sulman, I met an Iraqi student in England. "I know who you are," he said to me bitterly. "You built Sulman where my brother was done to death." When I asked him for his story, he told me that Sulman had been transformed into a desert concentration camp for political detainees, that his brother had been arrested for subversive political activities and had died there. He was under the impression that I had been responsible for the construction of Sulman as a political prison.

This little incident seemed to me symbolical of the sad transformation in British relations with Iraq which had taken place in recent years. For in the 1920's I was passionately devoted to Iraq. I had indeed done all in my power to cause the erection of the fort at Sulman, where it was a tower of refuge for the protection of many thousands of Iraqis, men, women and children. Yet here was I, thirty years later, remembered as the "imperialist" oppressor, who had built a prison for political offenders.

Thus was all our love and devotion distorted into hatred and oppression.

*   *   *   *   *

Soon after the affair at Al Riqai, a much larger Mutair raiding party descended upon a camp of seventy-five tents of Nejed Shammar at Al Aah. The victims were, it is true, subjects of Ibn Saud, but as they were camped in Iraq territory, we were responsible for their safety. Two desert police trucks from Sulman, each mounting a Vickers gun, set out in pursuit. The raiders had not only looted the herds, but had completely obliterated the camp. Twenty-five men of Shammar had been killed, though ten of the raiders had also lost their lives. The tents, foodstuffs, clothing and all the worldly possessions of the victims had been loaded on the looted flocks and carried away, leaving only a group of weeping women and children, sitting on the dusty desert ground.

The two police trucks, each carrying five men, overtook the raiders, driving great numbers of looted camels before them, in the open plain thirty miles south of Al Aah. The desert police vehicles were commercial Ford trucks, bought from the Ford agents in Baghdad, and had a fixed cab over the driver's seat. The Vickers guns had been mounted in the back of the trucks on an improvised mounting of wooden chocks bolted through the floor. They could only fire to the rear over the tail-board. As a result, we had been obliged to invent our own system of drill. It was a handicap that, when the trucks were advancing against an enemy, they could not fire, because the guns were only facing to the rear. Later on, we mounted a Lewis gun also in the seat beside the driver, but in 1929 no more guns were available. When, therefore, the vehicles came within effective range, they were obliged to turn about and halt before opening fire.

As soon as the raiders came in sight, the two trucks formed up line abreast and began rapidly to overtake them. When some five hundred yards from the mass of camel-riders and herds, the patrol commander raised the black and white pennant (for we had invented our own flag signals) and the two trucks swung right about in a cloud of dust and came to a halt. "Five hundred yards—fire!" yelled the sergeant in command.

The gunners adjusted their sights and pressed both thumbs on the triggers. "Tat-tat-tat-tat," barked the guns, "tat-tat-tat-tat."

The raiders, according to approved bedouin tactics, began a rearguard action. A dozen men slipped from the backs of their camels without checking speed, and opened fire on the trucks, then raced after their mounts, which had trotted on among their companions. Another party dropped to the ground, fired, and then over-took their comrades in a desperate sprint. Bullets began to whistle past the trucks, one of them splintering the wooden body, while another hit the chassis frame with a whack.

The trucks slipped into gear, swung round and gave chase again, thereby giving the raiders a few minutes' respite to recover their presence of mind after this unexpected onslaught. But the interval was a short one for the trucks had swung round and halted and were firing again. "Tat-tat-tat-tat," went the guns again. "*Al Aujan! Al Aujan!*" yelled the gunners. "Where are the Aujan?" "Tat-tat-tat-tat," rattled the Vickers guns.

In a minute or two, the trucks swung round again in pursuit. This time the commander did not just follow the retreating enemy, who by now were growing flustered. He inclined away to the left and drew up level with the great mass of galloping camels and riders, but some three hundred yards to their flank. The raiders were now disorganized and, although they continued to fire, many of their shots went wide. Up went the black and white pennant and the trucks again swung round. "Tat-tat-tat. Tat-tat-tat-tat."

Increasing confusion was evident amongst the Ikhwan. Some, mounted on swifter camels than the rest, emerged from the crowd, riding at full speed for the south and the Nejed frontier. Many of the looted camels, no longer driven forward by the riders, swung away to right or left, slowed down to a stop, gazed vacantly about them and finally stooped to graze as the battle swept on.

The men in the trucks were in a frenzy of excitement. "*Al Aujan! Al Aujan!*" they yelled at the tops of their voices. Their headgear had fallen off, their matted hair fell over their eyes, the sweat poured down their faces in the flaming desert heat. Even the drivers had caught the infection, leapt from their seats snatching their rifles, and stood out in the open desert firing into the masses of enemy camelmen, until recalled by the furious yells of the N.C.O.'s.

The raiders were now fleeing at full speed in complete confusion, making for a line of rocky cliffs, which they obviously thought would be impassable to wheels. Soon the ammunition was exhausted, for bedouins, though fine fighters, become so excited in action that it is always difficult to control their fire. Petrol and water were running low and this quick moving fight had carried them almost to the Nejed frontier. At length the pursuit was abandoned, and the trucks turned back. The sun was already low and the men turned to rounding up the flocks of looted camels and to loading up the plund-ered tents, carpets and household gear which had been scattered over the face of the desert during the battle.

These two actions, unworthy of mention in comparison to the mass slaughter of millions to which the "civilized" nations of today have

accustomed us, nevertheless produced a profound effect on the
situation in Arabia. The tables had been turned on the hitherto
dreaded Ikhwan who, after these battles, never again attempted to
raid into Iraq. Not only so, however, but throughout the summer,
the rebels had raided the tribes still loyal to Ibn Saud again and
again. The king appeared to have no effective reply to these summer
raids, unless it were to authorize his followers to raid back. To protect them from the attacks of marauding Mutair, Ateiba or Ajman
was beyond his power.

Meanwhile Shammar in Nejed had been raided more than once
by the Ikhwan. Only in the case of those camped in Iraq was the
loot recovered and the attack avenged, and this by a small force
consisting entirely of bedouins and without the aid of either British
forces or of the Iraq army. Moreover, whereas until eighteen months
before, Iraq's inability to control her tribes had been notorious and
had provoked frequent denunciations and sarcasms from the Nejdis,
now it was Ibn Saud's protection which was no longer effective and
tribes seeking safety from Ikhwan raids were fain to take refuge in
Iraq.

In reality, of course, Ibn Saud was still capable of raising large
forces of horse and camelmen for major operations, but such numerous levies, with no administrative organization behind them, were
unable to operate except in winter and that only when heavy rain
had filled the dry desert valleys with pools of water. In summer,
the nimble bedouin raiders, travelling light, could not be overtaken
by other camel-riders. It so happened that, in our light unarmoured
trucks mounting machine guns and manned by bedouins to whom
the desert was home, we had found the ideal weapon to deal with
summer camel raiding, although both Ibn Saud and a number of
senior officers in Iraq had strenuously opposed its development.

Meanwhile the Governor of Hail, Ibn Musaad, was still camped at
Al Jubai with his war banners, waiting until the cool weather and
the autumn rains should permit of a resumption of military operations. When he received news of the defeat of the Al Aah raid, he
was reported to have shaken his head and said "*Ya heif!* Alas!
The Aujan have outstripped us to victory and deprived us of our
glory."

In fact, however, Ibn Musaad's opportunity was not long delayed.
Azaiyiz, the eldest son of Feisal al Duweesh, set out with a large
raiding party of Mutair. The affairs at Al Riqai and Al Aah had
taught him to give the Iraq frontier a wide berth. Ibn Musaad, as
stated, was at Al Jubai, but the great wells at Umm al Rudhumma
and Lina were unoccupied. Azaiyiz decided to water there and to
raid Shammar on the Hazool. While the raiders were looting the
Shammar herds, Ibn Musaad saw his chance. Moving quickly for-

ward with a large force, he concealed his men in broken ground above the wells at Umm al Rudhumma.

Although hardy, intelligent and experienced in desert warfare, the bedouins were always too idle and negligent to be efficient fighters. Driving before them great flocks of camels looted from Shammar, the Mutair raiders, on their return journey, decided to water at the wells at Umm al Rudhumma. They had finished their supplies of water and, beneath the fiery glare of the August sun, many of the men were thirsty. Ibn Musaad had brought with him some fifteen hundred men, consisting of Shammar, Harab and the townspeople of Hail and its oases. They had dug trenches on ground commanding the wells and poured an intense fire into the advancing Ikhwan. A desperate struggle ensued. Ibn Musaad's men were more numerous, were dug in, and rested. The raiders were exhausted and thirsty and were unable to capture the trenches. Ibn Musaad gave no quarter. Every single raider was put to death, including Azaiyiz al Duweesh himself. Every Ikhwan engagement was a battle of extermination.

The summer fighting had inflicted heavy losses in men on the rebels, though they had obtained considerable amounts of loot from other tribes in Nejed. But the fighting men could not be re-placed, and the king's forces would obviously be in overwhelming numbers for the coming winter operations. The rebel defeats had been due to the Southern Desert police on the one hand and to Ibn Musaad on the other. In this direction, the Aujan and the Governor of Hail could claim equal honours.

*   *   *   *   *

In October, information was received of the final pacification of Ateiba, leaving Mutair and the Ajman alone in opposition to Ibn Saud. On 30th October, Feisal al Duweesh arrived in person at Jahra and asked to see the Shaikh of Kuwait and Colonel Dickson, the British Resident.[1] From the latter, he enquired whether he could leave his women and children on the border or in Kuwait, if he led the men of the rebel tribes to fight Ibn Saud in Nejed. The question was referred to the British Government, who returned an unsympathetic reply. The obviously unfriendly attitude of His Majesty's Government further increased the despair of the Duweesh, and indeed went far to terminate the rebellion.

[1] Dickson. *Kuwait and her Neighbours.*

XVIII

The Tables Turned

The Wahhabis have endeavoured, but in vain, to wean the bedouin from their religious indifference ... They have found devoted adherents among the settled Arabians, but not among the bedouin, who have preserved the true Arab character unalloyed ... Although the tribes immediately under the control of the Wahhabis were obliged to observe their religious duties with greater strictness and although some of them, to serve their own interests, assumed an appearance of zeal and even of fanaticism, still these bedouin did not become truly religious.　　　　DOZY, *The Moslems in Spain*

Take my word for it, if you had seen but one day of war, you would pray Almighty God that you might never see such a thing again.
　　　　　　　　　　　　　　　　　THE DUKE OF WELLINGTON

XVIII

THE TABLES TURNED

AT the beginning of December, 1929, the position of the Ikhwan rebels was an awkward one. British armoured cars had been sent to evict them from Kuwait territory, and they were once more moving southwards towards Lusafa and Jeriya. For the moment they believed themselves to be safe, their spies in Nejed having informed them that Ibn Saud's horses and camels were in too poor condition to allow of his undertaking an immediate advance. In Nejed, both horses and camels relied almost entirely on grazing, few people being able to afford to import grain to feed to horses. Thus a failure of the rains, and hence a lack of grazing, could immobilize an army which in other respects was ready for action. The rebels could not, however, reckon on the continuance of such a state of affairs, and as soon as heavy rain fell the grazing would doubtless improve. The position of the rebels, with Kuwait apparently closed to them and Ibn Saud massing overwhelming forces to the south, was anything but enviable.

Meanwhile also a coldness between Mutair and the Ajman had arisen, apparently from an exchange of recriminations caused by an unsuccessful attack on the Awazim in October.

Three courses appeared to be open to them:

(1) To surrender to Ibn Saud before he attacked them. Messengers had indeed been despatched to Ibn Saud with this object, and had returned with a reply to the effect that the surrender of Mutair and the Ajman would be accepted, and that nothing would be done to them except what was prescribed by the Muslim religious law. This cryptic answer was by no means reassuring. A considerable number of the rank and file, however, were in favour of unconditional surrender to the mercy of Ibn Saud. It was almost certain that he would exact from them a heavy fine in camels, but to lose their property and save their lives seemed to them preferable to the risk of losing both.

The principal leaders, however, Feisal al Duweesh, and Ali Ibn Ashwan of Mutair, and Naif Ibn Hithlain of the Ajman, expected no mercy of Ibn Saud, and, fearing that he would put them to death, preferred any solution rather than surrender.

(2) A second possible course was to attempt to break through to Trans-Jordan or Syria, where, it was stated, the Huwaitat and

the Ruwalla were prepared to afford asylum to the rebels. The rank and file of both Mutair and the Ajman, not being in fear for their lives, were categorically opposed to this course, which, however, was favoured by the principal leaders.

(3) The third course was to endeavour to obtain asylum in Iraq. I had recently returned from leave in England, and had not as yet been approached by the rebels, their previous efforts having been made in Kuwait. I had the reputation of understanding the old Arab customs of hospitality and asylum, and it was thought that I might grant protection to any who appealed for it. The Ikhwan failed to understand that government policy applied as much to me as to others.

The idea of obtaining asylum in Iraq appealed equally to the leaders and to the rank and file. To those who were toying with the idea of taking refuge in Trans-Jordan or Syria, asylum in Iraq offered a safe means of transit to the west through Iraq territory and out of reach of Ibn Saud. Otherwise a flank march from Lusafa to the Hazool,[1] with loyalist forces at Lina, seemed too precarious. To those who wished to make peace with the king, in order to return to their home country, asylum in Iraq offered a gain of time, which would allow them, behind the safe shield of government forces on the frontier, to bargain with Ibn Saud for terms.

Eventually, therefore, all parties agreed to make an attempt to secure temporary or permanent asylum in Iraq. After watering at Jeriya and Lusafa, the rebels moved north-west. The Duweesh and Mutair arrived in the Batin on 11th December, 1929, and camped between Al Ubaid and Adharaiyyat. Two days later, the Ajman entered the Batin at Abraq al Hibari, from the direction of Umm Amara Mahazool.

Meanwhile, on my return from leave, I communicated with the Iraq tribes, who were already clamouring to move out to the desert. The police were organized on much the same basis as in the previous year, although the Iraq army motor machine gun company was no longer with us. At the end of November, we moved out from Busaiya, and on 31st November I camped at Julaida, and the Iraq tribes scattered over the Neutral Area.

On 12th December, a Southern Desert police car patrol located Mutair in the Batin, where they had arrived the day before with their camps and herds. The cars succeeded in capturing two Mutairis, who had wandered some distance from their tents, and brought them back to our camp at Julaida for cross-questioning. The prisoners stated that the rebels desired the friendship and protection of the

---

[1] For the Hazool see map on page 298.

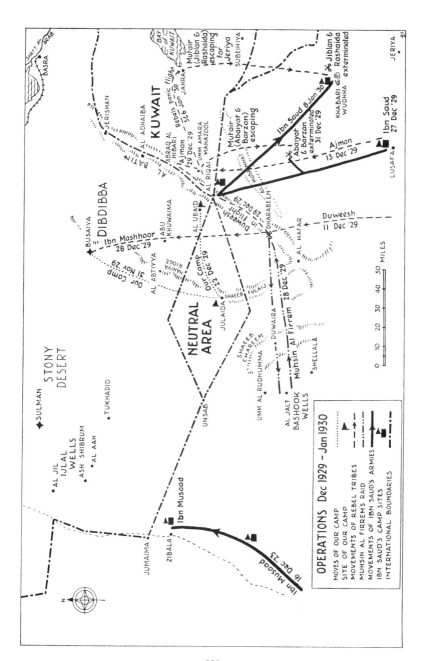

OPERATIONS Dec 1929 – Jan 1930

MOVES OF OUR CAMP	
SITE OF OUR CAMP	▲
MOVEMENTS OF REBEL TRIBES	
MUHSIN AL FIRREM'S RAID	
MOVEMENTS OF IBN SAUD'S ARMIES	
IBN SAUD'S CAMP SITES	▲ ■
INTERNATIONAL BOUNDARIES	

Iraq Government, and that the Duweesh had sent a deputation to negotiate.

Next day, the deputation arrived at our camp, under the leadership of Mushrif Ibn Lami, and bearing a letter from Feisal al Duweesh addressed to me. The letter contained merely protestations of friendship, and the somewhat surprising statement that Mutair "had always been considered to be natives of Iraq". Mushrif Ibn Lami made a verbal request for permission for the rebels to enter Iraq, where they proposed to become devoted subjects of the Iraq Government.

A number of loyalist Nejed tribes, chiefly Shammar, together with Ajami Ibn Suwait and his following of the Dhafeer, had been camped in Shaeeb Chareem,[1] when they heard of the Duweesh's arrival at Al Riqai. Fearing attack, they moved hastily to a position north of Julaida, in order to shelter behind our camp, where they pitched their tents on 13th December, the day on which the first deputation from the rebels arrived. Meanwhile the Iraq tribes were unconcernedly scattered over the Neutral Area quietly enjoying the grazing. To some of us, who had witnessed events in the Southern Desert for the previous eight years and could remember the panic-stricken flights of the Iraq tribes at the mere rumour of an Ikhwan raid, the contrast seemed striking, and indeed deeply moving. For here were those same Iraq tribes, previously scorned for their timidity, grazing far and wide with confidence, while, on the one hand, the Ikhwan rebels implored permission to surrender to us, and, on the other, the tribes loyal to Ibn Saud begged permission to camp close to our police tents, for protection from the rebels. Just two years before, the Duweesh had sworn a famous oath that he would cause the daggers of the Ikhwan to play in the bazaars of Basra.

Shammar, under Mishal Ibn Tawala, and our renegade Ajami Ibn Suwait, insisted on camping within sight of our tents. Ajami, a short time before, had been presented with an Ikhwan war banner by Ibn Saud, and brought it with him when he came to us for protection. One of the chiefs of the shepherd Zayyad, who happened to be in our camp, shook his head and smiled, as the Suwait unloaded and pitched their tents behind us:

"By Allah," he said, "during the last ten years, I never hoped to see an Ikhwan war banner leader, with his bairaq[2] tucked under his arm, camping for protection in the midst of the Zayyad."

Never indeed, during the previous eight years of terror, had we dreamed of so dramatic a turning of the tables.

Meanwhile, reports had been received from our spies to the effect

---

[1] Thus pronounced by the local tribes. The word should really be Kareem.
[2] Bairaq was the name given by Nejdis to their war banners.

that the Duweesh had stated his intention, should entry into Iraq be refused to him, to break his way through to the west, whatever the opposition, in order to find sanctuary in Trans-Jordan.

The sudden arrival of all the rebels at Al Riqai had placed my little camp in a somewhat precarious position. At a distance from Nejed, my small force with its police cars might doubtless be magnified by rumour into an army. But the emissaries from the Duweesh had now arrived in our tents, seen our vehicles and counted our men, of whom I had about forty. Indeed it was not impossible that Ibn Lami had been sent as much to ascertain our strength as to negotiate for terms. If the Duweesh from Al Riqai wished to break through to the west, his route lay across the Neutral Area and straight through our camp. If he wished to reach Trans-Jordan, it was indeed essential for him to start at once, before the rainy weather enabled Ibn Saud to march against him. In addition, the Iraq tribes, especially the shepherds, were dangerously scattered and it would take two or three days to concentrate them.

An immediate and curt refusal to admit the rebels into Iraq might, it seemed to me, cause the Duweesh with a part at least of the rebel tribes, to come sweeping across the Neutral Area in an attempt to break through to the west, a movement which, in view of the weakness of my camp and the dispersion of the Iraq tribes, might result in a disaster for us. I proposed, therefore, to temporize for a few days with the deputation, while I ordered up police reinforcements to my camp, and rallied the Iraq tribes around me. When, in this manner, we were in a suitable defensive posture, I would inform the deputation that Iraq was unable to afford them asylum.

Meanwhile several camps of Dhafeer were grouped at Adhaiba in the Batin, only a few miles from the Ajman who had arrived at Abraq al Hibari. A clash between the two tribes seemed more than probable. I accordingly signalled my appreciation of the situation to Baghdad, and suggested the despatch of a section of armoured cars to Adhaiba, to prevent fighting between the Dhafeer and the Ajman.

No reply to this signal was ever received by me, but on 15th December, two days later, I received a direct signal from the commander of an armoured car section, informing me that he was moving to Adhaiba. I assumed that he had been sent in answer to my request.

On 16th December, I proceeded to Adhaiba to arrange co-operation with the armoured cars, leaving Mushrif Ibn Lami and his deputation still awaiting his answer in our tents at Julaida. I felt fairly confident that the rebels would not undertake any further enterprises until Ibn Lami returned to them with the government reply.

On my arrival at Adhaiba, however, I discovered that two sections of armoured cars had been sent out, with direct orders from air headquarters to evict the rebels forthwith. I had not been informed by Baghdad that any such operation was contemplated nor even that armoured cars were being sent out, although the Iraq Government was in charge of the operations and I was its local representative. I was camped only fifty miles from the rebel tribes, yet without my knowledge the armoured cars had been ordered to attack these tribes.

The increasing amount of work in the desert had resulted in the appointment of a senior police officer to the post of commandant of police, Southern Desert. I had left this officer at Julaida. During my absence at Adhaiba, he received a signal from the ministry of the interior in Baghdad, ordering him to dismiss Mushrif Ibn Lami forthwith, and forbidding him to hold any further intercourse with the rebels. Next morning the armoured cars left Adhaiba to drive the Ajman from the Batin.

Thus the rebels' hopes of obtaining asylum in Iraq had been destroyed at a blow, and there seemed to be a possibility that they would now adopt the alternative course of breaking through to the west. I accordingly signalled Baghdad, suggesting that one section of armoured cars, of which three had now reached Adhaiba, be sent temporarily to Julaida, until the police and tribes could be better organized for the defence. No reply was ever received to this signal.

Affairs were in this situation when, on the evening of 17th December, while I was still at Adhaiba, I received a message from the commandant of police at Julaida, stating that large forces of Mutair and the Ajman had been located by a police car patrol at a point thirty-five miles east of Julaida. The tribesmen, the signal continued, on seeing the cars, had opened fire and unfurled their war banners, and were at that very moment advancing on Julaida, which they would probably attack that night.

The reports previously received of the possible intention of the rebel leaders to break through to the west, the fact that their deputation had been curtly dismissed and that armoured cars had already begun to drive back the Ajman all seemed to combine to make the commandant's report not improbable.

As a result of the commandant's signal, a copy of which had been sent to air headquarters direct, they ordered all three sections of armoured cars at Adhaiba to proceed on the next day, not to Julaida but to Al Abtiyya, where they were to form a defended camp. The police at Julaida, if attacked, were to retire to Al Abtiyya.

The detailed direction of the operations from an office in Baghdad, three hundred miles away, certainly involved difficulties, especially when we were so close to the enemy and the situation in the desert might change in an hour. The orders issued to the armoured cars seemed to me of doubtful value to us. The commandant reported that the rebels were advancing on his camp on the afternoon of 17th December and were only thirty-five miles away. It seemed to me that, if this were the case, the police camp would be attacked at dawn on the 18th. Yet the armoured cars were not ordered to leave Adhaiba until the morning of the 18th. By doing so, they would reach Al Abtiyya in the afternoon of the 18th, and Al Abtiyya was still thirty-five miles from Julaida. If, therefore, the rebels were really advancing on Julaida to attack it at dawn on the 18th, the armoured cars were unlikely to be in time. Not only so, but the police had been ordered that if attacked they were to retire from Julaida to Al Abtiyya, across thirty-five miles of open desert. There were forty desert police at Julaida, and the rebel Mutair alone could probably put three or four thousand men in the field. Moreover, half the police were in cars and half on camels, a difficult force to extricate and move thirty-five miles against odds of one hundred to one.

It seemed to me that the armoured cars were unlikely to be in time for the battle—if battle there were. Indeed, they never yet had been in time for any battle on the Nejed frontier. Whatever the situation at Julaida, we should have to handle it ourselves. I accordingly left Adhaiba immediately and, driving all night, reached Julaida before the first pale light appeared in the east. We stood by at dawn but nothing happened.

As soon, however, as it was broad daylight, and we stood down and could sit round the camp fire and make tea, it became obvious to me that the commandant's appreciation of the situation had been mistaken. He was a fine old man, and was to become a close friend of mine, but he had never been in the desert before. None of the rank and file of the camel corps—all bedouins—agreed with the commandant. They told me that what he had reported as a concentration of the Ajman and Mutair advancing to attack his camp had been Mutair moving camp a few miles to find fresh grazing. The incident was an unfortunate one from my point of view, because it supplied a further example to those who always claimed that every request for R.A.F. support was "only the usual panic". The question was not merely one of proving ourselves to be right or wrong—it was of essential operational importance. The belief held in Baghdad that half of our appeals were merely false alarms was not far from the truth, but the conclusions which we drew from it were diametrically opposite to each other.

When air headquarters received an appeal for help on the grounds that a report had been received that a raid was to take place, their tendency usually was to say: "It's probably only the usual panic. Let's wait for confirmation before taking action." Perhaps more often than not they were right. But half the time or in one case out of three, the report was correct and the R.A.F. missed the raid. Possibly aircraft were able even so to overtake the raiders two days later, and inflict some casualties, instead of destroying them. But never once in the years of operations in Iraq against the Ikhwan did armoured cars come into action, although they were the only weapon which would have inflicted a really decisive defeat. The reason, in my opinion, was that the armoured cars were never moved until a report was finally confirmed.

My argument, on the other hand, was that in this type of operation final confirmation could never be obtained until the battle began. If armoured cars were sent forward, on a plausible but not a finally confirmed report, twice out of three times they would have moved in vain and nothing would have happened, but the third time they would have got into the raiders. One such action, I believed, would have ended Ikhwan raiding into Iraq for ever, and have saved far-reaching international repercussions. But it never happened.

On the return of Mushrif Ibn Lami's deputation, the rebels were again torn by divided counsels, and were unable to make up their minds to any united course of action—a dilemma typically Arab. They were too individualistic to be able to work together. Every Arab wanted his own way, and refused to bow to the opinions of others or the voice of the majority—with the result that anarchy was with them the only alternative to autocracy. Eventually it was decided to send yet another deputation to Julaida, this time with a thoroughbred mare as a propitiatory gift to me. A new deputation was also sent to Ibn Saud, asking for more definite assurances than the previous reference to religious law. The new deputation to Julaida was under the leadership of Hazza Ibn Bedr al Duweesh, a nephew of Feisal. It reached our camp at Julaida on the morning of 18th December.

Meanwhile the concentration of the Iraq tribes had been completed and reinforcements of desert police from Sulman also reached our camp on 18th December. Thus the situation which, twenty-four hours before, the commandant's signal had depicted as alarming, was now re-established and well in hand. I signalled Baghdad that the commandant's telegram had been misleading, that a new deputation had arrived from the rebels, that our tribes were now concentrated and police reinforcements had arrived—in other words that the situation was now safe.

Meanwhile, however, a signal arrived from Baghdad, to the effect that the rebels must be allowed to use the wells in the Neutral Area. We received this telegram with not a little amazement. It was only a few hours since we had received a peremptory telegram to have nothing to do with the rebels. We were under the impression that we were to make things as difficult as possible for them, in order to help Ibn Saud. However, we informed Hazza al Duweesh of these instructions, which, as a matter of fact, greatly reduced the likelihood of an attack on ourselves. If the rebels were told that they could move freely in the Neutral Area, they would probably infer that we would not interfere with them if they crossed the area going west. They were most unlikely to attack the police, if they were satisfied that we would not intercept them.

In actual fact, however, their vacillations had already made it impossible for them to escape to the west, for Ibn Musaad with a large force had moved up from Al Jubai to Lina, and had thereby closed the trap. Their only escape route now lay through Iraq, from the Neutral Area to the Ijlal group of wells, via Tukhadid or Sulman. There was, however, no possibility of their attempting this route without the consent of the Iraq Government. With the police at Julaida now raised to seventy strong by the arrival of reinforcements from Sulman, the grant of permission to the rebels to use the Neutral Area, and the fact that the Iraq tribes were now grouped around us, our situation had been made secure. At the same time we were strategically placed to deal with all eventualities, for the arrival of Ibn Saud's forces could not now be much longer delayed.

Suddenly, however, a peremptory telegram was received from Baghdad ordering the withdrawal of my camp and the police, who were to be based on Busaiya, though an advanced camp might be formed near the frontier. It was difficult to understand the intention of the government. The police were already "based" on Busaiya with an advanced camp near the frontier. But the use of the word "withdrawal" suggested that Baghdad desired our camp to move, for some reason unknown to us. Possibly the signal was a delayed result of the commandant's previous panicky signal, which (though since proved erroneous) was only now beginning to take effect. For the police camp to move back to Busaiya would mean chaos. The Iraq tribes, abandoned to their own devices, would have scattered at their free will, and fighting between them and the rebels would immediately have broken out. There was, however, no water at the time between the Neutral Area and Busaiya (a point which had doubtless never occurred to the Baghdad headquarters who lived on the Tigris), and consequently no intermediate camp site was possible.

The telegram, however, was peremptory—a "withdrawal" of some kind must be made. Eventually on 22nd December, 1929, we moved back to the Haniya ridge, some twenty miles from Julaida. As there was no water near our new camp site, the tribes were unable to follow us, and scattered out of control all over the Neutral Area. Our own camp, consisting of seventy men with no supporting tribes in the vicinity, became once again dangerously exposed to attack. Moreover, when we had been camped on the well at Julaida, all of our eight armed cars were available for fighting patrols, reconnaissance or the martialling of the Iraq tribes. As soon as we moved, however, our efficiency went down rapidly. The guns were dismounted from four of the trucks, which had to be used to fetch water from Julaida, and only four vehicles were left for patrolling. Thenceforward we lost control of the tribes.

Meanwhile, on 20th December, a desert police car patrol encountered Ferhan Ibn Mashhoor, with a following of some sixty men and twenty women, moving towards Abu Khuwaima. A little behind him was Feisal Ibn Shiblan of Mutair. Both were warned in the strongest terms to leave Iraq territory. Ibn Shiblan apparently lost his nerve, and returned the same night to Al Riqai.

At the same time, the armoured cars, which had moved from Adhaiba to Al Abtiyya, had been ordered to return to Adhaiba, after the evaporation of the scare caused by the commandant's telegram. Near Abu Khuwaima, they encountered Ibn Mashhoor and camped for the night a mile from his tents. On hearing this information, I proceeded hastily to Abu Khuwaima, interviewed Ibn Mashhoor and warned him to leave Iraq. He replied, however, that he preferred to be killed by the government than by Ibn Saud. If he had to die, he said, he begged the government to order the armoured cars to shoot down his followers and himself at once.

On the following day, the Chief Air Staff Officer, Air Commodore Burnett, arrived by air at Abu Khuwaima from Baghdad. His arrival was of immense assistance to me. The facts of the situation in the desert, the intelligence reports and the grazing needs of our own tribes, on which our proposed movements were based, were perfectly easily explained verbally on the site. The insuperable difficulty in the past had always been to explain the situation to the many different authorities in Baghdad, British and Iraqi alike, when telegrams were the only vehicle, and when no freedom of action was allowed to those on the spot. Moreover I was too young and too junior to deal with such a senior headquarters. Had I been a colonel or a brigadier, my recommendations would have received more weight and would not have appeared to involve disrespect. Henceforward, however, with a senior R.A.F. officer beside me, all went smoothly. It is easy to be wise in retrospect. What I had of course needed all the time (but I was too inexperienced to know it) was an R.A.F. liaison officer with me, whose sole duty would have been to interpret our tribal situation to air headquarters. Alternatively I could have flown to Baghdad more frequently and thereby laid my views verbally before the R.A.F. and the Iraq Government. In the 1920's, however, no one was as air-minded as they have since become and it is by no means certain that, as a junior officer, I would have been allotted an aircraft so frequently. In fact, I was so engrossed in my local activities that I desired to avoid visiting Baghdad as far as possible.

In view of Ibn Mashhoor's refusal to move, he and his followers were disarmed on 23rd December, 1929. He, and the sixty followers still remaining with him, were of the Ruwalla tribe, whom the Iraq and British Governments reckoned to be Syrian subjects. It was accordingly decided that they were not covered by the pledge, given to Ibn Saud, that asylum would not be given to his rebellious subjects. Ferhan was sent to Busaiya by car for detention, while his camp and disarmed retainers followed under an escort of twenty camel police. They duly reached Busaiya and camped outside the fort on 28th December, 1929.

Ferhan Ibn Mashhoor offered a marked contrast to the Mutair and Ajman rebels. He had been brought up in wealth and comfort in the rich and powerful Shaalan family, who were chiefs of the great Ruwalla division of Aneza. His youth had been spent, partly in the tents of the Ruwalla, partly in the town house of Al Nouri Ibn Shaalan in Damascus. He was comparatively civilized, could drive a a car, and engaged me in a discussion on the relative merits of Buicks and Dodges.

On the other hand, again unlike many of the men of Mutair and the Ajman, he seemed to be genuinely infected with fanatical Wahhabi-ism. He endeavoured, at Abu Khuwaima, to save the souls of the desert police by giving them a religious talk. As, however, he began his homily with the words, "Three years ago, I myself, was a heathen like you are . . . ," he met with but little sympathy.

Meanwhile the second rebel deputation under Hazza al Duweesh had also been sent back by us, with a message to the effect that we were unable to afford them asylum in Iraq. The rebel counsels were still divided. None seemed capable of taking a decision. Signs of disintegration became apparent.

Two sectional leaders, Haif al Fughum and Sultan Ibn Muhailib, abandoned the Duweesh's cause and moved southwards to Jeriya, whence they sent messages of abject surrender to Ibn Saud. The Ajman, and the Diyaheen section of Mutair, were still at Abraq al Hibari, forty miles from the Duweesh at Dharabeen, and showed no signs of wishing to co-operate with him any further.

The Duweesh remained at Dharabeen, apparently paralysed by indecision. It seemed possible that he would remain there until Ibn Saud arrived and then flee helter-skelter into Iraq, in such a manner that he could not be turned back. He placed no scouts or pickets in front of his camp at Dharabeen, apparently relying entirely on his spies at Lusafa for warning of Ibn Saud's advance. It never seemed to occur to him that anyone would attack him, except Ibn Saud with his whole army.

Two months earlier, in late October, 1929, Muhsin al Firrem, a great shaikh of the Harab tribe,[1] had set out, at Ibn Saud's instigation, to raid the rebels in Kuwait territory. On learning however that news of his intention had leaked out and that the rebels were ready to receive him, he had lost his nerve and had returned home without attacking them. This futile effort had apparently provoked a scornful comment from Ibn Saud in public. The gibe had been duly reported to Muhsin, who set out once more in December, unknown to Ibn Saud, to wipe out the disgrace by a raid on the Duweesh.

On 22nd December, Muhsin al Firrem, with his war banners, arrived at Duwaira. On the 27th, he was at Shaeeb Fulaij. The delay in his advance was due to the fact that he had sent messengers to Shammar and to Ajami Ibn Suwait, who ten days before had fled to us for protection at Julaida, calling upon them to join him.

Meanwhile, on the 27th, while Muhsin al Firrem was in Shaeeb Fulaij, Ibn Saud with his main army arrived at Lusafa, whence he sent forward four cars to locate the position of the rebels. These cars entered Kuwait territory as far as Mahazool, where they captured a man of the Diyaheen section of Mutair, which was camped with the Ajman at Abraq al Hibari, and took him back to Lusafa for cross-questioning. He informed Ibn Saud of the fact that the Duweesh and Mutair were at Dharabeen. At this moment, therefore, Muhsin al Firrem, unknown to Ibn Saud, was in Shaeeb Fulaij, while Ibn Saud, unknown to Muhsin al Firrem, was at Lusafa. The staff work of the Saudi forces seemed to leave a good deal to be desired, especially as the king had with him some twenty-five cars, which could have been used for reconnaissance and communications.

Mishal Ibn Tawala and Ajami Ibn Suwait, leaving their camps under our protection, joined Muhsin al Firrem on 27th December in Shaeeb Fulaij, only twenty miles from the Duweesh's camp. We ourselves had learned, by bitter experience, to cover our front with horse and camel scouts thirty, forty or fifty miles ahead of us. Yet here was the great Duweesh himself allowing the enemy raiding force to assemble in a valley only twenty miles from his camp. Such were the casual undisciplined ways of the bedouins at war.

As soon as it was dark, Muhsin al Firrem and his allies advanced from Shaeeb Fulaij, Harab being on the right, Shammar and Ajami's Dhafeer on the left. Two hours before dawn, they came within striking distance of the Mutair camps. They halted in the dark, couched their camels and dismounted to wait for the daylight. Not a scout or a picket was on the look-out. All the Mutair camps

[1] It was Muhsin al Firrem who had raided at Sulman in December 1924, see page 136.

seemed to be sleeping peacefully, disturbed only by the occasional bark of a dog, or the flare up of a flame as some restless tribesman awoke and blew the embers of his tent fire to a blaze to warm his toes. Two miles away fate silently awaited the dawn to destroy the Duweesh's military reputation at a blow. With the first light the raiders remounted, the war banners were unfurled, and the bedouins, camelmen and horsemen together, poured like a raging torrent on to the sleeping camps.

As the men of Mutair leaped to their feet, the first thought that flashed through every mind was that their assailant was Ibn Saud, whose army, as they knew, outnumbered them hopelessly. The idea of resistance, therefore, probably never entered their minds. With the first instinct of bedouins, the Mutairis ran to their camels, their principal source of wealth. The women were not molested in these battles, and the sale of two or three camels would easily replace the tent and its simple furnishings. Soon the immense herds of the great lumbering camels were galloping down into the Batin in full stampede, abandoning the camps to the enemy.

The first brunt of Muhsin al Firrem's attack fell upon the Abaiyat and Rashaida sections, who lost almost all they possessed. Ajami Ibn Suwait's brand new war banner advanced on the Jiblan section. The Barzan, who were camped in a tributary valley going down into the Batin, were never seen by the raiders and escaped scot free. The camels of the Dushan and part of the Jiblan escaped across the Batin, and up past Al Riqai. All the camps were abandoned. Muhsin al Firrem planted his war banner outside the Duweesh's tent, while the latter's guest tent, a large one made of white canvas and said to have been a present from Ibn Sobah, was burnt by his victorious enemies. There was no resistance and few casualties. Perhaps some fifty men and boys were killed.

The attackers were probably afraid of a counter-attack when the fugitives realized that they had fled from other bedouin raiders, and not from Ibn Saud. Anyhow, they contented themselves with rounding up the vast number of camels which they had captured, probably about five thousand, for Mutair had accumulated immense herds as a result of their years of raiding. Then hastily ransacking the tents, Muhsin al Firrem and his companions retired once again to the west, driving their loot before them.

At the request of Air Commodore Burnett, I drove to Al Ubaid on 28th December, as the armoured cars had moved there, still intent on evicting the Ajman from Abraq al Hibari. Early on the 29th, I persuaded Naif Ibn Hithlain and the Ajman to move from Abraq al Hibari to Mahazool. They promised the next day to move back into Nejed territory at Al Riqai. In the afternoon I set out southwards from Al Ubaid towards Shaeeb al Auja, two miles north of which we encountered two Mutair fugitives on foot. A little farther on, we noticed a small group of men sitting disconsolately on the ground, round a small brushwood fire. One of them we recognized as Hazza al Duweesh, who had headed the second deputation to our camp. He rose and advanced towards our car to salute me. Behind him followed a thickset figure with an ungainly walk, a long brown beard, projecting teeth and cunning little eyes — the very face of the wicked ogre in a fairy story. It was none other than Feisal al Duweesh, the one-time terror of Arabia, who a year before, when he moved out his war banner from Artawiya, had declared that he would never return until he had seized Abu Hunaik, alive or dead.

The desert was dotted with scattered camels and herds, moving slowly up the Batin, the property of the raided Mutair camps from which they had been driven away in a wild stampede which eluded pursuit. A little farther on, we came upon a large and most striking herd of all black camels. It was the sharaf or "the honour", a famous black herd which had belonged to the Duweesh family for many generations. On days of battle, the honour had been used as a rallying point for Mutair, who boasted that it had never been captured by an enemy — an old piece of bedouin vainglory, smacking perhaps too much of worldly vanity.

During the night of 29th-30th December, fugitives from the followers of the Duweesh arrived in the Ajman camp at Mahazool. The following morning, the Ajman, not unexpectedly, refused to move to Al Riqai, as they had previously agreed to do.

The British and Iraq Governments, which had pledged themselves to Ibn Saud not to give asylum to the rebels, were finding the task less simple than they had thought. Indeed it was surprising to me that the rebels did not enter Iraq one evening after dark, march all night and keep marching all the next day until someone stopped them. They would probably by that time have arrived thirty or forty miles from the frontier. Then they could have sat down and refused to move, and invited the government to shoot them. Possibly the Ikhwan, so accustomed to massacre, imagined that the government would have killed them all, as they in their heyday had killed all who were not Wahhabis. Only Ibn Mashhoor, more familiar with the ways of governments, adopted this method and was successful.

Air Commodore Burnett was not a little perplexed at the Ajman refusal to move from Mahazool. After a discussion between us, he obtained the approval of the authorities to make an offer to the rebels, of which he and I together drafted the suggested terms.

The principal leaders were to surrender themselves and be interned. They would not subsequently be handed back to Ibn Saud, unless he agreed to spare their lives. Should he refuse to do so, they would be made to reside at a distance from the Iraq-Nejed frontier, both the British and the Iraq Governments guaranteeing that they would not be allowed to return to Nejed or the frontier area. The tribes were to surrender unconditionally, whereupon they would be mustered and disarmed, and a number of animals taken from them as compensation for loot previously raided by them from Iraq.

Should the rebels reject these terms, they would have been given their chance, and in that case they would be evicted by force, fire being opened if necessary. It seemed probable that the rebels might refuse to evacuate Iraq and Kuwait territory, unless fired upon.

Armed with these suggestions, Air Commodore Burnett flew to Baghdad, returning on 31st December, 1929. The terms suggested had been agreed to in Baghdad, except that we were ordered to promise the leaders that they would not, in any event, be handed back to Ibn Saud. This promise was substituted for our suggested formula, that they would not be handed back unless Ibn Saud agreed to spare their lives. The new wording appeared to me to be sailing rather close to the wind, in view of the pledge given to Ibn Saud that we would not grant asylum to the rebels. Meanwhile the chiefs, if they gave themselves up, were to be sent to Basra.

During these days, we were at times perplexed by the apparent contradictions contained in the orders from Baghdad. When we had spoken to the deputation led by Mushrif Ibn Lami, we had received peremptory orders to dismiss him and hold no converse with the rebels; then came an order to allow them to camp in the Neutral Area. Now we had suggested that the Ikhwan leaders might have to be interned in Iraq if Ibn Saud refused to pledge himself to spare their lives, but the government replied, ordering us to assure them that they would not in any case be handed back to Ibn Saud. Whereas at first the government had seemed to suspect us of leniency towards the Ikhwan, now it seemed to us that the government was acting in a manner contrary to the pledge which it had given, that it would not afford them asylum. Even if, on their arrival in Iraq, the rebel leaders had been interned at a distance from the frontier, there could not be the least doubt that Ibn Saud, suspicious as he was, would have accused Iraq of giving them sanctuary.

It seemed as though conflicting policies were giving rise to these vacillations. King Feisal doubtless wished to make matters easy for the rebels, because they were the enemies of Ibn Saud, who had seized the Hejaz from King Husain, his father. The British, and to a lesser extent, the Iraqi ministers, were anxious only for peace and reconciliation, and desired to appease Ibn Saud. Neither King Feisal nor the Iraqi or the British authorities seemed to me to give enough thought to the Iraq tribes, which had suffered so many losses and massacres at the hands of the Ikhwan.

On receipt of the orders from Baghdad, letters were written to

Feisal al Duweesh and Naif Ibn Hithlain, ordering them to report to Al Ubaid on safe conduct. The Duweesh, with the remnant of the Dushan and Jiblan sections, had meanwhile joined the Ajman at Mahazool. The Abaiyat and Barzan sections had decided to return to Nejed and surrender to Ibn Saud. Of them, we shall hear more later.

On 1st January, 1930, Feisal al Duweesh and Naif Ibn Hithlain reported to the camp at Al Ubaid, and the terms were explained to them. They were desperately anxious, before agreeing, to ascertain what their ultimate fate would be, but as I was ignorant of it myself, I was unable to enlighten them. The shaikhs were extremely suspicious of the order that they were to be despatched to Basra, and urgently requested permission to remain with their tribes, stating that, in this case, they and their tribes would agree to surrender. Eventually they requested twelve hours' grace, to return to their homes and consult their friends. They were given sixty hours to evacuate Kuwait and Iraq territory should the terms be refused, after which time they were warned that any of them found within those countries would be treated as hostile.

XIX

Unconditional Surrender

When the wicked, even mine enemies, and my foes, came upon me:
they stumbled and fell. Though an host of men were laid against me,
yet shall not my heart be afraid: and though there rose up war against
me, yet will I put my trust in him. . . .
And now shall he lift up mine head: above mine enemies round about
me.   *Psalm* xxvii

The moral law is written on the tablets of eternity; and for every
unrighteous deed, for cruelty or oppression, for lust or vanity, the
price has to be paid at last.   FROUDE

The best kind of revenge is not to be like him who did the injury.
                                        MARCUS AURELIUS ANTONINUS

For the operations described in this chapter, please see
map on page 313.

XIX

UNCONDITIONAL SURRENDER

NO further reply was received from the Duweesh or Ibn Hithlain as to whether our terms of surrender were accepted or not. On the morning of 3rd January, 1930, therefore, they were notified by us that our terms were assumed to have been rejected, and that they must consequently evacuate Iraq and Kuwait territory by dawn on 5th January. All the rebels thereupon struck camp and moved south through Umm Amara Mahazool. All this time, there was no news of Ibn Saud. Muhsin al Firrem was reported to be camped at Al Jalt with his war banners, and to be still engaged in dividing his enormous loot.

On the afternoon of 5th January, 1930, however, the leading rebels, after pitching camp at Umm Amara Mahazool, suddenly packed up once more, and set out at full speed towards Jahra, travelling all night and all the following day. The desert in their wake was strewn with camels and sheep, exhausted by this forced march, and abandoned in their flight. The reason for this sudden panic was not at first obvious to us. I was asked by the Air Commodore to accompany him and the armoured cars into Kuwait territory, permission for me to do so having been obtained from Ibn Sobah, and the Political Agent, Colonel Dickson, not having arrived. Otherwise, there being no Iraq tribes in Kuwait, I had neither the desire nor the right to enter that territory.

At sunrise on 6th January, the armoured car column, which I was accompanying, overtook the leading rebels in flight, fifteen miles west of Jahra. They were utterly demoralized, none of them knew where they were going, nor could any shaikhs be found, but all were equally bent on flying pell-mell to the north, away from Ibn Saud's army, which they imagined to be at their heels (unaware that he was obliged to halt at the frontier). We made an attempt to round up the fugitives, with but mediocre success, owing to their state of panic and the absence of any leaders. This applied especially to the Dushan, Rashaida and Jiblan sections, who had already been raided by Mushin al Firrem. The Ajman, who brought up the rear, were in slightly better shape.

As a man, I found something painful and humiliating in seeing other human beings reduced to such a state of abject fear. The (perhaps British) dislike which we instinctively feel at striking a man who is already beaten, made me apprehensive of the possibility that

329

we might be ordered to fire on this panic-stricken horde, or that we should hand them over to Ibn Saud to be butchered before our eyes. Yet at the same time, I could not but remember how often I had seen our own Iraq tribes in just such terror-stricken flight, intent on escaping from massacre by these same pitiless Ikhwan whom we now saw before us. This was poetic justice indeed—but far from feeling satisfaction, I felt distressed.

At midday, when I was still accompanying the armoured car column in its efforts to round up the fleeing Ikhwan, I was handed a wireless message picked up by the armoured cars and despatched by the small detachment which I had left at Al Ubaid. It announced laconically the arrival of Ibn Saud with his whole army at Al Riqai. This then had been the reason for the sudden panic flight of the rebels. Perhaps some Mutairi, of whom there were many with Ibn Saud, had slipped away from the royal forces and had warned his relatives in the rebel camp of Ibn Saud's proximity. I accordingly hastily left the armoured cars, who in any case were expecting the arrival of Colonel Dickson to assume political responsibility with the column, and hastened to return to Al Ubaid.

As already related, when Ibn Saud had arrived at Lusafa, he had sent four cars to reconnoitre for the rebels and these had captured a Mutairi and taken him back to the king for cross-questioning. He stated that the Duweesh was at Dharabeen. This was on 28th December. Ibn Saud decided to advance to the attack. Great precautions were taken to prevent the escape of spies from Lusafa to warn the rebels, apparently with complete success, as the king in reality did reach Al Riqai unexpectedly. In the interval, however, while Ibn Saud was preparing to advance, Muhsin al Firrem raided Mutair on 28th December, and the fugitives fled northwards into Kuwait. Consequently when Ibn Saud arrived, the Duweesh was no longer at Dharabeen.

Meanwhile, after Muhsin al Firrem's raid, the remainder of the Abaiyat section (Ali Ibn Ashwan) and the Barzan section (Ali abu Shuwairibat) decided to flee to Jeriya and appeal to Ibn Shuqair, who had made his peace with Ibn Saud, to intercede for them also. They were of course unaware that Ibn Saud was at that moment leaving Lusafa to meet them. On 31st December, 1929, the advanced guard of the royal army, consisting of four cars, located Ali Ibn Ashwan on the move, in an open plain south-east of Al Musannat. A car was sent back to report to Ibn Saud, and Muhammad, the king's third son, with the remaining cars, probably about twenty in all, immediately reinforced the advanced guard. The king's men were warned that, should any man spare the life of a Mutairi, his own life would be forfeit, and they were reminded that these were the men who had so often raided and looted them in the past. The king's cars encircled Ibn Ashwan and his followers from the north, while Ibn Saud with his main forces charged from the south. Ibn Ashwan and his relatives, surrounded and outnumbered, couched their camels in a compact mass, and fired steadily at their attackers, inflicting considerable casualties until they were eventually overwhelmed by numbers. Every single male Mutairi was killed, the women of course being left.

A halt was made after this action, and at sunset, two other scout cars returned to report that another tribal group was on the move on the south-east of the army. This was the Barzan section, which had crossed in front of Ibn Saud's army, ahead of Ibn Ashwan, and was making for Jeriya. Orders were issued for their pursuit and annihilation the next morning. Meanwhile, however, the Barzan had apparently become aware of the presence of Ibn Saud's army, and possibly of the fate of Ibn Ashwan. Ali Abu Shuwairibat[1] (of Ikhwan refugee fame) and Mutlaq Abu Hanaiya, the two headmen of the section, left their tribe at dusk, and riding through the night, slipped into the camp unidentified—presumably so large a mass of tribal levies without regular military organization made their apprehension difficult. Soon after midnight, they burst into Ibn Saud's tent and threw themselves at his feet. Having reached the asylum of his tent, their lives were spared.

These actions delayed the advance of Ibn Saud's army, and it was not until 5th January that he reached Al Riqai and camped there. He heard of Muhsin al Firrem's raid for the first time from Ali Abu Shuwairibat. On reaching Al Riqai, he found no rebels south of the frontier. His advanced guard, consisting of some forty horsemen and two hundred camelmen, penetrated into Kuwait territory as far as Mahazool. They came upon three Iraq tribesmen, two of whom they immediately killed with rifle fire and then dagger wounds, looting their rifles and riding camels. The third man made his escape. The rifles and camels were never returned.

On 5th January, after I had left Al Ubaid with Air Commodore Burnett to round up the fleeing rebels in Kuwait territory, three cars arrived at our post at Al Ubaid from Ibn Saud. They contained Yusuf al Yaseen, the Syrian lawyer and former journalist, whom we had already met at Jidda. With him were Turki as Sudairi, a relative of Ibn Saud, and Munowwakh Aba Ithnain, a shaikh of the Sebei tribe. When I arrived back at Al Ubaid, I found them awaiting me.

Yusuf al Yaseen was the spokesman of the party and presented me with a letter from the king, asking to know what steps would be taken by the British Government to fulfil their pledge not to allow the rebels to enter Kuwait. Yusuf al Yaseen added a verbal tirade on his own behalf, against the shortcomings of His Majesty's Govern-

[1]See page 107.

ment. I replied that, as I was an official of the Iraq Government, I was in no way concerned with the intentions of the British authorities, nor with the alleged activities of the Shaikh of Kuwait. There was therefore no advantage to be gained by reciting their misdemeanours to me. I, however, gave him a full account of all that had happened, and added that, as a private person and not the responsible official, I had no doubt that His Majesty's Government were determined to take every step to fulfil their pledges.

I agreed, at his request, to despatch wireless messages from Ibn Saud on the police mobile wireless set at Al Ubaid. Presumably the king had been unable to bring a wireless set with him, because many of the Ikhwan still considered wireless to be diabolical magic, incompatible with true religion. Yusuf al Yaseen thereupon wrote out two wireless messages, one addressed to the British High Commissioner in Baghdad and one to the Resident in the Persian Gulf. In both he requested on behalf of the king that the rebels be evicted from Kuwait or that Ibn Saud be given permission to enter Kuwait to attack them. In the event of His Majesty's Government failing to adopt one or other of these courses, Ibn Saud would be reluctantly compelled to return home, but in that event the responsibility for all future disturbances on the frontier would, of course, rest on the shoulders of those who had given asylum to the rebels (presumably the British Government).

These notes appeared to have been drafted by Yusuf al Yaseen himself, in his capacity of Ibn Saud's expert on foreign affairs. I have since often noticed what appears to me an unfortunate aspect of Arab diplomacy—their predilection for using threats in even the most ordinary affairs. I could not avoid the impression that this was a tactical mistake. We were working ourselves to the bone to comply with the king's wishes, and it was merely annoying to be told that, if we did not fulfil our pledges, it would be the worse for us. I could not help feeling that, if we could have dealt direct with King Abdul Aziz, he would not have adopted this tone, but, as at Jidda, his advisers were the channel of communications between us. Twenty years later, the Arab League were to commit the same tactical error in the discussions on the subject of Palestine in U.N.O. The world wanted to do the right thing, but it was aggravating to receive threats instead of explanations.

Between coming and going from us to Al Riqai, Yusuf al Yaseen and his party spent some three days in the post at Al Ubaid. He periodically launched into recriminations against the British Government, or against those of Iraq or Kuwait. A curious mixture of a modern Syrian journalist and a Wahhabi fanatic, he endeavoured, in a rash moment, to convert the commandant of police to the True Path. Hasan Fehmi Beg, however, appeared to know more of the

Qoran by heart than did the would-be missionary and the latter was somewhat put to confusion.

On one occasion, a flight of aircraft passed over our camp when Yusuf al Yaseen was present. He watched them for a short time disappearing to the south, and then requested an immediate interview with me, at which he delivered a violent protest, claiming that the aircraft had crossed the frontier. I replied that I had not the least idea whence the aircraft had come nor whither they were going, but that I would like him to understand that both the British and Iraq Governments had incurred great trouble and expense in these operations, solely in order to assist Ibn Saud. The interests of the two sides were identical. If, however, I added, he was on the look-out for chances to make protests, I was quite ready to follow the same method. To begin with, Ibn Saud's scout cars, and later on his advanced guard of horsemen and camelmen, had penetrated as far as Mahazool in Kuwait territory, a fact which both Hasan Fehmi Beg and I had abstained from reporting to our government, because we realized that the frontier was not demarcated, and the trespass might possibly have been unintentional. For the moment, this produced the desired effect.

The next day, 7th January, 1930, a party of horsemen from Ibn Saud's camp raided the Dhafeer in the Dibdibba, and drove off forty-five camels. Two police cars gave chase but reached the frontier at Shaeeb al Auja just in time to see the raiders drive the looted camels into the royal camp. A strong protest was immediately despatched to Ibn Saud, and, on the following morning, a letter of apology was received, accompanied however by only thirty-seven camels. The remainder were never heard of again.

The incident was troublesome at the time, because the Iraq tribes arrived at our tents in high indignation, demanding permission to raid an equal number of camels from Ibn Saud. As the king had some seven thousand men at Al Riqai, and we had twenty-four camel police at Al Ubaid, it seemed to me unnecessary to resort to arms. We told our tribes sternly to go back to their tents and not to be naughty. The incident, however, caused us, in a manner, a slight smile of amusement. At Jidda, the Nejed delegates had frequently advised us to give up trying to deal with bedouins, because Ibn Saud was the only man who could control such wild tribes. It was obvious that the king did not want his followers to steal our camels just at this moment, when to co-operate with us was the only chance he had of bringing his campaign to a successful conclusion. But, unlike the Iraq Government (we said to each other), his control over his wild bedouins was incomplete.

On the following day, an Iraq tribesman near Shaeeb al Auja, on our side of the frontier, came across a party of Nejed camelmen who demanded to know who he was. He foolishly replied that he was "from Abu Hunaik's tribes," an answer which drew a burst of rifle fire, and only luck and a fast riding camel saved his life. Other similar incidents followed.

Meanwhile Yusuf al Yaseen continued to come and go with protests. I tried to explain to him that we were trying very hard, and had no possible interest in deceiving Ibn Saud and in helping the rebels, who were the people who had been massacring our subjects for years. Many of his protests delivered to me, and others sent officially to the British and Iraq Governments during the previous year, attributed to them, but particularly to Iraq, evil ulterior motives of which in reality they were perfectly innocent. I assured Yusuf al Yaseen that we were not guided by the sinister intentions which he believed us to entertain. At first he retorted that all the Nejed protests had been based on statements made in the Iraqi press—presumably on the assumption that no government would allow the press of its country to write anything of which it did not approve. Eventually, however, he admitted to me that Ibn Saud had desired to multiply protests during 1928 and 1929, in order "to prove the evil effects of the existence of police posts in the Iraq deserts". I could not help thinking that if the king had really desired to multiply protests, he did so on the advice of his officials. King Abdul Aziz had given me the impression of a man of frank and open (even if of forcible or violent) speech. These rather tortuous methods did not seem to me to originate from his mind.

Yusuf al Yaseen's companions, Turki as Sudairi and Munowwakh Aba Ithnain, were more kindred spirits. They were open and sincere, with the frank and democratic candour of the Nejdi. Both said that Ibn Saud was very grateful for the help which the two governments were giving him in dealing with the rebels, and that his former suspicions of the motives of Iraq and of myself had completely vanished. How different the world would be if all nations realized that, in diplomacy, honesty, not guile, was the best policy!

The royal fleet of "armed cars" consisted principally of ancient Chevrolet trucks, the bodies of which had been mended here and there by nailing on patches made of pieces of petrol tins. They arrived at Al Riqai on their last tin of petrol, and as a result the royal army was reduced to immobility, except on horses and camels, until we supplied them with more petrol. His Majesty asked whether, if petrol was not obtainable, he could deposit the mechanical branch of his army with us at Al Ubaid for safe custody, "as your guests" as he gracefully put it. The campaign could be finished by horses and camels, he explained. Our administrative arrangements, however, dealt adequately with the crisis and the Nejed battle fleet left Al Riqai under its own power.

At this stage, an incident occurred which placed me in an embarrassing situation. I woke on the morning of 7th January to be told that a bedouin had crept into our camp in the small hours of the morning, and throwing himself into the tent where the police were sleeping (our "camp" consisted of only three tents), had seized the tent pole and shouted, "I am under the protection of this tent."[1]

We, as usual, had a black tent pitched beside our two white tents, as a guest tent. This house of hair was always filled with passing tribesmen, and Ibn Saud had doubtless taken the precaution of sending his spies over to enjoy our hospitality. I took no action to prevent this, because we had nothing to hide. Our new protégé proved to be one Abu Shijra, a member of the Ajman tribe, who had committed a peculiarly heinous crime. He had, it appeared, enjoyed hospitality in Ibn Saud's guest house in Riyadh and had left there to rob a caravan, while the king's salt was still in his stomach.

Within a few hours of his arrival, up roared a royal Buick with Yusef al Yaseen in high dudgeon. This time he really had material for a protest. Contrary to all the pledges solemnly given by the British and Iraq Governments, I was sheltering a rebel in my tent. I succeeded in putting him off for a time, and he went back to Al Riqai. Three hours later, however, I saw the Buick coming back. The desert police were outraged at the idea of giving up Abu Shijra. He would be killed immediately on reaching Ibn Saud's camp. He had appealed to their tent, not to mine. No Arab could honourably deny the right of sanctuary in his tent. I decided to make a clean breast of it. Before Yusef al Yaseen had time to deliver another protest, I told him that I had Abu Shijra in my tent, that he had appealed to that tent for protection and that I only asked Ibn Saud to grant me the right of sanctuary, which any Arab would claim. The message must have been delivered to the king, for no further protests were made to me, nor did he ever mention the incident to either the British or Iraq Governments. I was grateful to Ibn Saud for this generosity. Had he reported the affair I should probably have been in trouble, for neither of these governments would have accorded much respect to ancient Arab custom. I was not at that time aware that, a few days before, Ibn Saud himself had pardoned the two headmen of the Barzan Mutair, because they had, in a similar manner, burst into his tent and seized the tent pole.

It was with some relief that, on the morning of 8th January, 1930, we saw Ibn Saud's army apparently moving eastward out of the Batin. The water at Al Riqai had proved insufficient for his forces, and he moved to some large rainwater pools at Khabari

[1] This story was told more fully in *The Story of the Arab Legion*.

Wadhha. "God save us from our friends," I wrote in my diary for 8th January.

The total number of Ibn Saud's forces in the field in January, 1930, was difficult to estimate. No officer of ours visited his camp, and bedouins are erratic when cross-questioned regarding numbers.

The king's tent was said to be surrounded by about fifty others, presumably slaves, personal retainers and the bodyguard, whose numbers might thus be estimated at about four hundred. There were also other tents, possibly occupied by the town contingents and by notables and religious shaikhs. The bedouin tribal contingents bivouacked in the open, and their numbers were therefore more difficult to estimate. The contingents from oases and towns may have amounted to about three thousand, and the total with bedouin contingents to about seven or eight thousand men. This figure can, however, be scarcely more than a guess.

The principal contingents with Ibn Saud at Al Riqai were the following:

Townspeople of the provinces of Al Aridh, Washm and the Qaseem
Harab under Hijab Ibn Naheet (The other half of Harab with Muhsin al Firrem had gone home after his raid.)
Mutair loyalists. Meshari Ibn Busaiyis
Sebei
Qahtan
Dawasir
Ateiba loyalists under Ibn Rubaiyan and Menahi al Haidhal.

Meanwhile an independent army was holding the northern Hasa, with contingents from:

The Hasa townspeople
Beni Hajir
Beni Khalid
Al Murra.

Ibn Musaad was also in the field at Zibala, blocking the Duweesh's possible way of escape to Trans-Jordan. He had with him:

Townspeople of Hail and the Jebel Shammar oases
Ikhwan Shammar
(Many of the bedouin Shammar had already raided under Ibn Tawala with Muhsin al Firrem.)

On the total of the three armies, Ibn Saud may have had some sixteen thousand men in the field. On the other hand, the primitive methods of administration, the dependence on grazing because forage could not be carried, and the lack of water in the desert, would not have allowed the sixteen thousand men to have been used in one army. Even as it was, to water and feed such large forces in the desert in three widely dispersed armies, with no system of supplies, was no mean feat.

Ibn Saud's mechanized force, which accompanied his army to Al Riqai, consisted of between twenty-five and thirty vehicles. A number of these, as already described, were Chevrolet trucks, to which eight or ten negroes clung precariously. There was also a sprinkling of touring cars, amongst which a Buick and a new Ford were noticed (the back springs of the Ford were broken and the body was resting on the back axle, but all concerned appeared to be quite undismayed thereby). There were rumoured to be five machine guns, of unknown makes, in the royal camp.

* * * * *

The first news of the arrival of the Duweesh at Al Riqai and the flight of the Najd Shammar and Ajami Ibn Suwait to our police post at Julaida on 13th December, 1929, had produced great elation among the Iraq tribes. Firstly it was the outward and visible sign that their own government (now trusted, though so hated and suspected a few years before) were masters of the field. But the second reason for their jubilation was that they anticipated an early opportunity of recovering some at least of the crushing losses which they had suffered in the previous ten years. They at first anticipated an immediate attack by government forces on the rebels, and many tribal chiefs had hastened to our post at Julaida, begging to be allowed to join the expedition. When, however, the Mutair deputation arrived at Julaida seeking asylum in Iraq, they stated verbally that if their request were granted, they would hand over loot taken from the Iraq tribes. This news caused even greater enthusiasm, and for a time our tribes held high hopes of recovering their property without a struggle. Bitter disappointment ensued when the deputation was dismissed, without any negotiations on the return of loot, and the rebels were warned not again to enter Iraq.

During the previous two years, since Ajami Ibn Suwait had gone over to Ibn Saud, considerable jealousy had grown up between him and his following, and that portion of the Dhafeer which had remained in Iraq. Each party endeavoured to prove the advantages of the policy which it had adopted. Ajami's followers loudly proclaimed the vast rewards and the honourable treatment lavished upon them by Ibn Saud. Those who had remained in Iraq were equally zealous in describing the happy conditions which now prevailed in that country.

The presentation of an Ikhwan war banner to Ajami in the spring of 1929, caused considerable resentment in Iraq. Indeed, in view of the fact that Ibn Saud had recognized the Dhafeer as Iraq subjects in the Treaty of Muhammarah, this action did appear to be sailing rather close to the wind. The precipitous arrival of Ajami at Julaida early in December, with his war banner (as they said) tucked under his arm, gave rise to some mocking merriment among the Iraq half of the tribe, who hastened to point out that a dozen desert police cars seemed, in a tight corner, to be a safer refuge than Ibn Saud—war banners or no war banners.

But this jubilation turned again to indignation when Ajami, leaving his tents in safety by our police camp, unfurled his brand new war banner and joined Muhsin al Firrem's raid, while we forbade the Iraq tribes to attack the Ikhwan rebels. Not only so, but Ajami and his followers obtained from Mutair an undreamt-of amount of loot—the wealth Mutair had accumulated as a result of ten years of raiding Iraq. Ajami, the renegade, had now secured the lion's share of what properly should have gone to compensate Iraq. It was said that his personal booty amounted to between one hundred and fifty and two hundred camels. Returning in triumph with his hitherto virgin banner proudly unfurled, Ajami was reported to have taunted the Iraq tribesmen he encountered with the words, "You had better go home and sit with your wives."

Infuriated deputations poured into my little camp, vociferating that the government, by its prohibition of raiding, had destroyed their honour. Ajami, they shouted, with his tinpot banner, had won fame and wealth, while an Iraq government post protected his tents and women for him. The camels of Mutair were by right the property of the Iraq tribes, who had endured massacre and looting for so many years, and who had been debarred by government orders from recovering their property from the rebels. There was no reply which I could make to these complaints, because they were all true.

Jedaan Ibn Suwait who was a cousin of Ajami, and had remained in Iraq, took the law into his own hands with more courage than common sense, and attacked the Ajman, assembled at Mahazool, with a party of thirty men. The Ajman rallied and several hundred of them fell upon Jadaan, who was put to flight with a loss of three killed.

The arrival of Ibn Saud at Al Riqai was the sign for further effervescence. The next day, horsemen, camelmen and men on foot poured from all directions into our little camp at Al Ubaid. Some anticipated a combined attack on the rebels, and hoped to be in at the death. Others alleged that they had heard that "this southerner" (meaning Ibn Saud) was behaving too haughtily, and they thought he should be made to realize that the government also had its fighting tribes. There were soon several hundred ragged warriors round our tents.

The murder of two Iraqi tribesmen by Ibn Saud's scouts, and the subsequent raid by a party of his horsemen on the Dhafeer, only added fuel to the fire. I signalled urgently to Baghdad, suggesting that we be allowed to seize two thousand camels from the rebels, before we handed them all back to Ibn Saud. I calculated that the losses of the Iraq tribes in the Southern Desert had been equivalent to twenty-five thousand camels omitting the very heavy losses in human life. Thus two thousand camels would have represented only about eight per cent of their losses. It would, however, have temporarily allayed their resentment, and enabled them at least to feel that they and their government had taken action, just as much as had Ibn Saud and Ajami Ibn Suwait. No reply to my signal was received from Baghdad.

Those who estimated bedouin gains and losses in terms of loot alone were wide of the mark. Imaginative, hot-tempered, independent and proud as well as avaricious, honour was as dear to them as loot. Interminable stories of wars and raiding occupied long winter evenings round the camp fires, and were perpetuated in innumerable ballads. The man who sat quietly at home, while his peers were gaining fame and wealth, was scarcely worthy the name of a man.

Eventually Jedaan Ibn Suwait, and others of the Dhafeer and Shammar camped in Iraq, seeing the government still inactive, rode to Al Riqai and volunteered in Ibn Saud's army. Meanwhile Ajami Ibn Suwait rode past the police post at Al Ubaid, at the head of his following of the Dhafeer, with his banner ostentatiously displayed, and likewise joined Ibn Saud at Al Riqai. Now that the struggle was over, except for the shouting and the dividing of the spoils, everyone was anxious to unfurl his war banner on the winning side. A year before, when the rebels were in the field, they had been less conspicuous.

A fury of revenge had meanwhile seized even the shepherds of Iraq. Unaware of the exact situation, but hearing vaguely that Mutair were in the Batin, horse and foot poured across the Dibdibba to the east. Few had any definite idea of what they meant to do, but a general cry of "Mutair are defeated. Loot, revenge, kill," was in the air.

A desert police car, crossing the Dibdibba on its way from Busaiya to Al Ubaid, encountered an old shepherd, half bent with age and armed only with a stick, running across the desert towards the east. He waved to the car with his threadbare cloak and called: "*Ya walad!* Oh boy! Where is the Batin?"

"Straight in front of you, my uncle," answered one of the police. "What do you want there?"

"The Duweesh! The Duweesh!" shouted the old man, shaking his stick menacingly. "The Duweesh, he killed both my sons," and he shambled off across the vast desert, muttering to himself.

Those who regarded Iraq-Nejed relations as a mere political problem, and who had never seen the result of Ikhwan raids at first hand, could not visualize the agony, slaughter, terror and bereavement of those passionate times. But the Iraq tribes had endured all this for ten years, and it had eaten into their souls. As I have already said so often—massacre was the key to the situation.

The dead could not be brought to life again, but it seemed to me at least to be my duty to see that the victims of so much cruelty and terror obtained all that it was possible to obtain for them in material compensation. The British and Iraq Governments appeared to be more anxious to placate Ibn Saud than to defend the interests of their own subjects. I accordingly continued to bombard the ministry of the interior with requests for its sanction to some form of compensation for raid victims.

At length a somewhat half-hearted agreement was given for me to distribute to the Iraq tribes what rebel camels I could collect. The greater part of Mutair were already beyond our control, but we had at Busaiya, Ibn Mashhoor and Murdhi al Rufidi, with a number of looted flocks.

Eventually we collected a number of herds of camels at a place near Adhaiba. As far as possible, we summoned the victims of previous Ikhwan raids and distributed our loot between them. It was but a drop in the ocean, but it gave at least some slight satisfaction to those who, through the indifference of their government, had endured so much suffering.

*   *   *   *   *

When the rebels fled from Al Riqai to Jahra at the news of the approach of Ibn Saud, my active connection with them came to an end. The Shaikh of Kuwait, not the Iraq Government, was now responsible, and the forces available consisted of aircraft and armoured cars of the R.A.F. The rest of the story may therefore be briefly told.

The rebels, on reaching Jahra, were again torn by divided counsels. While attempting to round them up, the R.A.F. had dropped a few small bombs in front of them. Accustomed as they were to wholesale massacres, they conceived the idea that the government were about to exterminate them.

As a result, the majority of the Jiblan and Rashaida sections of Mutair decided to make a dash for Jeriya, intending to throw them-

selves on the mercy of Ibn Shuqair, who had made his peace with
Ibn Saud, and who, they hoped, would act as go-between and secure
favourable terms for them from the king. A few groups of the Ajman,
in the same manner, decided to try and reach the Hasa and join
Ibn Juma, a shaikh of their tribe who had remained loyal to Ibn
Saud. This considerable collection of tribes, with their women,
children and flocks were intercepted by Ibn Saud's army near
Khabari Wadhha on 9th January, 1930. Every man was killed and
all these sections were exterminated without mercy.

On the same day, 9th January, 1930, Naif Ibn Hithlain surrendered to the armoured car column at Jahra, and was sent in by air to
84 Squadron camp in Shaiba, where he passed the night in a small
tent pitched for him in front of the guard room. The next day, Feisal
al Duweesh and Jasir Ibn Lami also gave themselves up. All three
leaders were transferred to the Royal Indian Marine ship *Patrick
Stewart*, which was lying in the Shatt al Arab.

Meanwhile, also on 9th January, the R.A.F. were instructed to round
up the rebels from Jahra and shepherd them in a north-westerly
direction to near Jarishan, pending negotiations as to their fate.

On 20th January, the British Resident in the Persian Gulf,
accompanied by Air Commodore Burnett, flew from Shaiba and
landed on a special camp pitched by Ibn Saud, a short distance
north of where his army lay at Khabari Wadhha. On 25th January,
an agreement was reached to hand over the three rebel leaders to
Ibn Saud, and for the tribes still in Kuwait to return to Nejed.
Ibn Saud promised to spare the lives of the rebels and to temper with
mercy any punishment inflicted on the tribes, a clause which at
least saved the survivors from the complete extermination by
massacre which had proved to be the fate of those who had already
attempted to return to Nejed independently. Ibn Saud further
undertook to prevent any raids into Iraq in the future, a pledge
which he indeed faithfully observed. Finally he promised to settle
the claims of Iraq tribes for losses in past Ikhwan raids, a pious
hope which was never fulfilled.

The rebel leaders had meanwhile been transferred to the sloop
H.M.S. *Lupin*, which had then anchored in the Bay of Kuwait.
On 28th January, Feisal al Duweesh, Jasir Ibn Lami and Naif Ibn
Hithlain, were flown from Kuwait to Ibn Saud's camp at Khabari
Wadhha and were handed over. As the king had promised to spare
the lives of the three leaders, they were not immediately executed,
but were transferred to prison in Riyadh. They were all believed to
have died not long afterwards.

The agreement specified that all the rebel tribes in Kuwait were
to be returned to Ibn Saud complete with their flocks and herds.
R.A.F. armoured cars were charged with the task of herding them

back once more from Jarishan. They crossed the Kuwait-Nejed frontier on 8th February.

Their departure on these terms was a bitter disappointment to the Iraq tribes. The R.A.F. estimated that twenty thousand camels were handed back in this manner, a great part of them the product of loot taken from Iraq tribes. The British Government refused our request to seize any of these camels as compensation, on the grounds that Ibn Saud had stipulated their return complete, as an indispensable condition of his agreement to settle the claims of the Iraq tribes later on. The rebel tribes were therefore handed back with all their flocks, many of them the actual property of the Iraq tribes. If the victims of the Ikhwan raids had been lawyers or politicians, the nature of the settlement might have been different, but as the victims had been poor and inarticulate, they had no means of pressing their claims on the attention of the authorities.

* * * * *

The surrender of the rebels and the victorious termination of all our sufferings were, of course, greeted with an outburst of bedouin poetry. I have long ago forgotten most of these compositions but I recently discovered the following poem pinned into the leaves of my diary. It so happened that after the surrender of the rebels, I paid a visit to Aneza, in the Wadian district west of Kerbela. Here I established another desert post, at the well of Nukhaib, thereby enabling the Iraq Government to establish its control over all its deserts west of the Euphrates. The author of this poem was a man of Aneza, who had been with us in the Southern Desert. To his regret, he was left behind when I went to visit his tribe in the Wadian. The poem begins with a modern adaptation of the messenger introduction. The poet apostrophizes the pilot of an aircraft flying to Nukhaib.

> Flying to Nukhaib, O rider from the east,
> On wings than ostrich in her flight more swift,
> If I must stay, bear my *salaams* at least,
> To Glubb, from whom I ask a worthy gift.

> Like hawk which cleaves the highest heaven in flight,
> Then folds its wings and drops in some sweet valley,
> Thus in green plains he camps, his foes in sight;
> Chief of the desert, his tribes round him rally.

> He signals with his flags both black and red,
> We load our weapons, for we shall not fail;
> Our leader oft in battle stern has led,
> In fight our bullets fall like deadly hail.

He captured shaikhs who bore a famous name,
And to the government he brought them bound,
Before the Imam, he stripped Duweesh of fame,
Right gallant men for the Aujan he found.

His men are daring lads, a noble few,
How sweet to serve among them, girt in arms;
He speaks a word and ever it proves true:
His gifts are splendid—his no miser's alms.

This little poem shows many typical features of the bedouin ballad, though my halting English conveys no idea of the sonorous rhythm of the original. The line stating that we camped in green plains in sight of our enemies refers of course to our camping in the Neutral Area close to Mutair. The black and red flags were the signals which we invented for use between our armed trucks. The Imam is the title of Ibn Saud, before whose arrival the Duweesh had already been discredited. Like many bedouin poets, the author begins and ends his poem with a request for a gift. For thousands of years the end of every bedouin campaign had been celebrated in similar verses.

     *   *   *   *   *

The Nejed rebellion having been thus brought to a successful conclusion, the British Government were anxious to strike while the iron was hot by mediating in negotiations for a permanent peace between Ibn Saud and King Feisal of Iraq. Proposals were made for a meeting between the two kings. The suggestion soon encountered difficulties, for neither monarch would agree to visit the other, both considering that he who left his country to call on his neighbour would thereby admit his inferior status.

At length a solution acceptable to both parties was devised. It was suggested that the meeting take place on a ship of the Royal Navy in the Persian Gulf. To make certain that neither king obtained an unfair advantage, it was stipulated that the meeting place of the ships should be out of sight of land. This plan appeared to possess a number of advantages. The meeting would take place on completely neutral ground—on the deck of a British ship. Moreover, it was thought that the fact that the conference would be held on board a ship at sea would avoid the possibility of a competition in magnificence between the two rulers.

I was informed that I had been selected as a member of the entourage of King Feisal, whose suite consisted of the prime minister of Iraq, Naji Beg as Suwaidi, and the adviser to the ministry of the interior, Mr. (later Sir Kinahan) Cornwallis. The British Government was represented by the high commissioner, Sir Francis Humphreys, and by the air officer commanding, Air Vice-Marshal Sir Robert Brooke Popham.

On the evening of 21st February, 1930, three ships arrived at a rendezvous in the Persian Gulf, out of sight of land. Next morning the two kings met on board H.M.S. *Lupin*. It would be an exaggeration to say that they liked one another. So bitter had been the rivalry between their two families that it would have been foolish to expect an immediate friendship to spring up between them. Suffice it to say that they met and entertained one another with apparent affability.

A crisis arose at one stage which nearly caused the failure of the meeting. It was agreed that the two monarchs should exchange letters, but King Feisal refused to address Ibn Saud as king of the Hejaz. King Feisal's father, King Husain, had been driven from the throne of that country by Ibn Saud only four years earlier, and the latter now refused to accept any letter addressed to him which did not give him the title of king of the Hejaz and Nejed and its dependencies. It fell to Sir Francis Humphreys to pacify the ruffled feelings of the two monarchs. After no little trouble, both agreed to address one another without titles as "my dear brother". While the kings were occupied in these somewhat acid exchanges, their officials were engaged in drafting a Bon Voisinage Agreement, which was duly initialled in Baghdad a fortnight later.

While the *Lupin* meeting did not produce any emotional reconciliation between the Saud and sherifian families, the mere fact that the two rulers had met and parted amicably was no small triumph for British diplomacy, so often falsely accused of sowing discord instead of peace. Most important of all, the agreements negotiated on H.M.S. *Lupin* enjoyed the (nowadays rare) distinction of having led to permanent peace. Thirty years have elapsed since the Ikhwan war came to an end—years during which hostilities have never been renewed on the frontier between Nejed and Iraq.

These thirty years have witnessed the complete transformation of the greater part of Arabia. The invasion of the desert by aircraft and mechanical vehicles (an invasion for which we unknowingly paved the way) have reduced to impotence the wild tribes which formerly terrorized their settled neighbours. American oil fields are generously sprinkled over the desert and the sons of the Ikhwan warriors of yesterday are fain to work as labourers or mechanics in their once inviolate deserts. Soon all the battles and massacres, the glory, the terror and the gallantry, will be but vague memories of a past age. The fanatical Ikhwan movement has vanished, though the people of Nejed are still Wahhabis.

Times change and we must needs change with them. Yet many of the changes, so striking to the outward appearance, are still superficial. Beneath the surface, the men can scarcely as yet have changed—the wild, passionate, generous, hospitable and turbulent sons of the desert.

INDEX